THE WISDOM OF ADRIAN FORTESCUE

Adrian Fortescue

THE WISDOM OF ADRIAN FORTESCUE

Michael Davies

Roman Catholic Books

P.O. Box 2286 • Fort Collins, CO 80522

Dedication

This book is dedicated to the memory of
Adrian Willson, 1913-1998,
eldest son of Thomas Wilfred Willson
Doctor Fortescue's choirmaster and friend.
The help given to me by Adrian Willson
in writing my brief life of Doctor Fortescue
cannot be calculated.
Although he did not live to see its publication
he would have taken great satisfaction in this
commemoration
of a great priest whom he so loved and admired.

INTRODUCTION

Adrian Fortescue (1874-1923) was a priest of unique and remarkable talents who truly merited the title of genius. He was probably the most outstanding scholar among the clergy of the English-speaking world in the first three decades of this century. He was always referred to by his friends and parishioners as "the Doctor" in view of his triple doctorate. He will be referred to by this title in the book that follows. Dr. Fortescue could not only speak but lecture in eleven languages, was an authority on the classics, an artist of considerable talent, a recognized authority on heraldry, England's most talented calligrapher, a talented musician and composer, possessed an unrivalled knowledge of the Eastern Churches, and was certainly the greatest authority on the liturgy of the Roman Rite the English-speaking world has ever known. I have quoted him frequently in my own books on the liturgy, as a result of which I was contacted by Miss Norah Devine, the last infant baptized by him, who gave me some background information on his life. I was immediately captivated and began to gather further information. Mr Adrian Willson, son of Dr. Fortescue's choirmaster, and named after him, provided me with valuable documentation and many personal reminiscences, as did his brother Peter. I hope that my brief life of Dr. Fortescue which begins the book will inspire someone to write a full biography. The two principal sources for such a biography are the Westminster diocesan archives and those of Downside Abbey. The diaries of Doctor Fortescue at Downside Abbey, which are written in Latin, read in conjunction with the letters in the Westminster archives, provide a comprehensive source for a biography. There is also a substantial correspondence between Dr. Fortescue and Stanley Morison in the Fitzwilliam Museums, Cambridge.

The evident purpose of this book is to make available once

more Dr. Fortescue's scholarly exposition of the Mass of the Roman Rite as it was celebrated during his lifetime and, as he points out, as it had been celebrated in all essential respects since the pontificate of St. Gregory the Great at the end of the sixth century. The articles reprinted here have all been taken from the original *Catholic Encyclopaedia* published in the first decade of this century. The young priest had been invited to write these articles in 1906, at the age of thirty-two, upon the recommendation of Father Herbert Thurston, SJ who had been the first choice for the task. Father Thurston had so many other writing assignments to complete, including many other articles for the Encyclopaedia, that he was unable to accept this particular commission.

It could be argued that in view of the radical reform of the Mass of the Roman Rite following the Second Vatican Council, the articles of Dr. Fortescue would now constitute little more than an historical curiosity. Nothing could be further from the truth. Such articles as Liturgy, Rites, *Kyrie*, *Gloria*, Gradual, and Preface stand independent of the rite used, apart from the rubrical instructions cited by the Doctor. But in view of the great and expanding interest shown in the Traditional Mass, particularly by young people, there can be no doubt that it will respond to a widespread need. It will be of particular interest to the growing number of priestly societies and monastic communities which use exclusively the liturgical books predating the Second Vatican Council. The recent reprint of Dr. Fortescue's *Ceremonies of the Roman Rite Described* is circulating widely not only in these establishments, but in diocesan seminaries throughout the English-speaking world.[1] A reprint of his *The Early Papacy* has also been very well received.[2] Beautiful facsimile reproductions of the six liturgical books of the

---

[1]   Available from The Saint Austin Press, 296 Brockley Road, London, SE4 2RA, England.

[2]   Ibid.

Council of Trent, which are referred to frequently in this book, are now being published by the Libreria Editrice Vaticana. They should be in the library of every student of the history of the Roman Rite.[3]

I have used English spelling and punctuation throughout the book. The Doctor would have been horrified had it been otherwise! Where capitalization is concerned, I have conformed to the original text, which is not always consistent. This may be due to different editors having been responsible for the articles. There are also some inconsistencies in spelling, e.g. "Uniate" and "Uniat". I have drastically curtailed the references included in the original text. On far from infrequent occasions there are as many as four or five references for just one of Doctor Fortescue's sentences, all included within the text, and in most cases these are to sources to which the general reader would not have access. I have tended to confine references to such sources as St. Clement of Rome, Durandus, Justin Martyr, Duchesne, and *Patrologia Latina*, I have also inserted them as end notes rather than cluttering up the text. Where I have found it necessary to add explanatory footnotes of my own they are specified as coming from the Editor. I have also added a glossary which should be of help to all but the most erudite readers. Those who wish for detailed source material for any article should refer to *The Catholic Encyclopaedia*.

I offer my most sincere thanks to the following people whose generous help has made this book possible: Denis and Nora Devine, Father Ian Dickie, the Westminster Archivist, Dom Henry Foster, OSB, Librarian of Downside Abbey during my research there, Anthony de Melo, Dom Andrew Southwell, OSB, John Scruby, historian of Letchworth and an authority on typography, Harold Simms, the sacristan of St. Hugh, The Reverend Scott Reid, Father Philip Stark, Adrian

---

[3] Available from Libreria Editrice Vaticana, 00120 Città del Vaticano.

and Peter Willson, my son Adrian, and a gentleman who pre-
fers not to be named. To my great sorrow, Nora Devine and
Adrian Willson died before the book in which they had shown
such interest had been completed.

It is my hope that this will be the first of a series of books
making the wisdom of Adrian Fortescue available once more.
His articles on the Eastern liturgies alone provide sufficient
material for a second volume. By a happy coincidence I have
been able to complete this tribute to Adrian Fortescue on the
feast of the great Pope, to the brilliance of whose liturgical
reform he pays tribute in the pages that follow. The collect of
his Mass reads:

O God, who for the overthrowing
of the enemies of Thy Church,
and for the restoring of the beauty of Thy worship,
didst choose bless Pius as supreme Pontiff,
grant that we may be defended by his patronage
and so cleave to Thy service.
that overcoming all the snares of our enemies,
we may rejoice in Thy eternal peace.

Michael Davies
5 May 1999
Saint Pius V

CONTENTS

CONTENTS

ILLUSTRATIONS

PART ONE

ADRIAN FORTESCUE—
PRIEST AND SCHOLAR

Adrian Fortescue—Priest and Scholar

Early Life

ADRIAN FORTESCUE was born on 14 January 1874. His father, Edward Bowles Knottesford Fortescue, was the head of an old Midland county family of ancient lineage and high position. His landed estates were in Warwickshire, including Alvestone Manor, Stratford-on-Avon. The House of Fortescue is said to date from the Battle of Hastings (1066), where Richard le Fort, having saved the life of William the Conqueror by the shelter of his "strong shield", was henceforth known as Fort-Escu. In reference to this tradition, his descendants have taken for their motto, *Forte scutum salus ducum*—"A strong shield is the safety of leaders."

Edward Fortescue was a descendant of the namesake of his famous son, the martyr Blessed Adrian Fortescue. Sir Adrian had risen to favour at the court of Henry VIII partly through the fact that he was related to the influential Boleyn family; his mother was the aunt of Anne Boleyn. He accompanied Henry in wars against the French in 1513 and 1522 and was chosen by the King to attend Queen Catherine at "The Field of the Cloth of Gold" at Guisnes in 1520, when Henry entered into a treaty with Francis I of France. In 1532 Sir Adrian was admitted to the Knights of St John of Malta, but, as a married man, he would have been admitted only as a Knight of Honour and Devotion. It took considerable courage and integrity to become a member of an order established by papal authority, and with the militant defence of the Catholic faith as its purpose, at a time when Henry's relationship with

17

the papacy was near breaking-point. The king was to be excommunicated in the following year by Pope Clement VII, who had been an active knight himself before taking holy orders. Sir Adrian was arrested in 1534, the year of the Act of Supremacy, but released after a few months, perhaps due to his kinship with Anne Boleyn, who was herself executed two years later in 1536. In 1539 he was rearrested, confined to the Tower of London, and executed for sedition on 8 July of that year under an act of attainder, which saved King Henry the inconvenience of a trial. A portrait of the martyr is preserved in St. Paul's College at Rabat in Malta, with an inscription stating that Blessed Adrian died *ob constantem fidei Catholicae confessionem* (for his constancy in confessing the Catholic faith).

Edward Fortescue graduated from Oxford University in 1838, was ordained into the Church of England, and became a leading member of the High Church party. In view of the concern which his son Adrian was to show for liturgical perfection the following extract from an obituary is of considerable interest:

> Mr. Fortescue graduated at Oxford in 1838, and immediately after taking priest's orders he entered upon the sole charge of a small neglected hamlet called Wilmcote, near Stratford-on-Avon. Here he built a church, schools, and a parsonage-house, and at once set about the then arduous work of rendering Divine service in a manner somewhat more worthy of the honour of Him to whom it was offered than had hitherto been attempted in a country parish. So far as regards the High Church movement of our own times—Wilmcote was the first church outside of London, in which a surpliced choir was introduced, and it was the first in England wherein lights and a special vestment for the altar service were adopted.

In 1861, Mr. Fortescue accepted an invitation to become Dean of the newly founded Scottish Episcopalian Cathedral of St. Ninian's, Perth.[1] Provost Fortescue achieved a considerable reputation as a retreat-master and spiritual director. As a preacher and public speaker he had few if any equals, and no superior, among the Anglican clergy. The publication of the decrees of the First Vatican Council prompted him to reconsider very carefully Anglican claims to be a branch of the Catholic Church, and in 1872, he submitted to Rome and devoted himself to the cause of Catholic education until he died a few years later on 18 August 1877 at the early age of sixty-one. Such was the respect in which he was held within the Catholic Church that it was said that no funeral comparable to his had taken place since the death of Cardinal Wiseman in 1865. There is a fine memorial chapel with his arms and inscription in the Dominican Church at Haverstock Hill.

In 1877, after his father's death, Adrian was taken by his mother, Gertrude Mary Knottesford Fortescue, née Robins, to live at 40 Park Road (now Parkhill Road) at Haverstock Hill, near the Dominican Priory. She sent him to the Jesuit Preparatory School at Boulogne-sur-Mer in 1883 at the age of nine where he remained until Easter 1885, when he entered St. Charles' College, Bayswater. At the age of twelve Adrian suffered the sad loss of his mother who died on 6 December 1886. He went to live with his aunt, Miss Katherine Robins, who brought him up at 18 Darlaston Road, Wimbledon. Miss Robins died in Florence in 1907 at the age of sixty-nine, and is buried at San Miniato.

The Seminarian

In 1891 Adrian entered the Scots' College in Rome where, due to his exceptional musical talent, he was soon appointed organist. He was awarded the degree of Bachelor of Philosophy in 1892, and his Ph.D in 1894. In the same year he entered the Theological Faculty at Innsbruck University. In addition to his theological studies the young seminarian studied German and drawing, and travelled extensively during his holidays, walking, climbing, and sketching in Bavaria, Tyrol and

North Italy, France and England. A scheme of work for study in his free-time set out by him while studying at Innsbruck shows what an extraordinary, perhaps unique, student he was:

Plan of Study in Free Time

Jan. 1896-July 1896:	Modern Greek.
Vacations 1896:	Classical and Modern Greek grammar.
Oct. 1896-July 1897:	Greek: Italian.
Vacations 1897:	Hungarian.
Oct. 1897-July 1898:	Hungarian.
Vacations 1898:	Sanskrit.
Oct. 1898-July 1899:	Sanskrit.
Vacations 1899:	Sanskrit.
Oct. 1899-July 1900:	Icelandic.
Vacations 1900:	Icelandic.
If God spares me.	

His Ordination

Adrian Fortescue was ordained to the priesthood on 27 March 1898 by Simon, Prince Bishop of Brixen, whose secretary he became while continuing his studies. On 10 April 1898, Easter Sunday, the new priest sang his first Mass at 11 a.m. in the Jesuit Church at Wimbledon. He sang his second Mass the next day for the souls of his parents in the family chapel in the Dominican church at Haverstock Hill. Between 1899 and 1905 the young priest passed doctoral examinations in Moral Theology, Dogma, Church history, Canon Law, Arabic, and Biblical Science—passing the examination in Semitic Languages with great distinction, a rare achievement. On 10 June 1905 he was awarded the degree of Doctor of Divinity, making him the very rare recipient of a triple doctorate. The level of his scholarship was so exceptional that he was awarded a prize presented to him personally by the Emperor Franz Joseph himself. This was an award given rarely, and only to students who achieved the most exceptional level of scholarship. It is hardly surprising that his friends and parishioners tended to refer to him as "the Doctor", and this is the title that will be used throughout this account of his life.

In 1906, at the age of thirty-two, upon the recommendation of Father Herbert Thurston, S.J., he was asked to contribute articles on the liturgy to the original *Catholic Encyclopaedia*, a very great honour, particularly in view of the fact that he had not yet published any books. It is these articles which make up the present volume. The reader will certainly agree that they provide a treasure-house of historical scholarship of the very highest level. Taken as a whole, this book will certainly provide the most valuable treatise on the Mass available today. It has been both a privilege and an honour for me to compile and edit it.

The Scholar

In a tribute to the scholarship of Adrian Fortescue, Dr. J.G. Vance, Vice-President of St. Edmund's College, Old Hall, commented:

> Adrian was a man of such high attainment and of such breadth of interest that he may rightly be styled a genius. He knew so much, knew it so well, and loved the knowledge whole-heartedly. It was said long ago that we men become what we really know at least in the moment of vision. This was indeed true in the case of Adrian, who delivered himself of his knowledge as an artist "stung by the splendour of a sudden thought" gives us his vision of true beauty. He simply poured out his soul as he told men of what he at once knew and loved.

Adrian Fortescue was indeed a man of such high attainment in so many branches of learning that no one could better lay claim to the title of genius. He could not only speak but lecture in eleven languages. He had in many fields of scholarship the sureness of touch, the breadth of vision, the love of truth, and the absence of personal prejudice that make for genius in learning. His eager, vivid temperament, and his sensitivity of mind led him intuitively into the very heart of things, and what he knew he could impart in clear speech and vivid phrase. In addition to insight and depth he had an exceptionally broad range of interests, some indication of which can be obtained from the range of topics on which he lectured, included in the chronological account of his life. He loved the study of the East; was fascinated by the languages, customs, and religions of the Orientals, and knew the origin and history of the Eastern Churches, both Uniate and Orthodox, as few priests of the Roman Rite have ever done, as is made clear in his books upon the subject. He devoted many years to the study of Church history, of which he was so inspiring a master.

Hearing Dr. Fortescue lecture was an experience that could never be forgotten. His presentation of facts in lecturing was amazing in its discipline and power. He spoke without emotion, without rhetoric, and with practically no gestures. But, Dr. Vance wrote:

> In passages that excited his enthusiasm Adrian's lecturing was that of a genius. All sternness would disappear from his features, his voice lose any trace of a didactic tone, as his face portrayed fully and beautifully each feeling that his story evoked. These were the specially winning moments not to be forgotten. Little graceful gestures were now seen and his whole person would glow with enthusiasm for his subject, joy in its recital and power in its presentation. On these occasions he was little short of a magician and no audience could fail to be spellbound.

His Accomplishments

Adrian Fortescue was an authority on the classics. His erudition was admired by non-Catholics, who flocked to his lectures on such authors as Plato and Virgil. He also possessed a specialized knowledge of Dante and Boethius. His annotated edition of Book V of Boethius's *De Consolatione Philosophiae* was completed by his friend and colleague, Canon George Smith, and published posthumously in 1925. He was an artist of considerable talent, which he used in a range of subjects from a masterly study of Chartres Cathedral to exquisitely beautiful book-plates designed for his friends. His watercolours would merit a place in any art gallery. Dr. Fortescue was also a recognized authority on heraldry, and his own designs were widely admired. His cousin, Lady Winifred Fortescue, considered that the book-plate he designed for her was the most beautiful that she had ever seen, a judgement with which those who see it will be inclined to concur. It incorporates, in heraldic terms, the Fortescue arms, azure shield, a bend engrailed argent, plain cottised or, and the crest (see page 94). When Lady Winifred expressed her gratitude for its beauty, Adrian replied: "Ah, you see, I put love into it. They are my own arms." In her autobiography, *There's Rosemary, There's Rue*, Lady Winifred provides a fascinating insight into the character of Adrian Fortescue, revealing not only the extent to which this brilliant scholar was prepared to go to help his poor parishioners, but the extent of his sense of humour.

He was the most generous and unpractical man alive. He gave all his substance to needy parishioners, and having no fixed stipend but only the voluntary contributions of a poor parish, was always in difficulties about his church expenses and in despair over his inability to raise enough money to meet them. When he first confided this to me, I suggested that he should design book-plates for my customers and illuminate aphorisms on parchment or vellum to be used as book-markers, etc. This he did most exquisitely, handing them to me with a sardonic grin, and I was able to get him many orders and so ease his financial burden. In his simplicity, he thought me the most marvellous business woman the world has ever seen, and once advised his Cardinal "to let Peggy Fortescue run the diocese for him."

Lady Fortescue insisted that her cousin was the most generous and unpractical man alive. Edith Cowell, a writer and parishioner of St. Hugh, also refers to this in an obituary in *Catholic Truth*, making special mention of his refusal to accept Mass stipends or any fee for administering the sacraments:

> He was the most unpractical person born. He knew nothing about business, and cared nothing at all about money, preferring to live very frugally upon his small private means rather than to accept a fee for a baptism, or an offering for a Mass. He would have no buying or selling in or near the church in any circumstances whatsoever...

In an obituary which she wrote for *Blackfriars*, Miss Cowell referred to another of Dr. Fortescue's eccentricities, his insistence upon the classical pronunciation of Latin as used in English schools. She explains:

> He wrote, and had printed and distributed among the parishioners, a leaflet on the classical pronunciation of Latin. This was one of his whims. Newcomers to the choir who sang *ch* instead of *k* in *caeli*, or *v* instead of *w* in *ave* were scourged with whips, and he was so particular about the separate enunciation of each vowel in words like *saecula* that a strange priest coming to the church was heard innocently to regret that the choir sung in Cockney accents.

The Calligrapher

Lady Winifred's reference to her "customers" relates to an enterprise she had started more as a hobby than a business. She had been able to publicise it with "some circulars, beautifully written by Adrian Fortescue, reproduced and broadcasted among my friends." He was probably the most out-standing calligrapher of his era, and he influenced the William Morris-inspired Catholic-led renaissance in the art of printing which began in England at the beginning of this century. Dr. Fortescue had begun his study of calligraphy in 1899, when he began to attend the first classes of Edward Johnston at the London County Council School of Arts and Crafts. Johnston, who was born in Uruguay of Scottish descent, had arrived in London when the William Morris-inspired Arts and Crafts revival was at its height. He immediately came under the influence of W.R. Lethaby, founder and principal of the Central School of Arts and Crafts. Johnston based his calligraphy upon his personal research into medieval manuscripts, to which he had been introduced in 1898 by Sydney Cockerell, a notable authority on illuminated manuscripts and at one time the secretary and a close friend of William Morris. Johnston did more than any other individual to influence the renaissance in calligraphy and printing in this century. He did this through his books and his classes which were attended by many individuals who achieved fame in these fields, including Eric Gill, Grailey Hewitt, Stanley Morison, and Eleni Zompolides. Johnston's ambition was "to make living letters with a formal pen". He once remarked, "Our aim should be, I think, to make letters live...that men themselves may have more life."[2] Johnston's most celebrated achievement was a block letter based on classical Roman proportions and used exclusively by London Underground Railways for their famous posters. It was a private type for their use only. A few years later Eric Gill "designed" a virtually identical alphabet which became famous throughout the world as *Gill Sans-Serif*. Gill accepted that it was based on Johnston's Underground alphabet.

Dr. Fortescue was insistent upon the relationship between high standards of calligraphy and the art of typography. Among those influenced by him were Eric Gill and Bernard Newdigate

(1869-1944), whose Arden Press publications are among the cream of this century's English printing. When Newdigate set out to rescue his father's printing firm at Leamington in 1890 the only book types he found were not very inspiring "old style" and "modern" fonts. He did his best with these until 1905 when he was introduced to Caslon Old Face. This made such an impression on him that he became a master of its use, and his typographical style was influenced by it for the rest of his life.[3] The Arden Press moved to a modern works at Letchworth in 1907, where together with W.H. Smith's book-binding works, under the direction of Douglas Cockerell, it began an enterprise in commercial book production of the highest quality. "In 1908, when W.H. Smith exercised an option to buy the Arden Press, Newdigate remained with the firm and was able to concentrate more fully on book design. It was at this time that his friendship with Adrian Fortescue began to have an influence on the direction of his interests, especially in his growing regard for the work of William Morris at the Kelmscott Press."[4] Fortescue also imparted to Newdigate his lasting passion for calligraphy.[5] Newdigate had a particular flair for the use of Caslon types, and in 1951 during the Festival of Britain South Bank Exhibition, the 1905 Arden publication, *Of God and His Creatures*, designed by Bernard Newdigate, was included in an exhibition of one hundred of the most notable books printed in England this century. It is possible that *A History of the Holy Eucharist in Great Britain*, also designed by Newdigate and printed after he had moved the Arden Press to Letchworth in 1907, is an even more elegant example of the art of typography.[6] It is set in Caslon Old Face 14 point, with italic and swash capitals on the title page. In 1908, during Fortescue's first full year at Letchworth, Newdigate's Arden Press published his book *The Greek Fathers*. In 1912 Newdigate printed for the Catholic publishing firm of Burns and Oates a Missal with a preface by Adrian Fortescue, which became known as the "Fortescue Missal". It was certainly the most widely used Missal in Britain before the war and had already been printed twelve times by 1930. Fortescue not only wrote for Burns and Oates but also designed letters for the publisher some of which were in use until the firm closed down in the nineteen-sixties. The managing director of Burns and Oates was Wilfrid Meynell, the author and journalist, and husband of the celebrated essayist and poet Alice Meynell. Meynell valued the services of Newdigate as a book designer. He placed his youngest son, Francis, at the age of twenty-one, in charge of the design of books for Burns and Oates. It proved to be an inspired choice, and resulted in a most fruitful collaboration between the young Meynell and Newdigate. In 1913, Newdigate printed for Burns and Oates at the Arden Press an edition of *Ritus Servandus*, which was to be described by Stanley Morison as a "a splendid piece of typography".[7] Francis Meynell was extremely impressed by Fortescue, and in addition to his preface for the Missal, he was asked to contribute an introduction for *The Holy Week Book* in the *Liturgy for Layfolk* series, and an essay on hymns to accompany the collection *Pange Lingua*, both published in 1916.

Stanley Morison

The most celebrated of all those involved in calligraphy and typography who were influenced by Father Fortescue was Stanley Morison, the greatest typographer of this century, who made the Cambridge University Press famous throughout the world for the quality of its typography. Morison was typographical adviser to this press from 1923 to 1944, and 1947 to 1959. He was also employed by the London *Times* from 1929, and designed the famous Times New Roman type which was introduced in 1932 and used for more than sixty years. Morison, a convert, met Fortescue through the Burns and Oates circle of Newdigate, Francis Meynell, Fortescue, and Eric Gill the stone cutter, later celebrated as an artist and typographer. Gill's most celebrated work is the Stations of the Cross that he carved for Westminster Cathedral in London.

Morison was captivated heart, mind, and spirit by Adrian Fortescue, being deeply impressed by the other man's learning, and absorbing as much as possible from him. He even imitated the Doctor's somewhat eccentric manner of dressing—such as his flowing Chestertonian-style cloak, and his practice of studying at every possible opportunity—Morison began learning Greek in trains, buses, and trams in imitation of his idol, and even tried to imitate the way in which the Doctor spoke. In his biography of Morison, Nicholas Barker writes of Dr. Fortescue:

> He was tall, handsome, strong, learned, childish both in a strong sense of fun and in moments of weakness, brave, charming, impatient with fools and severe in his judgement of them, austere yet with an overwhelming sense for the good things of life, overbearing yet diffident, subtle in thought yet simple and forthright in speech and writing—in all, to Morison, a friend and master of overwhelming attraction. He was perhaps the only man, certainly the only Catholic priest Morison had met, who could understand and meet Morison at every inch of the long hard road by which he had come to the Church.[8]

Morison's Catholicism appeared at times to be eccentric or even unorthodox, but there is no doubt of his sincere devotion to the Faith that he had adopted. His biographer Nicholas Barker insists that for Morison the Catholic Church was the only one: "He would argue, attack and abuse, but never doubt. In a strong man his faith remained the strongest part."[9] He was devastated by the death of Dr. Fortescue in 1923:

> With his death Morison lost the first and last person to understand fully what the Church meant to him. It was a devotion as profound as unorthodox: "I wouldn't belong to this bunch of macaroni merchants for another second if it wasn't the way of laying hold on Christ," he roared at T. F. Burns,

consulting him, over lunch at the Holborn Restaurant, about his magazine, *Order*.[10]

A very fruitful collaboration between Meynell and Morison resulted in some exquisitely designed books. Morison discovered what are known as the "Fell" types. Dr. John Fell (1625-1686), an Anglican divine, had imported from Holland between 1667 and 1672, punches and types for the use of the University Press, Oxford, but they were neglected until rediscovered at the end of the nineteenth century.[11] Morison persuaded the Controller of the Oxford University Press to let him have two cases of the Fell type and used them in a 1915 edition of the *Ordo Administrandi Sacramenta*. This must certainly be one of the greatest typographical masterpieces of this century. It is to be hoped that there is an university foundation somewhere in the world with sufficient vision and sufficient funds to publish a facsimile edition. Some of the letters on the title page of the *Ordo* were designed specifically for the book by Gill as there was no suitable size in the Fell types. Meynell also persuaded Gill to engrave a device of "arms" of St. Thomas of Canterbury with the petition *Nos ne cesses Thoma tueri*. It became celebrated as the publisher's mark of Burns and Oates. In the centre were three choughs attributed posthumously to Thomas Becket, but Gill thought that they were martlets.[12]

A characteristic of books designed by Meynell and Morison is the use of printers' flowers. They can be seen in the Fortescue Missal, the *Ordo Administrandi Sacramenta*, in Challoner's *Meditations for Every Day in the Year*, published in the Fell type in 1924. One of the best things that they ever did was an edition of Chesterton's poems published by Burns and Oates in 1915 and printed by the Chiswick Press. The type was plain Caslon and the initial letter of each poem was designed specially for the book by Eric Gill. The red buckram cover embroidered with printers' flowers is simple but striking. They designed an almost equally beautiful book, also published by Burns and Oates and printed in Caslon by the Chiswick Press in the same year. This was *Pange Lingua*, a collection of Breviary hymns according to the texts used before the reform of Urban VIII. Where the content of this book is concerned, a twenty-nine page introduction by Fortescue can be appreciated as the Doctor at the top of his form, no more so than in his scathing indictment of Pope Urban VIII:

> In the seventeenth century came the crushing blow which destroyed the beauty of all Breviary hymns. Pope Urban VIII (Maffeo Barberini, 1623-1644) was a Humanist. In a fatal moment he saw that the hymns do not all conform to the rules of classical prosody. Attempts to reform them had been made before, but so far they had been spared. Urban VIII was destined to succeed in destroying them.[13] He appointed four Jesuits to reform the hymns, so that they should no longer offend Renaissance ears. The four Jesuits were Fabiano Strada, Tarquinio Galuzzi, Mathias Sarbiewski, Girolamo Petrucci. These four, in that faithful obedience to the Holy See which is the glory of their Society, with a patient care that one cannot help admiring, set to work to destroy every hymn in the Office. They had no concept of the fact that many of these hymns were written in metre by accent; their lack of understanding of those venerable types of Christian poetry is astounding. They could conceive no ideal but that of a school grammar of Augustan Latin. Wherever a line was not as Horace would have written it, it had to go. The period was hopelessly bad for any poetry;[14] these pious Jesuits were true children of their time. So they embarked on that fatal reform whose effect was the ruin of our hymns. They slashed and tinkered, they re-wrote lines and altered words, they changed the sense and finally produced the poor imitations that we still have in place of the hymns our fathers sang for over a thousand years. Indeed their confidence in themselves is amaz-

ing. They were not ashamed to lay their hands on Sedulius, on Prudentius, on St. Ambrose himself. Only in one or two cases does some sense of shame seem to have stopped their nefarious work. They left *Ave maris stella*, *Iam lucis orto sidere*, and St. Thomas Aquinas's hymns alone (they would have made pretty work of *Sacris solemniis*). In 1632 their mangled remnants were published. We still await the day when the Bull of publication will be revoked.[15]

Adrian Fortescue's calligraphy became more perfect with each succeeding year, and reached its apotheosis in an exquisitely written and illuminated collection of the music used in his church, which he compiled for the use of the organist at St. Hugh. He was an outstanding musician, and was not only a devoted student of hymnody, metre, and the ancient Latin hymns of the Church, but a composer of considerable talent, a talent which was not confined to religious works but extended even to humorous compositions. A memorial exhibition of Adrian Fortescue's work was organized in the Book Club, Commerce Avenue, Letchworth in June 1923. Simply to read the catalogue puts one in awe of the man. There are sections listing his books and pamphlets, notes for his lectures, music, writing and illuminations, book-plates, heraldic and other designs, vestments that he had designed, drawings, water-colours and pencil sketch books, and letters in many languages. There were, in fact, so many exhibits that they could not all be shown at the same time and needed to be changed frequently. All this had been achieved by a relatively young man who died at the age of forty-nine.

Early Appointments

On 28 November 1901 Dr. Fortescue was appointed as curate to St James', Colchester (*Camuloduni inter Orientales Anglos*). His personality was evidently incompatible with that of his parish priest, to whom he gave the name of the Reverend

Sophronius Scroggs, designating himself as "The Latin Clerk". On 1 January 1903 he told his friend Harold Burton of his problems, pointing out that: "Of course no respectable person takes any notice at all of this repugnant day. The year began on the first Sunday of Advent." With illustrations of all the characters involved, Sophronius Scroggs, the Latin Clerk, and one Smufkin, Esquire, he explained the situation in what he described as "the land of Egypt and the house of Bondage".

> Now I only write to inform you of the appalling fact that Mr. Scroggs is possessed by an unclean spirit. The spirit's name is Smufkin. So you see, as the Mousquetaire said: "Mon Dieu! Il-y-en a trois."—me, Scroggs and Smufkin. Smufkin occasionally gets loose, quarrels with Scroggs and is found wandering about the stairs—a blood curdling sight! Sometimes he comes and knocks at my door; I then leap up, lock the door and holy water the keyhole. Smufkin hates holy water. When I am not at home he steals my chocolates, and once I found him asleep in my chair. When I meet him on the stairs he kisses my hand (like Baugh) and asks for my blessing. I then say: "*Ignis, grando, nix, glacies, spiritus procellarum descendant super te et maneant semper.*" He is quite a well meaning unclean spirit. Oh, by the way I should have said il-y-en-a quatre- there is also Scroggs' housekeeper: she is the last surviving Gadarene Swine. Now there is going to be a cycle of stories about the Latin Clerk, Scroggs, Smufkin and the Gadarene Swine. You will get the first one when you are back at Ushaw—they must not be published in the Ushaw magazine, nor must they be told to those people whom Pius IX blandly described as "*canes extra Ecclesiam latrantes.*"

The Latin Clerk left Colchester in February 1903 and returned to the church where he had received his first appointment on 29 September 1899, the German Church of St. Boniface in Union Street, Whitechapel. In a letter to Harold Burton dated 5 March 1903 he mentioned that: "The irony of the situation was that poor Scroggs seemed really sorry that I went, and could not make out why I consented to go! How do you think he showed his affection? By trying to make me take £5 as a douceur! Faut-il être Anglais!" Fortescue's opinion of his new parish priest was no more flattering than that which he had held of Scroggs. Father Bernhard Schaefer was, according to Fortescue, "an exceeding pious person", but "a raving maniack, also a seer of visions and dreamer of dreams..."

> Quite compatible with his piety (which is perfectly genuine) is the fact that he is a liar, a calumniator and a receiver of stolen goods. However, the odd thing about it is that I really like him very much. He is such a blazing old fool, he blathers away such amazing tosh in his endless sermons, and he is generally such a palpable and imperial idiot that the cockles of my heart warm towards him.

Whitechapel, where Jack the Ripper operated, was one of the poorest and most racially mixed areas of London, but working there gave the scholarly young priest great satisfaction.

> I love these slums and all the German beggars. It is all just like old times again. I tramp down through the slush of Whitechapel Road, and sit in the awful filth of the rooms in which a whole family sleeps and eats and lives (and never a window open) and talk the most beautiful tongue on earth (save Greek) and have a real joy in knowing that I am doing something for Christ...Then at midday I interview the beggars who come here, every nation in Europe—Russians and Poles and Lithuanians, Italians, Czechs, Magyars and Roumanians; most of all of course the Chosen People, whom I love best of all, because though they are the poorest and dirtiest of all they always have that superb scorn for the Gentile that suggests Mount Zion and the glory of the things that are gone. Even when I give them alms, in their souls they know

that I am only "Goyi" and unclean (unclean! my word, if you could see them!), but they bless me with a beautiful Hebrew blessing that again suggests the holy city and the Dead Sea, Isaiah and Ezekiel and the Waters of Babylon where their fathers sat and wept—and all the while the roar of the dray-carts and trams, yelling hawkers and shrieking children goes on in Whitechapel Road outside.

Letchworth

After the temporary positions, interrupted by his doctoral examinations, Dr. Fortescue was eventually appointed, in November 1907, as Missionary Rector of Letchworth in Hertfordshire—the world's first garden city. He was to spend the rest of his life there. Under the direction of Ebenezer Howard, the founder, the two architects responsible for the planning of Letchworth were Raymond Unwin, who had been a supporter of William Morris's Socialist League, and Barry Parker, who had been very closely involved with Morris's Arts and Crafts Movement. Howard had witnessed the rebuilding of Chicago after the fire of 1871, and the laying out of its residential suburbs—notably Riverside, a pioneer "garden suburb". Howard's eventual plan, which did not transpire, was to build a series of garden cities each with a population limit of 32,000 and surrounded by an agricultural belt. Each garden city was to be self-contained for employment and social facilities. Six cities would form a cluster around a central city, population 58,000, linked to the others by a radial railway network. The utopian socialist nature of the concept is evident, and although the overall project was not realized, there can be no doubt of the complete success of the Letchworth project.

Letchworth provided a unique parish for a unique priest, but one less suited to his talents and his temperament could hardly be imagined. Work had begun on its construction in 1904. A large number of unemployed men were drafted from London to lay sewers and build roads and other service utilities. As there was no housing available the Corporation erected a number of wooden buildings called "the sheds" to house the workers. In 1907 Bernard Newdigate moved his Arden Press to Letchworth, bringing with him a number of Catholic employees. It is probable that it was their presence that made the establishment of a Catholic mission necessary. Dr. Fortescue's first task was to arrange for the construction of a temporary church, and while this was being done he offered Mass in one of the original sheds located near the railway line. Dr. Fortescue celebrated his first public Mass in the shed on 30 November 1907, the first Sunday of Advent. He described the building in his first visitation report:

> The shed is partitioned in two—one half is used as an infant school. There are broken windows and the children have kicked holes in the partition. The building is mean and ragged and against one wall there is a poor altar. The Blessed Sacrament is not reserved except on Sundays. A bedraggled curtain across one corner serves as a confessional. There are a dozen or more broken chairs, two or three benches, and a number of deal boards resting on bricks. There are twenty men, twenty-seven women and fifty-four children in the parish.

By May 1908, Dr. Fortescue had obtained a site for a new church in Pixmore Way which he built largely with his own money, as was the case with the presbytery, the land on which both were built, and many of the church furnishings. The church was designed by Sir Charles Spooner, R.I.B.A., and was dedicated to St. Hugh of Lincoln. Dr. Fortescue always insisted upon his church being referred to as "St. Hugh", and it made him very angry to hear it called St. Hugh's. He blessed the first stone on 21 June 1908 and celebrated Mass in the new building for the first time on 31 August. It was blessed by the Bishop of Amycla on 6 September, but could not be consecrated as it was intended to be a temporary structure until a larger church could be built. It was, in fact, used as the parish church from 1908 until 1963. The parish was too small to be self-supporting, and much of the income which kept it in being was provided by Dr. Fortescue throughout his fifteen years as parish priest with the income he earned from his writing, his lectures, and the sale of his art and calligraphy, as well as donations from his friends. Often he wrote furiously in weekly and monthly reviews for the sake of the few guineas that he would receive, which were so badly needed for the upkeep of St. Hugh. A very fine description of St. Hugh was included in a long tribute to Dr. Fortescue published in the Letchworth local paper on the occasion of his funeral:

> In three short years, owing to the enthusiasm of our well-loved priest, Dr. Adrian Fortescue, the church has become as nearly perfect as knowledge and love allied can make it. Built according to Byzantine ideas, of a type severe and dignified, its interior decorations a running pattern with a Latin inscription, picked out in black and white round three sides of the church, and one small stained glass window showing St. Francis preaching to the birds. The dossal curtains are of Morris tapestry, and form a background to the chief architectural beauty of the scheme, which consists of a ciborium or canopy built right over the altar, standing on four pillars, and reaching half-way down the chancel. Its roof is solid gilt, and reflects gloriously; the rest is heavily patterned in gesso-work, while its inscription, at once so simple and so suitable, runs in the official language of the Church: "Blessed are they who are called unto the marriage supper of the Lamb." A complete set of vestments, for fast and festival, have been presented; these, with the altar-frontals, were designed by the architect. The unstinted labour and skill expended on the needlework are seen in the splendid results, which add much to the splendour of worship, and a right interpretation "of things unseen".

The beautiful ciborium (baldachino) erected in April 1911, was the gift of Anne Weld. The altar crucifix, candlesticks, sanctuary lamp, and alabaster font, which Dr. Fortescue presented, were all designed by Sir Charles Spooner, and the statue of Our Lady sculpted by his sister, Mrs. Phoebe Stabler. The font was later fitted with a silver lining. These items can be seen in the new church which came into use in 1963. Dr. Fortescue's church is now used as a parish hall. The Latin inscription referred to in the report above, based on Solomon's prayer, was written in exquisite capitals around the walls below the ceiling: *QUICUMQUE ORAVERIT IN LOCO ISTO, EXAUDI DE HABITACULO TUO, ID EST, DE CAELIS PROPITIARE* (II Paralip. 6. 21). "Whosoever shall pray in this place, hear Thou from Thy dwelling place, that is, from heaven, and shew mercy." Until the splendid marble font, donated by Dr. Fortescue, was installed, he used a plain bright blue china bowl for baptisms. Ronan Purdom, and Adrian Willson, son of the choirmaster, were the first two babies to be baptized in it. The bowl was then used for many years to hold flowers before the statue of Our Lady.

The presbytery remains just as it was when built for Dr. Fortescue, but is now totally surrounded by houses, whereas when built it was situated in open fields. On one occasion the chimney was struck by lightning. The local postman, Bert Wheatley, knocked at the door to deliver some mail and was astonished when the door was opened by a man who appeared to be a chimney sweep, blackened with soot from head to toe. The two men had a good laugh at what had happened and the postman helped Dr. Fortescue to clean up the mess. He later told Adrian Willson that it was the first time that he had met the Doctor, and that they had got on very well together.

Dr. Fortescue's congregation was predominantly English until the granting of independence to Southern Ireland. This resulted in an influx of Irish parishioners who had been in the service of the Crown and whose lives would not have been safe had they remained in the new republic. Matthew Gallagher had been employed in the General Post-Office in Dublin when it was attacked by Sinn Fein and had played a prominent part in its defence, and so he and his family were evacuated to Letchworth when the republic was established. His arrival, with his wife and seventeen children, gave a considerable boost to the parish population. The other Irish Catholics who were resettled in Letchworth were members of the Royal Irish Constabulary, inspectors and sergeants, about forty families in all, thus doubling the Catholic population of Letchworth.

The Doctor's great ambition had been to build a permanent church for which he had drawn up his own plans, but this hope did not come to fruition due to his early and untimely death in 1923. The foundation stone of the new church of St. Hugh was laid by Cardinal Godfrey of Westminster on 7 April 1962. The Doctor's little church has been preserved as the parish hall, and it is considered to be one of Letchworth's buildings of greatest historic interest. A number of features from the old church can still be seen in the new one. In the Lady Chapel there are three stained glass windows depicting Our Lady, St. Hugh of Lincoln, and St. Lawrence, for whom Dr. Fortescue had a special devotion. The original baptismal font presented by Dr. Fortescue can be seen in the baptistry, and the sanctuary lamp, candlesticks, and the crucifix above the tabernacle were all removed from the old church. The most beautiful feature of the new church is Dr. Fortescue's baldacchino over the sanctuary. The Lady Chapel of the new church also contains an inscription carved in a tablet of Roman stone by Mr. R. Fincham to the memory of Adrian Fortescue. It is an exquisite example of lettering after the manner of Italian Renaissance "incised" inscription cutting, and also includes the Fortescue arms. It is of a quality which would more than have satisfied Dr. Fortescue's own exacting standards. Beside the inscription there is an exquisitely written translation on a varnished panel by Grailey Hewitt, a fellow student of the Doctor in the classes of Edward Johnston.

The Pastor

It is hard to imagine a scholar who produced even a fraction of Dr. Fortescue's literary output, not to mention his public lectures, teaching commitments, and other activities, being able to cope with the duties of a parish priest in a conscientious manner. But, in fact, very few parish priests can ever have carried out their duties more conscientiously than he did. Although his personal inclination was for the life of a scholar, his high sense of duty would never allow him to put his scholarly pursuits before the care of the souls entrusted to him. His visits to the poor and sick were paid with the most scrupulous regularity, no matter how busy he might be. He was never known to refuse to see a caller, however inconvenient it might be for him to interrupt his work. In his study there were four desks, and he would flit from one to another as the mood took him, writing a separate book on each. The desks were breast-high and he preferred to write standing, and even to read standing. One of these desks can be seen in the museum at Letchworth together with other relics of the Doctor, including samples of his calligraphy. Although much of the routine parish work was far from congenial to a scholar of his temperament, it was always done thoroughly. Everything that a parish priest could do, and many things that most could never have conceived or accomplished, were done devotedly throughout his fifteen years at St. Hugh.

Dr. Fortescue catechized his parishioners with extraordinary zeal. There can have been no parish in Europe where the faithful were better instructed in their religion, their liturgy, the lives of the saints, and all that concerns the worship of God. He took endless pains to ensure that every person in his parish understood his religion and appreciated the liturgy. He gave up two precious hours every Saturday evening to writing in his exquisite hand the parish notice-sheet for the week. In her obituary written for *Catholic Truth*, Edith Cowell wrote:

> He took as much pains over the weekly notice-sheet as some priests would over a sermon. He would make any old excuse to illuminate these sheets. On Christmas night, for instance, we would find a delicious picture of Letchworth, with all the windows dark except those of St Hugh (not "St. Hugh's" , mind).

In a letter written to an Anglican lady in Letchworth in August 1909, after making a retreat, Dr. Fortescue made clear how uncongenial he found parish work, and how desperately he wished that his superiors would recognize his scholarly aptitude and make it possible for him to pursue his studies in the interests of the Church, as would have been the case had he not been a secular priest, but had belonged to a religious order. He wrote:

> I am not really much good at parish work. There are lots of men who are really keen about it and good at it, who get a real personal interest in their people and children and school. I can't help the fact that I'm not made that way (though I suppose I could force myself to do my duty if I had to). In my heart I am not really a bit keen about poor people and working up a thriving parish, and young men's clubs, and schools. Of course I wish I were. Really whenever I have to do those things, in my heart I have wanted to get it all over so as to go back to my books. On the other hand I can do writing work and am good at it. That is rarer in England (among our people, I mean) and there is some want of it. I am sure that there is room for a few student-priests among us—there will never be more than very few. So if I am to go on as a secular priest it would seem to be more reasonable that I should do the kind of work I am naturally good at (that is wanted too) than what I should never do as well as heaps

of other men...In the retreat all the old dreams and ambitions came back. What should I have said ten years ago if I had been told that my life was to be that of a sort of country gentleman, good at amateur photography and popular at tea parties, with a lot of lady-friends? I know I have missed any real chance. I shall never now do anything really worth doing. The old childish dreams of a university professorship and great work for Catholic theology, building up a school and starting a great movement—or a bishopric and vast influence in Church politics! That is all gone. The Vienna people are right. I was going to become something tremendous, wonderful and then—one more disappointment—I just dropped out.

Dr. Fortescue's wishes were not granted by his superiors, and he was compelled to live out his all too brief life as a parish priest. Knowing how uncongenial he found parish work must increase our admiration for the dedication with which he fulfilled it, and despite the sentiments expressed in the letter that has just been quoted, there can be no doubt that he had grown to love his parish and his people before his untimely death in 1923, as his insistence upon being buried among them makes clear. Edith Cowell concluded her *Blackfriars* obituary with by remarking: "No one was ever—outwardly—less priestly; no one was ever—inwardly—more thoroughly a priest."

The Pontifical Biblical Commission

It is possible that Adrian Fortescue was forced to live out his life in a relatively insignificant parish because, as was the case with Newman, his intellect and his learning caused him to be regarded with suspicion and even envy by some of his ecclesiastical superiors. This is not surprising at a time when the anti-Modernist crusade was at its height, and his correspondence with Father Thurston makes clear that he considered the Vatican to be over-reacting to the heresy, particularly in the realm of biblical scholarship. He objected to the fact that no disagreement with or criticism of the decisions of the Pontifical Biblical Commission was permitted, but that these decisions did not carry the note of infallibility. His prudent reaction was to write nothing on such controverted aspects of the Scriptures as the Mosaic authorship of the entire Pentateuch, or the historicity of the first three books of Genesis. We must certainly be glad of this as his writing on the liturgy is of permanent and widespread interest, whereas anything that he might have written on the Scriptures would probably have been of interest only to scholars and might well have dated quickly and been of little interest today. In a letter dated 12 October 1911 to his close friend Father Harold Burton, also a contributor to *The Catholic Encyclopaedia*, Dr. Fortescue mentioned, with typical sardonic humour, his decision to avoid writing on the Scriptures. He had offered Burton some books that he no longer wanted:

> Some represent work I meant to do and have now finally abandoned. For instance you will observe some *biblica*. Time was when I was young & had no sense, *regnante Leone*, that I meant to read the Bible. The various decisions of the Pontifical Biblical Commission have long shown me that Christians had better leave that interesting volume altogether alone. Apparently there is very little you are allowed to say at all and what there is is not *tutum*. So, do you know the advice L. da Vinci gave to the hopelessly ugly man?—*Lasciare le donne e studiare la matematica* ("Forget women and study mathematics).

It is of no little interest to note that the positions of the Pontifical Biblical Commission which Dr. Fortescue found unconvincing were no longer insisted upon by the Holy See by the Pontificate of Pope Pius XII. They were never repudiated. It was not at that time the custom in the Vatican to say *Erravimus*. Dr. Fortescue's position could certainly be said to have been vindicated by the encyclical *Divino Afflante Spiritu* of Pope Pius XII.[16]

The Liturgy at St. Hugh

Dr. Fortescue's Mass was something to remember. It was slow: every word that was intended to be audible was perfect. All that was about the altar was exquisitely tended. He spent hours with his servers before great feasts, practising every detail of the ceremonies. The offices for Holy Week, for which he had a deep devotion, were carried out with every possible ceremony in St. Hugh. Dr. Fortescue grew to be very proud of his beautiful little church, so much of which he had designed and paid for personally. "It is the only church worth looking at west of Constantinople," he would claim vehemently.

The music at St. Hugh was of an uniquely high standard. To be a member of its choir was to receive a thorough musical education from the Doctor and his devoted choirmaster, Thomas Wilfred Willson, always known as Wilfred. Mr. Willson, a devout Anglican and an experienced musician, had been a boy chorister at St. Mary's Parish Church in Dover, and both a boy singer and later a bass singer at the Anglican Church in Calais. He had come to work in Letchworth in 1908 and lodged with a Catholic lady who told him that her parish priest needed a voluntary organist to play the harmonium. He called on Dr. Fortescue, offered his help, but made it clear that he would never become a Catholic. Within a year he was received into the Church! He became a close friend of the Doctor and was eventually appointed choirmaster as well as organist. He went on behalf of the Doctor to select the Positive Organ for the temporary church, which was later moved to the permanent church, and he designed and constructed the ingenious swell box for it.[17] He also made the beautiful oak pulpit, designed with the help of Dr. Fortescue, and an oak prie-dieu for the sanctuary. The two men became close friends, and after choir practice each Friday they would spend the evening together in Dr. Fortescue's study, smoking cigars, drinking coffee, and discussing everything under the sun. Their aim was to achieve musical perfection, and they must have come as near to achieving this as any parish choir has ever done. It is not without significance that the norms for music mandated by the Liturgy Constitution of the Second Vatican Council conformed almost exactly to the pattern established by Dr. Fortescue and Wilfred Willson at St. Hugh. Gregorian Chant was established as the norm, but polyphony was by no means excluded. The entire congregation was able to sing the ordinary of the Mass in plainchant, in accordance with the wishes of St. Pius X, but Dr. Fortescue and his choirmaster realized that although a good parish choir could be expected to master the various plainchant settings of the Ordinary of the Mass, the time required each week to learn the Propers from the *Liber Usualis* was rather more than lay members of an amateur choir could be expected to give, and so the Doctor adapted, and in some cases composed, simple chants to which parts of the Proper might be sung. During the First World War, when most of his male choristers were in the armed forces, Dr. Fortescue arranged all the part music for Holy Week for women's voices. There still exists in the church a beautiful leather-bound book of music written out by the Doctor in his exquisite hand and illuminated by him. It must certainly be one of the most sublime works of Catholic art produced in England since the Middle Ages.

In 1913 he compiled for his people a book of Latin hymns with, in most cases, his own English prose translations. It was set for him by Bernard Newdigate in Caslon type, and printed by Newdigate's sister, Mary, on the small printing press at her home, Astley Cottage, Letchworth. The Doctor himself supervised the printing. A second edition of the book published posthumously in 1924 is far more celebrated from a typographical standpoint. It was redesigned by Stanley Morison who retained the Caslon type, but with the brief introductions to each hymn printed in Caslon italic, to which Newdigate did not have access in 1913. This edition was printed by the Cambridge University Press which, at that time, under the guidance of Morison, was renowned throughout the world for the superlative quality of its printing. Morison's cover design is exceptionally striking. In the preface to his hymnbook, Dr. Fortescue wrote:

> I have gathered together all the hymns and chants which we usually sing with a double purpose. First, that anyone who knows the tune may join the singers; secondly, that those who do not sing may be able to follow, to know what is being sung. Every text has an English translation on the opposite page. If anyone does not understand Latin, he can use the translation as his own prayer, and so join in intention with those who sing...There is not, and there is never likely to be, any religious poetry in the world worthy to be compared with the hymns of the Latin office...our old Latin hymns are immeasurably more beautiful than any others ever composed. Other religious bodies take all their best hymns from us. It would be a disgrace if we Catholics were the only people who did not appreciate what is our property. And, from every point of view, we of the old Church cannot do better than sing to God as our fathers sang to Him during all the long Ages behind us. Nor shall we find a better expression of Catholic piety than these words, hallowed by centuries of Catholic use, fragrant with the memory of the saints who wrote them in that golden age when practically all Christendom was Catholic.

In view of the extent to which he deplored the changes made to the Breviary hymns during the Pontificate of Urban VIII, one might wonder whether Dr. Fortescue used the older versions in his book. Submissive to legitimate authority he did not. He writes:

> A great number of the hymns are taken from the Roman breviary. Many of these were altered in 1629, with the idea of

making them agree better with the laws of classical Latin poetry. Everyone now admits that this was a mistake. Much of the beauty of the older forms was lost and the hymns did not really become classical. We have reason to hope that the present reform of the breviary will also give us back the old form of the hymns. But meanwhile it seems necessary to keep the later text. This is the one best known, it is given in all hymn books and is still the only authorized form.

The War Years

During the war a number of Belgian refugees came to live in Letchworth, and the Doctor would write every notice in three languages, English, French, and Flemish. He would also preach in these three languages until the Belgians were able to return home at the end of the war. The notice-sheet also gave learned, and sometimes humorous, accounts of the saints whose feasts fell during the coming week, and detailed instructions for finding the Proper of the Mass, so that when, for instance, there were more than twenty-four Sundays after Pentecost, everyone knew that the parts sung by the choir were to be found in the Proper for the twenty-third Sunday, while the rest of the Proper followed that of the extra Sundays after Epiphany— and so on. The music for the following Sunday was also given, with the names and dates of the composers, and often a note on one or other of the hymns which were to be sung. Nothing was too good for the church that he loved.

On at least one occasion during the war, Dr. Fortescue had the opportunity of preaching once more in German, one of his favourite languages. In a letter to Sir John Fortescue he wrote:

I had a wonderful experience this morning. Unwilling I had to get another man to do my business here. I went away from my own church and my music and rode my bicycle a long way, to say Mass in a prisoners' camp. I did so in the attic of a granary, so badly lit that I could scarcely see the missal. The Catholic Germans had rigged up an altar of planks and thrown their blankets over it. They had made absurd bouquets of wild flowers, buttercups and dandelions and things, and put them in mugs. I heard their confessions, and said Mass, and preached, and gave them Communion. The whole thing fetched me enormously. When I think about the war on big lines, I eat fire, as every Englishman does; and I want Mr Hohenzollern (and especially Mr Hohenzollern Jun.) to be hanged. But there was no feeling of that kind this morning. It was like the catacombs—the low dark spaces and the rows of those nice peasants, Bavarians, Westphalians, Rheinlanders, kneeling on the ground all round their rough altar. A flood of old memories came with a rush as I talked to them in that beautiful dear language. It is a dear language to me in spite of all. I did nearly all my University in Austria and Germany (after Rome)—nine solid years, and the best nine years of my life (21 to 30), in which I was practically a German among Germans. At one time I spoke German far more easily than any other language. Now all that has faded. For years I have hardly used German in speaking at all, always Flemish. This morning I was back in the days when I said Mass at Innsbruck, and the morning light shone on the great white mountains. They sang the old hymns I have not heard for years—all day since the tune of *Hier liegt vor deiner Majestät* has been sounding in my head. Even the little German tricks of the man who served Mass and his funny German pronunciation of Latin brought back memories of Feri and Karel and dear Ernö and all those old friends with whom I used to chatter and climb mountains and argue. They are all lost to me now. I suppose they hate every Englishman like poison. Then I talked a bit to my prisoners and said I hoped they would soon be back in their own homes. So I came out into the bright sunlight and passed the barbed wire and the sentry— and I was in England again. It was like crossing a frontier, and about 15 years in a moment. This evening, as they were singing Compline, I heard the tune of *Hier liegt vor deiner Majestät* all the time, and the sound of cow-bells. I sat in my place by the altar, and looked out of the window at the evening light, and wondered if that light were shining with alp-glow on the Tirol mountains as it used to. When I began to preach to my own people it was an effort not to start in German.

Pacifism

As a result of the war a serious disagreement arose between Dr. Fortescue and Stanley Morison, but without in the least affecting their close friendship. Morison was an extreme pacifist and refused to serve his country even in a non-combatant role. He and Francis Meynell both declared themselves to be conscientious objectors in 1916. Newdigate and Fortescue took the opposite standpoint. Newdigate volunteered for service and was commissioned in the Royal Warwickshire Regiment. In 1916 Dr. Fortescue published a pamphlet entitled *Pacifism— A Word with Conscientious Objectors*. Without in any way calling into question the sincerity of Christian conscientious objectors such as Morison, he made it clear that in no way can the Christian religion be used legitimately to prevent a citizen from coming to the defence of his country in a just war, laying stress upon the fact that the war must be just. One short extract will demonstrate the force of his argument:

In the matter of taking human life, then, the whole question resolves itself to this: is there any good greater than a man's life, so that I may kill him, if necessary, for the sake of that good? The Pacifist implicitly says not. The idea which is the basis of his position is that human life is so precious a thing that no other good can ever compensate for its loss. If it were so, we should have to admit that the Pacifist is right. If human life is the supreme good, then no cause would justify a man in taking it. But the principle is false and can be shown to be false.

There are, on the contrary, many good things which out-weigh beyond measure the evil of the loss of one, two, twenty, or even a million human lives. Human life is so precious, so that certainly, only the very gravest cause can justify a man in taking it. That is not the issue between us and the Pacifist. The issue is whether it is the supreme good; so that nothing can ever be more valuable. To think so is his mistake. The good estate, peace, civilization of a whole country is a greater good than human life, or a number of human lives. It may be difficult in each case to measure the balance, to say exactly how many men's lives are equal to a certain other good. But the Pacifist's general principle is obviously false. When for instance the Huns, the real Huns this time, were over-running civilized Europe, to arrest the evils they were causing more than compensated for the loss of a number of Huns' lives. The Roman soldiers at Chalons were justified in taking lives, and in exposing their own, to save peaceful provinces of the Empire from the murder, rape, devastation that the Huns would otherwise cause. This is the issue in the question of every just war; is the good for which we fight sufficiently great to justify us in allowing the evils of war, as a necessary means to it? Of course it has not always been so. It would not be a sufficient reason to inflict so appalling an evil as war, merely to gratify the ambition of a Prince. This only means that not all wars are just. But there are good results which outweigh the evil of war, and so there are just wars.

The Man

Although he was capable of warm and enduring friend-ships, Adrian Fortescue was, by nature, a shy and sensitive man. He would mask this sensitivity by appearing in public to be brusque, sardonic, and even arrogant. Edith Cowell writes:

> Comparatively few people knew Dr. Fortescue personally. Even of these very few understood him. This was his fault,

not theirs, for, unlike most of us, his policy throughout life seems to have been to put his worst into the shop window, and keep his best hidden away in cupboards which he could rarely be persuaded to unlock.

It is in letters to his few intimate friends that the true Adrian Fortescue manifests himself. These letters make it clear that he enjoyed Christmas more than any other festival in the year. In one such letter dated 28 December 1909 he writes:

This Christmas was perfectly glorious and heavenly to me...I think that perhaps the best time of all is just before it begins always—the end of Christmas eve and the beginning of the holy night. The grey twilight drew in, and all day we were busy decking the church and preparing, and I had lots of confessions to hear, and we ate our fasting supper very late...I stood in my room at my desk with the light of the green lamp on my books and white walls and did nothing but think and look out of the window.

It was a heavenly night. Cold with a glimmer of frost on the grass and paths, and a bright moon sailing across the dark sky, and making strange shadows from trees, black and sharp across the silver, all black and silver underneath, and above the white quiet stars. I waited for matins alone and looked out over the silent night across the great field (over my fence)—*stille Nacht, heilige Nacht*.

And I saw again the long white twisting road that goes out from the Jaffa gate of Jerusalem, past Rachael's tomb, to Bethlehem, and the market place, and there the Nativity church and the huddled roofs, and the quiet fields outside where they were keeping the watches of the night by their sheep. It was very quiet and beautiful, and I thought of other years too and could hear bells ringing for matins across the sea and mountains in the cold night air at Innsbruck.

And I said the prayers before Mass—strange to be saying them in the evening. At eleven the church was lit up and warm

50

and we began matins. All the singing was quite beautiful: the *Invitatorium—Christus natus est nobis: venite adoremus*—twined and curved and twisted like garlands of beautiful strange sound, in the IVth mode, across the church. Then the glorious Christmas hymn—*Jesu redemptor omnium*; we sang...the first nocturn lessons to the old German chant with wonderful neums...You know—the Isaias lessons: *Puer natus est nobis et filius datus est nobis...et consurge, consurge Hierusalem...et ecce virgo concipiet et pariet filium et vocabitur nomen eius Emmanuel...* And the second and third nocturn lessons, beautiful homilies of the old Fathers, Leo and Ambrose and Augustine and the Christmas psalms and the responsories to beautiful tunes I had made myself, and then just before midnight the *Te Deum*.

Then we went to the sacristy and I vested and we came round through the garden and in at the big doors. In the garden I saw the blue cloud of the incense against the moonlight of the sky and the tall cross black outline against the stars and the pale flames of the acolytes' candles burning clear in the cold still air.

And we came up the church as they sang—quite beautifully—the Introit of midnight Mass, while the smoke of the incense and the black and silver cross slowly moved along. Then all that wonderful and strange Mass in the middle of the dark night. I sang the gospel about the shepherds and the crowd of the heavenly army, and the Christmas preface, under the dark garlands of holly and bay, while the thin white candles held up their flames among the lilies and the chrysanthema and shone on the white corporal and silver chalice.

And the choir's *Sanctus* rang out across the silent night, and from the windows the light shone out into the dark outside. Then the silence and the bell and the Canon: "Communicating and remembering the most sacred night when the unspotted Mother gave birth to the Saviour of the world, and honouring the memory first of that same glorious Virgin Mary,

mother of our God and Lord Jesus Christ, and of Thy blessed
Apostles and Martyrs Peter and Paul, Andrew, James..." And
the long rows of my nice little people kneeling at the altar
rails while I gave them Communion...And at half past one I
went to bed and did not sleep for excitement and saw it all
again, and our dear Lady laying Him in the manger—*haec
sacratissima nox*.

I said the dawn Mass at eight, as the grey winter light
shone in the east, and the third Mass at ten; and then was
utterly done and tired, but frightfully happy as I ate my tea
and toast. I did remember you too...and everyone I love, when
I stood before my altar all white and gold and gleaming under the tall candles in the holy night...

The Doctor would never show the depth of his religious
feeling. This was a matter between himself and God—a domain where none might ever pry. One might hear his splendid
enthusiasm for the liturgy, for the wonders of Holy Week, for
certain prayers at Mass, for Church Music, for the early martyrs, for St. Augustine, for a thousand things that affect the
Catholic Church and her history, but never the deeper things
of his spirit. He could not bring himself to make explicit in
public his fiery enthusiasm for the cause of Christ, and his rev-
erent awe for the things of God. But this could not be hidden
from those who were present when he offered Mass, or who
even saw him genuflect. Dr. Fortescue's reluctance to express
anything which smacked of emotion was reflected in his sermons, which were always short, carefully prepared, and packed
with instruction. Edith Cowell stated that he considered it ill-
bred to show one's love for the Church in public. His Lenten
sermons on the Passion were the one exception to this reticence, and they even attracted non-Catholics. Then, and almost only then, did he lay aside his reticence and speak words
which drew tears and made converts. He made a good many
converts at Letchworth, and took endless pains over their in-

struction. He did not strive for eloquence in his preaching. He was too honest intellectually, and too scrupulous, lest by any words of his he should call forth emotion which might hinder the free use of the reason.

The consideration shown by Adrian Fortescue for those who had won his friendship was made very clear by his role in the marriage of his choirmaster Wilfred Willson to Clare McDonnell. Miss McDonnell had come to live in Letchworth with another Catholic young lady at the suggestion of Dr. Fortescue, whom she sometimes met at the London home of his sister, Gertrude Squire. Miss McDonnell soon joined the choir and was introduced by Dr. Fortescue to his choirmaster, almost certainly in the hope of their eventual marriage. Mr. Willson's ultra-Protestant family was dismayed at his decision to become a Catholic, and even more so when he announced his intention of marrying a Catholic lady. They allowed Wilfred to continue to visit the family home, but he was forbidden to bring his prospective bride. The Doctor intervened, and he charmed the Willsons to such an extent that they actually came to the wedding and the reception, the latter taking place in the Doctor's study and spilling out into his garden. He not only organized the entire event but took and processed the wedding photographs. Their eldest son, Adrian, learned that the Doctor once told his mother that he had given her husband the two finest gifts of his life—the Catholic faith and the most charming young woman in the parish! Adrian Willson, who was named after the Doctor, remembers being present one day when Dr. Fortescue gave his father some advice on his education:

> When he grows up give him a good education. There are only three subjects a young man needs—Latin, fencing, and heraldry. Everything of importance is written in Latin; fencing sharpens the wits and a man never knows when he may need to defend himself; and heraldry because it makes such a fascinating hobby.

Adrian Fortescue was a stoutly built, full-blooded man, of great physical strength and of true manly virtue in the old classical sense. This stood him in good stead during the journeys to the wild and remote places that he loved so much. Twice at least he fought for his life. On one occasion he was engaged in a hand-to-hand struggle with some fanatical Albanian soldiers at Hebron, and he and his companions had to fight their way with bludgeons to their horses and gallop away, in Adrian's case with a broken collar-bone. On a second occasion the caravan with which he was travelling in Asia Minor, disguised as an Arab, was attacked by brigands, and in self-defence he killed an assailant with a pistol shot. He mentioned this incident in a letter to his close friend Father Harold Burton in 1907:

> I have just come back from a year spent in Syria, Mesopotamia, Asia Minor & Greece. I saw many and wonderful things. I rode long days across the great Syrian desert, alone among Arabs. I stood among the ruins of strange dead Greek cities in Asia Minor & slept on the bare earth under broken white columns where Diana of the Ephesians had once reigned as a mighty god. And I saw forests & climbed mountains and crept through deep passes in the heart of Asia Minor. I went a-pilgriming to the holy places too, said Mass at the holy sepulchre, spent the night of Maundy Thursday on the Mount of Olives & saw the Easter sun rise above the golden walls of Herod's temple. Then there were Damascus, the slow brown waters of the Euphrates, the orchards of Galilee, Cyprus (a heavenly island), the tawny pillars of the Athenian Acropolis, the fat plains & strange Byzantine monasteries of Thessaly; and—far most glorious of all—the line of domes and minarets, radiant, white & fretted like carved ivory against a hot grey-blue sky, that crown imperially Constantine's New Rome by the Bosphorus. So you see I have had a purple time. I have learned to talk Syrian Arabic quite well & some Turk-

ish. Greek I could talk already; & now I work at Persian like a horse, greatly hoping to go out again in a year or two & next time to reach Teheran & Shiraz. Also I made a heap of drawings and learned much about Mohammedan ideas. But I suffered a great hunger & thirst & heat, was under fire from robbers & Bedawin several times; once I saved my life by flight, leaving all my baggage to the spoiler, once I shot a man dead (a horrid memory); I had my shoulder smashed to bits in a fight at Hebron & lay six weeks sorely sick in the French hospital at Jerusalem, & I nearly died of malarial fever at Aleppo. Such is the outline. To hear more you must come to see me, as I very much hope you will. Now I shall not go back to Maldon, but I am to start a new mission at Letchworth in Hertfordshire—where this new Garden City place is. I am very pleased with the idea indeed.

The Humour of Dr. Fortescue

Dr. Fortescue had a highly developed sense of humour. A joke which he made every year about Christmas time, was a notice on Sunday morning that evergreens for the decoration of the church should be left in the presbytery garden on the afternoon of *O Rex Gentium*. In the evening he would announce with pained surprise that it appeared that there were actually some Catholics so appallingly ignorant that they had never heard of the Great O's, and consequently had to be told on which day *O Rex Gentium* came.[18] He once remarked that whenever a young boy told him in confession that he had committed simony by buying and selling benefices he knew that he had been reading the Catechism.

On Twelfth Night, 1908, Dr Fortescue granted a pardon to May Crickmer, with whose family he dined frequently. It reads:

> This is to certify that May Crickmer hereby receives full indulgence, pardon, remission, and forgiveness of all crimes,

offences, and misdemeanours committed by her before this Twelfthnight, 1908, on condition that the said May, Mary, or Bill Crickmer:

I, do humbly and heartily repent of the said crimes and of fences.;

II, do hereby make a firm and solid purpose of amendment for the future;

III, do pay the usual fees for pardons according to the accompanying tariff;

IV, do hereinafter walk in new paths and diligently amend her life.

In witness whereof we do hereto affix our sign and seal

Adrian Fortescue.

Twelfthnight, 1908.

At times he liked to play the *enfant terrible* and shock his friends. "What is the difference between X (a member of his congregation) and Balaam's ass? Answer: There is no difference." When reproached for comparing his parishioner to the ass he agreed that he had been uncharitable—to the donkey!

Dr. Fortescue took a particular delight in denigrating the Vatican Curia with remarks of the most outrageous nature. When he learned that Stanley Morison had arranged to visit Rome he wrote to him with the following advice:

Do not speak to any officials of the Curia, nor have any dealings with any of them. They are the lowest class of men that survives. If you go near them they will probably pick your pockets or try to sell you an indulgence. Remember me to the present Ordinary, if you see him. I am told he is a decent man. It was Leo XIII in my time.

When his friend Dr. Burton of St. Edmund's College was appointed an honorary Canon of Westminster, the Doctor wrote on 30 December 1917 to congratulate him—on the fact that he had not been made a *monsignore*:

I must speak with caution, since I fear the evil may yet fall on you. At any rate, so far you do not have to add a filthy Italian prefix to a decent English name. It is, of course, all right for an ass like Barton-Brown (who never fails to impress on me the majesty of a member of the Papal Household, the rights and precedence it gives him to be a *Cameriere*). Still, for a man who fears the God of Israel, it must be an awful thing to be classed among the sweepings of the Italian gutters who lurk around the back yards and latrines of the Vatican, their greasy palms outstretched for tips, their oily lips bubbling with servile lies in bad French. However—if you notice that I do not say a quarter of what I think on this subject, put it down to the matchless delicacy which forbids me to use adequate language about *Monsignori*, since I fear that after all some day they may land the putrid thing on you. If they do I will write and commiserate.

The Doctor avoided with horror all social functions and publicity. "I went to Westminster yesterday, but I smelt bishops and fled away," he remarked to his cousin, Lady Winifred. A letter written in 1917 to a Protestant lady from Letchworth, and a very close friend, shows how relaxed and amusing he could be. Mrs. Webb, his housekeeper had given him notice, and he asked his friend to find a new one for him:

If you can—this is what I want. I do not want a Roman Catholic. There are great difficulties about that, especially in a small country place. It is difficult for her to go to confession to her employer; also the danger is that she would become a great lady among her own class and gossip to them about all Father does. I would rather have someone quite outside my parish, with whom I have no relations except as her employer. I want an oldish and eminently respectable woman, one whose appearance will not make any danger of scandal (do not send me a fair young thing with her golden hair hanging down her back). All the same, I want someone not absolutely decrepit, respectable in every way, and capable. Edith says I shall have to demand the most exacting references. She should be a decent cook of the kind called plain, but not too infernally plain. I have suffered much from Mrs. Webb's plain cooking (which means nothing ever but cold mutton). She must be clean and economical and honest—in short have all the virtues—you know the sort of thing.

His friend did manage to find a housekeeper, and one wonders whether she was the one referred to by his cousin Lady Winifred: "Like all bachelors, Adrian was terrified of his housekeeper, who, as is the way with housekeepers of single men, tyrannised over him."

There was an occasion when Cardinal Bourne decided to require all the priests serving in his diocese who had been ordained abroad to submit to an examination. No exception was made for the most learned priest in the diocese, Adrian Fortescue with his triple doctorate. All the candidates duly finished their papers and departed, with the exception of Dr. Fortescue who continued to write and write and write. The Canon who was superintending the examination began to feel hungry, but, to his dismay, his remaining candidate produced a packet of sandwiches which be proceeded to eat with great relish while continuing to write. Finally, the hungry Canon could bear it no longer. He approached the candidate and enquired if he had nearly finished. Dr. Fortescue, with an amazed expression, answered that he had not as he was answering the question: "State what you know about the Arian heresy." It is to be hoped that, for the sake of the famished Canon, he did not go to the extent of writing down all that he knew about this particular topic. How wonderful it would be if Dr. Fortescue's paper could be found one day in the diocesan archives.

Dr. Fortescue realized that time is our most precious commodity, and he hated to waste so much as a second of it. When almost bullied by his doctor into taking a daily walk he chose the road to the Arlesey Asylum, because nothing on that dull and ugly route could possibly divert his thoughts from the Arabic dictionary he studied on the way there, and the Persian grammar that replaced it on the homeward journey. He did, however, have one weakness, if weakness it can be called, which was that of reading what were known as "sevenpenny novels" at the end of each day. These were works devoid of any intellectual content or literary merit. He was reproached for this by his friend Reginald Hine, a lawyer and author, who told the Doctor that he had another friend with a triple doctorate who shared the same weakness, but that when he went to the public library to select his weekly supply he would pretend that they were for his maids.

"Silly man," said Adrian, "he should own up. There's nothing wrong in it. It's dull to sleep with the Fathers, and you can't go to bed with the saints. The fact is one simply has to relax and unbend on something lighter, or else one's brain would bust."

On one occasion the Doctor gave a lecture on the subject of language in the Howard Hall, named after Ebenezer Howard, the founder of the first Garden City at Letchworth. He referred to Esperanto in somewhat scathing terms, as an artificial concept with no literature and no special appeal. An indignant Esperantist challenged the Doctor by recounting the manner in which he had obtained help at the Gare du Nord in Paris after seeing a passenger wearing an Esperanto badge. The Doctor replied that he had been at the Gare du Nord on many occasions, and had never had the least difficulty in making himself understood although he did not speak Esperanto. "How was that?" asked the Esperantist. "I speak French," explained the Doctor. He would certainly have reacted with angry disbelief if anyone had suggested to him that in the final decade of this century the Vatican would permit Mass to be celebrated in Esperanto to enable Catholics from different countries to worship together in a common language!

Mention has already been made of Dr. Fortescue's ability to present the fruits of his researches with great clarity. He had no patience whatsoever for verbosity or unnecessarily abstruse language, as he made clear in his uniquely witty manner in the preface to the best known of all his books, *Ceremonies of the Roman Rite Described* (which he wrote not as a labour of love but in order to obtain £100 for urgently needed work to be completed on his church). Until the publication of the Fortescue book, the Catholic clergy in England had relied upon a translation by the Reverend J.D. Dale of an Italian book written in 1839 by the Reverend G. Baldeschi, Master of Ceremonies in St. Peter's Basilica. "Unwillingly," wrote Fortescue, "one speaks ill of a work which has for so many years been the chief guide to Catholic ceremonies in England." He then proceeded, in the best Fortescue manner, to speak ill of it with the greatest possible gusto!

It is said that the test of a good translation is that it should read like an original work. According to this ideal Dale comes off very badly indeed. He has such a mania for using Italian words that a great part of his book is not really English at all, and can hardly be understood till one has translated it back into Italian. Not only does he use an Italian name on every possible occasion; when the words are English he translates with ruthless exactness all the gorgeous phrases of Italian grand style. For instance in Dale you do not bow to the celebrant, "you proceed to make the customary salutation"; you do not stand, you "retain a standing posture." Everyone "observes" to do everything: you observe not to kneel, you observe to retain a kneeling posture. The M.C. does not tell a man to do a thing, he apprizes him that it should be performed. The celebrant "terminates" the Creed; he genuflects in conjunction with the sacred Ministers—then he observes to assume a standing posture in conjunction with them. The M.C. goes about apprizing and comporting himself till he observes to perform the customary salutation. The subdeacon imparts the *Pax* in the same manner as it was communicated to him. Everyone exhibits a grave deportment. Imagine anyone talking like this. Imagine anyone saying that you ought to exhibit a deportment. Of course we have to "ascend" every time, the blessing is always "benediction," harmful becomes "deleterious," and so on. Frankly, I do not think I have ever read a book written in so atrocious a style. The only thing in its favour is that it is extremely funny. However, since the book is meant to be serious, it is a pity that someone did not apprize Dale to proceed to observe the customary use of language, in conjunction with people who write English.

There was an occasion when Dr. Fortescue was being shown one of the early cars (automobiles). Gingerly he pressed the klaxon horn, and jumped back at its raucous noise. "Good heavens," he exclaimed, "it sounds like the Canons of St. Peter's singing Terce." If Dr. Fortescue's opinion of the musical standards prevailing in the Basilica of St. Peter was not very high, he could be equally scathing about his own choir who adored him, and who received his comments in the spirit in which they were delivered. While on holiday in Sicily in 1913 he sent a postcard to his choirmaster saying that it had occurred to him to wonder what Mr. Willson was doing because he had taken part in a Byzantine liturgy and had thought of him "in the midst of their strange wailing"! In a similar vein he remarked that he was most intrigued with a line that he had discovered in a seventeenth century Protestant hymn: "The beastly creatures sing His praise." "I think," he explained, "that the gentleman really means the quadrupeds (though few of them really sing; John does). But is it not a heavenly line? It ought to be written up as a motto in the choir. Every time I hear you all at Compline I shall think of it."

The John referred to was the Doctor's cat. He was very fond of cats, and one was almost invariably curled up in a comfortable place in his study. When he knew that death was certain, his last words to a lady in his parish were: "If the worst comes to the worst you will look after John."

Boethius and The Uniate Eastern Churches

In 1919 Dr. Fortescue undertook a project to which he was to devote much of the remaining four years of his life. He explained it in a letter to Francis Meynell who worked with Stanley Morison for the Catholic publisher Burns & Oates:

> I write this to propose to you a plan that I have much at heart. I want you to print the Latin Text of Boethius: *de Consolatione Philosophiae*. First, it is really one of the most important books of later Latin. Perhaps you know already that it had an enormous influence through all the middle ages. St. Thomas Aquinas and a score of other famous people wrote commentaries on it. In those days everyone read this book. It is one of the most important sources of Dante. Boethius was really the man who first introduced the philosophy of Aristotle to the West. He is one of the chief sources of the whole school, or schools, of Catholic philosophy. He is the original source of a crowd of sayings, proverbs, axioms, and so on, repeated from him by Dante, and then by everyone since. For instance: "A sorrow's crown of sorrows is remembering happier things" was first said by Boethius in his *Consol(atione) Phil*. It is also an exceedingly beautiful little book, alternately in prose and poetry, full of fine things and beautiful verses. I verified in the Museum catalogue the other day that this book was printed over and over again, with commentaries and without, from the XVth to the XVIIIth centuries. But now comes the incredible fact. There is not a single edition of the Latin text now in print, anywhere in the world...

Dr. Fortescue proposed an edition that would be a masterpiece of typography, a beautiful edition that would bring great glory to the firm that published it. Morison shared Fortescue's enthusiasm for the project, which pleased the Doctor greatly. He replied to Morison on 24 March 1919:

> I am all eagerness for Boethius...Then I hope you will be so kind enough to look after the production of as pretty a book as possible. I have seen some work of the Pelican Press which I think beautiful. Would it be possible to have big versals (initial letters) and then to print some copies with the space for these left blank, so that one could fill them in by hand?

Fortescue had, by this time, come to reciprocate fully the admiration that Morison felt for him. He made this clear in a letter dated 17 February 1920 with the almost boyish ingenuousness which characterized so much of his personal correspondence:

> When I first heard of you I thought: "Who is this ass who has the cheek to talk to ME about writing or printing?" Now I have the most absolute, final, wholehearted trust in your judgement and taste in all such things, and I know that you know infinite streets more than I do about them. You see, at first you occurred to me only as a Burns and Oates person, whose ideal of fine printing would probably be the Granville series. Then I began to see the Fell type and other things; and I began to understand that you and Francis Meynell were not exactly the sort of people I had imagined...

The Fortescue *Boethius* had not been completed before the Doctor's death. It was made ready for publication by his friend Canon George D. Smith. Published by Burns and Oates and printed by the Cambridge University Press under the close personal supervision of Stanley Morison, it was indeed a masterpiece of typography. It would be hard to find a more striking example of elegance and simplicity than Morison's cover design. The edition, entirely in Latin, contains a life of Boethius, a chapter on his religious beliefs, and hundreds of notes by Dr. Fortescue. In a letter dated 26 March 1924, to Miss Ethel Elmes,[19] Canon Smith remarked:

> I must confess that much as I enjoyed doing the book, it is a great relief to have it done. I feel at the same time a certain nervousness as to whether it is all right, as to whether (as I have expressed it in the preface) "operi quae addidi non obfuere". One thing I am certain of, and that is that I have omitted none of the information contained in his notes. I have added a certain amount of my own—but only what I think the Holy Man would have added, if he had lived to complete the book. I think he will be pleased with what I have done. That he may be has been my wish all the time I was working at it, and I have always tried to imagine to myself his encouraging smile. Imagine his horror if he sees that I am allowing the book to go into press with a wrong reference somewhere. Still I do not suppose there has ever been a book without some mistake in it.

It is to be hoped that some wealthy university foundation may decide to produce a facsimile edition.

Canon Smith also undertook to bring to publication another unfinished work by the Doctor, *The Uniate Eastern Churches*. In his preface Canon Smith wrote:

> A few days before he died Dr. Fortescue expressed to me a wish that this work on the Uniate Churches should be published. He said that I might if I chose complete it, or else publish it as it stood; but he left little doubt in my mind which course he would prefer. I am therefore placing before the public his work in its incomplete state as it left the author's hands, with the certainty that in doing so I am fulfilling his wishes. Moreover, I am persuaded, and I think that not a few readers

will agree with me, that the unfinished work of Dr. Fortescue himself is preferable to any attempted completion by another hand.

The Last Days

Suddenly, in the midst of life, this amazing scholar was unexpectedly and cruelly called away with much of his work unfinished. On 20 December 1922 Dr. Fiddian, his general practitioner, diagnosed the presence of cancer in his patient and sent him to a Harley Street specialist on the very next day. Lady Winifred has written of the way in which she received the news:

> It was just before Christmas of the year 1922 that I received a thick envelope addressed to me in Adrian's matchless script. I opened it eagerly, but, after reading a few lines, the sunshine of the morning was blotted out and I sat in a quiet darkness of the spirit. Adrian, our strong vivid Adrian, feeling unwell for the first time in his robust life, had visited a specialist who had given him sentence of death—it might be a slow and hideous death.

Adrian Fortescue heard the "sentence of death", as he expressed it himself, passed upon him on 21st December 1922 by Sir Charles Gordon-Watson in Harley Street. The diagnosis was of one of the most hideous forms of cancer. In a letter written on St. Stephen's Day, 1922, to the President of St. Edmund's College, where he was Professor of Church History, he wrote:

> I have had what at first was a very great shock. After a good deal of trouble and some pain I have been to see a specialist in London, Sir Charles Gordon-Watson (who turns out to be a Catholic). It appears that I have cancer, apparently in a rather bad and advanced state. I am going to the hospital in Dollis Hill, probably on Jan. 3. There will be an operation. If

it succeeds they hope to prolong life for a bit; but they will leave me a horribly maimed and patched-up body. There seems little hope of a radical cure. Sir Charles warned me that, in any case, I can only hope for a very short bit of life now. Indeed the idea of what they are going to do to me revolts me more than death, so that I do not now feel that I much want to survive.

This was a shock at first. A week ago, as far as I knew, I was in perfect health, except for what I took for a little indigestion. I came out of Sir Charles's house after about a quarter of an hour's examination. I wandered down Harley Street and Wimpole Street in the grey light under drizzling rain, into Oxford Street among crowds of people buying Christmas presents; and all the time I was hearing loud the splash of the ferryman's oars. The first day or two was rather dreadful. I wandered about my room, took up a book and tried to read a page or two, then put it down. I could not settle down to Boethius or to arranging my notes or anything. What does all that matter to me now? So I have been through all the Christmas festivities, the music at Matins, and midnight Mass, the garland,* and little presents and cards arriving, with this in front of me all the time.

Now I am getting hardened to the idea. The very worst, when they have cut me open, will be death quite soon. I am used to the idea now, and it is much less difficult to bear than I would have thought...

I think it silly to make a fuss about so inevitable a thing as death; nor do I want now to work up an emotional crisis. I am spending these last days making my will, arranging things for my successor, sorting papers. I think I have already got over

---

* The garland—this refers to the custom of hanging a garland made of holly and ivy across the sanctuary at Christmas and Easter. This unusual custom was introduced at St. Hugh by Wilfred Willson who had been taught it as a choirboy in the Anglican parish church at Dover.

the pang of parting with work half done and the too many interests I had in life. Only let me say this: if I do not come back from Dollis Hill, if Azrael* has got me, I like now to remember how very kind and nice you, Vance, Flynn, George Smith and everyone there were to me always...I am going to spend the day before I go into the hospital with the OP# at Haverstock Hill (no Molinism" for me, thank you. Tell Vance that if my essence loses its existence I am firmly convinced that the existence will go walking about by itself. This, I believe, to be the authentic doctrine of the late Rev. T. Aquinas, OP). I shall make a general confession and get ready then. I suppose they will bring me Communion before the operation. Then I shall go down into unconsciousness in the hands of God and leave the rest to Him, whether it is to be a bit more life with a maimed body, or Azrael at once. If it is to be Azrael, I should like to think that you will all remember me kindly and say Mass for a soul that has no hope but in the mercy of God.

This letter exemplifies some of the finest aspects of the Doctor's character, his profound faith, his Christian resignation, his affection for his friends, and his sense of humour which even the prospect of impending death could not curb.

Dr. Fortescue duly celebrated the three Masses of Christmas, and on the next day, the Feast of St. Stephen, he baptized the daughter of Thomas and Elizabeth Devine. Soon after returning from Harley Street he had visited the Devines and told them that he had cancer and would have to prepare his final sermon, but despite his pain and anguish he remembered to ask whether their baby had been born. Nora Evalina had

---

* Azrael—the angel who separates the soul from the body at death.

OP—Order of Preachers, *i.e.* the Dominicans in whose priory at Haverstock Hill the memorial to his father can be seen.

" Molinism—a doctrine of grace taught be the Spanish Jesuit, Luis De Molina in the sixteenth century which was attacked fiercely by the Dominicans.

been born on the day that the cancer had been diagnosed. Her parents told her how moved they had been at the concern that their parish priest had shown for them in the midst of his pain and anguish, and his insistence on baptizing her himself, the last parishioner on whom he would confer this sacrament. The grave of Thomas and Elizabeth Devine can be seen very close to that of their beloved parish priest.

Dr. Fortescue preached a final sermon to his flock on 31st December—"Christ our Friend and Comforter". He explained the meaning of the Nativity in profound but simple terms. It picked, he said, from all births one birth for remembrance, and that not alone the birth of a human child, but the special visitation of God to Earth. This was the idea of the Epiphany-"Heaven had visited Earth," and this visitation is the foundation upon which the Christian religion rests. Everything in Heaven became incarnate in that birth and life. The Christian religion was not a system of difficult doctrines; all we had to do was love Christ and obey Him. We need not be great philosophers, nor worry ourselves with recondite facts; we have our gospels, and our Friend is portrayed in them. Everyone wants a friend, and Christ is the best of friends. One could not even be sure of one's own friends; they forget or go away; but whatever happens Christ will not leave us; He will keep us company even in sorrow and death. He will not take away all evil from our circumstance, or all trials from our path. These are the terms on which we are put into the world, and we do wrong to expect or claim security; no security exists for any mortal thing subject to the laws of nature. Christ's office is to comfort us through all, for He has been through all Himself. Our heaviest burden cannot be heavier than was His, nor our road harder than was His to His sacred feet. He had gone before us into all dark places, and will strengthen us in those we have to go through. The final outcome of all is good; no evil is infinite, for the world is not governed by an evil demon, but by a living God. Meanwhile the best road for us all

is the road of duty, the acceptance of tasks and their brave performance, irrespective of the pain or joy they might bring us.
In following this path we will have the comfort of our dear
Friend who will sustain us in weariness, cold and hunger. We
must say always: "He will never leave me." Each year we can
think this thought; "Heaven has visited earth."

Dr. Fortescue concluded his sermon with the words: "That
is all I have to say." In view of his impending death, this was
profoundly true in a sense that, probably, he did not intend.
Despite his awe-inspiring erudition, the faith of this great priest
had been basically a simple one, like that of such great saints
as the Curé d'Ars or St. Pius X. It was based not on a set of
abstract propositions but on a deep and personal relationship with Christ our Friend and Comforter. All that is necessary to save our souls is to love and obey Him, even when
He asks us to follow Him along the path of suffering that
His own sacred feet had taken for our salvation. That was
all that he had to say, and what is there that he or any other
preacher could have added to this simple message? Dr.
Fortescue was now about to live in his death what he had
preached in his life.

On 3 January 1923 Dr. Fortescue left Letchworth for
Dollis Hill Hospital, where he died of cancer on 11 February.
On the previous evening he had come to say good-bye to the
Willson family. Despite the anguish that he had been enduring he had remembered, as always, to send the children Christmas gifts. The children did not know the gravity of his illness,
and he appeared to them to be very cheerful. Adrian Willson
remembers the Doctor going into an adjoining room for a
private word with his mother, and when they emerged she was
brushing tears from her cheeks. Each in turn held the Doctor's
hands and wished him well, then he turned and walked down
the garden path into the darkness. When they saw him again
he was lying in his coffin. Before leaving St. Hugh for what
he knew would be the last time in his life, to take the train for

London, he bade his little church a lone and final farewell, and was seen kissing silently the altar-stone upon which he had so often offered that holy sacrifice about which he had written so profoundly.

It came as no surprise to his congregation, who prayed for him unceasingly, to learn from those who were with him in his last illness that his mind dwelt constantly, during those weeks of agony, on the sufferings of Our Lord, and that he many times refused morphine in his determination to persevere along the "royal road of pain"—one of the expressions he had used each year in his little church at Letchworth during his Lenten sermons on the Passion which had held the congregation spellbound. To preach upon the "royal road" is one thing, to walk upon it is another. This great priest died on 11 February 1923, at the age of forty-nine—with the name of Jesus on his lips.

It was mentioned above that Christmas was the favourite feast of Adrian Fortescue, and the fact that it was at this very season that he received his "sentence of death" gives added poignancy to the conclusion of a letter that he had written on St. Stephen's Day 1912:

> I had Willson to share the fasting supper. He and Britten got on very well (oddly enough), we sate and talked about music and things during those first heavenly hours of the night while waiting for matins. I left them and walked in the garden and remembered other Christmas nights at Rome and Innsbruck and Ongar and Cyprus. Then matins and the Isaiah lessons with their beautiful tune going up and ringing across the little church under the twined hoops of dark green and the scarlet berries. The Russian tunes for the Responsories were heavenly—odd jumping bits of tunes with strange modulations, sudden false relations and long hung-up discords, that made me see huge snow-covered steppes and churches with bright covered bulby domes, all glowing inside with tarnished

gilding and gay ikons in a haze of incense-smoke. They sang everything perfectly. Then just before midnight the crashing *Te Deum*—all bursts of thundering chord and marching sound, alternate with the old plainsong. And so at last they sang the Introit of the Christmas Mass as we came up the Church. The Lotti Mass was heavenly too—and nice funny archaic carols. They have learned to sing unaccompanied parts awful well. And all the Catholics came to Communion—first six children who made their first Communion, then all the servers and rows and rows of people. And I said beautiful purple patchious things about the holy night, and back at the end of the church the lights gleamed before the crib. And the music stopped and all the singers came to communion...all of them. And they sang a last little quiet hymn that I made up—about going to bed tired and happy, because again we have remembered the night on which He came down from heaven for us men and for our salvation, and about sleeping now till dawn in His care who lies in the manger and holds all the world in his little hands (I say, won't it be dreadful when I am dead and there is no one left to make beautiful hymns and music and things)—and so we came out into the quiet night and went to bed—very tired and awful happy.

Dr. Fortescue's funeral must have been the most impressive ever accorded to a parish priest in England, and manifested the great respect for him among Catholic and non-Catholic alike. Peter Willson, the second son of Wilfred Willson, was unable to be present as he was suffering from chickenpox. He remembers vividly being allowed to watch the funeral procession with his sister Pauline, two years his senior (who also had chickenpox), from an upstairs window as it passed through Letchworth to the cemetery, the cortège stretching for nearly a mile. It included bishops, large numbers of clergy, the choir of Westminster Cathedral, the choir, the clergy, and some boys from St. Edmund's College, members of the aristocracy and other dignitaries, members of the Fortescue family, and countless local people from Letchworth. After the funeral a group of mourners remained at the grave side. They included members of the parish choir and choristers from St. Edmund's College. They joined together in a spontaneous and moving rendition of "O Sacred Head Surrounded" from Bach's "St Matthew Passion", a favourite hymn of Adrian Fortescue. The Willson family remembered this, and it was sung at the Requiems of both Wilfred and Clare Willson.

We can learn more about the innermost reality of our faith, which is the Cross, from the life and the death of Adrian Fortescue than we can from his books. His complete candour, his high sense of honour, his generosity, and the strictness of his private life made him universally admired by people of all religions in Letchworth. Despite the wishes of his family that he should be laid to rest with his ancestors, he chose to be buried at Letchworth among his own parishioners, and he asked that his memorial card should bear the picture of the Good Shepherd.

No man is perfect, and Adrian Fortescue certainly had his caprices, prejudices, and impatience which were not always calculated to endear him to his fellows. A man of quite extraordinary learning, he found it hard to suffer fools gladly and was considered by some to maintain an arrogant assumption of superiority. In her *Catholic Truth Society* obituary, Edith Cowell remarked that: "He had no patience with stupidity, and literally stamped on humbug wherever he found it." His friend Reginald Hine commented on the short shrift given to those with the temerity to challenge even deliberately provocative statements made during the course of Dr. Fortescue's lectures:

> One after another they went down like ninepins. After a few withering words from him there was no more spirit left in them. The meetings would terminate in a hushed and awk-

ward silence with men of inferior minds dying to say something, but not daring.

Dr. Fortescue's acerbic sense of humour was particularly resented by those at whom it was aimed, but if he realized that he had been cruel he would give himself no peace until he had made amends. He was a scholar whose writing is of excellent and permanent value. He was a teacher of profound learning and of such charm that he commanded the attention and affection of his pupils. He was a parish priest who laboured without stint for his flock, and was rewarded with their devotion. He was gifted as a linguist to an exceptional, almost unique, degree. He was talented as a musician and as an artist, stood in the very first rank in the fields of calligraphy and heraldic design, and he was a fine theologian and a great author.

Adrian Fortescue is buried in the Catholic part of the cemetery in Letchworth, surrounded by the graves of his parishioners. It is only appropriate that Wilfred and Clare Willson, his closest friends in the parish, are buried in the next plot to him. The headstone of his grave is carved with the arms of his family and the words:

> HIC IACET
> ADRIANUS A FORTI SCUTO
> PRESBYTER
> WESTMONASTERIENSIS
> BEATAM SPEM EXSPECTANS

Around the tomb itself are carved the beautiful words from verse 8 of Psalm 25 which he had used each day at Mass for almost twenty-five years, and which express precisely the motivating force of his entire priestly life:

> DOMINE, DILEXI DECOREM DOMUS TUAE,
> ET LOCUM HABITATIONIS GLORIAE TUAE.

In a personal memoir, Sir John Fortescue, the military historian and librarian of Windsor Castle, wrote: "To me the most memorable thing in Adrian is not his intellectual power nor his versatility, amazing though both of them were, but his noble sense of duty and his steadfast endeavour never to fall short of the lofty standard which he had erected for himself." His very close friend, fellow-teacher at St. Edmund's College, Ware, Dr. J.G. Vance, described Adrian Fortescue as "one of the most distinguished, chivalrous and lovable of men". The most moving tribute to Doctor Fortescue that I have read came to me from Adrian Willson when he sent me the material which has provided so much of the information in this brief biography. Adrian was not quite ten years old when the Doctor died, and the fact that he made such a lasting impression upon a young boy of that age is a very striking testimony to the holiness and humanity of this great priest. Adrian Willson wrote to me in 1992:

> What I remember of Adrian Fortescue is still absolutely vivid. Going through the papers before sending them to you has been like reliving that old friendship as it was developing. I knew Adrian Fortescue the man—though I realized always that he was a great scholar too. I was too young to know a great deal about his writing.
>
> How privileged I was—I knew him from my first conscious existence. He baptized me. He heard my first confession. I served Low Masses for him. I played minor roles on the altar during Sung Mass and spectacular services—Holy Week, Easter, Christmas. I enjoyed his sermons and talks. As a small boy I had my hair tousled by him as we stood in his garden and talked. I saw some of his artistic work at the time he was engaged upon it. Often I had reason to be grateful for gifts received from him.
>
> I knew his study intimately. Row upon row of books covering the walls. Some treasured objects—many from his student days—and many pictures displayed. A pleasant back-

ground of cigar smoke. It is the picture I conjure up when I think of a really cultured person's den. I enjoyed his easy humour. I grew to love his music. I was a humble torch bearer at his last Midnight Mass. I was among the last of his friends to grip his hand on the evening before he went to Dollis Hill Hospital. I said my last good-bye to him as he lay in state in his open coffin in St. Hugh. With my mother I was in St. Hugh for his Requiem among that illustrious crowd of clerics and so many members of his family. My father was conducting those parts of the service which consisted of Adrian Fortescue's music. I think this explains our presence our presence inside when so many thousands were turned away. I formed part of that amazing funeral cortège sadly trudging along the Icknield way to the cemetery. I stood close to his grave as he was very slowly lowered into it. I heard the wonderful sound of his favourite hymn sung with such feeling by hundreds of absolutely devastated mourners.

Strangely I always thought of him as a friend rather than a parish priest. A natural leader with the respect of the whole community—not just the Catholic element. There was a big age-gap between us but it never seemed important. He could match the thoughts of a boy and make him feel absolutely at ease. I have lived under his shadow all my life, and still do.

Chapter Notes

[1] "Mr." is the correct title to be used when referring to Anglican clerics unless they possess such a title as "Canon". It is contrary to correct etiquette to refer to them as "Reverend": *e.g.* Reverend Jones accepted an invitation.

[2] E. Johnston, *Formal Penmanship*, ed. H. Child (Pentalic Corporation, New York, NY, 1971), p. 9.

[3] J. Moran, *Stanley Morison* (London, 1971), p. 40.

4 J.D. Scruby, *Bernard Newdigate: 1869-1944*, in "Albion", vol. 8, No. 3, Winter 1984.

5 N. Barker, *Stanley Morison* (London, 1972), p. 67.

6 *A History of the Holy Eucharist in Great Britain*, by T. E. Bridgett, CSSR, with notes by H. Thurston, S.J. (Letchworth, 1908).

7 J. Moran, p. 40.

8 N. Barker, pp. 66-67.

9 Ibid., p. 115.

10 Ibid., p. 114.

11 Fell, together with three others, contrived to maintain Anglican services during Cromwell's Commonwealth. After the Restoration he was made dean of Christ Church, Oxford, and eventually Bishop of Oxford. Thomas Brown's famous "I do not love thee, Doctor Fell" was directed at him.

12 J. Moran, p. 41.

13 It is to Urban VIII that the well known pasquinade refers: "*Quod non fecerunt barbari, fecerunt Barberini*"— "What the barbarians did not do the Barberini did." This did not refer Urban's reform of the Breviary but to his removal of bronze from the roof of the Pantheon to be used in St. Peter's.

14 Dr. Fortescue takes it for granted that his readers are aware of the fact that Urban VIII considered himself to be no mean poet and published well constructed but florid Latin poetry.

15 The pre-Urban VIII texts of the hymns of the Breviary were restored to the revised edition published after the Second Vatican Council.

16 The replies of the Pontifical Biblical Commission with a valuable commentary can be found in *A Catholic Commentary on Holy Scripture* (London, 1953) on pages 67-75. This may well be the most orthodox and most erudite commentary on the Scriptures yet published. It should be noted that the subsequent edition was drastically revised to accord with neo-modernist thinking.

17 Mr. Willson selected a Pattern 48 Positive-Organ from the Positive-Organ Company, 44 Mornington Crescent, London, NW, and Dr. Fortescue opted for extended payment at £8. 5. 0. per quarter.

18 The Great O's are the Greater Antiphons sung at the Magnificat in the office from 17 to 23 December. They are sung not in the penitential tone but in the solemn tone of great feasts. The seven antiphons all begin with O, beginning with *O Sapientia* on 17 December and ending with *O Emmanuel* on 23 December—hence the Great O's. *O Rex Gentium* comes on 22 December.

[19] Miss Ethel Elmes was one of Dr. Fortescue's closest friends. She was an intelligent, well educated, well read lady, free from affectation and steeped in Catholicism, who was able to discuss many topics with the Doctor at his own level. Miss Elmes was a tower of strength at St. Hugh. She looked after the sacristy and the sanctuary and ensured that everything necessary was always to hand. Any little thing that the Doctor needed to be done she would undertake. She would even teach boys to serve Mass. When the Doctor was admitted to Dollis Hill Hospital for the last few days of his life, Miss Elmes took accommodation in South Hampstead (17a Lambelle Road) to be near at hand in case there was anything that she could do for him. She would visit Letchworth every day or so to urge the parishioners of St. Hugh to meet in the church to pray for the doctor's recovery. Miss Elmes was the Doctor's executrix and wound up his estate with considerable success and dedication, and at her personal expense she arranged for the completion of some projects which the Doctor would not have wished to remain undone, such as the republication of *Latin Hymns* in the new edition designed by Stanley Morison. (Note supplied by Mr. Adrian Willson.)

A Chronology of the Life of Adrian Fortescue

1874   14 January. Birth of Adrian Fortescue.

1877   18 August. His father dies, aged 61. His mother goes to live at 40 Park Road, now Parkhill Road, Haverstock Hill.

1883   Attends Jesuit Preparatory School at Boulogne-sur-Mer, France.

1885   Easter. Attends St. Charles' College, Bayswater.

1886   6 December. His mother dies. Lives with his aunt, Miss Katherine Gertrude Mary Robins, at 18 Darlaston Road, Wimbledon.

1891   Enters Scots' College, Rome. Is appointed organist.

1892   July. Bachelor of Philosophy at Rome. During his vacations he has drawing lessons and studies German. Does much drawing in cathedral cities.

1894   Begins his reading of Dante which he continues until his death.

25 June. Ph.D., Rome.

2 October. Enters Theological College at Innsbruck. Spends holidays walking, climbing, and sketching in Bavaria, Tyrol and North Italy, and also sketching tours in France and England.

1896   16 July. Received tonsure and four minor orders at Darmstadt from Bishop Paul Haffner.

1897   18 July. Ordained Subdeacon at Brixen, Austria.

22 July. Ordained Deacon at Brixen.

1898   27 March. Ordained Priest at Brixen by Simon, Prince Bishop of Brixen.

10 April, Easter Sunday. Sings his first Mass at 11 a.m. in the Jesuit Church at Wimbledon.

11 April. Says his second Mass in the family chapel at the Dominican Church, Haverstock Hill, for the souls of his parents.

29 April. Returns to study in Innsbruck.

1899   28 February. Passes first Doctor's examination in Moral Theology.

Passes second Doctor's examination, Dogma. Spends two months assisting at churches in the Tyrol. Leaves Innsbruck after his five years' course. Spends the summer travelling in Hun gary with fellow students.

29 September. Is interviewed by Cardinal Vaughan at Mill Hill and accepts an appoint ment to the German Church at Whitechapel.

14 December. Begins calligraphy lessons in Edward Johnston's class on Thursday evenings at the London County Council School of Arts and Crafts.

1900   Writes notes on Church History, studies Canon Law, Hungarian, and Arabic.

9 November. Leaves the German Church, Whitechapel. Appointed to Walthamstow, residing at 3, Comely Bank Road.

1901   Resolves to study only Church History, Canon Law, Arabic until his final examinations in Innsbruck in May 1902.

17 June. Appointed Rector to St. Helen's, Chipping Ongar, Essex (*Angrae ad Castrum inter Orientales Saxones*).

1902   26-27 May. Returns to Innsbruck.

28 May. Passes final examination in Church History and Canon Law.

30 May. Passes final examination in Arabic.

7 June. Back in Ongar. Studies for final examinations in Biblical Studies and Hebrew.

28 November. Resigns Ongar. Unable to bear the expense of the Mission. Appointed as curate to St. James', Colchester (*Camuloduni inter Orientales Anglos*).

1903   26 February. Leaves Colchester and returns to German Church, Whitechapel (*Londinii inter Germanos*).

24 August. Appointed to Enfield (*Aerieopruti inter Centraliores Saxones*) during the absence of the Parish Priest, Father O'Gorman.

1904   7 April. Appointed to Witham, Essex (*Ad Aqua Separatoria inter Orientales Saxones*), during the absence of the Parish Priest, Canon Tuke, for six months.

1 October. Appointed to Maldon, Essex (*Meldurii inter eosdem Orientales Saxones*. Studies for his final examination for Doctor of Divinity.

1905   Writes a treatise on St. John's authorship of the Fourth Gospel for his Doctorate.

8 June. Final doctoral examination in Biblical Sciences at Innsbruck. He passes in Semitic Languages with distinction—a rare achievement.

10 June. Proceeds to the degree of Doctor of Divinity.

1 July. Returns to Maldon. Continues studying Arabic and begins work on his book, *The Orthodox Eastern Church*, which he completes in July 1906.

1906   Writes his first articles for *The Catholic Encyclopaedia*.

21 June. Is granted a year's leave of absence to study in Syria at St. Joseph's University, Beirut.

20 December to 7 January 1907. Travels in Cyprus.

1907   28 January. His aunt, Miss Katherine Robins, dies in Florence at The age of 69. She is buried at San Miniato.

26 March to 23 September. Travels in Jerusalem, Bethlehem, Galilee, Samaria, Asia Minor, Constantinople, Dalmatia, Venice, Florence, Milan, Paris.

29 November. Appointed to Letchworth in Hertfordshire where he remains for the rest of his life. Offers Mass in some sheds near the railway line.

1908   Writes articles for *Catholic Encyclopaedia*, and works on his books *The Greek Fathers* and *The Mass*. Studies Arabic every evening. Thomas Wilfred Willson, then an Anglican is appointed organist. He eventually becomes a Catholic and one of Dr. Fortescue's closest friends.

29 May. Work begins on site for new church.

21 June. Blesses first stone of his church.

30 August. Last Mass in The sheds.

6 September. Blessing by The Bishop of Amycla of the new church dedicated to St. Hugh.

12 September. Arranges a celebration of the Liturgy of St. John Chrysostom in Westminster Cathedral during the Eucharistic Congress.

1909   31 January. Compline sung for the first time at St. Hugh.

15 February. Moves into new house next to the church.

March. Begins pamphlet on Eastern Churches for Catholic Truth Society. Writes articles for *Catholic Encyclopaedia*. Trains his choir.

All Holy Week ceremonies including *Tenebrae* at St. Hugh.

Travels for a month in Holland and Germany.

24 December. Matins sung at St. Hugh prior to Midnight Mass.

1910   Buys the organ for St. Hugh in consultation with Thomas Wilfred Willson. Lectures in Letchworth and Cambridge on topics ranging from Mohammed to monasticism, writes articles for *The Tablet*, travels in Holland and Germany, and in November begins regular weekly readings of Dante which are continued until Christmas 1922.

1911   Writes articles for *The Tablet*, *The Catholic Encyclopaedia*, Hastings' *Encyclopaedia of Religion and Ethics*, and Dom Cabrol's *Dictionnaire d'Archéologie et de Liturgie*. Continues his work on *The Mass*, begins *The Lesser Eastern Churches*, and revises *The Orthodox Church* for its third edition. Begins teaching French at the Letchworth Boys' Club.

8 April. The new ciborium (baldachino) erected in St. Hugh is blessed.

1912   Studies Syriac. Begins a private class in German at Letchworth. Compiles the book *Latin Hymns* for use in St. Hugh. Finishes *The Lesser Eastern Churches*. Travels in Normandy. Gives many lectures, and instructs many converts. Writes much music for his choir, including the Russian settings for Responsories at Christmas Matins.

1913   Gives many lectures on topics ranging from "John

the Presbyter" to "Moslem History", writes many articles for *The Tablet*, conducts French and Italian classes in his house, preaches at St. James', Spanish Place on Sunday evenings, and on occasions at Westminster Cathedral in the mornings. Draws the illustrations for his book *The Lesser Eastern Churches*. His book *Latin Hymns*, compiled for the parishioners of St. Hugh, is published.

3 February–7 March. Holiday in Rome and Sicily. His last until 1922.

24 April. Public debate in the Howard Hall, Letchworth, on Esperanto.

November. Preaches at Westminster Cathedral in the mornings and at St. James', Spanish Place, in the evenings.

1914   Lectures on topics ranging from "The Philosophy of St. Thomas" to "The Dual Monarchy". Writes pamphlet *The Formula of Hormisdas* for the CTS, articles for *The Tablet* and *Encyclopaedia of Religion and Ethics*. Designs vestments for St. Hugh, most of which are now at St. Edmund's College, Ware.

1915   Studies Syriac and Flemish, delivers many lectures ranging from "The Alphabet" to "The Mormons in Utah".

Begins *The Ceremonies of the Roman Rite*. Preaches in Flemish and French for Belgian refugees in Letchworth.

1916   Gives lectures including "Christianity and War" and "Roumania". Writes articles for *Studies* and *The Tablet*. Works on *Ceremonies of The Roman Rite* and his *Organ Book* for St. Hugh. Writes the introduction "Concerning Hymns" for *Pange Lingua* by A. G.

McDougall. Publication of his pamphlet entitled *Pacifism—A Word with Conscientious Objectors*.

1917   Studies Syriac and Greek, writes articles for *The Tablet* and the *Dublin Review*, lectures at Cambridge on "*The Italo-Greeks*", and revises, corrects, and annotates the manuscript of W. C. Bishop, the liturgical historian, for his book *The Nestorians*.

1918   Lectures on topics ranging from "The Slavs" to "Socrates". Composes Mass Propers for his choir. Rearranges all the Holy Week part-music for the women's voices of his war-time choir. Revises *Ceremonies of the Roman Rite* for its second edition.

1919   Lectures on subjects ranging from "Flags" to "Boethius". Begins work on his edition of Boethius' *De Consolatione Philosophiae*.

         July-August. Appointed Consultor of the Congregation *Pro Ecclesia Orientali* and Professor of Church History at St. Edmund's College.

1920   Lectures on topics ranging from "The Essence of the Catholic Religion" to "On Learning Languages". Revises *The Early Papacy*, and revises and edits the manuscript of Jean Maspero's *Histoire des Patriarches d'Alexandrie*.

1921   Lectures on subjects ranging from "Charles III—The Young Pretender" to "Christ and Plato". Reads *Mincius Felix* with his Dante class.

1922   Lectures on topics ranging from "Turkey" to "The Death of the Gods". Designs and draws book-plates. Writes on the Church of Malabar for the *Cambridge History of India* Takes his final holiday in August in Austria and the Tyrol.

         20 December. Sees Dr. Fiddian.

21 December. Sees Sir Charles Gordon-Watson.

31 December. Preaches his final sermon at St. Hugh on "Christ our Friend and Comforter".

1923   3 January. Leaves for Dollis Hill.

5 January. First operation.

23 January. Second Operation.

11 February. Dies a few days after his 49th birthday. R.I.P.

Adrian Fortescue's Literary Work

CTS = Catholic Truth Society.

Books

The Orthodox Eastern Church (London, CTS, 1907).

The Greek Fathers (London, CTS, 1908).

The Liturgy of St. John Chrysostom (London, CTS, 1908).

The Mass: a Study of the Roman Rite (London, Longmans, 1912).

Latin Hymns (printed by Miss M. Newdigate at Astley Cottage, Letchworth, 1913). Redesigned by Stanley Morrison and reprinted in 1924.

Thomae a Kempis, *De Imitatione Christi, libri quattuor quos denuo recognouit,* Adrianus a Fortiscuto Presbyter ritus Latini (London, Methuen, 1919).

Preface to the *Roman Missal* (London, Burns & Oates, 1920).

La Messe, French translation by A. Boudinhon (Paris, 1920).

The Lesser Eastern Churches (London, CTS, 1913).

Donatism (London, Burns & Oates, 1917).

The Early Papacy (London, Burns & Oates, 1920).

The Ceremonies of the Roman Rite Described, with designs by the author (London, Burns & Oates, 1918).

The Uniate Eastern Churches (London, Burns & Oates, 1923). Published posthumously.

Boethius, *De Consolatione Philosophiae*, edited by A. Fortescue (London, Burns & Oates, 1925). Published posthumously with preface by Canon George Smith.

Pamphlets

How to Pronounce Latin (Letchworth, 1908).

Rome and Constantinople (London, CTS, 1908).

The Eastern Churches (London, CTS, 1909).

Pope Gregory VII (June, 1909).

The Branch Theory (London, CTS, 1910).

An Anglican on Reunion (London, CTS, 1910).

The Vestments of the Roman Rite (London, CTS, 1912).

Compline for Sunday (1914).

The Formula of Hormisdas (February, 1914).

Russia and the Catholic Church (London, CTS, 1915).

Vespers for Sunday (1915).

Mass in Time of War (1915).

Pacifism (London, CTS, 1916).

The Date of the Anglican Schism (London, CTS, 1917).

Catholic because Roman Catholic (1917)

Other Writing

Dr. Fortescue wrote countless articles for Catholic and non-Catholic journals and contributed many articles to several encyclopaedias (see Chronology). He also contributed to the following books:

Essay Concerning Hymns, prefixed to *Pange Lingua* by A. G. McDougall (London, Burns & Oates, 1916).

Essay on "The Rites of Holy Week", prefixed to *The Holy Week Book* (Burns & Oates, 1916).

Papers on "The Eastern Schism" and "Americanism" in *Folia Fugitiva*, edited by Rev. W.H. Cologan (London, Washbourne, 1907).

"The Orthodox Church and the Holy Eucharist", a lecture given during the Eucharistic Congress in London in 1908 and included in the book *Nineteenth Eucharistic Congress. Westminster 1908* (London, Sands & Company, 1909).

Histoire des Patriarches d'Alexandrie par Jean Maspero, revue et publiée par Adrian Fortescue et Gaston Wiet (Paris, Ecole des Hautes Etudes, Champion, 1923).

ILLUSTRATIONS
FIRST SECTION

adrian fortescue.

Blake Hall, 17–22 aug. 1903.

Dr. Fortescue on a sketching holiday in 1903.

Dr. Fortescue at the doorway of his church. His sigillum can be seen on the altar frontal. See the title page for a clear picture of the sigillum, and page 417 for an explanation of the letters IC, XC, NI, KA.

T.W. Willson about 1908

Claire McDonnell
who married Thomas Willson

A cope designed by Dr. Fortescue

One of Dr. Fortescue's four desks

St. Hugh and Dr. Fortescue's house soon after completion

Dr. Fortescue's Sigillum

The blessing of The New Fire during the Easter Vigil which took place in the morning at that time. It was restored to the evening by Pius XII in 1955.

The altar crucifix of white alabaster on a brass stand

The altar of repose. Part of the inscription in exquisite capitals around the walls can be seen

St. Hugh—Letchworth

The Funeral Cortège

Dr Fortescue's grave, showing also the grave of Thomas and Clare Willson

The memorial tablet to Adrian Fortescue in the Lady Chapel of the new church of St. Hugh, Letchworth. The inscription carved in Roman stone by Mr. R. Fincham reads:

Entreat the gracious mercy of God for the well-loved soul of ADRIAN FORTESCUE, D.D., first Rector of this church. Born on the 14th of January, 1874, he studied with no little success at London, Rome, and Innsbruck. After ordination to the priesthood he travelled widely in the East, gaining an intimate knowledge of the Oriental Rites, of which he was later nominated a consultor to the Holy See. Returning to England he cast his lot in this place, where he might duly build a church, with himself as a guide and pattern to his flock, might raise and adorn unto the Lord a temple of living stones. He gave lavishly of his unusual talents of intellect and learning, gladly devoting all in the simplicity of his heart to God and to his brethren. His ministry discharged, undismayed either by the severest bodily pain or by premature death, he fell asleep very peacefully in the Lord on 11th February 1923. It was his wish to lie buried among his own people in the neighboring cemetery, and there he awaits the blessed hope and the coming in the glory of our Lord Jesus Christ. May he rest in peace.

FORTE DVCVM

SCVTVM · SALVS

WINIFRED
FORTESCUE

A Bookplate designed by Dr. Fortescue for his cousin, Lady Winifred

PART TWO

ARTICLES BY DR. FORTESCUE

1

LITURGY

In this article the various Christian liturgies are considered only from the point of view of their relation to one another in the most general sense, and an account is given of what is known about the growth of a fixed liturgy as such in the early Church.

1. *Definition*. — Liturgy (*leitourgia*) is derived from a Greek composite word meaning originally "a public duty, a service to the state undertaken by a citizen". From this we have *leitourgos* "a man who performs a public duty", "a public servant", often used as equivalent to the Roman *lictor*. At Athens public services would be performed by the wealthier citizens at their own expense, such as the office of *gymnasiarch*, who superintended the gymnasium, that of *choregus*, who paid the singers of a chorus in the theatre, that of the *hestiator*, who gave a banquet to his tribe, of the *trierarchus*, who provided a warship for the state. The meaning of the word Liturgy is then extended to cover any general service of a public kind. In the Septuagint it is used for the public service of the temple (e.g., Ex., xxxviii, 27; xxxix, 12, etc.). Thence it comes to have a religious sense as the function of the priests, the ritual service of the temple (e.g., Joel, i, 9; ii, 17, etc.). In the New Testament this religious meaning has become definitely established. In Luke, i, 23, Zachary goes home when "the days of his *liturgy*" are over. In Heb., viii, 6, the high priest of the New

Law "has obtained a better *liturgy*", that is a better kind of public religious service than that of the Temple.

So in Christian use liturgy meant the public official service of the Church, that corresponded to the official service of the Temple in the Old Law. We must now distinguish two senses in which the word was and is still commonly used. These two senses often lead to confusion. On the one hand, liturgy often means the whole complex of official services, all the rites, ceremonies, prayers, and sacraments of the Church, as opposed to private devotions. In this sense we speak of the arrangement of all these services in certain set forms (including the canonical hours, administration of sacraments, etc.), used officially by any local church, as the liturgy of such a church—the Liturgy of Antioch, the Roman Liturgy, and so on. So liturgy means rite; we speak indifferently of the Byzantine Rite or the Byzantine Liturgy. In the same sense we distinguish the official services from others by calling them liturgical; those services are liturgical which are contained in any of the official books (see **LITURGICAL BOOKS**) of a rite. In the Roman Church, for instance, Compline is a liturgical service, the Rosary is not. The other sense of the word liturgy, now the common one in all Eastern Churches, restricts it to the chief official service only—the Sacrifice of the Holy Eucharist, which in our rite we call the Mass. This is now practically the only sense in which *leitourgia* is used in Greek, or in its derived forms (e.g., Arabic *al-liturgiah*) by any Eastern Christian. When a Greek speaks of the "Holy Liturgy" he means only the Eucharistic Service. For the sake of clearness it is perhaps better for us too to keep the word to this sense, at any rate in speaking of Eastern ecclesiastical matters; for instance, not to speak of the Byzantine canonical hours as liturgical services. Even in Western Rites the word "official" or "canonical" will do as well as "liturgical" in the general sense, so that we too may use Liturgy only for the Holy Eucharist. It should be noted also that, whereas we may speak of our Mass quite correctly as the

Liturgy, we should never use the word Mass for the Eucharistic Sacrifice in any Eastern rite. Mass (*missa*) is the name for that service in the Latin Rites only. It has never been used either in Latin or Greek for any Eastern rite. Their word, corresponding exactly to our Mass, is *Liturgy*. The Byzantine Liturgy is the service that corresponds to our Roman Mass; to call it the Byzantine (or, worse still, the Greek) Mass is as wrong as naming any other of their services after ours, as calling their *Hesperinos* Vespers, or their *Orthros* Lauds. When people go even as far as calling their books and vestments after ours, saying Missal when they mean *Euchologion* (see **GLOSSARY**), alb when they mean *sticharion*, the confusion becomes hopeless.

2. *The Origin of the Liturgy.*—At the outset of this discussion we are confronted by three of the most difficult questions of Christian archaeology, namely: From what date was there a fixed and regulated service such as we can describe as a formal Liturgy? How far was this service uniform in various Churches? How far are we able to reconstruct its forms and arrangement?

With regard to the first question it must be said that an Apostolic Liturgy in the sense of an arrangement of prayers and ceremonies, like our present ritual of the Mass, did not exist. For some time the Eucharistic Service was in many details fluid and variable. It was not all written down and read from fixed forms, but in part composed by the officiating bishop. As for ceremonies, at first they were not elaborated as now. All ceremonial evolves gradually out of certain obvious actions done at first with no idea of ritual, but simply because they had to be done for convenience. The bread and wine were brought to the altar when they were wanted, the lessons were read from a place where they could best be heard, hands were washed because they were soiled. Out of these obvious actions ceremony developed, just as our vestments developed out of the dress of the first Christians. It follows then of course that, when there was no fixed Liturgy at all, there could be no question of absolute uniformity among the different Churches.

And yet the whole series of actions and prayers did not depend solely on the improvisation of the celebrating bishop. Whereas at one time scholars were inclined to conceive the services of the first Christians as vague and undefined, recent research shows us a very striking uniformity in certain salient elements of the service at a very early date. The tendency among students now is to admit something very like a regulated Liturgy, apparently to a great extent uniform in the chief cities, back even to the first or early second century. In the first place the fundamental outline of the rite of the Holy Eucharist was given by the account of the Last Supper. What our Lord had done then, that same thing He told His followers to do in memory of Him. It would not have been a Eucharist at all if the celebrant had not at least done as our Lord did the night before He died. So we have everywhere from the very beginning at least this uniform nucleus of a Liturgy: bread and wine are brought to the celebrant in vessels (a plate and a cup); he puts them on a table—the altar; standing before it in the natural attitude of prayer he takes them in his hands, gives thanks, as our Lord had done, says again the words of institution, breaks the Bread and gives the consecrated Bread and Wine to the people in communion. The absence of the words of institution in the Nestorian Rite is no argument against the universality of this order. It is a rite that developed quite late; the parent liturgy has the words.

But we find much more than this essential nucleus in use in every Church from the first century. The Eucharist was always celebrated at the end of a service of lessons, psalms, prayers, and preaching, which was itself merely a continuation of the service of the synagogue. So we have everywhere this double function; first a synagogue service Christianised, in which the holy books were read, psalms were sung, prayers said by the bishop in the name of all (the people answering "Amen" in Hebrew, as had their Jewish forefathers), and homilies, explanations of what had been read, were made by the bishop or priests, just as they had been made in the synagogues by the learned men and elders (e.g.. Luke, iv, 16-27). This is what was known afterwards as the Liturgy of the Catechumens. Then followed the Eucharist, at which only the baptised were present. Two other elements of the service in the earliest time soon disappeared. One was the love-feast (*agape*) that came just before the Eucharist (see **GLOSSARY**); the other was the *spiritual exercises*, in which people were moved by the Holy Ghost to prophesy, speak in divers tongues, heal the sick, by prayer, and so on. This function—to which I Cor., xiv, 1-14, and the *Didache* (see **GLOSSARY**), x, 7, etc., refer—obviously opened the way to disorders; from the second century it gradually disappears. The Eucharistic *Agape* seems to have disappeared at about the same time. The other two functions remained joined and still exist in the liturgies of all rites. In them the service crystallised into more or less set forms from the beginning. In the first half the alternation of lessons, psalms, collects, and homilies leaves little room for variety. For obvious reasons a lesson from a Gospel was read last, in the place of honour as the fulfilment of all the others; it was preceded by other readings whose number, order, and arrangement varied considerably (See **LESSONS IN THE LITURGY**). A chant of some kind would very soon accompany the entrance of the clergy and the beginning of the service. We also hear very soon of litanies of intercession said by one person, to each clause of which the people answer with some short formula (see **KYRIE ELEISON**). The place and number of the homilies would also vary for a long time. It is in the second part of the service, the Eucharist itself, that we find a very striking crystallisation of the forms, and a uniformity even in the first or second century that goes far beyond the mere nucleus described above.

Already in the New Testament—apart from the account of the Last Supper—there are some indexes that point to liturgical forms. There were already readings from the Sacred Books (I Tim., iv, 13; I Thess., v, 27; Col., iv, 16) there were sermons (Act., xx, 7), psalms and hymns (I Cor., xiv, 26; Col., iii, 16; Eph., v, 19). I Tim., ii, 1-3, implies public liturgical prayers for all classes of people. People lifted up their hands at prayers (I Tim., ii, 8), men with uncovered heads (I Cor., xi, 4), women covered (*ibid.*, 5). There was a kiss of peace (I Cor., xvi, 20; II Cor., xiii, 12; I Thess., v, 26). There was an offertory of goods for the poor (Rom., xv, 26; II Cor., ix, 13) called by the special name "communion". The people answered "Amen" after prayers (I Cor., xiv, 16). The word Eucharist has already a technical meaning (*ibid.*). The famous passage, I Cor., xi, 20-9, gives us the outline of the breaking of bread and thanksgiving (Eucharist) that followed the earlier part of the service. Heb., xiii, 10 (cf. I Cor., x, 16-21), shows that to the first Christians the table of the Eucharist was an altar. After the consecration prayers followed (Acts, ii, 42). St. Paul "breaks bread" (= the consecration), then communicates, then preaches (Acts, xx, 11). Acts, ii, 42, gives us an idea of the liturgical *Synaxis* in order: They "persevere in the teaching of the Apostles" (this implies the readings and homilies), "communicate in the breaking of bread" (consecration and communion) and "in prayers". So we have already in the New Testament all the essential elements that we find later in the organised liturgies: lessons, psalms, hymns, sermons, prayers, consecration, communion. It has been thought that there are in the New Testament even actual formulae used in the liturgy. The *Amen* is certainly one. St. Paul's insistence on the form "For ever and ever, Amen"—Rom., xvi, 27; Gal., i, 5; I Tim., i, 17; cf. Heb., xiii, 21; I Pet., i, 11; v, 11; Apoc., i, 6, etc.) seems to argue that it is a liturgical form well known to the Christians whom he addresses, as it was to the Jews. There are other short hymns (Rom., xiii, 11-12; Eph., v, 14; I Tim.,

iii, 16; II Tim., ii, 11-13), which may well be liturgical formulae.

In the Apostolic Fathers the picture of the early Christian
Liturgy becomes clearer; we have in them a definite and to
some extent homogeneous ritual. But this must be understood.
There was certainly no set form of prayers and ceremonies such
as we see in our present Missals and *Euchologia*; still less was
anything written down and read from a book. The celebrating
bishop spoke freely, his prayers being to some extent impro-
vised. And yet this improvising was bound by certain rules. In
the first place, no one who speaks continually on the same
subjects says new things each time. Modern sermons and modern extempore prayers show how easily a speaker falls into set
forms, how constantly he repeats what come to be, at least for
him, fixed formulae. Moreover, the dialogue form of prayer
that we find in use in the earliest monuments necessarily supposes some constant arrangement. The people answer and echo
what the celebrant and the deacons say with suitable exclamations. They could not do so unless they heard more or less the
same prayers each time. They heard from the altar such phrases
as: "The Lord be with you", or "Lift up your hearts", and it
was because they recognised these forms, had heard them often before, that they could answer at once in the way expected.

We find too very early that certain general themes are constant. For instance our Lord had given thanks just before He
spoke the words of institution. So it was understood that every celebrant began the prayer of consecration—the Eucharistic Prayer—by thanking God for His various mercies. So we
find always what we still have in our modern prefaces—a prayer
thanking God for certain favours and graces that are named,
just where that preface comes shortly before the consecration.[1]
An intercession for all kinds of people also occurs very early,
as we see from references to it.[2] In this prayer the various classes
of people would naturally be named in more or less the same
order. A profession of faith would almost inevitably open that

part of the service in which only the faithful were allowed to take part.[3] It could not have been long before the archetype of all Christian prayer—the Our Father—was said publicly in the Liturgy. The moments at which these various prayers were said would very soon become fixed. The people expected them at certain points, there was no reason for changing their order, on the contrary to do so would disturb the faithful. One knows too how strong conservative instinct is in any religion, especially in one that, like Christianity, has always looked back with unbounded reverence to the golden age of the first Fathers. So we must conceive the Liturgy of the first two centuries as made up of somewhat free improvisations on fixed themes in a definite order; and we realise too how naturally under these circumstances the very words used would be repeated—at first no doubt only the salient clauses—till they become fixed forms. The ritual, certainly of the simplest kind, would become stereotyped even more easily. The things that had to be done, the bringing up of the bread and wine, the collection of alms and so on, even more than the prayers, would be done always at the same point. A change here would be even more disturbing than a change in the order of the prayers.

A last consideration to be noted is the tendency of new Churches to imitate the customs of the older ones. Each new Christian community was formed by joining itself to the bond already formed. The new converts received their first missionaries, their faith and ideas from a mother Church. These missionaries would naturally celebrate the rites as they had seen them done, or as they had done them themselves in the mother Church. And their converts would imitate them, carry on the same tradition. Intercourse between the local Churches would further accentuate this uniformity among people who were very keenly conscious of forming one body with one Faith, one Baptism, and one Eucharist. It is not then surprising that the allusions to the Liturgy in the first Fathers of various countries, when compared, show us a homogeneous rite at any rate in its main outlines, a constant type of service, though it was subject to certain local modifications. It would not be surprising if from this common early Liturgy one uniform type had evolved for the whole Catholic world. We know that that is not the case. The more or less fluid ritual of the first two centuries crystallised into different liturgies in East and West; difference of language, the insistence on one point in one place, the greater importance given to another feature elsewhere, brought about our various rites. But there is an obvious unity underlying all the old rites that goes back to the earliest age. The medieval idea that all are derived from one parent rite is not so absurd, if we remember that the parent was not a written or stereotyped Liturgy, but rather a general *type* of service.

3. *The Liturgy in the First Three Centuries.*—For the first period we have of course no complete description. We must reconstruct what we can from the allusions to the Holy Eucharist in the Apostolic Fathers and apologists. Justin Martyr alone gives us a fairly complete outline of the rite that he knew. The Eucharist described in The Teaching of the Twelve Apostles—the *Didache* (most authorities now put the date of this work at the end of the first century) in some ways lies apart from the general development. We have here still the free "prophesying", the Eucharist is still joined to the *Agape*, the reference to the actual consecration is vague. The likeness between the prayers of thanksgiving and the Jewish forms for blessing bread and wine on the Sabbath points obviously to derivation from them.[4] It has been suggested that the rite here described is not our Eucharist at all; others think that it is a private Eucharist distinct from the official public rite. On the other hand, it seems clear from the whole account in chapters ix and x that we have here a real Eucharist, and the existence of private celebrations remains to be proved. The most natural explanation is certainly that of a Eucharist of a very archaic nature, not fully described. At any rate we have these liturgical

points from the book. The "Our Father" is a recognised formula: it is to be said three times every day. The Liturgy is a eucharist and a sacrifice to be celebrated by breaking bread and giving thanks on the "Lord's Day" by people who have confessed their sins. Only the baptised are admitted to it. The wine is mentioned first, then the broken bread; each has a formula of giving thanks to God for His revelation in Christ with the conclusion: "To thee be glory for ever." There follows a thanksgiving for various benefits; the creation and our sanctification by Christ are named; then comes a prayer for the Church ending with the form: "*Maranatha. Amen*"; in it occurs the form: "*Hosanna* to the God of David" (x, 5-6).

The First Epistle of Clement to the Corinthians (written probably between 90 and 100) contains an abundance of liturgical matter, much more than is apparent at the first glance (see **GLOSSARY: CLEMENT**). That the long prayer in chapters lix-lxi is a magnificent example of the kind of prayers said in the liturgy of the first century has always been admitted; that the letter, especially in this part, is full of liturgical forms is also evident. The writer quotes the *Sanctus* (Holy, holy, holy Lord of Sabaoth; all creation is full of his glory) from Is., vi, 3, and adds that "we assembled in unity cry (this) as with one mouth".[5] The end of the long prayer is a doxology invoking Christ and finishing with the form: "now and for generations of generations and for ages of ages. Amen".[6] This too is certainly a liturgical formula. There are many others. But we can find more in I Clement than merely a promiscuous selection of formulae. A comparison of the text with the first known Liturgy actually written down, that of the Eighth Book of the *Apostolic Constitutions* (written long afterwards, in the fifth century in Syria) reveals a most startling likeness (see **GLOSSARY**). Not only do the same ideas occur in the same order but there are whole passages—just those that in I Clement have most the appearance of liturgical formulae—that recur word for word in the *Apostolic Constitutions*.

In the *Apostolic Constitutions* the Eucharistic prayer begins, as in all liturgies, with the dialogue: "Lift up your hearts", etc. Then, beginning: "It is truly meet and just", comes a long thanksgiving for various benefits corresponding to what we call the preface. Here occurs a detailed description of the first benefit we owe to God—the creation. The various things created—the heavens and earth, sun, moon and stars, fire and sea, and so on, are enumerated at length.[7] The prayer ends with the *Sanctus*. I Clement, xx, contains a prayer echoing the same ideas exactly, in which the very same words constantly occur. The order in which the creatures are mentioned is the same. Again the *Apostolic Constitutions*[8] introduces the *Sanctus* in the same way as I Clement, where the author actually says he is quoting the Liturgy.[9] This same preface in the *Apostolic Constitutions*, remembering the Patriarchs of the Old Law, names Abel, Cain, Seth, Henoch, Noe, Salmon, Lot, Abraham, Melchisedech, Isaac, Jacob, Moses, Josue. The parallel passage in I Clement names Enoch, Noe, Lot, Salmon, Abraham, Rahab, Josue:[10] We may note at once two other parallels to this list containing again almost the same list of names—Hebrews xi, 4-31, and Justin.[11] The long prayer in I Clement is full of ideas and actual phrases that come again in the *Apostolic Constitutions*.[12] It is not only with the Liturgy of the *Apostolic Constitutions* that I Clement has these extraordinary resemblances. I Clement, lix, 4, echoes exactly the clauses of the celebrant's prayer during the intercession in the Alexandrine Rite (Greek St. Mark). These parallel passages cannot all be mere coincidences.

The question then occurs: What is the relation between I Clement and—in the first place—the Liturgy of the *Apostolic Constitutions*? The suggestion that first presents itself is that the later document (the *Apostolic Constitutions*) is quoting the earlier one (I Clement), but it is exceedingly unlikely. In that case the quotations would be more exact, the order of I Clement would be kept; the prayers in the Liturgy have no appearance of being quotations or conscious compositions of fragments from earlier books; nor, if the *Apostolic Constitutions* were quoting I Clement, would there be reduplications such as we have seen above? There was a certain uniformity of type in the earliest Liturgy in the sense described above, not a uniformity of detail, but one of general outline, of the ideas expressed in the various parts of the service, with a strong tendency to uniformity in certain salient expressions that recurred constantly and became insensibly liturgical formulae. This type of liturgy (rather than a fixed rite) may be traced back even to the first century. It is seen in Clement of Rome, Justin, etc.; perhaps there are traces of it even in the Epistle to the Hebrews. And of this type we still have a specimen in the *Apostolic Constitutions*. It is not that that rite exactly as it is in the *Constitutions* was used by Clement and Justin. Rather the *Constitutions* give us a much later (fifth century) form of the old Liturgy written down at last in Syria after it had existed for centuries in a more fluid state as an oral tradition. Thus, Clement, writing to the Corinthians (that the letter was actually composed by the Bishop of Rome, as Dionysius of Corinth says in the second century, is now generally admitted) uses the language to which he was accustomed in the Liturgy; the letter is full of liturgical ideas and reminiscences. They are found again in the later crystallisation of the same rite in the *Apostolic Constitutions*. So that book gives us the best representation of the Liturgy as used in Rome in the first two centuries.

This is confirmed by the next witness, Justin Martyr. Justin (died about 164), in his famous account of the Liturgy, describes it as he saw it at Rome. The often quoted passage is:

1. We lead him who believes and is joined to us, after we have thus baptised him, to those who are called the brethren, where they gather together to say prayers in common for ourselves, and for him who has been enlightened, and for all who

are everywhere. . . .2. We greet each other with a kiss when the prayers are finished. 3. Then bread and a cup of water and wine are brought to the president of the brethren, and he having received them sends up praise and glory to the Father of all through the name of his Son and the Holy Ghost, and makes a long thanksgiving that we have been made worthy of these things by him; when these prayers and thanksgivings are ended all the people present cry "Amen". . . .5. And when the president has "given thanks" (already a technical name for the Eucharist) and all the people have answered, those whom we call deacons give the bread and wine and water for which the "thanksgiving" (Eucharist) has been made to be tasted by those who are present and they carry them to those that are absent... This food is called by us the Eucharist.[13] (The well-known passage about the Real Presence follows, with the quotation of the words of Institution.) 3. On the day which is called that of the Sun a reunion is made of all those who dwell in the cities and fields; and the commentaries of the Apostles and writings of the prophets are read as long as time allows. 4. Then, when the reader has done, the president admonishes us in a speech and excites us to copy these glorious things. 5. Then we all rise and say prayers and, as we have said above, when we have done praying bread is brought up and wine and water; and the president sends up prayers with thanksgiving for the men, and the people acclaim, saying "Amen", and a share of the Eucharist is given to each and is sent to those absent by the deacons.[14]

This is by far the most complete account of the Eucharistic Service we have from the first three centuries. Putting it all together we have the scheme of the service:

1. Lessons (lxvii, 3).
2. Sermon by the bishop (lxvii, 4).
3. Prayers for all people (lxvii, 5; lxv, 1).
4. Kiss of peace (lxv, 2).

5. Offertory of bread and wine and water brought up by the deacons (lxvii, 5; lxv, 3).
6. Thanksgiving prayer by the bishop (lxvii, 5; lxv, 3).
7. Consecration by the words of institution (lxv, 5; lxvi, 2-3).
8. Intercession for the people (lxvii, 5; lxv, 3).
9. The people end this prayer with *Amen* (lxvii, 5; lxv, 3).
10. Communion (lxvii, 5; lxv, 5).

This is exactly the order of the Liturgy in the *Apostolic Constitutions*. Moreover, as in the case of I Clement, there are many passages and phrases in Justin that suggest parallel ones in the *Apostolic Constitutions*—not so much in Justin's account of the Liturgy as in other works in which Justin, like Clement, may be supposed to be echoing well-known liturgical phrases.

We have, then, in Clement and Justin the picture of a Liturgy at least remarkably like that of the *Apostolic Constitutions*. That the Liturgy of the *Apostolic Constitutions* as it stands is Antiochene, and is closely connected with the Rite of Jerusalem, is certain. It would seem, then, that it represents one form of a vaguer type of rite that was in its main outline uniform in the first three centuries.

4. *The Parent Rites, from the Fourth Century.*—From about the fourth century our knowledge of the Liturgy increases enormously. We are no longer dependent on casual references to it: we have definite rites fully developed. The more or less uniform type of Liturgy used everywhere before crystallised into four parent rites from which all others are derived. The four are the old Liturgies of Antioch, Alexandria, Rome, and Gaul. It will be enough here to trace an outline of their general evolution.

The development of these liturgies is very like what happens in the case of languages. From a general uniformity a number of local rites arise with characteristic differences. Then one of these local rites, because of the importance of the place that uses it, spreads, is copied by the cities around, drives out its rivals, and becomes at last the one rite used throughout a more or less extended area. We have then a movement from vague uniformity to diversity and then a return to exact uniformity. Except for the Gallican Rite the reason of the final survival of these liturgies is evident. Rome, Alexandria, and Antioch are the old patriarchal cities. As the other bishops accepted the jurisdiction of these three patriarchs, so did they imitate their services. The Liturgy, as it crystallised in these centres, became the type for the other Churches of their patriarchates. Only Gaul and north-west Europe generally, though part of the Roman Patriarchate, kept its own rite (Gallican) till the seventh and eighth centuries.

Alexandria and Antioch are the starting points of the two original Eastern rites. The earliest form of the Antiochene Rite is that of the *Apostolic Constitutions*, written down in the early fifth century. From what we have said it seems that this rite has best preserved the type of the primitive use. From it is derived the Rite of Jerusalem (till the Council of Chalcedon, 451, Jerusalem was in the Antiochene Patriarchate), which then returned to Antioch and became that of the patriarchate. We have this liturgy (called after St. James) in Greek and in Syriac. The Alexandrine Rite differs chiefly in the place of the great intercession. This too exists in Greek and the language of the country, in this case Coptic. In both cases the original form was certainly Greek, but in both the present Greek forms have been considerably influenced by the later Rite of Constantinople. A reconstruction of the original Greek is possible by removing the Byzantine additions and changes, and comparing the Greek and Syriac or Coptic forms. Both these liturgies have given rise to numerous derived forms. The Gallican Rite is certainly Syrian in its origin. There are also very striking parallels between Antioch and Alexandria, in spite of their different arrangements. It may well be, then, that all four rites are to be considered as modifications of that most ancient use, best preserved at Antioch.

In any case the old Roman Rite is not exactly that now used. Our Roman Missal has received considerable additions from Gallican sources. The original rite was simpler, more austere, had practically no ritual beyond the most necessary actions. It may be said that our present Roman Liturgy contains all the old nucleus, has lost nothing, but has additional Gallican elements. The original rite may be in part deduced from references to it as early as the fifth century.[15] It is represented by the Leonine and Gelasian Sacramentaries, and by the old part of the Gregorian book (see **LITURGICAL BOOKS**). The Roman Rite was used throughout Central and Southern Italy. The African use was a variant of that of Rome. In the West, however, the principle that rite should follow patriarchate did not obtain till about the eighth century. The pope was Patriarch of all Western (Latin) Europe, yet the greater part of the West did not use the Roman Rite. The North of Italy whose centre was Milan, Gaul, Germany, Spain, Britain, and Ireland had their own Liturgies. These Liturgies are all modifications of a common type; they may all be classed together as forms of what is known as the Gallican Rite. Where did that rite come from? It is obviously Eastern in its origin: its whole construction has the most remarkable conformity to the Antiochene type, a conformity extending in many parts to the actual text with the corresponding litany in the Antiochene Liturgy. It used to be said that the Gallican Rite came from Ephesus brought by the founders of the Church of Lyons, and from Lyons spread throughout North-Western Europe. This theory cannot be maintained. It was not brought to the West till its parent rite was fully developed, had already evolved a complicated ceremonial, such as is inconceivable at the time when the Church of Lyons was founded (second century). It must have been imported about the fourth century, at which time Lyons had lost all importance. Milan has been suggested as the centre from which it radiated, and the Cappadocian Bishop of Milan, Auxentius (355-74), as the man who introduced this Eastern Rite to the West. In spreading over Western Europe the rite naturally was modified in various Churches. When we speak of the Gallican Rite we mean a type of liturgy rather than a stereotyped service.

The Milanese Rite still exists, though in the course of time it has become considerably romanized.[16] For Gaul we have the description in two letters of St. Germanus of Paris (d. 576). Spain kept the Gallican Rite longest; the Mozarabic Liturgy still used at Toledo and Salamanca represents the Spanish use.[17] The British and Irish Liturgies, of which not much is known, were apparently Gallican too. From Lindisfarne the Gallican Use spread among the Northern English converted by Irish monks in the sixth and seventh centuries.

5. *The Derived Liturgies.*—From these four types—of Antioch, Alexandria, Rome, and the so-called Gallican Rite—all liturgies still used are derived. This does not mean that the actual liturgies we still have under those names are the parents; once more we must conceive the sources as vaguer, they are rather types subject always to local modification, but represented to us now in one form, such as, for instance, the Greek St. James or the Greek St. Mark Liturgy. The Antiochene type, apparently the most archaic, has been also the most prolific of daughter liturgies. Antioch first absorbed the Rite of Jerusalem (St. James), itself derived from the primitive Antiochene use shown in the *Apostolic Constitutions* (see **JERUSALEM, LITURGY OF**). In this form it was used throughout the patriarchate till about the thirteenth century. A local modification was the Use of Cappadocia. About the fourth century the great Byzantine Rite was derived from this. The Armenian Rite is derived from an early stage of that of Byzantium. The Nestorian Rite is also Antiochene in its origin, whether derived directly from Antioch, or Edessa, or from Byzantium at an early stage. The Liturgy of Malabar is Nestorian. The Maronite Use is that of Antioch considerably romanised. The other Eastern parent rite, of Alexandria, produced the numerous Coptic Liturgies and those of the daughter Church of Abyssinia.

In the West the later history of the Liturgy is that of the gradual supplanting of the Gallican by the Roman, which, however, became considerably gallicanised in the process. Since about the sixth century conformity with Rome becomes an ideal in most Western Churches. The old Roman use is represented by the Gelasian Sacramentary (see **LITURGICAL BOOKS**). This book came to Gaul in the sixth century, possibly by way of Arles and through the influence of St. Caesarius of Arles. It then spread throughout Gaul and received Gallican modifications. In some parts it completely supplanted the old Gallican books. Charles the Great (742-814) was anxious for uniformity throughout his kingdom in the Roman use only. He therefore procured from Pope Adrian I (772-795) a copy of the Roman Sacramentary. The book sent by the pope was a later form of the Roman Rite (the *Sacramentarium Gregorianum*). Charles imposed this book on all the clergy of his kingdom. But it was not easy to carry out his orders. The people were attached to their own customs. So someone, possibly Alcuin, added to Adrian's book a supplement containing selections from both the older Gelasian book and the original Gallican sources. This composition became then the service-book of the Frankish Kingdom and eventually, as we shall see, the Liturgy of the whole Roman Church.

In Spain Bishop Profuturus of Braga wrote in 538 to Pope Vigilius (537-55) asking his advice about certain liturgical matters. The pope's answer shows the first influence of the Roman Rite in Spain. In 561 the national Synod of Braga imposed Vigilius's ritual on all the kingdom of the Suevi. From this time we have the mixed Rite (Roman and Gallican) of Spain. Later, when the Visigoths had conquered the Suevi

(577-584), the Church of Toledo rejected the Roman elements and insisted on uniformity in the pure Gallican Rite. Nevertheless Roman additions were made later; eventually all Spain accepted the Roman Rite (in the eleventh century) except the one corner, at Toledo and Salamanca, where the mixed (Mozarabic) Rite is still used. The great Church of Milan, apparently the starting-point of the whole Gallican Use, was able to resist the influence of the Roman Liturgy. But here too, in later centuries the local rite became considerably romanised (St. Charles Borromeo, d. 1584), so that the present Milanese (Ambrosian) use is only a shadow of the old Gallican Liturgy. In Britain St. Augustine of Canterbury (597-605) naturally brought with him the Roman Liturgy. It received a new impetus from St. Theodore of Canterbury when he came from Rome (668), and gradually drove out the Gallican Use of Lindisfarne.

The English Church was very definitely Roman in the Liturgy. There was even a great enthusiasm for the rite of the mother Church. So Alcuin writes to Eanbald of York in 796: "Let your clergy not fail to study the Roman order; so that, imitating the Head of the Churches of Christ, they may receive the blessing of Peter, Prince of the Apostles, whom our Lord Jesus Christ made the chief of his flock"; and again: "Have you not plenty of books written according to the Roman use?" Before the Conquest the Roman service-books in England received a few Gallican additions from the old rite of the country.

So we see that at the latest by the tenth or eleventh century the Roman Rite has driven out the Gallican except in two sees (Milan and Toledo), and is used alone throughout the West, thus at last verifying here too the principle that rite follows patriarchate. But in the long and gradual supplanting of the Gallican Rite the Roman was itself affected by its rival, so that when at last it emerges as sole possessor it is no longer the old pure Roman Rite, but has become the gallicanised Roman Use that we now follow. These Gallican additions are all of the nature of ceremonial ornament, symbolic practices, ritual adornment. Our blessings of candles, ashes, palms, much of the ritual of Holy Week, sequences, and so on are Gallican additions; The original Roman Rite was very plain; simple, practical. Its characteristics were essentially soberness and sense. Once these additions were accepted at Rome they became part of the (new) Roman Rite and were used as part of that rite everywhere.

When was the older simpler use so enriched? We have two extreme dates. The additions were not made in the eighth century when Pope Adrian sent his Gregorian Sacramentary to Charlemagne. The original part of that book contains still the old Roman Mass. They were made by the eleventh century, as is shown by the *Missale Romanum Lateranense* of that time. The additions made to Adrian's book (by Alcuin) in the Frankish Kingdom came back to Rome (after they had become mixed up with the original book) under the influence of the successors of Charlemagne, and there supplanted the older pure form.

6. *Later Medieval Liturgies.*—We have now arrived at the present state of things. It remains to say a word about the various medieval uses the nature of which has often been misunderstood. Everyone has heard of the old English uses—Sarum, Ebor, etc. People have sometimes tried to set them up in opposition to what they call the "modern" Roman Rite, as witnesses that in some way England was not "Roman" before the Reformation. This idea shows an astonishing ignorance of the rites in question. These medieval uses are in no sense really independent rites. To compare them with the Gallican or Eastern Liturgies is absurd. They are simply cases of what was common all over Europe in the later Middle Ages, namely slight (often very slight) local modifications of the parent Rite of Rome. As there were Sarum and Ebor, so there were Paris, Rouen, Lyons, Cologne, Trier Rites. All these are simply Roman, with a few local peculiarities. They had their own saints' days, a trifling variety in the Calendar, some extra Epistles, Gospels, sequences, prefaces, certain local (generally more exuberant) details of ritual. In such insignificant details as the sequence of liturgical colours there was diversity in almost every diocese. No doubt, some rites (as the Dominican use, that of Lyons, etc.) have rather more Gallican additions than our normal Roman Liturgy. But the essence of all these late rites, all the parts that really matter (the arrangement, Canon of the Mass, and so on) are simply Roman. Indeed they do not differ from the parent rite enough to be called derived properly. Here again the parallel case of languages will make the situation clear. There are really derived languages that are no longer the same language as their source. Italian is derived from Latin, and Italian is not Latin. On the other hand, there are dialectic modifications that do not go far enough to make a derived language. No one would describe the modern Roman dialect as a language derived from Italian; it is simply Italian, with a few slight local modifications. In the same way, there are really new liturgies derived from the old ones. The Byzantine Rite is derived from that of Antioch and is a different rite. But Sarum, Paris, Trier, etc. are simply the Roman Rite, with a few local modifications.

Hence the justification of the abolition of nearly all these local varieties in the sixteenth century. However jealous one may be for the really independent liturgies, however much one would regret to see the abolition of the venerable old rites that share the allegiance of Christendom (an abolition by the way that is not in the least likely ever to take place), at any rate these medieval developments have no special claim to our sympathy. They were only exuberant inflations of the more austere ritual that had better not have been touched. Churches that use the Roman Rite had better use it in a pure form; where the same rite exists at least there uniformity is a reasonable ideal. To conceive these late developments as old compared with the original Roman Liturgy that has now again taken their place, is absurd. It was the novelties that Pius V abolished; his reform was a return to antiquity. In 1570 Pius V published his revised and restored Roman Missal that was to be the only form for all Churches that use the Roman Rite. The restoration of this Missal was on the whole undoubtedly successful; it was all in the direction of eliminating the later inflations, farced *Kyries* and *Glorias*, exuberant sequences, and ceremonial that was sometimes almost grotesque. In imposing it the pope made an exception for other uses that had been in possession for at least two centuries. This privilege was not used consistently. Many local uses that had a prescription of at least that time gave way to the authentic Roman Rite; but it saved the Missals of some Churches (Lyons, for instance) and of some religious orders (the Dominicans, Carmelites, Carthusians). What is much more important is that the pope's exception saved the two remnants of a really independent Rite at Milan and Toledo. Later, in the nineteenth century, there was again a movement in favour of uniformity that abolished a number of surviving local customs in France and Germany, though these affected the Breviary more than the Missal. We are now witnessing a similar movement for uniformity in plainsong (the Vatican edition). The Monastic Rite (used by the Benedictines and Cistercians) is also Roman in its origin. The differences between it and the normal Roman Rite affect chiefly the Divine Office.

7. *Table of Liturgies.*—We are now able to draw up a table of all the real liturgies used throughout the Christian world. The various Protestant Prayerbooks, *Agendae*, Communion-services, and so on, have of course no place in this scheme, because they all break away altogether from the continuity of liturgical development; they are merely compilations of random selections from any of the old rites imbedded in new structures made by various Reformers.

In the First Three Centuries:-

A fluid rite founded on the account of the Last Supper combined with a Christianised synagogue service showing, however, a certain uniformity of type and gradually crystallising into set forms. Of this type we have perhaps a specimen in the Liturgy of the second and eighth books of the Apostolic Constitutions.

Since the Fourth Century:-

The original indetermined rite forms into the four great liturgies from which all others are derived. These liturgies are:

I. *ANTIOCH*
  1. Pure in the *Apostolic Constitutions* (in Greek).
  2. Modified at Jerusalem in the Liturgy of St. James.
     a. The Greek St. James, used once a year by the Orthodox at Zacynthus and Jerusalem.
     b. The Syriac St. James, used by the Jacobites and Syrian Uniats.
     c. The Maronite Rite, used in Syriac.
  3. The Chaldean Rite, used by Nestorians and Chaldean Uniats (in Syriac).
     a. The Malabar Rite, used by Uniats and Schismatics in India (in Syriac).
  4. The Byzantine Rite, used by the Orthodox and Byzantine Uniats in various languages.
  5. The Armenian Rite, used by Gregorians and Uniats (in Armenian).

II. *ALEXANDRIA*
  1. a. The Greek Liturgy of St. Mark, no longer used.
     b. The Coptic Liturgies, used by Uniat and schismatical Copts.
  2. The Ethiopic Liturgies, used by the Church of Abyssinia.

III. *ROME*

1. The original Roman Rite, not now used.
2. The African Rite, no longer used.
3. The Roman Rite with Gallican additions used (in Latin) by nearly all the Latin Church.
4. Various later modifications of this rite used in the Middle Ages, now (with a few exceptions) abolished.

IV. *THE GALLICAN RITE*

1. Used once all over North-Western Europe and in Spain (in Latin).
2. The Ambrosian Rite at Milan.
3. The Mozarabic Rite, used at Toledo and Salamanca.

Chapter Notes

1. *I Apology*, xiii, lxv.
2. *Ibid.*, xiv, lxv.
3. *Ibid.*, xiii, lxi.
4. The "Berakoth" treatise of the Talmud; cf. Sabatier, *La Didache* (Paris, 1885), p. 99.
5. *I Clement Ad Cor.*, xxxiv, 7.
6. *Ibid.*, lxi, 3.
7. *Apost. Const.,* VIII, xii, 6-27.
8. *Ibid.,* VIII, xii, 27,
9. *I Clement ad Cor.*, xxxiv, 5-6.
10. *Ibid.*, ix-xii.
11. Justin, *Dialogue with the Jew Trypho*, xix, cxi, cxxxi, cxxxviii.
12. Compare for instance *I Clement ad Cor.*, lix, 2-4, with the *Apostolic Constitutions* VIII, x, 22-xi, 5 (which is part of the celebrant's prayer during the litany of the faithful: and xiii, 10 (prayer during the litany that follows the great intercession).lix, 2-4, with the *Apostolic Constitutions* VIII,

x, 22-xi, 5 (which is part of the celebrant's prayer during the litany of the faithful: and xiii, 10 (prayer during the litany that follows the great intercession).

[13] *I Apology*, LXV,1; LXVI.

[14] *Ibid*., LXVII,3.

[15] *Letters of Gelasius I* in Thiel, *Epistolae Rom. Pontificum*, I, cdlxxxvi, "Innocent I to Decennius of Eugubium", written in 416, in P.L., XX, 551; Pseudo-Ambrose, *De Sacramentis*, IV, 5.

[16] The Milanese (Ambrosian) Rite was drastically reformed after the Second Vatican Council (Ed.).

[17] The Mozarabic liturgy was also drastically reformed after the Second Vatican Council (Ed.).

2

RITES

1. *Name and Definition.*—*Ritus* in classical Latin means, primarily, the form and manner of any religious observance, so Livy, 1,7: *Sacra diis aliis albano ritu, graeco Herculi ut ab Evandro instituta erant* (Romulus) *facit*; then, in general, any custom or usage. In English the word "rite" ordinarily means the ceremonies, prayers, and functions of any religious body, whether pagan, Jewish, Moslem, or Christian. But here we must distinguish two uses of the word. We speak of any one such religious function as a rite—the rite of the blessing of palms, the coronation rite, etc. In a slightly different sense we call the whole complex of the services of any Church or group of Churches a rite—thus we speak of the Roman Rite, Byzantine Rite, and various Eastern rites. In the latter sense the word is often considered equivalent to liturgy (see **LITURGY**) which, however, in the older and more proper use of the word is the Eucharistic Service, or Mass; hence for a whole series of religious functions "rite" is preferable.

A Christian rite, in this sense, comprises the manner of performing all services for the worship of God and the sanctification of men. This includes therefore: (1) the administration of sacraments, among which the service of the Holy Eucharist, as being also the Sacrifice, is the most important element of all; (2) the series of psalms, lessons, prayers, etc., divided into separate unities, called "hours", to make up together the Divine Office; (3) all other religious and ecclesiastical functions, called sacramentals. This general term includes blessings of persons (such as a coronation, the blessing of an abbot, various ceremonies performed for catechumens, the reconciliation of public penitents, Benediction of the Blessed Sacrament, etc.), blessings of things (the consecration of a church, altar, chalice, etc.), and a number of devotions and ceremonies, e.g. processions and the taking of vows. Sacraments, the Divine Office, and sacramentals (in a wide sense) make up the rite of any Christian religious body. In the case of Protestants these three elements must be modified to suit their theological opinions.

2. *Difference of Rite.*—The Catholic Church has never maintained a principle of uniformity in rite. Just as there are different local laws in various parts of the Church, whereas certain fundamental laws are obeyed by all, so Catholics in different places have their own local or national rites; they say prayers and perform ceremonies that have evolved to suit people of the various countries, and are only different expressions of the same fundamental truths. The essential elements of the functions are obviously the same everywhere, and are observed by all Catholic rites in obedience to the command of Christ and the Apostles, thus: in every rite baptism is administered with water and the invocation of the Holy Trinity; the Holy Eucharist is celebrated with bread and wine, over which the words of institution are said; penance involves the confession of sins. In the amplification of these essential elements, in the accompanying prayers and practical or symbolic ceremonies, various customs have produced the changes which make the different rites. If any rite did not contain one of the essential notes of the service it would be invalid in that point, if its prayers or ceremonies expressed false doctrine it would be heretical. Such rites would not be tolerated in the Catholic Church. But, supposing uniformity in essentials and in faith, the authority of the Church has never insisted on uniformity of rite; Rome has never resented the fact that other people have their own expressions of the same truths. The Roman Rite is the most venerable, the most archaic, and immeasurably the most important of all, but our fellow-Catholics in the East have the same right to their traditional liturgies as we have to ours. Nor can we doubt that other rites too have many beautiful prayers and ceremonies, which add to the richness of Catholic liturgical inheritance. To lose these would be a misfortune second only to the loss of the Roman Rite. Leo XIII in his Encyclical, *Praeclara* (20 June, 1894), expressed the traditional attitude of the papacy when he wrote of his reverence for the venerable rites of the Eastern Churches and assured the schismatics, whom he invited to reunion, that there was no jealousy of these things at Rome; that for all Eastern customs "we shall provide without narrowness".

At the time of the Schism, Photius and Cerularius hurled against Latin rites and customs every conceivable absurd accusation. The Latin fast on Saturday, Lenten fare, law of celibacy, confirmation by a bishop, and especially the use of unleavened bread for the Holy Eucharist were their accusations against the West. Latin theologians replied that both were right and suitable, each for the people who used them, that there was no need for uniformity in rite if there was unity in faith, that one good custom did not prove another to be bad, thus defending their customs without attacking those of the East. But the Byzantine patriarch was breaking the unity of the Church, denying the primacy, and plunging the East into schism. In 1054, when Cerularius's schism had begun, a Latin bishop, Dominic of Gradus and Aquileia, wrote concerning it to Peter III of Antioch. He discussed the question Cerularius had raised, the use of azymes at Mass, and carefully explained that, in using this bread, Latins did not intend to disparage the Eastern custom of consecrating leavened bread, for there is a symbolic reason for either practice. "Because we know that the sacred mixture of fermented bread is used and lawfully observed by the most holy and orthodox Fathers of the Eastern Churches, we faithfully approve of both customs and confirm both by a spiritual explanation."[1] These words represent very well the attitude of the papacy towards other rites at all times. Three points, however may seem opposed to this and therefore require some explanation: the supplanting of the old Gallican Rite by that of Rome almost throughout the West, the modification of Uniat rites, the suppression of the later medieval rites.

The existence of the Gallican Rite was a unique anomaly. The natural principle that rite follows patriarchate has been sanctioned by universal tradition with this one exception. Since the first organisation of patriarchates there has been an ideal of uniformity throughout each. The close bond that joined bishops and metropolitans to their patriarch involved the use of his liturgy, just as the priests of a diocese follow the rite of their bishop. Before the arbitrary imposition of the Byzantine Rite on all Orthodox Churches no Eastern patriarch would have tolerated a foreign liturgy in his domain. All Egypt used the Alexandrine Rite, all Syria that of Antioch-Jerusalem, all Asia Minor, Greece, and the Balkan lands, that of Constantinople. But in the vast Western lands that make up the Roman patriarchate, north of the Alps and in Spain, various local rites developed, all bearing a strong resemblance to each other, yet different from that of Rome itself. These form the Gallican family of liturgies. Abbot Cabrol, Dom Cagin, and other writers of their school think that the Gallican Rite was really the original Roman Rite before Rome modified it. Most writers, however, maintain with Mgr. Duchesne, that the Gallican Rite is Eastern, Antiochene in origin.[2] Certainly it has numerous Antiochene peculiarities, and when it emerged as a complete rite in the sixth and seventh centuries (in Germanus of Paris, etc.), it was different from that in use at Rome at the time. Non-Roman liturgies were used at Milan, Aquileia, even at Gubbio at the gates of the Roman province. Innocent I (401-17) naturally protested against the use of a foreign rite in Umbria; occasionally other popes showed some desire for uniformity in their patriarchate, but the great majority regarded the old state of things with perfect indifference. When other bishops asked them how ceremonies were performed at Rome they sent descriptions (so Pope Vigilius to Profuturus of Braga in 538), but were otherwise content to allow different uses. St. Gregory I (590-604) showed no anxiety to make the new English Church conform to Rome, but told St. Augustine to take whatever rites he thought most suitable from Rome or Gaul.[3]

Thus for centuries the popes alone among patriarchs did not enforce their own rite even throughout their patriarchate. The gradual romanisation and subsequent disappearance of Gallican rites were (beginning in the eighth and ninth centuries), the work not of the popes but of local bishops and kings who naturally wished to conform to the use of the Apostolic See. The Gallican Rites varied everywhere (Charles the Great gives this as his reason for adopting the Roman Use), and the inevitable desire for at least local uniformity arose. The bishops' frequent visits to Rome brought them in contact with the more dignified ritual observed by their chief at the tomb of the Apostles, and they were naturally influenced by it in their return home. The local bishops in synods ordered conformity to Rome. The romanising movement in the West came from below. In the Frankish kingdom Charles the Great, as part of his scheme of unifying, sent to Adrian I for copies of the Roman books, commanding their use throughout his domain. In the history of the substitution of the Roman Rite for the Gallican the popes appear as spectators, except perhaps in Spain and much later in Milan. The final result was the application in the West of the old principle, for since the pope was undoubtedly Patriarch of the West it was inevitable that sooner or later the West should conform to his rite. The places, however, that really cared for their old local rites (Milan, Toledo) retain them even now.[4]

It is true that the changes made in some Uniat rites by the Roman correctors have not always corresponded to the best liturgical tradition. There are, as Mgr. Duchesne says, "corrections inspired by zeal that was not always according to knowledge",[5] but they are much fewer than is generally supposed and have never been made with the idea of romanising. Despite the general prejudice that Uniat rites are mere mutilated hybrids, the strongest impression from the study of them is how little has been changed. Where there is no suspicion of false doctrine, as in the Byzantine Rite, the only change made was the restoration of the name of the pope where the schismatics had erased it. Although the question of the procession of the Holy Ghost has been so fruitful a source of dispute between Rome and Constantinople, the *Filioque* clause was certainly not contained in the original creed, nor did the Roman authorities insist on its addition. So Rome is content that Eastern Catholics should keep their traditional form unchanged, though they believe the Catholic doctrine. The *Filioque* is only sung by those Byzantine Uniats who wish it themselves, as the Ruthenians. Other rites were altered in places, not to romanize but only to eradicate passages suspected of heresy. All other Uniats came from Nestorian, Monophysite, or Monothelete sects, whose rites had been used for centuries by heretics. Hence, when bodies of these people wished to return to the Catholic Church their services were keenly studied at Rome for possible heresy. In most cases corrections were absolutely necessary. The Nestorian Liturgy, for instance, did not contain the words of institution, which had to be added to the Liturgy of the converted Chaldees. The Monophysite Jacobites, Copts, and Armenians have in the *Trisagion* (see **GLOSSARY**) the fateful clause: "who wast crucified for us", which has been the watchword of Monophysitism ever since Peter the Dyer of Antioch added it (470-88). If only because of its associations this could not remain in a Catholic Liturgy.

In some instances, however, the correctors were over scrupulous. In the Gregorian Armenian Liturgy the words said by the deacon at the expulsion of the catechumens, long before the Consecration: "The Body of the Lord and the Blood of the Saviour are set forth (or "are before us") were in the Uniat Rite changed to: "are about to be before us". The Uniats also omit the words sung by the Gregorian choir before the Anaphora: "Christ has been manifested amongst us (has appeared in the midst of us)," and further change the cherubic hymn because of its anticipation of the Consecration. These misplacements are really harmless when understood, yet any reviser would be shocked by such strong cases. In many other ways also the Armenian Rite shows evidence of Roman influence. It has unleavened bread, our confession and *Judica* psalm at the beginning of Mass, a *Lavabo* before the Canon, the last Gospel, etc. But so little is this the effect of union with Rome that the schismatical Armenians have all these points too. They date from the time of the Crusades, when the Armenians, vehemently opposed to the Orthodox, made many advances towards Catholics. So also the strong romanising of the Maronite Liturgy was entirely the work of the Maronites themselves, when, surrounded by enemies in the East, they too turned towards the great Western Church, sought her communion, and eagerly copied her practices. One can hardly expect the pope to prevent other Churches from imitating Roman customs. Yet in the case of Uniats he does even this. A Byzantine Uniat priest who uses unleavened bread in his Liturgy incurs excommunication. The only case in which an ancient Eastern rite has been wilfully romanised is that of the Uniat Malabar Christians, where it was not Roman authority but the misguided zeal of Alexius de Menezes, Archbishop of Goa, and his Portuguese advisers at the Synod of Diamper (1599) which spoiled the old Malabar Rite.

The Western medieval rites are in no case (except the Ambrosian and Mozarabic Rites), really independent of Rome.

They are merely the Roman Rite with local additions and modifications, most of which are to its disadvantage. They are late, exuberant, and inferior variants, whose ornate additions and long interpolated tropes, sequences, and farcing destroy the dignified simplicity of the old liturgy. In 1570 the revisers appointed by the Council of Trent restored with scrupulous care and, even in the light of later studies, brilliant success, the pure Roman Missal, which Pius V ordered should alone be used wherever the Roman Rite is followed. It was a return to an older and purer form. The medieval rites have no doubt a certain archaeological interest, but where the Roman Rite is used it is best to use it in its pure form. This too only means a return to the principle that rite should follow patriarchate. The reform was made very prudently, Pius V allowing any rite that could prove an existence of two centuries to remain (Bull, *Quo primum*, 19 July, 1570, printed first in the Missal), thus saving any local use that had a certain antiquity. Some dioceses (e.g. Lyons) and religious orders (Dominicans, Carthusians, Carmelites), therefore keep their special uses, and the independent Ambrosian and Mozarabic Rites, whose loss would have been a real misfortune (see **LITURGY; MASS, LITURGY OF THE**) still remain.

Rome then by no means imposed uniformity of rite. Catholics are united in faith and discipline, but in their manner of performing the sacred functions there is room for variety based on essential unity, as there was in the first centuries. There are cases (e.g. the Georgian Church) where union with Rome has saved the ancient use, while the schismatics have been forced to abandon it by the centralising policy of their authorities (in this case Russia). The ruthless destruction of ancient rites in favour of uniformity has been the work not of Rome but of the schismatical patriarchs of Constantinople. Since the thirteenth century Constantinople in its attempt to make itself the one centre of the Orthodox Church has driven out the far more venerable and ancient Liturgies of Antioch and Alexandria and has compelled all the Orthodox to use its own late derived rite. The Greek Liturgy of St. Mark has ceased to exist; that of St. James has been revived for one or two days in the year at Zakynthos and Jerusalem only. The Orthodox all the world over must follow the Rite of Constantinople. In this unjustifiable centralisation we have a defiance of the old principle, since Antioch, Jerusalem, Alexandria, Cyprus, in no way belong to the Byzantine Patriarchate. Those who accuse the papacy of sacrificing everything for the sake of uniformity mistake the real offender, the oecumenical patriarch.

3. *The Old Rites*.—Catholic and Schismatical.—A complete table of the old rites with an account of their mutual relations will be found in the article **LITURGY**. Here it need only be added that there is a Uniat body using each of the Eastern rites. There is no ancient rite that is not represented within the Catholic Church. The rite a bishop or priest follows is no test at all of his religion. Within certain broad limits a member of any Eastern sect might use any rite, for the two categories of rite and religion cross each other continually. They represent quite different classifications: for instance, liturgically all Armenians belong to one class, theologically a Uniat Armenian belongs to the same class as Latins, Chaldees, Maronites, etc., and has nothing to do with his Gregorian (Monophysite) fellow-countrymen. Among Catholics the rite forms a group; each rite is used by a branch of the Church that is thereby a special, though not separate, entity. So within the Catholic unity we speak of local Churches whose characteristic in each case is the rite they use. Rite is the only basis of this classification. Not all Armenian Catholics or Byzantine Uniats obey the same patriarch or local authority; yet they are "Churches," individual provinces of the same great Church, because each is bound together by their own rites. In the West there is the vast Latin Church, in the East the Byzantine, Chaldean, Coptic, Syrian, Maronite, Armenian, and Malabar

Uniat Churches. It is of course possible to subdivide and to speak of the national Churches (of Italy, France, Spain, etc.,) under one of these main bodies (see **LATIN CHURCH**). In modern times rite takes the place of the old classification in patriarchates and provinces.

4. *Protestant Rites*.—The Reformation in the sixteenth century produced a new and numerous series of rites, which are in no sense continuations of the old development of liturgy. They do not all represent descendants of the earliest rites, nor can they be classified in the table of genus and species that includes all the old liturgies of Christendom. The old rites are unconscious and natural developments of earlier ones and go back to the original fluid rite of the first centuries (see **LIT-URGY**). The Protestant rites are deliberate compositions made by the various Reformers to suit their theological positions, as new services were necessary for their prayer-meetings. No old liturgy could be used by people with their ideas. The old rites contain the plainest statements about the Real Presence, the Eucharistic Sacrifice, prayers to saints, and for the dead, which are denied by Protestants. The Reformation occurred in the West, where the Roman Rite in its various local forms had been used for centuries. No Reformed sect could use the Ro-man Mass; the medieval derived rites were still more ornate, explicit, in the Reformers' sense superstitious. So all the Prot-estant sects abandoned the old Mass and the other ritual func-tions, composing new services which have no continuity, no direct relation to any historic liturgy. However, it is hardly pos-sible to compose an entirely new Christian service without borrowing anything. Moreover, in many cases the Reformers wished to make the breach with the past as little obvious as could be. So many of their new services contain fragments of old rites; they borrowed such elements as seemed to them harmless, composed and re-arranged and evolved in some cases services that contain parts of the old ones in a new order. On the whole it is surprising that they changed as much as they did. It would have been possible to arrange an imitation of the Roman Mass that would have been much more like it than anything they produced.

They soon collected fragments of all kinds of rites, Eastern, Roman, Mozarabic, etc., which with their new prayers they arranged into services that are hopeless liturgical tangles. This is specially true of the Anglican Prayer-books. In some cases, for instance, the placing of the *Gloria* after the Communion in Edward VI's second Prayer-book, there seems to be no object except of a love of change. The first Lutheran services kept most of the old order. The Calvinist arrangements had from the first no connection with any earlier rite. The use of the vulgar tongue was a great principle with the Reformers. Luther and Zwingli at first compromised with Latin, but soon the old language disappeared in all Protestant services. Luther in 1523 published a tract, "Of the order of the service in the parish"), in which he insists on preaching, rejects all "unevangelical" parts of the Mass, such as the Offertory and idea of sacrifice, invocation of saints, and ceremonies, and denounces private Masses (*Winkelmessen*), Masses for the dead, and the idea of the priest as a mediator.[6] Later in the same year he issued a *Formula missae et communionis pro ecclesia Vittebergensi*, in which he omits the preparatory prayers, Offertory, all the Canon to *qui pridie*, from *Unde et memores* to the Pater, the Embolism (see **GLOSSARY**) of the Lord's Prayer, fraction, *Ite missa est*. The Preface is shortened, the *Sanctus* is to be sung after the words of institution which are to be said aloud, and meanwhile the elevation may be made because of the weak who would be offended by its sudden omission. At the end he adds a new ceremony, a blessing from Num., vi, 24-6. Latin remained in this service.

Karlstadt began to hold vernacular services at Wittenberg since 1521.[7] In 1524 Kaspar Kantz published a German service on the lines of Luther's *Formula missae*, so also Thomas

Münzer, the Anabaptist, in 1523 at Alstedt. A number of compromises began at this time among the Protestants, services partly Latin and partly vernacular. Vernacular hymns took the place of the Proper (Introit, etc.). At last in 1526 Luther issued an entirely new German service, *Deudsche Messe und ordnung Gottis diensts* to be used on Sundays, whereas the *Formula missae*, in Latin, might be kept for week-days. In the *Deudsche Messe* "a spiritual song or German psalm" replaces the Introit, then follows *Kyrie eleison* in Greek three times only. There is no *Gloria*. Then come the Collects, Epistle, a German hymn, Gospel, Creed, Sermon, Paraphrase of the Lord's Prayer, words of institution with the account of the Last Supper from I Cor., xi, 20-9, Elevation (always kept by Luther himself in spite of Karlstadt and most of his colleagues), Communion, during which the *Sanctus* or a hymn is sung, Collects, the blessing from Numbers, vi, 24-6. Except the *Kyrie*, all is in German; azyme bread is still used but declared indifferent; Communion is given under both kinds, though Luther preferred the unmixed chalice. This service remained for a long time the basis of the Lutheran Communion function, but the local branches of the sect from the beginning used great freedom in modifying it. The Pietistic movement in the eighteenth century, with its scorn for forms and still more the present Rationalism, have left very little of Luther's scheme. A vast number of *Agendae, Kirchenordnungen*, and Prayer-books issued by various Lutheran consistories from the sixteenth century to our own time contain as many forms of celebrating the Lord's Supper. Pastors use their own discretion to a great extent, and it is impossible to foresee what service will be held in any Lutheran church. An arrangement of hymns, Bible readings (generally the Nicene Creed), a sermon, then the words of institution and Communion, prayers (often extempore), more hymns, and the blessing from Numbers vi, make up the general outline of the service.

Zwingli was more radical than Luther. In 1523 he kept a form of the Latin Mass with the omission of all he did not like in it, chiefly because the town council of Zurich feared too sudden a change, but in 1525 he overcame their scruples and issued his *Action oder bruch (=Brauch) des nachtmals)*. This is a complete breach with the Mass, an entirely new service. On Maundy Thursday the men and women are to receive communion, on Good Friday those of "middle age", on Easter Sunday only the oldest *(die alleraltesten)*. These are the only occasions on which the service is to be held. The arrangement is: a prayer said by the pastor facing the people, reading of I Cor., xi, 20-9, *Gloria in Excelsis*, "The Lord be with you" and its answer, reading of John, vi 47-63, Apostles' Creed, an address to the people, Lord's Prayer, extempore prayer, words of institution, Communion (under both kinds in wooden vessels), Ps. CXIII, a short prayer of thanksgiving; the pastor says: "Go in peace". On other Sundays there is to be no Communion at all, but a service consisting of prayer, Our Father, sermon, general confession, absolution, prayer, blessing. Equally radical was the Calvinist sect. In 1535 through Farel's influence the Mass was abolished in Geneva.[8] Three times a year only was there to be a commemorative Supper in the baldest form; on other Sundays the sermon was to suffice. In 1542 Calvin issued *La forme des prières ecclésiastiques*, a supplement to which describes *La manière de célébrer la cène*. This rite, to be celebrated four times yearly, consists of the reading of I Cor., xi, an excommunication of various kinds of sinners, and long exhortation. "This being done, the ministers distribute the bread and the cup to the people, taking care that they approach reverently and in good order." Meanwhile a psalm is sung or a lesson read from the Bible, a thanksgiving follows, and a final blessing. Except for their occurrence in the reading of I Cor., xi, the words of institution are not said. There is no kind of Communion form. It is hardly possible to speak of rite at all in the Calvinist body.

The other ritual functions kept by Protestants (baptism, confirmation as an introduction to Communion, marriage, funerals, appointment of ministers) went through much the same development. The first Reformers expunged and modified the old rites, then gradually more and more was changed until little remained of a rite in our sense. Psalms, hymns, prayers, addresses to the people in various combinations make up these functions. The Calvinists have always been more radical than the Lutherans. The Anglican body stands somewhat apart from the others, inasmuch as it has a standard book, almost unaltered since 1662. The first innovation was the introduction of an English litany under Henry VIII in 1544. Cranmer was preparing further changes when Henry VIII died. Under Edward VI (1547-53) many changes were made at once: blessings, holy water, the creeping to the Cross were abolished, Mass was said in English, and in 1549 the first Prayer-book, arranged by Cranmer, was issued. Much of the old order of the Mass remained, but the Canon disappeared to make way for a new prayer from Lutheran sources. The *Kölnische Kirchenordnung* composed by Melanchthon and Bucer supplied part of the prayers. The changes are Lutheran rather than Calvinist. In 1552 the second Prayer-book took the place of the first. This is the present Anglican Book of Common Prayer and represents a much stronger Protestant tendency. The commandments take the place of the Introit and *Kyrie* (kept in the first book), the *Gloria* is moved to the end, the Consecration-prayer is changed so as to deny the Sacrifice and Real Presence, the form at the Communion becomes: "Take and eat this in remembrance that Christ died for thee, and feed on him in thy heart by faith with thanksgiving" (similarly for the chalice). In 1558 Elizabeth's Government issued a new edition of the second Prayer-book of Edward VI with slight modifications of its extreme Protestantism. Both the Edwardine forms for communion are combined. In 1662 a number of revisions were made. In particular the ordination forms received additions defining the order to be conferred. A few slight modifications (as to the lessons read, days no longer to be kept) have been made since.

THE WISDOM OF ADRIAN FORTESCUE

The Anglican Communion service follows this order: The Lord's Prayer, Collect for purity, Ten Commandments, Collect for the king and the one for the day, Epistle, Gospel, Creed, sermon, certain sentences from the Bible (meanwhile a collection is made), prayer for the Church militant, address to the people about Communion, general confession and absolution, the comfortable words (Matt., xi, 28; John, iii, 16; 1 Tim., i, 15; I John, ii, 1), Preface, prayer, ("We do not presume"), Consecration-prayer, Communion at once, Lord's Prayer, Thanksgiving-prayer, "Glory be to God on high", blessing. Very little of the arrangement of the old Mass remains in this service, for all the ideas Protestants reject are carefully excluded. The Book of Common Prayer contains all the official services of the Anglican Church, baptism, the catechism, confirmation, marriage, funeral, ordination, articles of religion, etc. It has also forms of morning and evening prayer, composed partly from the Catholic Office with many modifications and very considerably reduced. The Episcopal Church in Scotland has a Prayer-book, formed in 1637 and revised in 1764, which is more nearly akin to the first Prayer-book of Edward VI and is decidedly more High-Church in tone. In 1789 the Protestant Episcopal Church of America accepted a book based on the English one of 1662, but taking some features from the Scotch services. The Anglican service-books are now the least removed from Catholic liturgies of those used by any Protestant body. But this is saying very little. The Non-jurors in the eighteenth century produced a number of curious liturgies which in many ways go back to Catholic principles, but have the fault common to all Protestant services of being conscious and artificial arrangements of elements selected from the old rites, instead of natural developments.[9] The Irvingites have a not very successful service-book of this type.[10] Many Methodists use the Anglican book; the other later sects have for the most part nothing but loose arrangements of hymns, readings, extempore prayers, and a sermon that can hardly be called rites in any sense.

5. *Liturgical Language.*—The language of any Church or rite, as distinct from the vulgar tongue, is that used in the official services and may or may not be the common language. For instance the Rumanian Church uses liturgically the ordinary language of the country, while Latin is used by the Latin Church for her Liturgy without regard to the mother tongue of the clergy or congregation. There are many cases of an intermediate state between these extremes, in which the liturgical language is an older form of the vulgar tongue, sometimes easily, sometimes hardly at all, understood by people who have not studied it specially. Language is not rite. Theoretically any rite may exist in any language. Thus the Armenian, Coptic, and East Syrian Rites are celebrated always in one language, the Byzantine Rite is used in a great number of tongues, and in other rites one language sometimes enormously preponderates but is not used exclusively. This is determined by church discipline. The Roman Liturgy is generally celebrated in Latin. The reason why a liturgical language began to be used and is still retained must be distinguished in liturgical science from certain theological or mystic considerations by which its use may be explained or justified. Each liturgical language was first chosen because it was the natural language of the people. But languages change and the Faith spreads into countries where other tongues are spoken. Then either the authorities are of a more practical mind and simply translate the prayers into the new language, or the conservative instinct, always strong in religion, retains for the liturgy an older language no longer used in common life. The Jews showed this instinct, when, though Hebrew was a dead language after the Captivity, they continued to use it in the Temple and the synagogues in the time of Christ, and still retain it in their services. The Moslem, also conservative, reads the Koran in classical Arabic, whether he be Turk, Persian, or Afghan. The translation of the church service is complicated by the difficulty of determining when the language in which it is written, as Latin in the West and Hellenistic Greek in the East, has ceased to be the vulgar tongue. Though the Byzantine services were translated into the common language of the Slavonic people that they might be understood, this form of the language (Church-Slavonic) is no longer spoken, but is gradually becoming as unintelligible as the original Greek. Protestants make a great point of using languages "understanded of the people", yet the language of Luther's Bible and the Anglican Prayer-book is already archaic.

6. *History*.—When Christianity appeared Hellenistic Greek was the common language spoken around the Mediterranean. St. Paul writes to people in Greece, Asia Minor, and Italy in Greek. When the parent rites were finally written down in the fourth and fifth centuries Eastern liturgical language had slightly changed. The Greek of these liturgies (*Apostolic Constitutions* VIII, St. James, St. Mark, the Byzantine Liturgy) was that of the Fathers of the time, strongly coloured by the Septuagint and the New Testament. These liturgies remained in this form and have never been recast in any modern Greek dialect. Like the text of the Bible, that of a liturgy once fixed becomes sacred. The formulae used Sunday after Sunday are hallowed by too sacred associations to be changed as long as more or less the same language is used. The common tongue drifts and develops, but the liturgical forms are stereotyped. In the East and West, however, there existed different principles in this matter. Whereas in the West there was no literary language but Latin till far into the Middle Ages, in the East there were such languages, totally unlike Greek, that had a position, a literature, a dignity of their own hardly inferior to that of Greek itself. In the West every educated man spoke and wrote Latin almost to the Renaissance. To translate the Liturgy into a Celtic or Teutonic language would have seemed

as absurd as to write a prayer-book now in some vulgar slang. The East was never hellenised as the West was latinised. Great nations, primarily Egypt and Syria, kept their own languages and literatures as part of their national inheritance. The people, owing no allegiance to the Greek language, had no reason to say their prayers in it, and the Liturgy was translated into Coptic in Egypt, into Syriac in Syria and Palestine. So the principle of a uniform liturgical language was broken in the East and people were accustomed to hear the church service in different languages in different places. This uniformity once broken never became an ideal to Eastern Christians and the way was opened for an indefinite multiplication of liturgical tongues.

In the fourth and fifth centuries the Rites of Antioch and Alexandria were used in Greek in the great towns where people spoke Greek, in Coptic or Syriac among peasants in the country. The Rite of Asia Minor and Constantinople was always in Greek, because here there was no rival tongue. But when the Faith was preached in Armenia (from Caesarea) the Armenians in taking over the Caesarean Rite translated it of course into their own language. And the great Nestorian Church in East Syria, evolving her own literature in Syriac, naturally used that language for her church services too. This diversity of tongues was by no means parallel to diversity of sect or religion. People who agreed entirely in faith, who were separated by no schism, nevertheless said their prayers in different languages. Melchites in Syria clung entirely to the Orthodox faith of Constantinople and used the Byzantine Rite, yet used it translated into Syriac. The process of translating the Liturgy continued later. After the Schism of the eleventh century, the Orthodox Church, unlike Rome, insisted on uniformity of rite among her members. All the Orthodox use the Byzantine Rite, yet have no idea of one language. When the Slavs were converted the Byzantine Rite was put into Old Slavonic for them; when Arabic became the only language spoken in Egypt and Syria, it became the language of the Liturgy in those countries. For a long time all the people north of Constantinople used Old Slavonic in church, although the dialects they spoke gradually drifted away from it. Only the Georgians, who are Slavs in no sense at all, used their own language. In the seventeenth century as part of the growth of Rumanian national feeling came a great insistence on the fact that they were not Slavs either. They wished to be counted among Western, Latin races, so they translated their liturgical books into their own Romance language. These represent the old classical liturgical languages in the East.

The Monophysite Churches have kept the old tongues even when no longer spoken; thus they use Coptic in Egypt, Syriac in Syria, Armenian in Armenia. The Nestorians and their daughter-Church in India (Malabar) also use Syriac. The Orthodox have four or five chief liturgical languages: Greek, Arabic, Church-Slavonic, and Rumanian. Georgian has almost died out. Later Russian missions have very much increased the number. They have translated the same Byzantine Rite into German, Esthonian, and Lettish for the Baltic provinces, Finnish and Tartar for converts in Finland and Siberia, Eskimo, a North American Indian dialect, Chinese, and Japanese. Hence no general principle of liturgical language can be established for Eastern Churches, though the Nestorians and Monophysites have evolved something like the Roman principle and kept their old languages in the liturgy, in spite of change in common talk. The Orthodox services are not, however, everywhere understood by the people, for since these older versions were made language has gone on developing. In the case of converts of a totally different race, such as Chinese or Red Indians, there is an obvious line to cross at once and there is no difficulty about translating what would otherwise be totally unintelligible to them. At home the spoken language gradually drifts away from the form stereotyped in the Liturgy, and it is difficult to determine when the Liturgy ceases to be understood. In more modern times with the growth of new sects the conservative instinct of the old Churches has grown. The Greek, Arabic, and Church-Slavonic texts are jealously kept unchanged, though in all cases they have become archaic and difficult to follow by uneducated people. Lately the question of liturgical language has become one of the chief difficulties in Macedonia. Especially since the Bulgarian Schism the Phanar at Constantinople insists on Greek in church as a sign of Hellenism, while the people clamour for Old-Slavonic or Rumanian.

In the West the whole situation is different. Greek was first used at Rome, too. About the third century the services were translated into the vulgar tongue, Latin (see **MASS, LITURGY OF THE**), which has remained ever since. There was no possible rival language for many centuries. As the Western barbarians became civilised they accepted a Latin culture in everything, having no literatures of their own. Latin was the language of all educated people, so it was used in church, as it was for books or even letter-writing. The Romance people drifted from Latin to Italian, Spanish, French, etc., so gradually that no one can say when Latin became a dead language. The vulgar tongue was used by peasants and ignorant people only; but all books were written, lectures given, and solemn speeches made in Latin. Even Dante (d. 1321) thought it necessary to write an apology for Italian (*De vulgari eloquentia*). So for centuries the Latin language was that, not of the Catholic Church, but of the Roman patriarchate. When people at last realised that it was dead, it was too late to change it. Around it had gathered the associations of Western Christendom; the music of the Roman Rite was composed and sung only to a Latin text; and it is even now the official tongue of the Roman Court. The ideal of uniformity in rite extended to language also, so when the rebels of the sixteenth century threw over the old language, sacred from its long use, as they threw over the old rite and old laws, the Catholic Church, conservative in all these things, would not give way to them. As a bond of union among the many nations who make up the Latin partiarchate, she retains the old Latin tongue with one or two small exceptions. Along the Eastern coast of the Adriatic Sea the Roman Rite has been used in Slavonic (with the Glagolitic letters) since the eleventh century, and the Roman Mass is said in Greek on rare occasions at Rome.

It is a question how far one may speak of a special liturgical Latin language. The writers of our Collects, hymns, Prefaces, etc., wrote simply in the language of their time. The style of the various elements of the Mass and Divine Office varies greatly according to the time at which they were written. We have texts from the fourth or fifth to the twentieth century. Liturgical Latin then is simply late Christian Latin of various periods. On the other hand the Liturgy had an influence on the style of Christian Latin writers second only to that of the Bible. First we notice Hebraisms (*per omnia saecula saeculorum*), many Greek constructions (*per Dominum nostrum*, meaning "for the sake of", ...) and words (*Eucharistia, litania, episcopus*), expressions borrowed from Biblical metaphors (*pastor, liber praedestinationis, crucifigere carnem, lux, vita, Agnus Dei*), and words in a new Christian sense (*humilitas, compunctio, caritas*). St. Jerome in his Vulgate more than any one else helped to form liturgical style. His constructions and phrases occur repeatedly in the non-Biblical parts of the Mass and Office. The style of the fifth and sixth centuries (St. Leo I, Celestine I, Gregory I) forms perhaps the main stock of our services. The mediaeval Schoolmen (St. Thomas Aquinas) and their technical terminology have influenced much of the later parts, and the Latin of the Renaissance is an important element that in many cases overlays the ruder forms of earlier times. Of this Renaissance Latin many of the Breviary lessons are typical examples; a comparison of the earlier forms of the hymns with the improved forms drawn up by order of Urban VIII (1623-44) will convince any one how disastrous its influence was. The tendency to write inflated phrases has not yet stopped: almost any modern Collect compared with the old ones in the Gelasian Sacramentary will show how much we have lost of style in our liturgical prayers.

7. Use of Latin.—The principle of using Latin in church is in no way fundamental. It is a question of discipline that evolved differently in East and West, and may not be defended as either primitive or universal. The authority of the Church could change the liturgical language at any time without sacrificing any important principle. The idea of a universal tongue may seem attractive, but is contradicted by the fact that the Catholic Church uses eight or nine different liturgical languages. Latin preponderates as a result of the greater influence of the Roman patriarchate and its rite, caused by the spread of Western Europeans into new lands and the unhappy schism of so many Easterns.[11] Uniformity of rite or liturgical language has never been a Catholic ideal, nor was Latin chosen deliberately as a sacred language. Had there been any such idea the language would have been Hebrew or Greek. The objections of Protestants to a Latin Liturgy can be answered easily enough. An argument often made from I Cor., xiv, 4-18, is of no value. The whole passage treats of quite another thing, prophesying in tongues that no one understands, not even the speaker (see 14: "For if I pray in a tongue, my spirit prayeth, but my understanding is without fruit"). The other argument, from practical convenience, from the loss to the people who do not understand what is being said, has some value. The Church has never set up a mysterious unintelligible language as an ideal. There is no principle of sacerdotal mysteries from which the layman is shut out. In spite of the use of Latin the people have means of understanding the service. That they might do so still better if everything were in the vulgar tongue may be admitted, but in making this change the loss would probably be greater than the gain.

By changing the language of the Liturgy we should lose the principle of uniformity in the Roman patriarchate. According to the ancient principle that rite follows patriarchate, the Western rite should be that of the Western patriarch, the Roman Bishop, who uses the local rite of the city of Rome. There is a further advantage in using it in his language, so the use of Latin in the West came about naturally and is retained through conservative instinct. It is not so in the East. There is a great practical advantage to travellers, whether priests or laymen, in finding their rite exactly the same everywhere. An English priest in Poland or Portugal could not say his Mass unless he and the server had a common language. The use of Latin all over the Roman patriarchate is a very obvious and splendid witness of unity. Every Catholic traveller in a country of which he does not know the language has felt the comfort of finding that in church at least everything is familiar and knows that in a Catholic church of his own rite he is at home anywhere. Moreover, the change of liturgical language would be a break with the past. It is a witness of antiquity of which a Catholic may well be proud that in Mass today we are still used to the very words that Anselm, Gregory, Leo sang in their cathedrals. A change of language would also abolish Latin chant. Plainsong, as venerable a relic of antiquity as any part of the ritual, is composed for the Latin text only, supposes always the Latin syllables and the Latin accent, and becomes a caricature when it is forced into another language with different rules of accent.

These considerations of antiquity and universal use always made proportionately (since there are the Eastern Uniat rites) but valid for the Roman patriarchate may well outweigh the practical convenience of using the chaos of modern languages in the liturgy. There is also an aesthetic advantage in Latin. The splendid dignity of the short phrases with their rhythmical accent and terse style redolent of the great Latin Fathers, the strange beauty of the old Latin hymns, the sonorous majesty of the Vulgate, all these things that make the Roman Rite so dignified, so characteristic of the old Imperial City where the Prince of the Apostles set up his throne, would be lost altogether in modern English or French translations. The impossibility of understanding Latin is not so great. It is not a secret, unknown tongue, and till quite lately every educated person understood it. It is still taught in every school. The Church does not clothe her prayers in a secret language, but rather takes it for granted that people understand Latin. If Catholics learned enough Latin to follow the very easy style of the Church language all difficulty would be solved. For those who cannot take even this trouble there is the obvious solution of a translation. The Missal in English is one of the easiest books to procure; the ignorant may follow in that the prayers that lack of education prevents their understanding without it.

The liturgical languages used by Catholics are:

1. *Latin* in the Roman, Milanese, and Mozarabic Rites (except in parts of Dalmatia).

2. *Greek* in the Byzantine Rite (not exclusively).

3. *Syriac* in the Syrian, Maronite, Chaldean, and Malabar Rites.

4. *Coptic* in the Coptic Rite.

5. *Armenian* by all the Churches of that rite.

6. *Arabic* by the Melchites (Byzantine Rite).

7. *Slavonic* by Slavs of the Byzantine Rite and (in Glagolitic letters) in the Roman Rite in Dalmatia.

8. *Georgian* (Byzantine Rite).

9. *Rumanian* (Byzantine Rite).

7. Liturgical Science.—a. *Rubrics.* The most obvious and necessary study for ecclesiastical persons is that of the laws that regulate the performance of liturgical functions. From this point of view liturgical study is a branch of canon law. The rules for the celebration of the Holy Mysteries, administration of sacraments, etc., are part of the positive law of the Church, just

147

as much as the laws about benefices, church property, or fasting, and oblige those whom they concern under pain of sin. As it is therefore the duty of persons in Holy orders to know them, they are studied in all colleges and seminaries as part of the training of future priests, and candidates are examined in them before ordination. Because of its special nature and complication liturgical science in this sense is generally treated apart from the rest of canon law and is joined to similar practical matters (such as preaching, visiting the sick, etc.) to make up the science of pastoral theology. The sources from which it is learned are primarily the rubrics of the liturgical books (the Missal, Breviary, and Ritual). There are also treatises which explain and arrange these rubrics, adding to them from later decrees of the S. Congregation of Rites.

7. *History*.—The development of the various rites, their spread and mutual influence, the origin of each ceremony, etc., form a part of church history whose importance is becoming more and more realised. For practical purposes all a priest need know are the present rules that affect the services he has to perform, as in general the present laws of the Church are all we have to obey. But just as the student of history needs to know the decrees of former synods, even if abrogated since, as he studies the history of earlier times and remote provinces of the Church, because it is from these that he must build up his conception of her continuous life, so the liturgical student will not be content with knowing only what affects him now, but is prompted to examine the past, to inquire into the origin of our present rite and study other rites too as expressions of the life of the Church in other lands. The history of the liturgies that deeply affect the life of Christians in many ways, that are the foundation of many other objects of study (architecture, art, music, etc.) is no inconsiderable element of church history. In a sense this study is comparatively new and not yet sufficiently organised, though to some extent it has always ac-

companied the practical study of liturgy. The great mediaeval liturgists were not content with describing the rites of their own time. They suggested historical reasons for the various ceremonies and contrasted other practices with those of their own Churches. Benedict XIV's treatise on the Mass discusses the origin of each element of the Latin liturgy. This and other books of seventeenth and eighteenth-century liturgiologists are still standard works. So also in lectures and works on liturgy in our first sense it has always been the custom to add historical notes on the origin of the ceremonies and prayers.

But interest in the history of liturgy for its own sake and systematic study of early documents is a comparatively new thing. In this science England led the way and still takes the foremost place. It followed the Oxford Movement as part of the revived interest in the early Church among Anglicans. Besides the practical instruction that forms a part of pastoral theology, lectures on liturgical history would form a valuable element of the course of church history. As part of such a course other rites would be considered and compared. There is a fund of deeper understanding of the Roman Rite to be drawn from its comparison with others, Gallican or Eastern. Such instruction in liturgiology should include some notion of ecclesiology in general, the history and comparison of church planning and architecture, of vestments and church music. The root of all these things in different countries is the liturgies they serve and adorn.

8. *Dogmatic Value*.—The dogmatic and apologetic value of liturgical science is a very important consideration to the theologian. It must, of course, be used reasonably. No Church intends to commit herself officially to every statement and implication contained in her official books, any more than she is committed to everything said by her Fathers. For instance, the Collect for St. Juliana Falconieri (19 June) in the Roman Rite refers to the story of her miraculous communion before her death, told at length in the sixth lesson of her Office, but the truth of that story is not part of the Catholic Faith. Liturgies give us arguments from tradition even more valuable than those from the Fathers, for these statements have been made by thousands of priests day after day for centuries. A consensus of liturgies is, therefore, both in space and time a greater witness of agreement than a consensus of Fathers, for as a general principle it is obvious that people in their prayers say only what they believe. This is the meaning of the well-known axiom: *Lex orandi lex credendi*. The prayers for the dead, the passages in which God is asked to accept this Sacrifice, the statements of the Real Presence in the oldest liturgies are unimpeachable witnesses of the Faith of the early Church as to these points. The Bull of Pius IX on the Immaculate Conception (*Ineffabilis Deus*, 8 December 1854) contains a classical example of this argument from liturgy. Indeed there are few articles of faith that cannot be established or at least confirmed from liturgies. The Byzantine Office for St. Peter and St. Paul (29 June) contains plain statements about Roman primacy. The study of liturgy from this point of view is part of dogmatic theology. Of late years especially dogmatic theologians have given much attention to it. Christian Pesch, S.J., in his *Praelectiones theologiae dogmaticae* quotes the liturgical texts for the theses as part of the argument from tradition. There are then these three aspects under which liturgiology should be considered by a Catholic theologian, as an element of canon law, church history, and dogmatic theology. The history of its study would take long to tell. There have been liturgiologists through all the centuries of Christian theology. Briefly the state of this science at various periods is this:

Liturgiologists in the Ante-Nicene period, such as Justin Martyr, composed or wrote down descriptions of ceremonies performed, but made no examination of the sources of rites. In the fourth and fifth centuries the scientific study of the subject began. From the sixth to the eighth centuries we have valuable texts (the Sacramentaries and *Ordines*) and a liturgical treatise of St. Isidore of Seville.[12] The Carolingian revival of the eighth and ninth centuries began the long line of medieval liturgiologists. In the eleventh century Berno of Constance (*Micrologus* in P.L., CLI, 974-1022), in the twelfth Rupert of Deutz (*De divinis officiis* in P.L., CLXX, 9-334), Honorius of Autun (*Gemma animae* and *De Sacramentis* in P.L., CLXXII), John Beleth (*Rationale div. offic.* in P.L., CCII, 9-166), and Beroldus of Milan (ed. Magistretti, Milan, 1894) carry on the tradition. In the thirteenth century William Durandus of Mende (*Rationale divinorum officiorum*); see **DURANDUS**) is the most famous of all the medieval liturgiologists. There is then a break till the sixteenth century. The discussions of the Reformation period called people's attention again to liturgies, either as defences of the old Faith or as sources for the compilation of reformed services. From this time editions of the old rites were made for students, with commentaries.

Chapter Notes

[1] Will, *Acta et scripta quae de controversiis ecclesiae graecae et latinae saec. XI composita extant*, Leipzig, 1861, 207.

[2] Duchesne, pp. 84-89.

[3] *Ep.* xi, 64, in P.L., LXXVII, 1186-7.

[4] The rites of Milan and Toledo were revised drastically following the second Vatican Council. (Ed.)

[5] Duchesne, p. 69.

[6] *Von ordenung gottis diensts ynn der gemeind* in Clemen, "*Quellenbuch zur prakt. Theologie*", I, 24-6.

[7] Karlstadt (c. 1480-1541), a German Reformer so named from his birthplace, his real name being Andreas Bodenstein. His theological position changed from that of an ardent Thomist to the most extreme of all the

Reformers. On Christmas Day 1521 he celebrated the first Protestant Communion Service with neither vestments nor canon nor elevation, the laity receiving Communion under both kinds. Karlstadt married and his extreme views brought him into conflict with Luther who termed him the new Judas. He was forced to leave Germany and spent the rest of his life in Switzerland (Ed.).

8 Guillaume Farel (1489-1565), Swiss Reformer. In 1530 he introduced the Reformation to Neuchâtel with iconclastic violence. In 1535 he led the struggle which established the Reformation at Geneva, and in the following year persuaded Calvin to settle in Geneva, declaring him to be a preacher and teacher of theology. For the rest of his life his fortunes were linked to those of Calvin, who disapproved of Farel's marriage at the age of 69 to a young widow from Rouen (Ed.).

9 Nonjurors is the title given to bishops and priests of the Church of England who refused to take the Oaths of Allegiance and Supremacy to William and Mary as by doing so they would have broken their oath to James II. James II had been deprived of his throne solely because of his Catholic Faith. His Protestant daughter Mary and her husband William of Orange (in the Netherlands) were invited to England to assume the throne in 1688 by seven British notables (the "Immortal Seven") and James was forced to escape to France. Support for James continued in Scotland and Ireland, the final defeat of the Jacobites (*Iacobus* or *Jacobus* is the Latin for James) coming with the Battle of the Boyne in 1690 and the surrender of Limerick in 1691. The Jacobite movement continued until the defeat of his grandson Charles Edward (Bonnie Prince Charlie) at Culloden in 1746. The refusal of the non-jurors, 9 bishops and 400 priests, to break their oath to James manifested great integrity. They were divided on the question of worshipping in their parish churches and in many cases devised their own liturgies which were illegal (Ed.).

10 Edward Irving (1792-1834) was a minister of the Church of Scotland associated with the foundation of the "Catholic Apostolic Church". He was a brilliant preacher whose magnetic personality attracted large congregations, and who later became preoccupied with millenarian ideas. He was expelled from the Church of Scotland in 1833. His followers had, by then, constituted themselves as the "Catholic Apostolic Church", but they accorded him only an inferior rank in the sect which had been founded largely through his influence (Ed.).

11 A. Fortescue, *The Orthodox Eastern Church* (London, 1907), p. 431.

12 *De eccl. officiis*, P.L., LXXXIII.

3

Liturgical Books

Under this name we understand all the books, published by the authority of any church, that contain the text and directions for her official (liturgical) services. It is now the book that forms the standard by which one has to judge whether a certain service or prayer or ceremony is official and liturgical or not. Those things are liturgical, and those only, that are contained in one of the liturgical books. It is also obvious that any church or religion or sect is responsible for the things contained in its liturgical books in quite another sense than for the contents of some private book of devotion, which she at most only allows and tolerates. The only just way of judging of the services, the tone, and the ethos of a religious body, is to consult its liturgical books. Sects that have no such official books are from that very fact exposed to all manner of vagaries in their devotion, just as the absence of an official creed leads to all manner of vagueness in their belief. In this article the liturgical books of the Roman Rite are described first, then a short account is given of those of the other rites

1. *The First Traces of Liturgical Books*.—Our present convenient compendiums—the Missal, Breviary, and so on—were formed only at the end of a long evolution. In the first period (lasting perhaps till about the fourth century) there were no books except the Bible, from which lessons were read and

psalms were sung. Nothing was written, because nothing was fixed. Even after certain forms had become so stereotyped as to make already what we should call a more or less fixed liturgy, it does not seem that there was at first any idea that they should be written down. Habit and memory made the celebrant repeat more or less the same forms each Sunday; the people answered his prayers with the accustomed acclamations and responses—all without books.

It has been much discussed at what period we have evidence of written liturgies, and it has been claimed that no books were written even by the fourth century. This argument is based on a passage in St. Basil (d. 379), who distinguishes between the written teaching of the Apostles (in the Bible) and the unwritten tradition, and quotes liturgical functions as belonging to this: "Who", he asks, "of the saints has written down for us the words of the Sacred Invocation in the consecration of the bread and chalice?"[1] Another argument is that no mention is made of liturgical books in the acts of martyrs (who are required to give up their holy books, that is, always, the Bible), or in the quarrels about the books with the Donatists in the fourth century. Other scholars argue against this opinion at length, and defend the view that liturgies were written down at the beginning of the fourth century, claiming that there were liturgical books back to the time of the Apostolic Fathers. The argument from St. Basil may be dismissed at once. He is only explaining the well-known distinction between the two sources of revelation, Scripture and tradition. Tradition is distinct from Scripture; it may include other written books, but not the Bible. By "saints" he means only the writers of Scripture, and therefore his statement is that the Eucharistic Invocation is not in the Bible. As for the Donatists, there is, on the contrary, evidence that both they and the Catholics had liturgical books at that time. Optatus of Mileve, writing about the year 370 against them, says: "You have no doubt cleaned the palls (linen cloths used in Mass), tell me what you have done with the books?"[2]

What were these books? Both palls and books had been taken from the Catholics, both were used in the liturgy. The books were not the Bible, because the Donatists thought them polluted. So there were other liturgical books besides the Bible. Augustine too reproaches the Donatists with being in schism with the very churches whose names they read in the "holy books".[3] So also a synod at Hippo in Africa (in 393) forbids anyone to write down the prayers of other Churches and use them, until he has shown his copy to the more learned brethren.

That some prayers were occasionally written down from the first age is evident. Prayers are quoted in the Apostolic Fathers.[4] This does not, however, prove the existence of liturgical books. It is claimed that the exact quotations made by the Fathers as far back as the second century prove that the liturgy was already written down, and that such quotations could only be made from written books. This argument does not seem very convincing. We know that formulae, especially liturgical formulae, can become very definite and well-known before they are put in a book. A more solid reason for the existence of a written liturgy at any rate by the fourth century is the comparison of the liturgy of the eighth book of the Apostolic Fathers with the Byzantine Rite of St. Basil. Proclus (d. 446) says that Basil (d. 379) modified and shortened the liturgy because it was too long for the people. There is no reason to doubt what he says. The liturgy shortened by Basil was that of Antioch, of which we have the oldest specimen in the *Apostolic Constitutions* see **GLOSSARY**). A comparison of this (especially the Thanksgiving-prayer) with that of St. Basil shows in effect that Basil is much shorter. It does not seem likely that, after Basil's necessary shortening, anyone should have taken the trouble to write out the discarded long form. Therefore, the liturgy of the *Apostolic Constitutions* was written before Basil's reform, although it is incorporated into a work not finally compiled till the early fifth century.

Our conclusion then is that at any rate by the middle of the fourth century there were written liturgies, and therefore liturgical books of some kind, however incomplete. How long before that anything was written down we cannot say. We conceive portions of the rite written out as the occasion required. Evidently one of the first things to be written was the diptychs containing the lists of persons and churches for whom prayers were to be said. These diptychs were used liturgically—the deacon read them—in all rites down to the Middle Ages. Augustine's argument against the Donatists refers to the diptychs.[5] The diptychs were two tablets folded like a book; on one side the names of the living, on the other those of the dead were written. They have now disappeared and the names are said from memory. But the Byzantine Rite still contains the rubrics: "The deacon remembers the diptychs of the departed"; "He remember the diptychs of the living". No doubt the next thing to be written out was the collection of prayers said by the celebrant (Sacramentaries and *Euchologia*), then indications for the reader (*Comites, Capitularia, Synaxaria*) and the various books for the singers (Antiphonaries, books of *Troparia*), and finally the rubrical directions (*Ordines, Typika*).

2. History of The Roman Liturgical Books.—So far the development went on in parallel lines in East and West. When we come to the actual books we must distinguish between the various rites, which have different groups and arrangements. In the Roman Rite the first complete books we know are the Sacramentaries (*Sacramentaria*). A Sacramentary is not the same thing as a Missal. It contains more on the one side, less on the other. It is the book for the celebrant. It contains all and only the prayers that he says. At the time that these books were written it was not yet the custom for the celebrant also to repeat at the altar whatever is sung by the ministers or choir. Thus Sacramentaries contain none of those parts of the Mass, no Lessons, no Introits, Graduals, Offertories and so on, but only the Collects, Prefaces, Canon, all that is strictly the celebrant's part. On the other hand they provide for his use at other occasions besides Mass. As the celebrant is normally supposed to be a bishop, the Sacramentary supplies him with the prayers he wants at ordinations, at the consecration of a church and altar, and many exorcisms, blessings, and consecrations that are now inserted in the Pontifical and Ritual. That is the order of a complete Sacramentary. Many of those now extant are more or less fragmentary.

The name *Sacramentarium* is equivalent to the other form, also used (for instance, in the Gelasian book), *Liber Sacramentorum*. The form is the same as that of the word *Hymnarium*, for a book of hymns. Gennadius of Marseilles (fifth century) uses both. He says of Paulinus of Nola: "*Fecit et sacramentarium et hymnarium.*"[6] The word *sacramentum* or *sacramenta* in this case means the Mass. *Sacramenta celebrare* or *facere* is a common term for saying Mass. So St. Augustine (d. 430) remarks that we say "*Sursum corda*" "*in sacramentis fidelium*", that is at Mass,[7] and two schismatics of the fifth century complain to the Emperors Gratian and Theodosius that Pope Damasus (366-384) will not allow them to say Mass; but they do so all the same, because "*salutis nostrae sacramenta facienda sunt*".[8] A number of Sacramentaries of the Roman Rite are still extant, either complete or in part. Of these the most important are the three known by the names Leonine, Gelasian, and Gregorian. Their date, authorship, place and original purpose have been much discussed. What follows is a compilation of the views of recognized scholars.

The so-called *Sacramentarium Leonianum* is the oldest. Only one manuscript of it is known, written in the seventh century. This manuscript was found in the library of the cathedral chapter of Verona, was published by Joseph Bianchini in 1735 in the fourth volume of his edition of *Anastasius Bibliothecarius*, and was by him attributed arbitrarily to St. Leo I (440-61). The Leonine Sacramentary represents a pure Roman use with no Gallican elements. But it is not a book compiled for use at the altar. The hopeless confusion of its parts shows this. It is a fragment, containing no Canon nor Ordinary of the Mass, but a collection of Propers (Collects, Secrets, Prefaces, Postcommunions, and *Orationes super populum*), of various Masses with ordination forms, arranged according to the civil year. It begins in the middle of the sixth Mass for April, and ends with a blessing for the font "*In ieiunio mensis decimi*" (i.e. the winter Ember-days). In each month groups of Masses are given, often very large groups, for each feast and occasion. Thus, for instance, in June we find twenty-eight Masses for St. Peter and St. Paul, one after another, each headed: "*Item alia*". There are fourteen for St. Lawrence, twenty-three for the anniversary of a bishop's consecration, and so on. Evidently the writer has compiled as many alternative Masses for each occasion as he could find. In many cases he shows great carelessness. He inserts Masses in the wrong place. Many of his Masses *in natali episcoporum* have nothing at all to do with that anniversary, and are really Masses for Sundays after Pentecost; in the middle of a Mass of St. Cornelius and St. Cyprian he has put the preface of a Mass of St. Euphemia, a Mass for the new civil year is inserted among those for martyrs; Masses for St. Stephen's day (26 December) with evident allusions to Christmas are put in August, obviously through a confusion with the feast of the finding of his relics (3 August). That the collection is Roman is obvious. It is full of local allusions to Rome. For instance, one of the collects to be said by a bishop in the anniversary of his consecration could only be used by the pope of Rome: "Lord God...who although Thou dost not cease to enrich with many gifts Thy Church spread throughout the world, nevertheless dost look more favourably upon the see of Thy blessed Apostle Peter, as Thou hast desired that it should be most exalted, etc." The Preface for St. John and St. Paul remembers that they are buried within "the boundaries of this city"; the Masses of the

Patrons of Rome, St. Peter and St. Paul, continually allude to the city (so the preface in the twenty-third Mass: "who, foreseeing that our city would labour under so many troubles, didst place in it the chief members of the power of the Apostles", and so on continually.

The "Gelasian Sacramentary" exists in several manuscripts. It is a Roman book more or less Gallicanized. The various manuscripts represent different stages of this Gallican influence (see **RITES**). The oldest form extant is a book written in the seventh or early eighth century for use in the abbey of St. Denis at Paris. This is now in the Vatican library.[9] The book does not in any old manuscript bear the name of Gelasius; it is called simply *Liber Sacramentorum Romanae ecclesiae*. It is much more complete than the Leonine Sacramentary. It consists of three books each marked with a not very accurate title. Book I (The Book of Sacraments in the order of the year's cycle) contains Masses for feasts and Sundays from Christmas Eve to the octave of Pentecost (there are as yet no special Masses for the season after Pentecost), together with the ordinations, prayers for all the rites of the catechumenate, blessing of the font at Easter Eve, of the oil, dedication of churches, and reception of nuns. Book II (Prayers for the Feasts of Saints) contains the Proper of Saints throughout the year, the Common of Saints, and the Advent Masses. Book III (Prayers and the Canon for Sundays) contains a great number of Masses marked simply "For Sunday" (i.e. any Sunday), the Canon of the Mass, what we should call votive Masses (e.g. for travellers, in time of trouble, for kings, and so on), Masses for the Dead, some blessings (of holy water, fruits, trees and so on), and various prayers for special occasions. An old tradition ascribes what is evidently this book to Pope Gelasius I [492-6].[10] Gennadius says he composed a book of Sacraments.[11] It was, however, composed in the Frankish kingdom. All the local Roman allusions (for instance, the Roman Stations) have been omitted. On Good Friday the prayers read: "Let us pray for our most

159

Christian Emperor (the compiler has added) "or king", and again: "Look down mercifully on the Roman (or the Frankish) Empire." There are also Gallican additions.

We know most about the third of these books, the so-called "Gregorian Sacramentary". Charlemagne, anxious to introduce the Roman Rite into his kingdom, wrote to Pope Adrian I between the years 781 and 791 asking him to send him the service-book of the Roman Church. The book sent by the pope is the nucleus of the Gregorian Sacramentary. It was then copied a great number of times, so that there are many versions of it, containing additions made by the various scribes. The original book sent by Adrian to Charlemagne is easily distinguished from the additions. The first who began to supplement Adrian's book from other sources (a certain Frankish Abbot named Grimold) was a conscientious person and carefully noted where his additions begin. At the end of the original book he adds a note, a *prefatiuncula* beginning with the word *Hucusque*: " So far (*Hucusque*) the preceding book of Sacraments is certainly that edited by the holy Pope Gregory." Then come two supplements, one (according to Pamelius) by Abbot Grimold and the other by Alcuin. The supplements vary considerably in the codices. Eventually their matter became incorporated in the original book. But in the earlier versions we may take the first part, down to the *prefatiuncula*, as being the book sent by Adrian. How far it is that of Gregory I is another question. This book then has three parts: (1) The Ordinary of the Mass; (2) the Propers for the year beginning with Christmas Eve. They follow the ecclesiatical year; the feasts of saints (days of the month in the civil year) are incorporated in their approximate places in this. The Roman Stations are noted. There are still no Masses for the Sundays after Epiphany and Pentecost; (3) the prayers for ordinations. There are no votive Masses or requiems. Is its attribution to St. Gregory I (590-604) correct? That Gregory did much to reform the liturgy is certain. A constant tradition ascribes such a work to him, as to Gelasius. John the Deacon (eighth century) in his life of Gregory expresses this tradition: "He collected the Sacramentary of Gelasius in one book, leaving out much, changing little, adding something".[12] Pope Adrian himself, in sending the book to Charlemagne, says that it is composed "by our holy predecessor the divinely speaking Pope Gregory". That the essential foundation of this Sacramentary goes back to St. Gregory, indeed to long before his time, is certain. Nor need we doubt that he made such changes as are claimed for him by his biographer, and that these changes stand in this book. But it is not his work untouched. It has additions made since his time, for instance his own feast (12 March) and other feasts not kept at Rome before the seventh century. Evidently then the book sent by Pope Adrian has gone through the inevitable development; succeeding centuries since Gregory have added to it. It represents the Roman Rite of the time when it was sent—the eighth century. We have said that, when it arrived in the Frankish kingdom, it began to receive supplements. It must be remembered of course that the writers who copied it had not in view the future needs of students. The books they made were intended for practical use at the altar. So they added at the end of Adrian's "Sacramentary" whatever other Masses and prayers were wanted by the churches for which they wrote. These supplements are taken partly from the Gelasian book, partly from Gallican sources. We have also noted that the additions were at first carefully distinguished from the original book, eventually incorporated in it. Between the ninth and eleventh centuries the book so composed returned to Rome, took the place of the original pure Roman Rite, and so became the foundation of our present Roman Missal. Besides these three most important Sacramentaries there are other fragments, the *Missale Francorum*, written in the seventh or eighth century, the "Ravenna Roll" of doubtful date (sixth to eleventh century).

At the same time as the Sacramentaries, books for the readers and choir were being arranged. Gradually the *Comes* or *Liber*

Comicus that indicated the texts of the Bible to be read developed into the *Evangelarium* and *Lectionarium* (see **GOSPEL IN THE LITURGY** and **LESSONS IN THE LITURGY**.) The homilies of Fathers to be read were collected in the *Homilaria*, the Acts of the Martyrs read on their feasts, in *Martyrologia*. The book of psalms was written separately for singing, then arranged in order, as the psalms were sung through the week, in the *Psalterium* that now forms the first part of our Breviary. The parts of the Mass sung by the choir (Introit, Gradual, Offertory, Communion) were arranged in the *Liber Antiphonarius* (or *Gradualis*), the Antiphons and Responsories in the Office formed the *Liber Responsalis*, or *Antiphonarius Officii*, as distinct from the *Antiphonarius Missae*. Throughout the early Middle Ages such collections were copied with local modifications all over Western Europe. Hymns (in our sense) were introduced into the Roman Rite about the fifth or sixth century. Those of the Mass were written in the Gradual, those of the Divine Office at first in the Psalter or Antiphonary. But there were also separate collections of hymns, called *Hymnaria*, and *Libri Sequentiales* (or *troponarii*), containing the sequences and additions (farcing) to the *Kyrie* and *Gloria*, etc. Other services, the Sacraments (Baptism, Confirmation, Penance, Marriage, Extreme Unction), the Visitation of the Sick, the Burial Service, all manner of blessings, were written in a very loose collection of little books called by such names as *Liber Agendorum*, *Agenda*, *Manuale*, *Benedictionale*, *Pastorale*, *Sacerdotale*, *Rituale*, the predecessors of our Ritual. Their number and variety is enormous.

Finally there remained the rubrics, the directions not about what to say but what to do. This matter would be one of the latest to be written down. Long after the more or less complicated prayers had to be written and read, tradition would still be a sufficient guide for the actions. The books of prayers (Sacramentaries, Antiphonaries, etc.) contained a few words of direction for the most important and salient things to be done—elementary rubrics. For instance the Gregorian Sacramentary tells priests (as distinct from bishops) not to say the *Gloria* except on Easter Day; the celebrant chants the preface *excelsa voce*, and so on.[13] In time, however, the growing elaborateness of the papal functions, the more complicated ceremonial of the Roman Court, made it necessary to draw up rules of what custom and etiquette demanded. These rules are contained in the *Ordines*—precursors of our *Caeremoniale Episcoporum*. The *Ordines* contain no prayers, except that, where necessary, the first words are given to indicate what is meant. They supplement the Sacramentary and choir books, with careful directions about the ritual.

During the Middle Ages these books were rearranged for greater convenience and developed eventually into the books we know. The custom of Low Mass changed the Sacramentary into a Missal. At Low Mass the celebrant had to supplement personally what was normally chanted by the deacon and subdeacon or sung by the choir. This then reacted on High Mass, so that here too the celebrant began to say to himself in a low voice what was sung by someone else. For this purpose he needed texts that were not in the old Sacramentary. That book was therefore enlarged by the addition of lessons (Epistle and Gospel, etc.) and the chants of the choir (Introit, Gradual, etc.). So it becomes a *Missale plenarium*, containing all the text of the Mass. Isolated cases of such Missals occur as early as the sixth century. By about the twelfth century they have completely replaced the old Sacramentaries. But Lectionaries and Graduals (with the music) are still written for the readers and choir.

In the same way, but rather later, compilations are made of the various books used for saying the Divine Office. Here too the same motive was at work. The Office was meant to be sung in choir. But there were isolated priests, small country churches without a choir, that could not afford the library of books required for saying it. For their convenience compendiums were made since the eleventh century. Gregory VII

(1073-85) issued a compendium of this kind that became very popular.

First we hear of *Libri nocturnales* or *matutinales*, containing all the lessons and responses for Matins. To these are added later the antiphons and psalms, then the collects and all that is wanted for the other canonical hours too. At the same time epitomes are made for people who recite the office without the chant. In these the Psalter is often left out; the clergy are supposed to know it by heart. The antiphons, versicles, responsories, even the lessons are indicated only by their first words. The whole is really a kind of concise index to the Office, but sufficient for people who said it day after day and almost knew it by heart. Such little books are called by various names—*Epitomata*, *Portiforia*, and then especially *Breviaria divini officii* (Abbreviations of the Divine Office). They were used mostly by priests on journeys. In the twelfth century the catalogue of the library of Durham Cathedral includes "a little travelling breviary" (*breviarium parvum itinerarium*). In 1241 Gregory IX says in a Bull for the Franciscan order: "You have (the Divine Office) in your Breviaries." The parts of these Breviaries were filled up eventually so as to leave nothing to memory, but the convenient arrangement and the name have been kept. It is curious that the word Breviary, which originally meant only a handy epitome for use on journeys and such occasions, has come to be the usual name for the Divine Office itself. A priest "says his breviary" that is, recites the canonical hours.

The development of the other books took place in much the same way. The Missals now contained only the Mass and a few morning services intimately connected with it. Daily Mass was the custom for every priest; there was no object in including all the rites used only by a bishop in each Missal. So these rites apart formed the Pontifical. The other non-Eucharistic elements of the old Sacramentary combined with the *Libri Agendarum* to form our Ritual. The Council of Trent

(1545-63) considered the question of uniformity in the liturgical books and appointed a commission to examine the question. But the commission found the work of unifying so many and so varied books impossible at the time, and so left it to be done gradually by the popes. The Missal and Breviary were reformed very soon (see next paragraph), the other books later. The latest work was the production of the *Caeremoniale Episcoporum*. John Burchard, Master of Ceremonies to Sixtus IV (1471-84), combined the old *Ordines Romani* into an *Ordo servandus per sacerdotem in celebratione missae* (Rome, 1502), and arranged the rubrics of the Pontifical. Other editions of the rubrics were made at intervals, till Clement VIII (1592-1605) issued the *Caeremoniale Episcoporum* (in 1600). All the books have been constantly revised and re-edited with additions down to our own time.

3. *The Present Roman Liturgical Books*.—The official books of the Roman Rite are seven—the Missal, Pontifical, Breviary, Ritual, *Caeremoniale Episcoporum*, *Memoriale Rituum*, and Martyrology. These contain all and only the liturgical services of this rite. Several repeat matter also found in others. Other books, containing extracts from them, share their official character inasmuch as the texts conform to that of the original book. Such secondary liturgical books are the Lectionary and Gradual (with musical notes) taken from the Missal, the Day Hours (*Horae diurnae*) of the Breviary, the Vesperal, Antiphonary and other choir-books (with notes), also extracted from the Breviary, various Benedictionals and *Ordines* taken from the Ritual or Pontifical.

(a) The Roman Missal (*Missale Romanum*), as we now have it, was published by Pope Pius V by the Bull *Quo primum* of 14 July, 1570. A commission, opened by the Council of Trent under Pius IV (1559-65), consisting of Cardinal Bernardine Scotti, Thomas Goldwell, Bishop of St. Asaph (one of the last two English bishops of the old Catholic line), Giulio Poggi, and others, had then finished its task of revising the book. Clement VIII (1592-1605) formed a new commission (Baronius, Bellarmine, and others) to restore the text which printers had again corrupted, and especially to substitute the new Vulgate (1590) texts for those of the *Itala*[14] *(see GLOS-SARY)* in the Missal; he published his revision by the Bull *Cum sanctissimum* on 7 July, 1604. Urban VIII (1623-44) again appointed a commission to revise chiefly the rubrics, and issued a new edition on 2 September, 1634 (Bull *Si quid est*). Leo XIII (1878-1903) again made a revision in 1884. These names stand for the chief revisions; they are those named on the title-page of our Missal (*Missale Romanum ex decreto SS. Concilii Tridentini restitutum S. Pii V Pont. Max. iussu editum, Clementis VIII, Urbani VIII et Leonis XIII auctoritate recognitum*). But the continual addition of Masses for new feasts goes on. There are few popes since Pius V who have not authorized some additions, made by the Sacred Congregation of Rites, to the Missal or its various supplements. The reigning pope, Pius X, has issued the chants of the Vatican Edition in the Gradual. As far as these affect the Missal they have again produced new editions of it. Moreover a commission now sitting is considering a further revision of the text. It is believed that when the commission for restoring the text of the Vulgate has completed its work, that text will be issued in the lessons of the Missal, thus making again a new revision. But, in spite of all these modifications, our Missal is still that of Pius V. Indeed its text goes back to long before his time to the Gallicanized Gregorian "Sacramentary" of the ninth to the eleventh century, and, in its essential characteristics, behind that to the Gelasian book of the sixth century, and so back into the mist that hangs over the formation of the Roman Rite in the first centuries.

The Missal begins with the Bulls of Pius V, Clement VIII, and Urban VIII. Then come the approbation of the bishop in whose diocese it is printed and a few of the most important decisions of the Sacred Congregation of Rites. A long explanation of the Gregorian Calendar follows, containing much astronomical information. This is headed: *De anno et eius partibus*. The two Paschal tables follow (Julian and Gregorian), a table of movable feasts for a number of future years and the Roman Calendar of feasts. Then come three sets of rubrics, first *Rubricae generales Missae*, containing the more general rules in twenty paragraphs (these were made by Burchard, revised by the commissions of Pius V, Clement VIII, Urban VIII); then the *Ritus servandus in celebratione missae*, in thirteen paragraphs or chapters. This latter gives exact directions for High or Low Mass, whether celebrated by a bishop or priest. Third come the directions about what to do in case of various accidents or defects, headed *De defectibus in celebratione missae occurrentibus*, in ten chapters. A private preparation and thanksgiving for Mass follow "to be made at the opportunity of the priest". The prayers said while vesting come at the end of the preparation. Lastly, figures show the way to incense the altar and oblation. Shorter and special rubrics for various occasions are inserted (in red) in the text.

Then follows the text of the Missal. The first part contains the "Proper of the time" (*Proprium temporis*) from the first Sunday of Advent to the last after Pentecost. The Proper of each Mass is given in order of the ecclesiastical year, that is the Masses of each Sunday and other day (vigils, ember-days, *feriae* in Lent) that has a proper Mass. Only Christmas and its cycle of feasts (to the octave of the Epiphany), although fixed to days of the civil year (25 Dec., etc.), come in this part. Certain rites, not Eucharistic, but connected closely with the Mass, are in their place in the Missal, such as the blessing of ashes, candles, and palms, all the morning services of Holy Week (except the Vespers of Thursday and Friday). After the service of Holy Saturday the whole Ordinary of the Mass with the Canon is inserted. This is the (almost) unchanging framework into which the various Propers are fitted. Its place in the book has

varied considerably at different times. It is now put here, not
so much for mystic or symbolic reasons, as because it is a convenient place, about the middle where a book lies open best.
The eleven proper Prefaces, and all changes that can occur in
the Canon (except the modifications on Maundy Thursday),
are printed here in the Ordinary. Then follows Easter Day and
the rest of the year in order. The second part of the Missal
contains the Proper of Saints (*Proprium missarum de sanctis*),
that is, the feasts that occur on days of the civil year. It begins
with the Vigil of St. Andrew (29 November), as occurring at
about the beginning of Advent, and continues (leaving out
Christmas and its cycle) regularly through the months to the
feasts of St. Silvester and St. Peter of Alexandria (26 November).

The third part is always paged anew in brackets, [I], etc. It
contains the Common Masses (*Commune sanctorum*), that is,
general Masses for Apostles, Martyrs and so on, that are very
commonly used for saints of each class, often with proper Collect, Secret, and Postcommunion. Most saints' days give the
rubric: "All of the Common of a Confessor Pontiff (or whatever it may be) except the following prayers". A collection of
votive Masses of various kinds follows, ending with the Mass
for a wedding (*Pro Sponso et Sponsa*), then thirty-five sets of
prayers (*Orationes diversae*) that may be used on certain occasions in Mass, according to the rubrics. The four Masses for
the dead come next, then twelve sets of prayers for the dead.
Then the rite of blessing holy water and the *Asperges* ceremony.
Eleven forms of blessings (Sacramentals) used by priests, blessings of vestments, altar-linen, and the tabernacle or ciborium
(used by bishops and by priests having a special faculty), and
the prayers (Collect, Secret, *Hanc igitur*, Postcommunion) said
at ordination Masses end the old part of the Missal. There follow, however, the ever-growing supplements. Of these first
come a collection of votive Masses appointed by Pius IX for
each day of the week, then special Masses allowed for certain

dioceses (*Missae aliquibus in locis celebrandae*), now forming a second Proper of Saints nearly as long as the old one; and finally with the Missal is bound up another supplement (paged with asterisks, I., etc.) for whatever country or province or religious order uses it. The Missal contains all the music used by the celebrant at the altar (except the obvious chants of *Dominus vobiscum*, Collects, etc.) that are given once for all in the *Caeremoniale Episcoporum*) in its place. The new (Vatican) edition gives the various new chants at the end.

The Lectionary (*Lectionarium Romanum*) contains the Epistles and Gospels from the Missal, the Gradual (*Graduale Romanum*), all the choir's part (the Proper, Introit, etc., and the common, *Kyrie*, etc. with music. Religious orders that have a special rite (Dominicans, Carmelites, Carthusians) have of course their special Missals, arranged in the same way.

(b) The Pontifical (*Pontificale Romanum*) is the bishop's book. It was issued by Benedict XIV (1740-58) on 25 March, 1752, and revised by Leo XIII in 1888. It has three parts and an appendix. Part I contains the rites of Confirmation, the tonsure, the seven ordinations, the blessing of abbots, abbesses, nuns, coronation of kings and queens, and blessing of a knight (*miles*). Part II contains the services for laying foundation-stones, consecrating churches, altars, chalices, many episcopal blessings (of vestments, vessels, crosses, statues, bells, weapons, and flags), the seven penitential psalms, and the litany. Part III contains the publication of movable feasts on the Epiphany, the expulsion of public penitents on Ash Wednesday and their reconciliation on Maundy Thursday, the order of synods, degradations from each order, excommunication and absolution from it, of the journeys of prelates (prayers to be said then), of visitation of parishes, solemn reception of bishops, legates, emperors, kings, and such people down to a "Princess of great power", the old episcopal scrutiny, a ceremony for the first shaving of a clerk's beard and a little rite for making or degrading a singer (*psalmista* or cantor). The appendix of the Pontifical contains the various rites of baptism by a bishop, the ordinations without music, marriage performed by a bishop, the pontifical absolution and blessing after the sermon at High Mass, the "Apostolic Benediction", and a blessing of Holy Water to reconcile a church after it has been execrated (polluted). A supplement adds the consecration of a church with many altars, of an altar alone, and of a portable altar—all without the chant. A number of extracts from the Pontifical are made, the ordination rites, consecration of a church, and so on. These are not specially authorized; they are authentic if they conform to the original.

(c) The Breviary (*Breviarium Romanum*) contains all the Divine Office without chant. It has been revised by the same popes (Pius V, Clement VIII, Urban VIII, Leo XIII) as the Missal. It begins with the Bulls, the chapter about the calendar, the paschal tables, tables of movable feasts, calendar, like the Missal. Then follow the general rubrics (*Rubricae generales breviarii*) in thirty-six chapters, giving full directions for the recital of the office, occurrence of feasts, and so on. Further tables of occurrences, prayers to be said before and after the office, and a table of absolutions and blessings end the introductory matter. The actual text begins with the psalter, that is the psalms arranged for the week, with their normal antiphons and hymns. First come Matins and Lauds for Sunday; then Prime, Terce, Sext, and None, then Matins and Lauds for each weekday. After Lauds for Saturday follow Vespers for each day, then Compline. This ends the *Psalterium*. The offices for each day follow, arranged exactly as in the Missal (Proper of the season, Proper of saints, Common of saints, votive Offices and Offices for the dead, the supplement for certain places, and a local supplement). After the Office for the dead some extraneous matter is inserted, namely the Gradual psalms, litany, prayers for the dying, blessing for the dying, grace at meals, and prayers for clerics on a journey. At the end of the whole book come the prayers before and after Mass and two private litanies (of the Holy Name and of the Blessed Virgin).

As the Breviary, in spite of its name, is now a very large and cumbersome book, it is generally issued in four parts (Winter, Spring, Summer, Autumn). This involves a good deal of repetition; the whole Psalter occurs in each part, and all feasts that may overlap into the next part have to be printed twice. The first volume only (Winter, which begins with Advent) contains the general rubrics. It is now also usual to reprint the psalms that occur in the Common of saints instead of merely referring back to the Psalter. Many other parts are also reprinted in several places. On the number and judicious arrangement of these reprints depends the convenience of any particular edition of the Breviary. Already in the Middle Ages the countless manuscripts of the Breviary are fond of promising the purchaser that he will find all the offices complete without references ("*omnia exscripta sine recursu*", "*tout le long sans recquerir*"), a statement that the writer, after examining a great number of them, has never once found true. The chief book excerpted from the Breviary is the "Day Hours" (*Horae diurnae breviarii Romani*), containing everything except Matins, which with its lessons forms the main bulk of the book. For singing in choir various books with music exist, representing still more or less the state of things before Breviaries were invented. The complete *Liber Antiphonarius* contains all the antiphons, hymns, and responses throughout the Office. From this again various excerpts are made. For the offices most commonly sung in churches we have the Vesperal (*Vesperale Romanum*), containing Vespers and Compline. The monastic orders (Benedictines, Cistercians, Carthusians, etc.), the Dominicans, Franciscans, Premonstratensians, and several local dioceses still have their own Breviaries.

(d) The Ritual (*Rituale Romanum*) contains all the services a priest needs besides those of the Missal and Breviary. This book especially was the least uniform in the Middle Ages. Almost every diocese had its own Ritual, or Agenda. Paul V

issued in 1614 a book meant to be used everywhere; Benedict
XIV revised it in 1752. The Roman Ritual contains ten titles
(*tituli*) and an appendix nearly as big again as all the rest. Title
I gives general directions for administering sacraments; II gives
all the forms for baptism; III for penance; IV for the Holy
Eucharist; V for extreme unction and the care of the sick; VI
relates to funerals and gives the Office for the dead from the
Breviary; VII relates to matrimony; VIII contains a large collection of blessings for various objects; IX deals with processions; X with exorcisms and forms for filling up in the books
of the parish (the books of baptism, confirmation, marriage,
the state of souls, and the dead). The appendix (paged anew
with asterisks) gives additional directions for the sacraments,
some decrees and prayers and a large collection of blessings,
first "unreserved", then those to be used only by priests who
have a special faculty, those reserved to certain religious orders, and many "newest blessings". There is still a great want
of uniformity in the use of this book. Many countries, provinces, and dioceses have their own Ritual or *Ordo administrandi
Sacramenta*, etc.

(e) The Ceremonial of Bishops (*Caeremoniale Episcoporum*)
in spite of its title contains much matter needed by other people
than bishops. It is entirely a book of rubrical directions, succeeding the old *Ordines Romani*. Much of it is already contained in the rubrics of the Missal, Pontifical, and Ritual. It
was first issued by Clement VIII in 1600, then revised by Innocent X (1650), Benedict XIV at various dates (finally 1752),
and Leo XIII (1882). It has three books. The first contains
general directions for episcopal functions, and for the bishop's
attendants (master of ceremonies, sacristan, canons, and so on).
Then come full directions for everything connected with Mass,
the altar, vestments, ceremonies, etc., finally the order of a
synod. Book II is all about the Divine Office, its chanting in
choir and all the ritual belonging to it, as well as certain special functions (the blessing of candles, ashes, palms, the Holy

Week services, processions, etc.). Book III is about various extra-liturgical functions, visits of bishops to governors of provinces, solemn receptions and so on, finally conduct for cardinals. The book continually gives directions, not only for bishops but for priests, too, at these functions. It is also here that one finds some of the most ordinary chants used by any celebrant (e.g., the *Dominus vobiscum*, Collects, I, 27; *Confiteor*, II, 39). The *Caeremoniale Episcoporum* is thus the official and indispensable supplement to the rubrics of the Missal, Breviary, Ritual, and Pontifical.

(f) The Memorial of Rites (*Memoriale Rituum*) or Little Ritual (*Rituale parvum*) is the latest of these official books. It gives directions for certain rites (the blessing of candles, ashes, palms, the Holy Week services) in small churches where there are no ministers (deacon and subdeacon). The Missal always supposes the presence of deacon and subdeacon at these functions; so there was doubt and confusion about them when carried out by a single priest. Benedict XIII (1724-30) published this book in 1725 to remove the confusion in the smaller parish churches of Rome. Pius VII (1800-23) extended it to all small churches of the Roman Rite in 1821. It is therefore the official norm for all such services without ordained ministers.

(g) The Martyrology (*Martyrologium Romanum*) is an enlarged calendar giving the names and very short account of all saints (not only martyrs) commemorated in various places each day. The earliest known martyrologies go back to the fourth century. In the Middle Ages there were, as usual, many versions of the book. Our present Roman Martyrology was arranged in 1584 by Cardinal Baronius under Gregory XIII, and revised four times, in 1628, 1675, 1680, and (by Benedict XIV) 1748. It is read in choir at Prime.

4. *Liturgical Books of Other Western Rites.*—The other two surviving rites in the West (of Milan and the Mozarabic Rite) have gone through the same development as the Roman—from

Sacramentaries, Lectionaries, Psalters, and Antiphonaries to Missals, Pontificals, and Breviaries. Only of course their books contain their own prayers and ritual. None of the Eastern Churches has yet made such compendiums of its books as our Missal and Breviary. All their books are still in the state that ours were in the days of Sacramentaries, Antiphonaries, and so on. One reason for this is that in the East our reduplications are unknown. There the priest does not also say at the altar the parts sung by the readers and choir. Nor has there been any development (except a rudimentary beginning, chiefly among the Uniats) of private recitation of the Office. So their books are only wanted for the choir; the various readers and singers use different volumes of what in some rites is quite a large library.

The Byzantine Books are the *Typikon*, a kind of perpetual calendar with directions for all services, the *Euchologion*, containing all the priest wants for the Holy Liturgy and other sacraments and rites (almost exactly the old Latin Sacramentary). The *Triodion*, *Pentekostarion*, *Oktoechos*, and *Horologion* contain the choir's part of the Liturgy and Office throughout the year. The *Menaia* and *Menologion* contain the saints' offices; the *Psalterion* explains itself. The *Apostolos* and *Evangelion* contain the Liturgical lessons. Each national Church has its own editions in its liturgical language. In the very vague state of most of their books one can only say in general that these churches have an indefinite collection, each service having its own book. These are then collected and arranged in all kinds of groups and compendiums by various editors. The Uniat compendiums have a natural tendency to imitate the arrangement of the Roman books. The most obvious cases of liturgical books are always the Lectionaries, then the Book of Liturgies. The others are mostly in a very vague state.

The Nestorian Books (all in Syriac) are the Liturgy (containing their three liturgies), the Gospel (*Euangelion*), Apostle

(*Shlicha*) and Lessons (*Kariane*), the *Turgama* (Interpretation), containing hymns sung by deacons at the liturgy (our Graduals and Sequences), the David (*Dawidha* = Psalter), *Khudhra* (= "cycle", containing antiphons, responsories, hymns, and collects for all Sundays), *Kash Kol* (= "Collection of all"; the same chants for week-days), *Kdham u-Wathar* (= "Before and after"; certain prayers, psalms, and collects most often used, from the other books), *Gezza* ("Treasury", services for feast-days), *Abu-Halim* (the name of the compiler, containing collects for the end of the Nocturns on Sundays), *Bautha d'Ninwaie* ("Prayer of the Ninevites", a collection of hymns ascribed to St. Ephraem, used in Lent). The Baptism Office (*Taksa d'Amadha*) is generally bound up with the Liturgies. The *Taksa d'Siamidha* has the ordination services. The *Taksa d'Husaia* contains the office for Penance, the *Kthawa d'Burrakha* is the marriage service, the *Kahneita*, the burial of clergy, the *Annidha* that of laymen. Lastly the *Khamis* and *Warda* are further collections of hymns. Naturally not every church possesses this varied collection of books.

The Coptic Books (in Coptic with Arabic rubrics, and generally with the text transliterated in Arabic characters too) are the *Euchologion* (*Kitab al-Khulagi almuqaddas*), very often (but quite wrongly) called Missal. This corresponds to the Byzantine *Euchologion*. Then the Lectionary called *Katamarus*, the *Synaksar*, containing legends of saints, the "Deacon's Manual", an Antiphonary (called *Difnari*), the Psalter, *Theotokia* (containing offices of the B.V.M.), *Doxologia*, collections of hymns for the choir and a number of smaller books for the various other offices.

The Ethiopic service-books are (except the Liturgy) the least known of any. Hardly anything of them has been published, and no one seems yet to have made a systematic investigation of liturgical manuscripts in Abyssinia. Since the Ethiopic Rite is derived from the Coptic, one may conjecture that their books correspond more or less to the Coptic books. One may also no doubt conjecture that their books are still in the primitive state of (more or less) a special book for each service.

The Jacobite (and Uniat) Syrian Rite has never been published as a whole. A fragment of the liturgy was published in Syriac and Latin at Antwerp (1572) by Fabricius Boderianus.

The Maronites have an abundance of liturgical books for their romanized Syrian Rite. These books are all referred to in Roman terms (Missal, Ritual, Pontifical, etc.). All Maronite books are in Syriac and Karshuni.

The Armenian Liturgical Books are quite definitely drawn up, arranged, and authorized. They are the only other set among Eastern Churches whose arrangement can be compared to those of the Byzantines. There are eight official Armenian service-books: (1) the Directory, or Calendar, corresponding to the Byzantine *Typikon*. (2) the Manual of Mysteries of the Sacred Oblation (=an *Euchologion*), (3) the Book of Ordinations, often bound up with the former, (4) the Lectionary, (5) the Hymn-book (containing the variable hymns of the Liturgy), (6) the Book of Hours (containing the Divine Office and, generally, the deacon's part of the Liturgy), (7) the Book of Canticles (containing the hymns of the Office), (8) the *Mashdotz*, or Ritual (containing the rites of the sacraments).

In conclusion it will be noticed that the Eastern and older Western liturgical books consider rather the person who uses them than the service at which they are used. The same person has the same book, whatever the function may be. On the other hand the later Western books are so arranged that all the service (whoever may be saying it) is put together in one book; our books are arranged by services, not according to their users. This is the result of our modern Western principle that every one (or at any rate the chief person, the celebrant) says everything, even if it is at the same time said by some one else.

Chapter Notes

1 *De Spir. Sancto*, c. xxvii, in P.G., XXXII, 187.

2 *De schism. Donat.* , V, Vienna edition, 1893, p. 153.

3 *Epp.* LII and LIII.

4 *Didache*, IX, X; *I Clement Ad Cor.*, LIX,3—LXI.

5 *Epp.* LII and LIII.

6 *De viris illustribus*, XLVIII.

7 *De Dono Persev.*, XIII, 33.

8 Faustinus and Marcellinus, *Lib. prec. ad Imp.*, in PL, XIII, 98.

9 MS. *Reginae* 316.

10 Walafrid Strabo, ninth century, *De rebus eccl.*, XX; John the Deacon, *Vita S. Gregorii*, II, xvii.

11 *De vir. illust.*, XCVI.

12 II, xvii.

13 P.L., LXXVIII, 25.

14 The old pre-Vulgate Latin text of the Bible (Ed.).

ILLUSTRATIONS
SECOND SECTION

Title page of the "Fortescue Missal" designed by Bernard Newdigate

The Missal

Compiled by lawful authority
from the Missale Romanum
A new edition
agreeable with the
Vatican Typical Edition
and with a preface by
Adrian Fortescue

Together with a supplement
containing the
Additional Masses used
in English-speaking countries
and those for the
greater feasts of the
Principal Religious Orders.

London
Burns Oates & Washbourne Ltd
MCMXXII

FIGURES USED IN THE PLANS

The Bishop, even when he wears no mitre

The Celebrant wearing a chasuble

The Celebrant in cope

The Deacon

The Subdeacon

Master of Ceremonies

Thurifer with incense

Thurifer not bearing incense

Cross-bearer

First and Second Acolytes with their candles

Acolytes without candles

Torch-bearers

Assistants in copes (pluvialistae) at the divine office

Cantor

Assistant Priest

Assistant Deacons

Mitre-bearer

Crozier-bearer

Book-bearer

Candle-bearer

Train-bearer

Server at Low Mass

Dr. Fortescue's celebrated symbols to assist those involved in liturgical ceremonies which he drew for his best known book *The Ceremonies of the Roman Rite Described,* the twelfth edition of which was published in 1962. It was, and still is, regarded as the ultimate authority by Masters of Ceremonies striving for perfection in the celebration of the traditional Roman liturgy. Whenever a problem arose their instinctive reaction was: "Look it up in Fortescue". The illustration of the figures used here comes from the 1917 First Edition.

Dr. Fortescue's drawing of the instruments used in the Byzantine Liturgy, facing page 409 of *The Orthodox Eastern Church.*

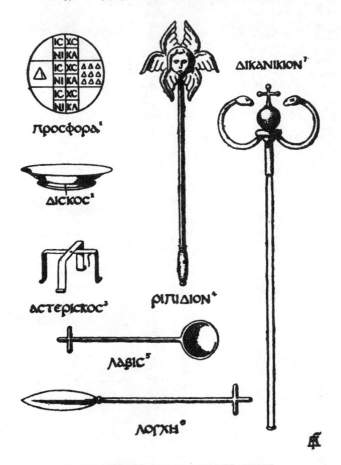

INSTRUMENTS USED IN THE BYZANTINE LITURGY.

1. The Holy Bread. 2. The Paten. 3. The Asterisk. 4. The Fan.
5. The Spoon. 6. The Holy Spear. 7. The Bishop's Staff.

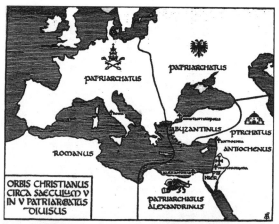

Dr. Fortescus's map of the five patriarchates in the fifth century facing page 49 of *The Orthodox Eastern Church* (1908). It depicts the five chief sees of Christendom, Rome, Alexandria, Antioch, Constantinople, and Jerusalem. It is an excellent example of his superb calligraphy, and his initials can be found in the bottom right hand corner.

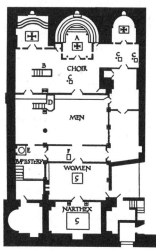

Dr. Fortescue's plan of the church of Abu Sargah at old Cairo

Dr. Fortescue's drawing of the church of St. Hripsime at Etshmiadzin, frontispiece to The Lesser Eastern Churches (1913). His initials can be found on the wall in the foreground

The Patriarchal Church at Etshmiadzin from *The Lesser Eastern Churches* (1913)

A superb example of Dr. Fortescue's calligraphy. It was written for the laying of the foundation stone of the Catholic Church at Royston in 1916, and includes the arms of Pope Benedict XV, Cardinal Bourne, Royston Priory and Mgr. Barton Brown

IN NOMINE DEI AMEN

Post divturnam viduitatem, prioratu canonicorum ordinis sancti augustini ab impio rege henrico viii anno m.d.xxxvi dissoluto, populo post schisma filiae eius sine legitimo pastore relicto, tandem restaurata a eccle- sia catholica huius civitatis crucis roisae, regnantibus apostoli- co domino benedicto pp.xv francisco cardinali bourne archiepisco- po vvestmonasteriensi, cura henrici barton brown cubicularii inti- mi sanctitatis eiusdem domini apostolici primi rectoris catholici hu- ius civitatis post dirum naufragium saeculi decimi sexti, hic primarius lapis ecclesiae sancto thomae cantuariensi et beatis martyribus anglorum dicatae, invocata beatissima trinitate, die vii kal. sept. anni domini mcmxvi positus est ab eodem eminentissimo ac reverendissimo domino, domino francisco presbytero cardinali titulo sanctae pudentianae vvestmona- steriensi archiepiscopo feliciter, quae ecclesia veluti surculus ex avita radice floreat in laudem dei omnipotentis ad utilitatem animarum ad fidem catholicam propagandam

There are several references to his articles for
The Catholic Encyclopedia in these pages from Dr. Fortescue's diary

| 4 | SATURDAY, JANUARY 4, 1908. | 1st Week. | 2nd Week. | SUNDAY, JANUARY 5, 1908. | 6 |

(4-362)

Breves dissertationes de Cuculla deq. Conceleb-
-ratione (250 vocab.) scribo p Cath. Enc.; unde
tota haec series nunc finita se. de Collecta.
Communione (Antiph.). Concelebratione. Con-
-fiteor, Cuculla. Horrende friget his diebus
ōuaq. tenentur artico gelu. H.6 in sacellum
ut excipiam confessiones; ibi socio Bernardo
Hewdigate instauramus novum lampadem;
verum geluit + oleum! Eppus drindelanus
mittit ephemer. Tablet quae stinet secundā
dissertationem de libro meo "Orth. E. Ch."
laudatoriam satis.

(5-361) 2nd after Christmas.

Lessons.
Matins—Isaiah xlii. Matthew iv, 12 v 23.
Eveuoug—Isaiah xliii, or xliv.; Acta III.

Dom. Oct. S. Thomae Cant.
Ordo solitus, sc. h.8.15 distribuo S. Commun., h.10
ago sacrum, ?ciono de festo Natū.Dīi. H.3.30
catechizo parvulos, h.6.30 rosarium + Ben. Ssmi
Pessime cantant. Post missam + Ben. Ssmi
conor populum docere cantum 'Adoremus'?
psalmo 'Laudate Dñum'. Oes dissertationes
p Enc. Cathol. demum finitas expedio exscrip-
-toribus typographicis. Vesp. ad coenā accedunt
Courtneius + Maia Crickmer, quibus? amoene
ludo usq. h.11 noctis, Courtneio vestiente se
vestibus meis arabicis, quas feret mox in festivi
-tate ap. Cockerells.

A page from Dr. Fortescue's *Organ Book*

COMPLINE

Pp.56-72.

Except in Eastertide, except also the possibility of Preces,+ the Anthem of the B.Virgin at the end, the
office of Compline on Sunday is always the same. (There is a change at the Responsory in Passiontide).
Everything sung by Lector, Cantors or Priest is unaccompanied; all sung by choir accompanied.
Play as people + procession come in + while the silent prayer is said before the altar. As soon as Pr. is
at his seat give note to Lector (Bb; p.56). After the blessing, ch:'Amen' (A-Bb). After the lesson,ch: 'Deo
gratias (p.56). Pr : 'Adiutorium nostrum'. Accompany Response (p.56). Then are said the Lord's Prayer
silently + 'Confiteor' +c between Pr.+ people. No organ. After the prayer 'Indulgentiam'π + 'Amen',
give note (Bb) for ⅴ. 'Conuerte nos' π (p.57). Accompany answers (ib.). Then give note (f.). Cantors sing
Ant. 'Miserere' + first verse of psalm : 'Cum inuocarem'. Accompany from v.2 on. Three psalms follow
straight on, sung alternately by ch.+ people. Pr. sings with people. Verse 1 of each has the initial ca-
-dence (p.59). Ch. sings Ant. at the end : 'Miserere mihi' +c (p.60). Then go on at once to Hymn: 'Te
lucis'. NB. Its last verse may vary for the feast, octave or season. After the hymn give note for the
Chapter. Ch. answers: 'Deo gratias'. Give note (f., in Advent Bb, p.61,72.); Cantors sing Responsory :
'In manus tuas'. Ch. answers. Give note (Bb) for ⅴ 'Custodi nos' π. Ch. sings answer. Give note (f.); Cantors
sing Ant. 'Salua nos' + the first verse : 'Nunc dimittis' π. Accompany from v.2. Ch. sings v.2 + then alter-
-nately with people. Ch. sings Ant. at the end. On all Sundays on which there is no double kept or
commemorated, nor an Octave a series of versicles called Preces follows (p.63). Give note (Bb) + ac-
-company Responses. Then (or immediately after the Ant. 'Salua nos', if there are no Preces) Pr.
'Dñus uobiscum', ch. answers. Pr. sings the Collect ; ch. 'Amen' (do-do). Pr. again : 'Dñus uobiscum',
Ch. answers. Cantors : 'Benedicamus Dño'; ch. 'Deo gratias', (p.65). Give note (f.); Pr: 'Benedicat et
custodiat nos' +c. Ch: 'Amen' (e-f). Then the Anthem of our Lady for the Season (p 66-67).
Generally sermon follows. No organ.
for Passiontide see p.16.   for Eastertide see p.17.

LIBRI LECTI MENSE SEPT.

ElllLane: The Manners & Customs of the Modern Egyptians; optimus liber omnino.
gKrüger: Das Papsttum; optimus & hic.
Mason: The Four Feathers.
Sclleyman: The Abbess of Vlaye.
Harder: Arabische Grammatik; sat multum inde discebam.

Entry from Dr. Fortescue's diary. It begins by listing the books he had read in September. The entry for 1 October 1909 refers to a choir practice followed by a discussion with Thomas Wilfred Willson, and that for 4 October to an entry for the *Catholic Encyclopedia*, i.e. Jerusalem from AD 71 to AD 1099. See volume VIII, pp. 355-361.

OCTOBER 1909

❡1 oct. par. Adhuc perficio picturas. Advenit Bernardus Newodigate qui hic deget usque diem lunæ ædibus eius interim clausis absente sorore. Vesp. se exercent cantores postea sloquor cum Clllllson de more.
❡3 oct. Dom. XVIII post Pent. Sol. s. rosarii. Conciono de historia s. eucharistiæ medio æuo, de berengario. Coeno ap. crickmeres præsente cyrillo mileham cognato maice.
❡4 oct. lun. S. francisci. finita demum perfectione picturarum relatarum ex itinere in qua nimium iam triui tempus incipio scribere dissertationem de historia Hierusalem a fine regni latini (1187) usque dies nostros pro cathol. encyclopædia americana.
❡7 oct. iou. Londinum. In museo britan. uiso georgio fratre nonnullos libros aspicio. Prandeo cum CDCobham præsente fHacket cognato eius presb. capellano ca-

The entry in Dr. Fortescue's diary describing the blessing by the
Bishop of Amycla of the new church dedicated to St. Hugh of Lincoln

Cfr appendicem I, in fine.

250	SUNDAY, SEPTEMBER 6, 1908.	37th Week.

(350-116) 13th after Trinity.

Lessons.
Matins—1 Kings xiii. to v 40; 1 Cor. xv. to v 35.
Evensong—2 Kings ii. to v 26; or iv. v 8 to v 38; Mark vii. v 24 to viii. v 10.

Dom. XIII post Pent.
fausta omnino dies. Hodie sacrata noua ecclesia. Mane Arhimandrita Kalημιαυκίω ornatum & ego exspectamus Eppum Amyclanum in statione uice ferreæ. H. 10.30 Eppus benedicit ecclesiæ, ego celebro missa solem, Car. Newdigate diacono. f. Atthill et Hithin locū tenente subdiacono. 4 cantores e choro cathedralis splendidissime canunt Palestrinæ missā 'æterna Xti munera'. Postea celebrat Arhimandrita, me canente responsa, Squire ministro. Tunc seq. prandium & orationes in diuersorio; multi adsunt. Postea sloquimur in horto diuersorii. H. 6.24 abeunt Clara & parvulis, Eppus & alii. H. 6.30 Completorium & Ben. ssmi, pulchernime canentibus 4 cantoribus. Mane Eppus, vesp. C. Newdigate concionant. Demum coeno in diuersorio & fennes & Squire.
'Ημέρα μεγαλοπρεπής.

37th Week.	MONDAY, SEPTEMBER 7, 1908.	251

(251-115)

In nova eccl. Car. Newdigate h. 7, Arhimandrita h. 7.30, ego h. 8 celebramus. lentaculo adsunt Arsenius & dña fenner. Mane abeunt Arsenius (in ædes anhieppales), fennes, Squire &c. Postea per reliquū diem post tantam turbationem pacifice sloquor & canis Dina & Carolo. Et illi vesp. abeunt. Manet adhuc magna res ordinanda scil. liturgia byzantina celebranda sabb. in eccl. cathedrali.

Music for the Liturgy of St. John Chrysostom arranged by Dr. Fortescue in
Westminster Cathedral during the Eucharistic Congress on 12 September 1908

Liturgia byzantina, Westmonasterii, sab. 12 sept. 1908.

Tres antiphonae post cuvarτὰc in initio.

Antiphona I

Lector recitat Ps. 91 : ᾿Αγαθὸν τὸ ἐξομολογεῖσθαι (ed Lit. Chrys. edit. o
P. de Meester, p. 216) in sol.

Chorus post Stich. 1, 2, 3 resp : [Ison ▪ sol.]

Ταῖς πρεσβείαις τῆς Θεοτόκου, Cῶτερ, cῶ-cov ἡμᾶς.

Sed 4ta vice, post Δόξα πατρί : [Ison ▪ sol]

Ταῖς πρεσβείαις τῆς Θεοτόκου, Cῶτερ, cῶcov ἡμᾶς

Antiphona II

Lector recitat Ps. 92 : ῾Ο Κύριος ἐβασίλευσεν (ib. p. 220) in 4 Stich ⁀n:
in sol.

Chorus sua vice cantat : [Ison ▪ sol]

Cῶ-cov ἡμᾶς υἱε Θεοῦ, ὁ ἄρ-τε οὐράνιε, ψάλ-λουτάς coι

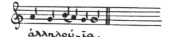

ἀλληλού-ϊα.   Seq. statim ῾Ο μονογενής.

A Composition by Dr. Fortescue

Page from Dr. Fortescue's own copy of Latin Hymns in which he has interleaved the music

THE CITY OF GOD

3. Portæ nitent margarítis
   ádytis paténtibus;
   et uirtúte meritórum
   illuc introdúcitur
   omnis qui ob Christi nomen
   hic in mundo prémitur.

4. Tunsiónibus, pressúris
   expolíti lápides
   suis coaptántur locis
   per manus artíficis;
   dispponúntur permansúri
   sacris ædifíciis.

5. Glória et honor Deo
   usquequáque altíssimo,
   una Patri, Filióque,
   ínclyto Paráclito,
   cui laus est et potéstas
   per ætérna sǽcula.

A composition by Dr. Fortescue

4

JERUSALEM, LITURGY OF

The Rite of Jerusalem is that of Antioch. That is to say, the Liturgy that became famous as the use of the patriarchical church of Antioch, that through the influence of that Church spread throughout Syria and Asia Minor, and was the starting point of the development of the Byzantine rite, is itself originally the local liturgy, not of Antioch, but of Jerusalem. It is no other than the famous liturgy of St. James. That it was actually composed by St. James the Less, as first Bishop of Jerusalem, is not now believed by any one; but two forms in it show that it was originally used as local rite of the city of Jerusalem. There is a reference to the Cross among the prayers for catechumens—"Lift up the horn of the Christians by the power of the venerable and life-giving cross"—that is always supposed to be a reference to St. Helena's invention of the True Cross at Jerusalem in the early fourth century. If so, this would also give an approximate date, at any rate for that prayer. A much clearer local allusion is in the Intercession, after the *Epiklesis* (see **EPIKLESIS**): "We offer to thee, O Lord, for thy holy places which thou hast glorified by the divine appearance of thy Christ and by the coming of thy Holy Spirit" (these are the various sanctuaries of Palestine) "especially for holy and glorious Sion, mother of all Churches" (Sion, in Christian language, is always the local Church of Jerusalem: "and for thy holy Catholic and Apostolic Church throughout the whole world", which always may mean, "throughout the whole Empire"). This reference, then, the only one to any local Church in the whole liturgy—the fact that the Intercession, in which they pray for every kind of person and cause, begins with a prayer for the Church of Jerusalem, is a sure index of the place of origin.

We have further evidence in the catechetical discourses of St. Cyril of Jerusalem. These were held about the year 347 or 348 in the Church of the Holy Sepulchre. It is obvious that they describe the liturgy known to his hearers there. Allowing for certain reticences, especially in the earlier instructions given to catechumens (the *disciplina arcani*), and for certain slight differences, such as time always brings about in a living rite, it is evident that Cyril's liturgy is the one we know as that of St. James. As an obvious example one may quote Cyril's description of the beginning of the *Anaphora* (corresponding to our Preface). He mentions the celebrant's versicle, "Let us give thanks to the Lord", and the answer of the people, "Meet and just". He then continues: "After this we remember the sky, the earth and the sea, the sun and the moon, the stars and all creation both rational and irrational, the angels, archangels, powers, mights, dominations, principalities, thrones, the many-eyed Cherubim who also say those words of David: Praise the Lord with me. We remember also the Seraphim, whom Isaias saw in spirit standing around the throne of God, who with two wings cover their faces, with two their feet and with two fly; who say: Holy, holy, holy Lord of Sabaoth. We also say these divine words of the Seraphim, so as to take part in the hymns of the heavenly host."[1] This is an exact description of the beginning of the Anaphora in the Liturgy of St. James. We have, then, certain evidence that our St. James's Liturgy is the original local rite of Jerusalem. A further question as to its origin leads to that of its relation to the famous liturgy in the eighth book of the *Apostolic Constitutions*. That the two are related is obvious. It seems also obvious that the *Apostolic Constitutions* rite is the older; St. James must be considered a later, enlarged, and expanded form of it. But the liturgy of the *Apostolic Constitutions* is not Palestinian, but Antiochene. The compiler was an Antiochene Syrian; he describes the rite he knew in the north, at Antioch. The St. James's Rite, then, is an a adaptation of the other (not necessarily of the very one we have in the *Apostolic Constitutions*, but of the old Syrian rite, of which the Apostolic Constitutions give us one version) made for local use at Jerusalem. Then it spread throughout the patriarchate. It must always be remembered that, till the Council of Ephesus (431), Jerusalem belonged to the Patriarchate of Antioch. So this liturgy came to Antioch and there displaced the older rite of the *Apostolic Constitutions*. Adopted unchanged at Antioch (the local allusion to "holy and glorious Sion" was left unaltered), it imposed itself with new authority as the use of the patriarchal Church. The earliest notices of an Antiochene Rite that we possess show that it is this one of St. James. There is no external evidence that the *Apostolic Constitutions'* rite was ever used anywhere; it is only from the work itself that we deduce that it is Syrian and Antiochene. Under its new name of Liturgy of Antioch, St. James's Rite was used throughout Syria, Palestine, and Asia Minor. When Jerusalem became a patriarchate it kept the same use.

The Liturgy of St. James exists in Greek and Syriac. It was probably at first used indifferently in either language, in Greek in the Hellenized cities, in Syriac in the country. Of the relation of these two versions we can say with certainty that the present Greek form is the older. The existing Syriac liturgy is a translation from the Greek. There is good reason to suppose that at Jerusalem, as everywhere else, the primitive liturgical language was Greek. The schismatical Monophysite Churches formed in the fifth and sixth centuries in Syria kept St. James's Rite in Syriac. The Orthodox used it in Greek till it was supplanted by the daughter-rite of Constantinople about the twelfth century. At present the old Rite of Jerusalem is used, in Syriac, by the Jacobites and Uniat Syrians, also in a modified form in Syriac by the Maronites. The Greek version has been restored among the Orthodox at Jerusalem for one day in the year—31 December.

Chapter Notes

[1]   *Catech. Myst.*, V, 6.

5

LATIN CHURCH

The word Church (*ecclesia*) is used in its first sense to express the whole congregation of Catholic Christendom united in one Faith, obeying one hierarchy in communion with itself. This is the sense of Matthew, xvi,18; xviii, 17; Eph., v, 25-27, and so on. It is in this sense that we speak of the *Church* without qualification, say that Christ founded one Church, and so on. But the word is constantly applied to the various individual elements of this union. As the whole is *the* Church, the universal Church, so are its parts the Churches of Corinth, Asia, France, etc. This second use of the word also occurs in the New Testament (Acts, xv, 41; II Corinthians, xi, 28; Apocalypse, i :4, 11, etc.). Any portion then that forms a subsidiary unity in itself may be called a local Church. The smallest such portion is a diocese-thus we speak of the Church of Paris, of Milan, of Seville. Above this again we group metropolitical provinces and national portions together as units, and speak of the Church of Africa, of Gaul, of Spain. The expression "Church of Rome", it should be noted, though commonly applied by non-Catholics to the whole Catholic body, can only be used correctly in this secondary sense for the local diocese (or possibly the province) of Rome, mother and mistress of all Churches. A German Catholic is not, strictly speaking, a member of the Church of Rome but of the Church of Cologne, or Munich-Freising, or whatever it may be, in union with and under the obedience of the Roman Church (although, no doubt, by a further extension *Roman Church* may be used as equivalent to *Latin Church* for the patriarchate).

The word is also used very commonly for the still greater portions that are united under their patriarchs, that is for the patriarchates. It is in this sense that we speak of the Latin Church. The Latin Church is simply that vast portion of the Catholic body which obeys the Latin patriarch, which submits to the pope, not only in papal, but also in patriarchal matters. It is thus distinguished from the Eastern Churches (whether Catholic or Schismatic), which represent the other four patriarchates (Constantinople, Alexandria, Antioch, Jerusalem), and any fractions broken away from them. The Latin patriarchate has always been considerably the largest. Now, since the great part of Eastern Christendom has fallen into schism, since vast new lands have been colonized, conquered or (partly) converted by Latins (America, Australia, etc.), the Latin part of the Catholic Church looms so enormous as compared with the others that many people think that everyone in communion with the pope is a Latin. This error is fostered by the Anglican branch theory, which supposes the situation to be that the Eastern Church is no longer in communion with Rome. Against this we must always remember, and when necessary point out, that the constitution of the Catholic Church is still essentially what it was at the time of the Second Council of Nicaea (787; see also canon 21 of Constantinople IV in 869).[1] Namely, there are still the five patriarchates, of which the Latin Church is only one, although so great a part of the Eastern ones have fallen away. The Eastern Churches, small as they are, still represent the old Catholic Christendom of the East in union with the pope, obeying him as pope, though not as their patriarch. All Latins are Catholics, but not all Catholics are Latins. The old frontier passed just east of Macedonia, Greece (Illyricum was afterwards claimed by Constantinople), and Crete, and cut Africa west of Egypt. All to the west of this was the Latin Church.

We must now add to Western Europe all the new lands occupied by Western Europeans, to make up the present enormous Latin patriarchate. Throughout this vast territory the pope reigns as patriarch, as well as by his supreme position as visible head of the whole Church with the exception of very small remnants of other uses (Milan, Toledo, and the Byzantines of Southern Italy), his Roman Rite is used throughout according to the general principle that rite follows the patriarchate, that local bishops use the rite of their patriarch. The medieval Western uses (Paris, Sarum and so on), of which people at one time made much for controversial purposes, were in no sense really independent rites, as are the remnants of the Gallican use at Milan and Toledo. These were only the Roman Rite with very slight local modifications. From this conception we see that the practical disappearance of the Gallican Rite, however much the archaeologist may regret it, is justified by the general principle that rite should follow patriarchate. Uniformity of rite throughout Christendom has never been an ideal among Catholics; but uniformity in each patriarchate is. We see also that the suggestion, occasionally made by advanced Anglicans, of a "Uniate" Anglican Church with its own rite and to some extent its own laws (for instance with a married clergy) is utterly opposed to antiquity and to consistent canon law. England is most certainly part of the Latin patriarchate. When Anglicans return to the old Faith they find themselves subject to the pope, not only as head of the Church but also as patriarch. As part of the Latin Church England must submit to Latin canon law and the Roman Rite just as much as France or Germany. The comparison with Eastern Rite Catholics rests on a misconception of the whole situation. It follows also that the expression *Latin* (or even *Roman*) *Catholic* is quite justifiable, inasmuch as we express by it that we are not only Catholics but also members of the Latin or Roman patriarchate. An Eastern Rite Catholic on the other hand is a Byzantine, or Armenian, or Maronite Catholic. But a person who is in schism with the Holy See is not, of course, admitted by Catholics to be any kind of Catholic at all.

Chapter Notes

1 *Corp. Jur. can.*, dist. xxii, c. vii.

6

ROMAN RITE (*RITUS ROMANUS*)

The Roman Rite is the manner of celebrating the Holy Sacrifice, administering Sacraments, reciting the Divine Office, and performing other ecclesiastical functions (blessings, all kinds of Sacramentals, etc.) as used in the city and Diocese of Rome. The Roman Rite is the most widespread in Christendom. That it had advantages possessed by no other, the most archaic antiquity, unequalled dignity, beauty, and the practical convenience of being comparatively short in its services will not be denied by any one who knows it and the other ancient liturgies. But it was not the consideration of these advantages that led to its extensive use; it was the exalted position of the see that used it. The Roman Rite was adopted throughout the West because the local bishops, sometimes kings or emperors, felt that they could not do better than use the rite of the chief bishop of all, at Rome. And this imitation of Roman liturgical practice brought about in the West the application of the principle (long admitted in the East) that rite should follow patriarchate. Apart from his universal primacy, the pope has always been unquestioned Patriarch of the West. It was then the right and normal thing that the West should use his liturgy. The irregular and anomalous incident of liturgical history is not that the Roman Rite has been used, practically exclusively, in the West since about the tenth or eleventh century, but that before that there were other rites in the pope's patriarchate. Not the disappearance but the existence and long toleration of the Gallican and Spanish (Mozarabic) rites is the difficulty (see **RITES**). Like all others, the Roman Rite bears clear marks of its local origin. Wherever it may be used, it is still Roman in the local sense obviously composed for use in Rome. Our Missal marks the Roman stations, contains the Roman saints in the Canon (see **CANON OF THE MASS**), honours with special solemnity the Roman martyrs and popes. Our feasts are constantly anniversaries of local Roman events, of the dedication of Roman churches (All Saints, St. Michael, S. Maria ad Nives, etc.). The Collect for Sts. Peter and Paul (29 June) supposes that it is said at Rome (the Church which "received the beginnings of her Faith" from these saints is that of Rome), and so on continually. This is quite right and fitting; it agrees with all liturgical history. No rite has ever been composed consciously for general use. In the East there are still stronger examples of the same thing. The Orthodox all over the world use a rite full of local allusions to the city of Constantinople.

The Roman Rite evolved out of the (presumed) universal, but quite fluid, rite of the first three centuries during the (liturgically) almost unknown time from the fourth to the sixth. In the sixth we have it fully developed in the Leonine, later in the Gelasian, Sacramentaries. How and exactly when the specifically Roman qualities were formed during that time will, no doubt, always be a matter of conjecture (see **LITURGY; MASS, LITURGY OF THE**). At first its use was very restrained. It was followed only in the Roman province. North Italy was Gallican, the South, Byzantine, but Africa was always closely akin to Rome liturgically. From the eighth century gradually the Roman usage began its career of conquest in the West. By the twelfth century at latest it was used wherever Latin obtained, having displaced all others except at Milan and in retreating parts of Spain. That has been its position ever since. As the rite of the Latin Church it is used exclusively in the Latin Patriarchate, with three small exceptions at

Milan, Toledo, and in the still Byzantine churches of Southern Italy, Sicily, and Corsica. During the Middle Ages it developed into a vast number of derived rites, differing from the pure form only in unimportant details and in exuberant additions. Most of these were abolished by the decree of Pius V in 1570 (see **MASS, LITURGY OF THE**). Meanwhile, the Roman Rite had itself been affected by, and had received additions from, the Gallican and Spanish uses it displaced. The Roman Rite is now used by every one who is subject to the pope's patriarchal jurisdiction (with the three exceptions noted above); that is, it is used in Western Europe, including Poland, in all countries colonised from Western Europe: America, Australia, etc., by Western (Latin) missionaries all over the world, including the Eastern lands where other Catholic rites also obtain. No one may change his rite without a legal authorisation, which is not easily obtained. So the Western priest in Syria, Egypt, and so on uses his own Roman Rite, just as at home. On the same principle Catholics of Eastern rites in Western Europe, America, etc., keep their rites; so that rites now cross each other wherever such people live together. The language of the Roman Rite is Latin everywhere except that in some churches along the Western Adriatic coast it is said in Slavonic and on rare occasions in Greek at Rome (see **RITES**). In derived forms the Roman Rite is used in some few dioceses (Lyons) and by several religious orders (Benedictines, Carthusians, Carmelites, Dominicans). In these their fundamentally Roman character is expressed by a compound name. They are the *Ritus Romano-Lugdunensis*, *Romano-monasticus*, and so on.

7

The Liturgy of the Mass

1. *Name and Definition.*—The Mass is the complex of prayers and ceremonies that make up the service of the Eucharist in the Latin rites. As in the case of all liturgical terms the name is less old than the thing. From the time of the first preaching of the Christian Faith in the West, as everywhere, the Holy Eucharist was celebrated as Christ had instituted it at the Last Supper, according to His command, in memory of Him. But it was not till long afterwards that the late Latin name *Missa*, used at first in a vaguer sense, became the technical and almost exclusive name for this service.

In the first period, while Greek was still the Christian language at Rome, we find the usual Greek names used there, as in the East. The commonest was *Eucharistia*, used both for the consecrated bread and wine and for the whole service. Clement of Rome (d. about 101) uses the verbal form still in its general sense of "giving thanks", but also in connection with the Liturgy.[1] The other chief witness for the earliest Roman Liturgy, Justin Martyr (d. c. 167), speaks of Eucharist in both senses repeatedly.[2] After him the word is always used, and passes into Latin (*eucharistia*) as soon as there is a Latin Christian literature. It remains the normal name for the sacrament throughout Catholic theology, but is gradually superseded by *Missa* for the whole rite. Clement calls the service "rite" and "oblation", with, however, a shade of different meaning. These and the other usual Greek names in the Catacombs, with their not yet strictly technical connotation, are used during the first two centuries in the West as in the East. With the use of the Latin language in the third century came first translations of the Greek terms. While *eucharistia* is very common, we also find its translation *gratiarum actio; benedictio* occurs too; (*sacrificium*, generally with an attribute, *divina sacrificia, novum sacrificium, sacrificia Dei*), is a favourite expression of St. Cyprian. We also find *Solemnia, Dominica solemnia, Prex, Oblatio, Coena Domini, Spirituale ac coeleste sacramentum, Dominicum, Officium,* even *Passio,* and other expressions that are rather descriptions than technical names.

All these were destined to be supplanted in the West by the classical name *Missa*. The first certain use of it is by St. Ambrose (d. 397). He writes to his sister Marcellina describing the troubles of the Arians in the years 385 and 386, when the soldiers were sent to break up the service in his church: The next day (it was a Sunday) after the lessons and the tract, having dismissed the catechumens, I explained the creed (*symbolum tradebam*) to some of the competents (people about to be baptized) in the baptistery of the basilica. There I was told suddenly that they had sent soldiers to the Portiana basilica. . . But I remained at my place and began to say Mass (*missam facere coepi*). While I offer (*dum offero*) I hear that a certain Castulus has been seized by the people."[3]

It will be noticed that *missa* here means the Eucharistic Service proper, the Liturgy of the Faithful only, and does not include that of the Catechumens. Ambrose uses the word as one in common use and well known. There is another, still earlier, but very doubtfully authentic instance of the word in a letter of Pope Pius I (from c.142 to c.157): "Euprepia has handed over possession of her house to the poor, where . . . we make Masses with our poor" (*cum pauperibus nostris . . . missas agimus*). The authenticity of the letter, however, is very doubtful. If *Missa* really occurred in the second century in the sense it now has, it would be surprising that it never occurs in the third. We may consider St. Ambrose as the earliest certain authority for it.

From the fourth century the term becomes more common. For a time it occurs nearly always in the sense of *dismissal*. St. Augustine (d. 430) says: "After the sermon the dismissal of the catechumens takes place" (*post sermonem fit missa catechumenorum*).[4] The Synod of Lerida in Spain (524) declares that people guilty of incest may be admitted to church *usque ad missam catechumenorum,* that is, till the catechumens are dismissed. The same expression occurs in the Synod of Valencia at about the same time. Etheria (fourth century) calls the whole service, or the Liturgy of the Faithful, *missa* constantly. So also Innocent I, (401-17), Leo I (440-61). Although from the beginning the word *Missa* usually means the Eucharistic service or some part of it, we find it used occasionally for other ecclesiastical offices too. In St. Benedict's (d. 547) Rule *fiant missae* is used for the dismissal at the end of the canonical hours. In the Leonine Sacramentary (sixth century, see **LITURGICAL BOOKS),** the word in its present sense is supposed throughout. The title *item alia*, at the head of each Mass means *Item alia Missa*. The Gelasian book (sixth or seventh century, see **LITURGICAL BOOKS**) supplies the word: *Item alia missa, Missa Chrismatis, Orationes ad missa (sic) in natale Sanctorum*, and so on throughout. From that time it becomes the regular, practically exclusive, name for the Holy Liturgy in the Roman and Gallican Rites.

The origin and meaning of the word, once much discussed, is not really doubtful. We may dismiss at once such fanciful explanations as that *missa* is the Hebrew *missah* ("oblation"), or in the Greek "initiation", or the German *Mess* ("assembly", "market"). Nor is it the participle feminine of *mittere*, with a noun understood (*oblatio missa ad Deum, congregatio missa,* i.e. *dimissa*. It is a substantive of a late form for *missio*. There are many parallels in medieval Latin, *collecta, ingressa, confessa, accessa, ascensa*—all for forms in -io. It does not mean an offering (*mittere*, in the sense of handing over to God), but the dismissal of the people, as in the versicle: *Ite missa est* ("Go the dismissal is made"). It may seem strange that this unessential detail should have given its name to the whole service. But there are many similar cases in liturgical language. *Communion, confession, breviary* are none of them names that express the essential character of what they denote. In the case of the word *missa* we can trace the development of its meaning step by step. We have seen it used by St. Augustine, synods of the sixth century, and Hincmar of Reims for "dismissal". *Missa Catechumenorum* means the dismissal of the catechumens. It appears that *missa fit* or *missa est* was the regular formula for sending people away at the end of a trial or legal process. Avitus of Vienne (d. 523) says: "In churches and palaces or law-courts the dismissal is proclaimed to be made (*missa fieri pronuntiatur*) when the people are dismissed from their attendance." So also St. Isidore of Seville: "At the time of the sacrifice the dismissal is (*missa tempore sacrificii est*) when the catechumens are sent out, as the deacon cries: "If any one of the catechumens remain, let him go out, and thence it is the dismissal (*et inde missa*)." As there was a dismissal of the catechumens at the end of the first part of the service, so was there a dismissal of the faithful (the baptized) after the Communion. There were, then, a *missa catechumenorum* and a *missa fidelium*, both, at first, in the sense of dismissals only. So Florus Diaconus (d. 860): "*Missa* is understood as nothing but *dimissio*, that is, *absolutio*, which the deacon pronounces when the people are dismissed from the solemn service. The deacon cried out and the catechumens were sent (*mittebantur*), that is, were dismissed outside (*id est, dimittebantur foras*). So the *missa catechumenorum* was made before the action of the Sacrament i.e., before the *Canon Actionis*), the *missa fidelium* is made after the consecration and communion (*post confectionem et participationem*)."[5] Note the difference of tense: in Florus's time the dismissal of the catechumens had ceased to be practised—

"the *missa catechumenorum* was made" but "the *missa fidelium* is made".

How this word gradually changed its meaning from dismissal to the whole service, up to and including the dismissal, is not difficult to understand. In the texts quoted we see already the foundation of such a change. To stay till the *missa catechumenorum* is easily modified into: to stay for, or during, the *missa catechumenorum*. So we find these two *missae* used for the two halves of the Liturgy. Ivo of Chartres (d. 1116) has forgotten the original meaning, and writes: "Those who heard the *missa catechumenorum* evaded the *missa sacramentorum.*" The two parts are then called by these two names. As the discipline of the catechumenate is gradually forgotten, and there remains only one connected service, it is called by the long familiar name *missa*, without further qualification. We find, however, through the Middle Ages, the plural *missae, missarum solemnia,* as well as *missae sacramentum* and such modified expressions also. Occasionally the word is transferred to the feast-day. The feast of St. Martin, for instance, is called *Missa S. Martini.* It is from this use that the German *Mess, Messtag,* and so on are derived. The day and place of a local feast was the occasion of a market. *Kirmess* (Flemish *Kermis,* French *kermesse*) is *Kirch-mess,* the anniversary of the dedication of a church, the occasion of a fair. The Latin *missa* is modified in all Western languages (Italian, *messa*; Spanish, *misa*; French, *messe*; German, *Messe*, etc.). The English form before the Conquest was *maesse,* then Middle English, *messe, masse*—"It nedith not to speke of the masse ne the seruise that thei hadde that day"[6] —"And whan our parish masse was done..."[7] It also existed as a verb: "to mass" was to say Mass; "massing-priest" was a common term of abuse at the Reformation.

It should be noted that the name Mass (*missa*) applies to the Eucharistic service in the Latin rites only. Neither in Latin nor in Greek has it ever been applied to any Eastern rite. For them the corresponding word is Liturgy (*liturgia*).

It is a mistake that leads to confusion, and a scientific inexactitude, to speak of any Eastern Liturgy as a Mass.

2. *The Origin of the Mass.*—The Western Mass, like all Liturgies, begins, of course, with the Last Supper. What Christ then did, repeated as he commanded in memory of Him, is the nucleus of the Mass. As soon as the Faith was brought to the West the Holy Eucharist was celebrated here, as in the East. At first the language used was Greek. Out of that earliest Liturgy, the language being changed to Latin, developed the two great parent rites of the West, the Roman and the Gallican (see **LITURGY**). Of these two the Gallican Mass may be traced without difficulty. It is so plainly Antiochene in its structure, in the very text of many of its prayers, that we are safe in accounting for it as a translated form of the Liturgy of Jerusalem-Antioch, brought to the West at about the time when the more or less fluid universal Liturgy of the first three centuries gave place to different fixed rites (see **LITURGY: GALLICAN RITE**). The origin of the Roman Mass, on the other hand, is a most difficult question. We have here two fixed and certain data: the Liturgy in Greek described by St. Justin Martyr (died c. 165), which is that of the Church of Rome in the second century, and, at the other end of the development, the Liturgy of the first Roman Sacramentaries in Latin, in about the sixth century. The two are very different. Justin's account represents a rite of what we should now call an Eastern type, corresponding with remarkable exactness to that of the *Apostolic Constitutions* (see **LITURGY**). The Leonine and Gelasian Sacramentaries show us what is practically our present Roman Mass. How did the service change from the one to the other? It is one of the chief difficulties in the history of liturgy. During the last few years, especially, all manner of solutions and combinations have been proposed. We will first note some points that are certain, that may serve as landmarks in an investigation.

Justin Martyr, Clement of Rome, Hippolytus (d. 235), and Novatian (c. 250) all agree in the Liturgies they describe, though the evidence of the last two is scanty. Justin gives us the fullest liturgical description of any Father of the first three centuries (see **LITURGY**). He describes how the Holy Eucharist was celebrated at Rome in the middle of the second century; his account is the necessary point of departure, one end of a chain whose intermediate links are hidden. We have hardly any knowledge at all of what developments the Roman Rite went through during the third and fourth centuries. This is the mysterious time where conjecture may, and does, run riot. By the fifth century we come back to comparatively firm ground, after a radical change. At this time we have the fragment in the *De Sacramentis* of the Pseudo-Ambrose, (about 400), and the letter of Pope Innocent I (401-17) to Decentius of Eugubium. In these documents we see that the Roman Liturgy is said in Latin and has already become in essence the rite we still use. A few indications of the end of the fourth century agree with this. A little later we come to the earliest Sacramentaries (Leonine, fifth or sixth century; Gelasian, sixth or seventh century) and from then the history of the Roman Mass is fairly clear. The fifth and sixth centuries therefore show us the other end of the chain. For the interval between the second and fifth centuries, during which the great change took place, although we know so little about Rome itself, we have valuable data from Africa. There is every reason to believe that in liturgical matters the Church of Africa followed Rome closely. We can supply much of what we wish to know about Rome from the African Fathers of the third century, Tertullian (d. c. 220), St. Cyprian (d. 258), the Acts of St. Perpetua and St. Felicitas (203), and St. Augustine (d. 430). The question of the change of language from Greek to Latin is less important than it might seem. It came about naturally when Greek ceased to be the usual language of the Roman Christians. Pope Victor I (190-199), an African, seems to have been the first to use Latin at Rome. Novatian writes Latin. By the second half of the third century the usual liturgical language at Rome seems to have been Latin, though fragments of Greek remained for many centuries. Other writers think that Latin was not finally adopted till the end of the fourth century. No doubt, for a time both languages were used. The Creed was sometimes said in Greek, some psalms were sung in that language, the lessons on Holy Saturday were read in Greek and Latin as late as the eighth century. There are still such fragments of Greek (*Kyrie eleison*, *Agios O Theos*) in the Roman Missal. But a change of language does not involve a change of rite. Novatian's Latin allusions to the Eucharistic Prayer agree very well with those of Clement of Rome in Greek (see **GLOSSARY: CLEMENT**), and with the Greek forms in the *Apostolic Constitutions*, VIII. The Africans, Tertullian, St. Cyprian, etc., who write Latin, describe a rite very closely related to that of Justin and the *Apostolic Constitutions*. The Gallican Rite shows how Eastern, how "Greek", a Latin Liturgy can be. We must then conceive the change of language in the third century as a detail that did not much affect the development of the rite. No doubt the use of Latin was a factor in the Roman tendency to shorten the prayers, leave out whatever seemed redundant in formulas, and abridge the whole service. Latin is naturally terse, compared with the rhetorical abundance of Greek. This difference is one of the most obvious distinctions between the Roman and the Eastern Rites.

If we may suppose that during the first three centuries there was a common Liturgy throughout Christendom, variable, no doubt, in details, but uniform in all its main points, which common Liturgy is represented by that of the eighth book of the *Apostolic Constitutions*, we have in that the origin of the Roman Mass as of all other liturgies (see **LITURGY**). There are, indeed, special reasons for supposing that this type of liturgy was used at Rome. The chief authorities for it (Clement, Justin, Hippolytus, Novatian) are all Roman. Moreover, even the present Roman Rite, in spite of later modifications, retains certain elements that bear a remarkable resemblance to the Liturgy of the *Apostolic Constitutions*. For instance, at Rome there neither is nor has been a public Offertory prayer. The *Oremus* said just before the Offertory is the fragment of quite another thing, the old prayers of the faithful, of which we still have a specimen in the series of collects on Good Friday. The Offertory is made in silence while the choir sings part of a psalm. Meanwhile the celebrant says private Offertory prayers which in the old form of the Mass are the Secrets only. The older Secrets are true Offertory prayers. In the Byzantine Rite, on the other hand, the gifts are prepared beforehand, brought up with the singing of the *Cherubikon* (see **GLOSSARY**), and offered at the altar by a public *Synapte* (see **GLOSSARY**) of deacon and people, and a prayer once sung aloud by the celebrant (now only the *Ecphonesis* (see **GLOSSARY**),is sung aloud). The Roman custom of a silent offertory with private prayer is that of the Liturgy of the *Apostolic Constitutions*. Here too the rubric says only: "The deacons bring the gifts to the bishop at the altar," and "The Bishop, praying by himself silently with the priests . . ." No doubt in this case, too, a psalm was sung meanwhile, which would account for the unique instance of silent prayer. The *Apostolic Constitutions* order that at this point the deacons should wave fans over the oblation (a practical precaution to keep away insects). This, too, was done at Rome down to the fourteenth century. The Roman Mass, like the *Apostolic Constitutions* has a washing of hands just before the Offertory. It once had a kiss of peace before the Preface. Pope Innocent I, in his letter to Decentius of Eugubium (416), remarks on this older custom of placing it *ante confecta mysteria* (before the Eucharistic prayer). That is its place in the *Apostolic Constitutions*. After the Lord's Prayer, at Rome, during the fraction, the celebrant sings: *Pax Domini sit semper vobiscum*. It seems that this was the place to which the kiss of peace was first moved (as in Innocent I's letter). This greeting, unique in the Roman Rite, occurs again only in the *Apostolic Constitutions*. Here it comes twice: after the Intercession and at the kiss of peace. The two Roman prayers after the Communion, the Postcommunion and the *Oratio super populum* (*ad populum* in the Gelasian Sacramentary) correspond to the two prayers, first thanksgiving, then a prayer over the people in the *Apostolic Constitutions*.

There is an interesting deduction that may be made from the present Roman Preface. A number of Prefaces introduce the reference to the angels (who sing the *Sanctus*) by the form *et ideo*. In many cases it is not clear to what this *ideo* refers. Like the *igitur* at the beginning of the Canon, it does not seem justified by what precedes. May we conjecture that something has been left out? The beginning of the Eucharistic prayer in the *Apostolic Constitutions*, the part before the *Sanctus*, our Preface, is much longer, and enumerates at length the benefits of creation and various events of the Old Law. The angels are mentioned twice at the beginning as the first creatures and then again at the end abruptly, without connection with what has preceded in order to introduce the *Sanctus*. The shortness of the Roman Prefaces seems to make it certain that they have been curtailed. All the other rites begin the Eucharistic prayer (after the formula: "Let us give thanks") with a long thanksgiving for the various benefits of God which are enumerated. We know, too, how much of the development of the Roman Mass is due to a tendency to abridge the older prayers. If then we suppose that the Roman Preface is such an abridgement of that in the *Apostolic Constitutions*, with the details of the Creation and Old Testament history left out, we can account for the *ideo*. The two references to the angels in the older prayers have met and coalesced. The *ideo* refers to the omitted list of benefits, of which the angels, too, have their share. The parallel between the orders of angels in both liturgies is exact: *...cum Angelis et Archangelis, cum Thronis et Dominationibus, cumque omni militia caelestis exercitus....sine fine dicentes.*

Another parallel is in the old forms of the *Hanc igitur* prayer. Two early Roman forms of this prayer have been found in Sacramentaries at Vauclai and Rouen. The older form is much longer and has plainly the nature of an intercession, such as we find in the Eastern rites at the end of the Anaphora. The form is: *Hanc igitur oblationem servitutis nostrae sed et cunctae familiae tuae, quaesumus Domine placatus accipias, quam tibi devoto offerimus corde pro pace et caritate et unitate sanctae ecclesiae, pro fide catholica...pro sacerdotibus et omni gradu ecclesiae, pro regibus...*("Therefore, O Lord, we beseech Thee be pleased to accept this offering of our service and of all Thy household which we offer Thee with devout heart for the peace, charity, and unity of Holy Church, for the Catholic Faith...for the priests and every order of the Church, for kings...") and so on, enumerating a complete list of people for whom prayer is said. This, then, supplies another missing element in the Mass. Eventually the clauses enumerating the petitions were suppressed—no doubt because they were thought to be a useless reduplication of the prayers *Te igitur, Communicantes* and the two Mementos, and the introduction of this Intercession (*Hanc igitur...placatus accipias*) was joined to what seems to have once been part of a prayer for the dead (*diesque nostros in tua pace disponas*, etc).

We still have a faint echo of the old intercession in the clause about the newly-baptized interpolated into the *Hanc igitur* at Easter and Whitsuntide. The beginning of the prayer has a parallel in the *Apostolic Constitutions* VIII (the beginning of the deacon's Litany of Intercession). The prayer containing the words of Institution in the Roman Mass (*Qui pridie...in mei memoriam facietis*) has just the constructions and epithets of the corresponding text in the *Apostolic Constitutions*. It is true that we can find parallel passages with other liturgies too, notably with that of Jerusalem—St. James (see **JERUSALEM, LITURGY OF**). There are several forms that correspond to those of the Egyptian Rite, such as the Roman *de tuis donis ac* *datis* in the *Unde et memores*: "... *offerimus praeclarae maiestati tuae de tuis donis ac datis*" is found exactly in the Coptic form: "Before Thine holy glory we have set Thine own gift of Thine own." But this does not mean merely that there are parallel passages between any two rites. The similarities of the *Apostolic Constitutions* are far more obvious than those of any other. The Roman Mass, even apart from the testimony of Justin Martyr, Clement, Hippolytus, Novatian, still bears evidence of its development from a type of liturgy of which that of the *Apostolic Constitutions* is the only perfect surviving specimen (see **LIT-URGY**). There is reason to believe, moreover, that it has since been influenced both from Jerusalem-Antioch and Alexandria, though many of the forms common to it and these two may be survivals of that original fluid universal rite which have not been preserved in the *Apostolic Constitutions*. It must always be remembered that no one maintains that the *Apostolic Constitutions'* Liturgy is word for word the primitive universal liturgy.

But between this original Roman Rite (which we can study only in the *Apostolic Constitutions*) and the Mass as it emerges in the first Sacramentaries (sixth to seventh century) there is a great change. Much of this change is accounted for by the Roman tendency to shorten. The *Apostolic Constitutions* has five lessons; Rome has generally only two or three. At Rome the prayers of the faithful after the expulsion of the catechumens and the Intercession at the end of the Canon have gone. Both no doubt were considered superfluous since there is a series of petitions of the same nature in the Canon. But both have left traces. We still say *Oremus* before the Offertory, where the prayers of the faithful once stood, and still have these prayers on Good Friday in the collects. And the *Hanc igitur* is a fragment of the Intercession. The first great change that separates Rome from all the Eastern rites is the influence of the ecclesiastical year. The Eastern liturgies remain always the same except for the lessons, *Prokeimenon* (Gradual-verse), and one or two other slight modifications. On the other hand the Roman

Mass is profoundly affected throughout by the season or feast on which it is said. We have the authority of Pope Vigilius (537-555) for the fact that in the sixth century the order of the Mass was still hardly affected by the calendar. The influence of the ecclesiastical year must have been gradual. The lessons were of course always varied, and a growing tendency to refer to the feast or season in the prayers, Preface, and even in the Canon, brought about the present state of things, already in full force in the Leonine Sacramentary. That Damasus was one of the popes who modified the old rite seems, however, certain. St. Gregory I (590-604) says he introduced the use of the Hebrew Alleluia from Jerusalem. It was under Damasus that the Vulgate became the official Roman version of the Bible used in the Liturgy; a constant tradition ascribes to Damasus's friend St. Jerome (d. 420) the arrangement of the Roman Lectionary. Mgr Duchesne thinks that the Canon was arranged by this pope.[8] A curious error of a Roman theologian of Damasus's time, who identified Melchisedech with the Holy Ghost, incidentally shows us one prayer of our Mass as existing then, namely the *Supra quae* with its allusion to *summus sacerdos tuus Melchisedech*.

3. *The Mass from the Fifth to the Seventh Century.*—By about the fifth century we begin to see more clearly. Two documents of this time give us fairly large fragments of the Roman Mass. Innocent I (401-17), in his letter to Decentius of Eugubium (about 416) alludes to many features of the Mass. We notice that these important changes have already been made: the kiss of peace has been moved from the beginning of the Mass of the Faithful to after the Consecration, the Commemoration of the Living and Dead is made in the Canon, and there are no longer prayers of the faithful before the Offertory (see **CANON OF THE MASS**). We notice especially that in Innocent's time the prayer of intercession follows the Consecration (see **CANON OF THE MASS**). The author of the

treatise *De Sacramentis* (wrongly attributed to St. Ambrose), says that he will explain the Roman Use, and proceeds to quote a great part of the Canon. (the text is given in **CANON OF THE MASS**). From this document we can reconstruct the following scheme: The Mass of the Catechumens is still distinct from that of the faithful, at least in theory. The people sing *Introibo ad altare Dei* as the celebrant and his ministers approach the altar (the Introit). Then follow lessons from Scripture, chants (Graduals), and a sermon (the Catechumens' Mass). The people still make the Offertory of bread and wine. The Preface and Sanctus follow (*laus Deo defertur*), then the Prayer of Intercession (*oratione petitur pro populo, pro regibus, pro ceteris*) and the Consecration by the words of Institution (*ut conficitur ven. sacramentum...utitur sermonibus Christi*). From this point (*Fac nobis hanc oblationem adscriptam, ratam, rationabilem...*) the text of the Canon is quoted. Then come the Anamnesis (*Ergo memores...*), joined to it the prayer of oblation (*offerimus tibi hanc immaculatam hostiam...*), i.e., practically our *Supra quae* prayer, and the Communion with the form: *Corpus Christi*. R. *Amen*, during which Psalm 22 is sung. At the end the Lord's Prayer is said.

In the *De Sacramentis*, then, the Intercession comes before the Consecration, whereas in Innocent's letter it came after. This transposition should be noted as one of the most important features in the development of the Mass. The *Liber Pontificalis* contains a number of statements about changes in and additions to the Mass made by various popes, as for instance that Leo I (440-61) added the words *sanctum sacrificium, immaculatam hostiam* to the prayer *Supra quae*, that Sergius I (687-701) introduced the *Agnus Dei*, and so on. These must be received with caution; the whole book still needs critical examination. In the case of the *Agnus Dei* the statement is made doubtful by the fact that it is found in the Gregorian Sacramentary (whose date, however, is again doubtful). A constant tradition ascribes some great influence on the Mass to Gelasius I (492-6). Gennadius says he composed a Sacramentary; the *Liber Pontificalis* speaks of his liturgical work, and there must be some basis for the way in which his name is attached to the famous *Gelasian Sacramentary*. What exactly Gelasius did is less easy to determine.

We come now to the end of a period at the reign of St. Gregory I (590-604). Gregory knew the Mass practically as we still have it. There have been additions and changes since his time, but none to compare with the complete recasting of the Canon that took place before him. At least as far as the Canon is concerned, Gregory may be considered as having put the last touches to it. His biographer John the Deacon, says that he "collected the Sacramentary of Gelasius in one book, leaving out much, changing little, adding something for the exposition of the Gospels". He moved the Our Father from the end of the Mass to before the Communion, as he says in his letter to John of Syracuse:

> We say the Lords' Prayer immediately after the Canon (*mox post precem*)...It seems to me very unsuitable that we should say the Canon [*Prex*] which an unknown scholar composed (*quam scholasticus composuerat*) over the oblation, and that we should not say the prayer, handed down by our Redeemer himself over His body and blood.[9]

He is also credited with the addition: *diesque nostros* etc. to the *Hanc igitur* (see **CANON OF THE MASS**). Benedict XIV says that "no pope has added to, or changed the Canon since St. Gregory." There has been an important change since, the partial amalgamation of the old Roman Rite with Gallican features; but this hardly affects the Canon. We may say safely that a modern Catholic who could be carried back to Rome in the early seventh century would—while missing some features to which he is accustomed—find himself on the whole quite at home with the service be saw there.

This brings us back to the most difficult question: Why and when was the Roman Liturgy changed from what we see in Justin Martyr to that of Gregory I? The change is radical, especially as regards the most important element of the Mass, the Canon. The modifications in the earlier part, the smaller number of lessons, the omission of the prayers for and expulsion of the catechumens, of the prayers of the faithful before the Offertory and so on, may be accounted for easily as a result of the characteristic Roman tendency to shorten the service and leave out what had become superfluous. The influence of the calendar has already been noticed. But there remains the great question of the arrangement of the Canon. That the order of the prayers that make up the Canon is a cardinal difficulty is admitted by every one. The old attempts to justify their present order by symbolic or mystic reasons have now been given up. The Roman Canon as it stands is recognized as a problem of great difficulty. It differs fundamentally from the Anaphora of any Eastern rite and from the Gallican Canon. Whereas in the Antiochene family of liturgies (including that of Gaul) the great Intercession follows the Consecration, which comes at once after the *Sanctus*, and in the Alexandrine class the Intercession is said during what we should call the Preface before the *Sanctus*, in the Roman Rite the Intercession is scattered throughout the Canon, partly before and partly after the Consecration. We may add to this the other difficulty, the omission at Rome of any kind of clear Invocation of the Holy Ghost (*Epiklesis*). So far it has been admitted on all sides that the Roman and Gallican rites belong to different classes; the Gallican Rite approaches that of Antioch very closely, the origin of the Roman one being the great problem.

We conclude, then, that at Rome the Eucharistic prayer was fundamentally changed and recast at some uncertain period between the fourth and the sixth and seventh centuries. During the same time the prayers of the faithful before the Offertory disappeared, the kiss of peace was transferred to after the Consecration, and the *Epiklesis* was omitted or mutilated into our Supplices prayer. We must then admit that between the years 400 and 500 a great transformation was made in the Roman Canon.

4. From the Seventh Century to Modern Times.—After Gregory the Great (590-604) it is comparatively easy to follow the history of the Mass in the Roman Rite. We have now as documents first the three well known Sacramentaries. The oldest, called Leonine, exists in a seventh-century manuscript. Its composition is ascribed variously to the fifth, sixth, or seventh century (see **LITURGICAL BOOKS**). It is a fragment wanting the Canon, but as far as it goes, represents the Mass we know (without the later Gallican additions). Many of its collects, secrets, post-communions, and prefaces are still in use. The Gelasian book was written in the sixth, seventh, or eighth century; it is partly Gallicanized and was composed in the Frankish Kingdom. Here we have our Canon word for word. The third Sacramentary, called Gregorian, is apparently the book sent by Pope Adrian I to Charlemagne, probably between 781 and 791. It contains additional Masses since Gregory's time and a set of supplements gradually incorporated into the original book, giving Frankish (i.e. older Roman and Gallican) additions. Mr Edmund Bishop explains the development of the Roman Rite from the ninth to the eleventh century in this way:

> The (pure) Roman Sacramentary sent by Adrian to Charlemagne was ordered by the king to be used alone throughout the Frankish kingdom. But the people were attached to their old use, which was partly Roman (Gelasian) and partly Gallican. So when the Gregorian book was copied they (notably Alcuin, d. 804) added to it these Frankish supplements. Gradually the supplements became incorporated into the original book. So composed it came back to Rome (through the influence of the Carolingian emperors) and became the use of the Roman Church.[10]

The *Missale Romanum Lateranense* of the eleventh century shows this fused rite complete as the only one in use at Rome. The Roman Mass has thus gone through this last change since Gregory the Great, a partial fusion with Gallican elements.

The Roman *Ordines* are valuable sources that supplement the Sacramentaries. They are descriptions of ceremonial without the prayers (like the *Caeremoniale Episcoporum*), and extend from the eighth to the fourteenth or fifteenth centuries. The first (eighth century) and second (based on the first, with Frankish additions) are the most important (see **LITURGICAL BOOKS**). From these and the Sacramentaries we can reconstruct the Mass at Rome in the eighth or ninth century. There were as yet no preparatory prayers said before the altar. The Pope, attended by a great retinue of deacons, subdeacons, acolytes, and singers, entered while the Introit psalm was sung. After a prostration the *Kyrie eleison* was, sung, as now with nine invocations (see **KYRIE ELEISON**); any other litany had disappeared. The *Gloria* followed on feasts (see *GLORIA IN EXCELSIS*) The Pope sang the prayer of the day (see **COLLECT**), two or three lessons followed (see **LESSONS IN THE LITURGY**), interspersed with psalms (see **GRADUAL**). The prayers of the faithful had gone, leaving only the one word *Oremus* as a fragment. The people brought up the bread and wine while the Offertory psalm was sung; the gifts were arranged on the altar by the deacons. The Secret was said (at that time the only Offertory prayer) after the Pope had washed his hands. The Preface, *Sanctus*, and all the Canon followed as now. A reference to the fruits of the earth led to the words *per quem haec omnia*, etc. Then came the Lord's Prayer, the Fraction with a complicated ceremony, the kiss of peace, the *Agnus Dei* (since Pope Sergius, 687-701), the Communion under both kinds, during which the communion psalm was sung (see **COMMUNION-ANTIPHON**), the Post-Communion Prayer, the dismissal (see **ITE MISSA EST**), and the procession back to the sacristy.

It has been explained how this (mixed) Roman Rite gradually drove out the Gallican Use (see **LITURGY**). By about the tenth or eleventh century the Roman Mass was practically the only one in use in the West. Then a few additions (none them very important) were made to the Mass at different times. The Nicene Creed is an importation from Constantinople. It is said that in 1014 the Emperor Henry II (1002-24) persuaded Pope Benedict VIII (1012-24) to add it after the Gospel. It had already been adopted in Spain, Gaul, and Germany. All the present ritual and the prayers said by the celebrant at the Offertory were introduced from France about the thirteenth century—before that the Secrets were the only Offertory Prayers. There was considerable variety as to these prayers throughout the Middle Ages until the revised Missal of Pius V (1570). The incensing of persons and things is again due to the Gallican influence; it was not adopted at Rome till the eleventh or twelfth century. Before that time incense was burned only during processions (the entrance and Gospel procession). The three prayers said by the celebrant before his communion are private devotions introduced gradually into the official text. Here too there was great diversity right through the Middle Ages till Pius V's Missal. The latest additions to the Mass are its present beginning and end. The psalm *Judica me*, the Confession, and the other prayers said at the foot of the altar, are all part of the celebrant's preparation, once said (with many other psalms and prayers) in the sacristy, as the *Praeparatio ad Missam* in the Missal now is. There was great diversity as to this preparation till Pius V established our modern rule of saying so much only before the altar. In the same way all that follows the *Ite missa est* is an afterthought, part of the thanksgiving, not formally admitted till Pius V.

We have thus accounted for all the elements of the Mass. The next stage of its development is the growth of numerous local varieties of the Roman Mass in the Middle Ages. These medieval rites (Paris, Rouen, Trier, Sarum, and so on all over

Western Europe) are simply exuberant local modifications of the old Roman rite. The same applies to the particular uses of various religious orders (Carthusians, Dominicans, Carmelites etc.). None of these deserves to be called even a derived rite; their changes are only ornate additions and amplifications; though certain special points, such as the Dominican preparation of the offerings before the Mass begins, represent more Gallican influence. The Milanese and Mozarabic liturgies stand on quite a different footing; they are the descendants of a really different rite—the original Gallican—though they too have been considerably Romanized (see **LITURGY**).

Meanwhile the Mass was developing in other ways also. During the first centuries it had been a common custom for a number of priests to concelebrate; standing around their bishop, they joined in his prayers and consecrated the oblation with him. This is still common in the Eastern rites. In the West it had become rare by the thirteenth century. St. Thomas Aquinas (d. 1274) discusses the question, "Whether several priests can consecrate one and the same host."[11] He answers, of course, that they can, but quotes as an example only the case of ordination. In this case only has the practice been preserved. At the ordination of priests and bishops all the ordained concelebrate with the ordainer. In other cases concelebration was in the early Middle Ages replaced by separate private celebrations. No doubt the custom of offering each Mass for a special intention helped to bring about this change. The separate celebrations then involved the building of many altars in one church and the reduction of the ritual to the simplest possible form. The deacon and subdeacon were in this case dispensed with; the celebrant took their part as well as his own. One server took the part of the choir and all the other ministers, everything was said instead of being sung, the incense and kiss of peace were omitted. So we have the well-known rite of low Mass (*missa privata*). This then reacted on the high Mass (*missa solemnis*), so that at high Mass too the celebrant himself recites everything, even though it also be sung by the deacon, subdeacon, or choir. The custom of the intention of the Mass further led to Mass being said every day by each priest. But this has by no means been uniformly carried out. On the one hand we hear of an abuse of the same priest saying Mass several times in the day, which medieval councils constantly forbid. Again, many most pious priests did not celebrate daily. Bossuet (d. 1704), for instance, said Mass only on Sundays, Feasts, every day in Lent, and at other times when a special ferial Mass is provided in the Missal.[12] There is still no obligation for a priest to celebrate daily, though the custom is now very common. The Council of Trent desired that priests should celebrate at least on Sundays and solemn feasts (Session XXIII, chapter 14). Celebration with no assistants at all (*missa solitaria*) has continually been forbidden, as by the Synod of Mainz in 813. Another abuse was the *missa bifaciata* or *trifaciata*, in which the celebrant said the first part, from the *Introit* to the Preface, several times over and then joined to all one Canon, in order to satisfy several intentions. This too was forbidden by medieval councils. The *missa sicca* (dry Mass) was a common form of devotion used for funerals or marriages in the afternoon, when a real mass could not be said. It consisted of all of the Mass except the Offertory, Consecration and Communion. The *missa nautica* and *missa venatoria*, said at sea in rough weather and for hunters in a hurry, were kinds of dry Masses. In some monasteries each priest was obliged to say a dry Mass after the real (conventual) Mass. Since the reform of Pius V the dry Mass has gradually disappeared. The Mass of the Presanctified (*missa praesanctificatorum*) is a very old custom described by the Quinisext Council (Second Trullan Synod, 692). It is a Service (not really a Mass at all) of Communion from an oblation consecrated at a previous Mass and reserved. It is used in the Byzantine Church on the week days of Lent (except Saturdays); in the Roman Rite only on Good Friday.

Finally came uniformity in the old Roman Rite and the abolition of nearly all the medieval variants. The Council of Trent considered the question and formed a commission to prepare a uniform Missal. Eventually, the Missal was published by Pius V by the Bull *Quo primum* (still printed in it) of 14 July, 1570. That is really the last stage of the history of the Roman Mass. It is Pius V's Missal that is used throughout the Latin Church, except in a few cases where he allowed a modified use that had a prescription of at least two centuries. This exception saved the variants used by some religious orders and a few local rites as well as the Milanese and Mozarabic liturgies. Clement VIII (1604), Urban VIII (1634), and Leo XIII (1884) revised the book slightly in the rubrics and the texts of Scripture (see **LITURGICAL BOOKS**). Pius X has revised the chant (1908). But these revisions leave it still the Missal of Pius V. There has been since the Middle Ages unceasing change in the sense of additions of Masses for new feasts, the Missal now has a number of supplements that still grow (see **LITUR-GICAL BOOKS**), but liturgically these additions represent no real change. The new Masses are all built up exactly on the lines of the older ones.

We turn now to the present Roman Mass, without comparison the most important and widespread, as it is in many ways the most archaic service of the holy Eucharist in Christendom.

5. *The Present Roman Mass*.—The ritual of the Mass is affected by (1) the person who celebrates, (2) the day or the special occasion on which it is said, (3) the kind of Mass (high or low) celebrated. But in all cases the general scheme is the same. The normal ideal may be taken as high Mass sung by a priest on an ordinary Sunday or feast that has no exceptional feature.

Normally, Mass must be celebrated in a consecrated or blessed Church (private oratories or even rooms are allowed for special reasons: and at a consecrated altar (or at least on a consecrated altar-stone), and may be celebrated on any day in the year except Good Friday (restrictions are made against private celebrations on Holy Saturday, and in the case of private oratories for certain great feasts) at any time between dawn and midday. A priest may say only one Mass each day, except that on Christmas Day he may say three, and the first may (or rather, should) then be said immediately after midnight. In some countries a priest may also celebrate three times on All Souls' Day (2 November). Bishops may give leave to a priest to celebrate twice on Sundays and feasts of obligation, if otherwise the people could not fulfil their duty of hearing Mass. In cathedral and collegiate churches, as well as in those of religious orders who are bound to say the Canonical Hours every day publicly, there is a daily Mass corresponding to the Office and forming with it the completed cycle of the public worship of God. This official public Mass is called the *conventual* Mass; if possible it should be a high Mass, but, even if it be not, it always has some of the features of high Mass. The time for this conventual Mass on feasts and Sundays is after Terce has been said in choir. On Simples and *feriae* the time is after Sext; on *feriae* of Advent, Lent, on Vigils and Ember days after None. Votive Masses and the Requiem on All Souls' Day are said also after None; but ordinary requiems are said after Prime. The celebrant of Mass must be in the state of grace, fasting from midnight, free of irregularity and censure, and must observe all the rubrics and laws concerning the matter (azyme bread and pure wine), vestments, vessels, and ceremony.

The scheme of high Mass is this: the procession comes to the altar, consisting of thurifer, acolytes, master of ceremonies, subdeacon; deacon, and celebrant, all vested as the rubrics direct. First, the preparatory prayers are said at the foot of the altar; the altar is incensed, the celebrant reads at the south (Epistle) side the Introit and *Kyrie*. Meanwhile the choir sing the Introit and *Kyrie*. On days on which the *Te Deum* is said in the office, the celebrant intones the *Gloria in excelsis*, which is continued by the choir. Meanwhile the deacon, and subdeacon recite it, after which they may sit down until the choir has finished. After the greeting *Dominus vobiscum*, and its answer *Et cum spiritu tuo*, the celebrant chants the collect of the day, and after it as many more collects as are required either to commemorate other feasts or occasions, or are to be said by order of the bishop, or (on lesser days) are chosen by himself at his discretion from the collection in the Missal, according to the rubrics. The subdeacon chants the Epistle and the choir sings the Gradual. Both are read by the celebrant at the altar, according to the present law that he is also to recite whatever is sung by any one else. He blesses the incense, says the *Munda cor meum* prayer, and reads the Gospel at the north (Gospel) side. Meanwhile the deacon prepares to sing the Gospel. He goes in procession with the subdeacon, thurifer, and acolytes to a place on the north of the choir, and there chants it, the subdeacon holding the book, unless an ambo be used. If there is a sermon it should be preached immediately after the Gospel. This is the traditional place for the homily, after the lessons. On Sundays and certain feasts the Creed is said next, just as was the *Gloria*. At this point before or after the Creed (which is a later introduction, as we have seen), ends in theory the Mass of the Catechumens. The celebrant at the middle of the altar chants *Dominus vobiscum* and *Oremus*—the last remnant of the old prayers of the faithful. Then follows the offertory. The bread is offered to God with the prayer *Suscipe, sancte pater*; the deacon pours wine into the chalice and the subdeacon water. The chalice is offered by the celebrant in the same way as the bread (*Offerimus tibi Domine*), after which the gifts, the altar, the celebrant, ministers, and people are all incensed. Meanwhile the choir sings the Offertory. The celebrant washes his hands saying the *Lavabo*. After another offertory prayer (*Suscipe, sancta Trinitas*), and an address to the people (*Orate fratres*) with its answer which is not sung (it is a late addition), the celebrant says the secrets corresponding to the collects. The last secret ends with an *Ecphonesis* (*Per omnia saecula saeculorum*). This is only a warning of what is coming. When prayers began to be said silently, it still remained necessary to mark their ending, that people might know what is going on. So the last clauses were said or sung aloud. This so-called *Ecphonesis* is much developed in the Eastern rites. In the Roman Mass there are three cases of it—always the words: *Per omnia saecula saeculorum*, to which the choir answers *Amen*. After the *Ecphonesis* of the Secret comes the dialogue, *Sursum Corda*, etc., used with slight variations in all rites, and so the beginning of the Eucharistic prayer which we call the Preface, no longer counted as part of the Canon. The choir sings and the celebrant says the *Sanctus*. Then follows the Canon, beginning *Te igitur* and ending with an *Ecphonesis* before the Lord's Prayer. All its parts are described in the article **CANON OF THE MASS**. The Lord's Prayer follows, introduced by a little clause (*Praeceptis salutaribus moniti*) and followed by an embolism (see **LIBERA NOS**), said silently and ending with the third *Ecphonesis*. The Fraction follows with the versicle *Pax domini sit semper vobiscum*, meant to introduce the kiss of peace. The choir sings the *Agnus Dei*, which is said by the celebrant together with the first Communion prayer, before he gives the kiss to the deacon. He then says the two other Communion prayers, and receives Communion under both kinds. The Communion of the people follows. Meanwhile the choir sings the Communion (see **COMMUNION-ANTIPHON**). The chalice is purified and the post-Communions are sung, corresponding to the collects and secrets. Like the collects, they are introduced by the greeting *Dominus vobiscum* and its answer, and said at the south side. After another greeting by the celebrant the deacon sings the dismissal (see **Ite missa est**). There still follow, however, three later additions, a blessing by the celebrant, a short prayer that God may be pleased with the sacrifice (*Placeat tibi*), and the Last Gospel, normally the beginning of St. John (see **GOSPEL IN THE LITURGY**). The procession goes back to the sacristy.

This high Mass is the norm; it is only in the complete rite with deacon and subdeacon that the ceremonies can be understood. Thus, the rubrics of the Ordinary of the Mass always suppose that the Mass is high. Low Mass, said by a priest alone with one server, is a shortened and simplified form of the same thing. Its ritual can be explained only by a reference to high Mass. For instance, the celebrant goes over to the north side of the altar to read the Gospel, because that is the side to which the deacon goes in procession at high Mass; he turns round always by the right, because at high Mass he should not turn his back to the deacon, and so on. A *sung* Mass (*Missa Cantata*) is a modern compromise. It is really a low Mass, since the essence of high Mass is not the music but the deacon and subdeacon.

The ritual of the Mass is further affected by the dignity of the celebrant, whether bishop or only priest. There is something to be said for taking the Pontifical Mass as the standard, and explaining that of the simple priest as a modified form, just as a low Mass is a modified form of high Mass. On the other hand historically the case is not parallel throughout; some of the more elaborate pontifical ceremony is an afterthought, an adornment added later. Here it need only be said that the main difference of the pontifical Mass (apart from some special vestments) is that the bishop remains at his throne (except for the preparatory prayers at the altar steps and the incensing of the altar) till the Offertory; so in this case the change from the Mass of the Catechumens to that of the Faithful is still clearly marked. He also does not put on the maniple till after the preparatory prayers, again an archaic touch that marks them as being outside the original service. At low Mass the bishop's rank is marked only by a few unimportant details and by the later assumption of the maniple. Certain prelates, not bishops, use some pontifical ceremonies at Mass. The pope again has certain special ceremonies in high Mass, of which some represent remnants of older customs. Of these we note especially that he makes his Communion seated on the throne and drinks the consecrated wine through a little tube called *fistula*.

Durandus (see **DURANDUS**) and all the symbolic authors distinguish various parts of the Mass according to mystic principles. Thus it has four parts, corresponding to the four kinds of prayer named in I Tim., ii, 1. It is an *Obsecratio* from the Introit to the Offertory, an *Oratio* from the Offertory to the *Pater Noster*, a *Postulatio* to the Communion, a *Gratiarum actio* from then to the end (see **MASS, SACRIFICE OF**). The Canon especially has been divided according to all manner of systems some very ingenious. But the distinctions that are really important to the student of liturgy are, first the historic division between the Mass of the Catechumens and Mass of the Faithful, already explained, and then the great practical distinction between the changeable and unchangeable parts. The Mass consists of an unchanged framework into which at certain fixed points the variable prayers, lessons, and chants are fitted. The two elements are the *Common* and the *Proper of the day* (which, however, may again be taken from a common Mass provided for a number of similar occasions, as are the Commons of various classes of saints). The Common is the Ordinary of the Mass (*Ordinarium Missae*), now printed and inserted in the Missal between Holy Saturday and Easter Day. Every Mass is fitted into that scheme; to follow Mass one must first find that. In it occur rubrics directing that something is to be said or sung, which is not printed at this place. The first rubric of this kind occurs after the incensing at the beginning: "Then the Celebrant signing himself with the sign of the cross begins the Introit." But no Introit follows. He must know what Mass he is to say and find the Introit, and all the other proper parts, under their heading among the large collection of Masses that fill the book. These Propers or variable parts are first the four chants of the choir, the Introit, Gradual (or tract, Alleluia, and perhaps after it a Sequence), Offertory, and Communion; then the lessons (Epistle, Gospel, sometimes Old Testament lessons too), then the prayers said by the celebrant (Collect, Secret, post-Communion; often several of each to commemorate other feasts or days). By fitting these into their places in the Ordinary the whole Mass is put together. There are, however, two other elements that occupy an intermediate place between the Ordinary and the Proper. These are the Preface and a part of the Canon. We have now only eleven prefaces, ten special ones and a common preface. They do not then change sufficiently to be printed over and over again among the proper Masses, so all are inserted in the Ordinary; from them naturally the right one must be chosen according to the rubrics. In the same way, five great feasts have a special clause in the *Communicantes* prayer in the Canon, two (Easter and Whitsunday) have a special *Hanc Igitur* prayer, one day (Maundy Thursday) affects the *Qui pridie* form. These exceptions are printed after the corresponding prefaces; but Maundy Thursday, as it occurs only once, is to be found in the Proper of the day (see **CANON OF THE MASS**).

It is these parts of the Mass that vary, and, because of them, we speak of the Mass of such a day or of such a feast. To be able to find the Mass for any given day requires knowledge of a complicated set of rules. These rules are given in the rubrics at the beginning of the Missal. In outline the system is this. First a Mass is provided for every day in the year, according to the seasons of the Church. Ordinary week days (*feriaee*) have the Mass of the preceding Sunday with certain regular changes; but *feriae* of Lent, rogation and ember-days, and vigils have special Masses. All this makes up the first part of the Missal called *Proprium de tempore*. The year is then overladen, as it were, by a great quantity of feasts of saints or of special events determined by the day of the month (these make up the *Proprium Sanctorum*). Nearly every day in the year is now a feast of some kind; often there are several on one day. There is then constantly coincidence (*concurrentia*) of several possible Masses on one day. There are cases in which two or more conventual Masses are said, one for each of the coinciding offices. Thus, on *feriae* that have a special office, if a feast occurs as well, the Mass of the feast is said after Terce, that of the *feria* after None. If a feast falls on the Eve of Ascension Day there are three Conventual Masses—of the feast after Terce, of the Vigil after Sext, of Rogation day after None. But, in churches that have no official conventual Mass and in the case of the priest who says Mass for his own devotion, one only of the coinciding Masses is said, the others being (usually) commemorated by saying their collects, secrets, and post-Communions after those of the Mass chosen. To know which Mass to choose one must know their various degrees of dignity. All days or feasts are arranged in this scale: *feria*, simple, semidouble, double, greater double, double of the second class, double of the first class. The greater feast then is the one kept: by transferring feasts to the next free day, it is arranged that two feasts of the same rank do not coincide. Certain important days are privileged, so that a higher feast cannot displace them. Thus nothing can displace the first Sundays of Advent and Lent, Passion and Palm Sundays. These are the so-called first-class Sundays. In the same way nothing can displace Ash Wednesday or any day of Holy Week. Other days (for instance the so-called second-class Sundays, that is the others in Advent and Lent, *Septuagesima, Sexagesima, and Quinqugesima*) can only be re-placed by doubles of the first class. Ordinary Sundays count as semidoubles, but have precedence over other semidoubles. The days of an Octave are semidoubles; the octave day is a double. The octaves of Epiphany, Easter, and Pentecost (the original three greatest feasts of all) are closed against any other feast. The displaced feast is commemorated, except in the case of a great inferiority: the rules for this are given among the *Rubricae generales* of the Missal (VII: *de Commemorationibus*). On semidoubles and days below that in rank other collects are always added to that of the day to make up an uneven number. Certain ones are prescribed regularly in the Missal, the celebrant may add others at his discretion. The bishop of the diocese may also order collects for special reasons (the so-called *Orationes imperatae*). As a general rule the Mass must correspond to the office of the day, including its commemorations. But the Missal contains a collection of Votive Masses, that may be said on days not above a semidouble in rank. The bishop or pope may order a votive Mass for a public cause to be said on any day but the very highest. All these rules are explained in the rubrics of the Missal. There are two other Masses which, inasmuch as they do not correspond to the office, may be considered a kind of votive Mass: the Nuptial Mass (*missa pro sponso et sponsa*), said at weddings, and the Requiem Mass, said for the faithful departed, which have a number of special characteristics (see **NUPTIAL MASS** and **REQUIEM MASS**). The calendar (*Ordo*) published yearly in each diocese or province gives the office and Mass for every day.

That the Mass, around which such complicated rules have grown, is the central feature of the Catholic religion needs hardly to be said. During the Reformation and always the Mass has been the test. The word of the Reformers: "It is the Mass that matters", was true. The Cornish insurgents in 1549 rose against the new religion, and expressed their whole cause in their demand to have the Prayer-book Communion Service taken away and the old Mass restored. The long persecution of Catholics in England took the practical form of laws chiefly against saying Mass; for centuries the occupant of the English throne was obliged to manifest his Protestantism, not by a general denial of the whole system of Catholic dogma, but by a formal repudiation of the doctrine of Transubstantiation and of the Mass. As union with Rome is the bond between Catholics, so is our common share in this, the most venerable rite in Christendom, the witness and safeguard of that bond. It is by

his share in the Mass in Communion that the Catholic pro-
claims his union with the great Church. As excommunication
means the loss of that right in those who are expelled so the
Mass and Communion are the visible bond between people,
priest, and bishop, who are all one body who share the one
Bread.

Chapter Notes

1 *I Clement Ad Cor.*, XXXVIII, 4.

2 *I Apology*, LXV, 3, 5; LXVI, §1; LXVII, 5.

3 *I Epistle*, XX, 4-5.

4 Sermon XLIX, P.L., XXXVIII, 324.

5 P.L., CXIX, 72.

6 *Merlin* in the Early English Text Society, II, 375.

7 *Sir Cauline*, Child's Ballads, III, 175.

8 Duchesne, pp. 168-169.

9 P.L., LXXVII, 956.

10 E. Bishop, "The Earliest Roman Massbook", *Dublin Review*, 1894, pp.
241-301.

11 *Summa Theologica*, III , Q, 82, ad 2.

12 Jacques Bénigne Bossuet (1627-1704) Bishop of Meaux, preacher and
controversialist. He studied under St Vincent de Paul and was ordained
at Metz in 1652 where he spent seven years in study, controversy with
Protestants, and preaching. He converted Marshal Turenne from Protestantism in 1668 and acted as tutor to the Dauphin from 1670-81. His
complete works extend to thirty-one volumes and his *History of the Variations of the Protestant Churches* (2 vols. 1688) is a masterly exposition of
the errors of this heresy. Bossuet is undoubtedly one of the greatest
preachers of all time. His funeral orations on Henrietta Maria (1669),
Henriette Anne d'Angleterre (1670), and the Prince de Condé (1687)
are classics (Ed.).

8

INTROIT

Introit. The Introit (*Introitus*) of the Mass is the fragment of a psalm with its antiphon sung while the celebrant and ministers enter the church and approach the altar. In all Western rites the Mass began with such a processional psalm since the earliest times of which we have any record. As it was sung by the choir it is not, of course, to be found in sacramentaries; but introits are contained in the first antiphonaries known (the Gregorian Antiphonary at Montpellier, the St. Gall manuscript, that represent a seventh-century tradition). The First Roman *Ordo* (sixth to seventh century) says that as soon as the candles are lit and everything is ready, the singers come and stand before the altar on either side, "and presently the leader of the choir begins the antiphon for the entrance (*antiphona ad introitum*)". As soon as the deacons hear his voice they go to the pope, who rises and comes from the sacristy to the altar in procession.[1] There is every reason to suppose that as soon as the Western liturgies were arranged in definite forms, the entrance was always accompanied by the chant of a psalm, which from that circumstance was called at Rome *Introitus* or *Psalmus* or *Antiphona ad Introitum*. The old Gallican Rite called it *Antiphona ad Praelegendum*; at Milan it is the *Ingressa*; in the Mozarabic, Carthusian, Dominican, and Carmelite books, *Officium*. The Introit was a whole psalm sung with the *Gloria Patri* and *Sicut erat* verses, preceded and followed by an antiphon in the usual way. No doubt originally it was sung as a

232

solo while the choir repeated a response after each verse (the *psalmus responsorius* of which we still have an example in the *Invitatorium* at Matins), then the later way of singing psalms (*psalmus antiphonarius*) was adopted for the Introit too. The *Liber Pontificalis* ascribes this antiphonal chant at the Introit to Pope Celestine I (422-32): "He ordered that the psalms of David be sung antiphonally (*antiphonatim*, by two choirs alternately) by all before the Sacrifice, which was not done before; but only the epistle of St. Paul was read and the holy Gospel." The text seems even to attribute the use of the Introit psalm in any form to this pope. Medieval writers take this idea from the *Liber Pontificalis*: "Pope Celestine ordered psalms to be sung at the entrance (*ad introitum*) of the Mass. Pope Gregory (I) afterwards composed antiphons in modulation for the entrance of the Mass."[2] It is perhaps safest to account for our Introit merely as a development of the processional psalm sung during the entrance of the celebrant and his ministers, as psalms were sung in processions from very early times. But it soon began to be curtailed. Its object was only to accompany the entrance, so there was no reason for going on with it after the celebrant had arrived at the altar. Already in the First Roman *Ordo* as soon as the pope is ready to begin Mass he signs to the choir-master to leave out the rest of the psalm and go on at once to the *Gloria Patri*. Since the early Middle Ages the psalm has been further shortened to one verse.[3] So it received the form it still has, namely: an antiphon, one verse of a psalm, *Gloria Patri, Sicut erat*, the antiphon repeated. In the Milanese Rite the antiphon of the *Ingressa* is not repeated except in Requiem Masses; on the other hand, in some medieval uses it was repeated several times. On great feasts the Carmelites still repeat it twice at the end. The antiphon is taken as a rule from the Psalter (Durandus calls such introits *regulares* [see **DURANDUS**]); sometimes (e.g., second and third Christmas Mass, Ascension-Day, Whit-Sunday, etc.) from another part of the Bible; more rarely (Assumption, All Saints, many

Masses of Our Lady, *Salve sancta parens*, Requiems, etc.) it is a composition by some later writer. The verse of the psalm in the earlier introits is the first (obviously still a fragment of the whole), except that when the antiphon itself is the first verse the "psalm" is the next (twelfth and fifteenth Sundays after Pentecost, etc.). In later times it has become common to choose a suitable verse regardless of this rule (e.g. the Crown of Thorns Mass for Friday after Ash Wednesday, St. Ignatius Loyola on 31 July, etc.). The text of the psalms used in the introits (as throughout the Missal) is not the Vulgate but the *Itala*. In Paschal time two Alleluias are added to the antiphon, sometimes (Easter Day, Low Sunday, the Third and Fourth Sundays after Easter, etc.) there are three. In Requiems and Masses *de tempore* in Passiontide, when the Psalm *Judica* is not said, there is no *Gloria Patri* at the Introit. On Holy Saturday and at the chief Mass on Whitsun Eve (when the prophecies are read) there is no Introit at all. The reason of this is obvious. The Introit accompanies the entrance; but on these occasions the celebrant has been at the altar for some time before Mass begins. We name Masses (that is the complex of changeable prayers that make up the *Proprium*) from the first words of the Introit by which they begin. Thus the Mass for the first Sunday of Advent is called *Ad te levavi*; the two Masses of the Sacred Heart are distinguished as *Miserebitur* and *Egredimini*; a Mass for the dead is spoken of as a Requiem, and so on. There is nothing corresponding to our Introit in the Eastern rites. In all of them the liturgy begins quite differently. The preparation (vesting, preparation of the offerings) takes place in the sanctuary, so there is no procession to the altar.

Ritual Of The Introit.— At high (or sung) Mass till quite lately the rule had obtained that the choir did not begin the Introit till the celebrant began the first prayers at the foot of the altar. Now the new Vatican Gradual (1908) has restored the old principle, that it is to be sung while the procession moves from the sacristy to the altar. (*De ritibus servandis in cantu missae* in the introduction.) It should therefore be begun as soon as the head of the procession appears in the church. One or more cantors sing to the sign *, all continue; the cantors alone sing the first half of the psalm and the V. *Gloria Patri* (*ibid.*). The celebrant, having finished the preparatory prayers at the altar-steps, goes up to the altar and kisses it (saying meanwhile the two short prayers, *Aufer a nobis* and *Oramus te*); then, going to the left (Epistle) side, he reads from the Missal the Introit, just as it is sung. This is one of the continual reactions of low Mass on high Mass. When the custom of low Mass began (in the early Middle Ages) the celebrant had to supply all the parts of deacon, subdeacon, and choir himself. Then, as he became used to saying these parts, he said them even at high Mass too they were, besides, chanted by others. So this rule has obtained that everything is said by the celebrant. The recital of the Introit should be considered as the real beginning of Mass, since what has gone before is rather of the nature of the celebrant's preparation. For this reason he makes the sign of the cross at its first words, according to the general rule of beginning all solemn functions (in this case the Mass) with that sign. At Requiem Masses he makes the cross not on himself but over the Missal, *quasi aliquem benedicens*, says the rubric.[4] This is understood as directing the blessing to the souls in purgatory. At low Mass there is no change here, save the omission of the chant by the choir.

Chapter Notes

[1] *Ordo Rom I*, p. 128.

[2] Honorius of Autun, *Gemma animae*, P.L. CLXXII.

[3] Durandus, IV, 5.

[4] *Rit. cel.*, XIII, I.

9

CONFITEOR

The *Confiteor* (so called from the first word, *confiteor*, I confess) is a general confession of sins; it is used in the Roman Rite at the beginning of Mass and on various other occasions as a preparation for the reception of some grace.

1. *History of the Confiteor*.—It is first heard of as the preparation for sacramental confession and as part of the preparation for Mass. Both the original Eastern liturgies begin with a confession of sin made by the celebrant. The first Roman *sacramentaries* and *ordos* tell us nothing about this preparation; they all describe the Mass as beginning at the Introit. The *Confiteor* in some form was probably from an early date one of the private prayers said by the celebrant in the sacristy before he began Mass. But the Sixth Roman *Ordo*, written apparently in the tenth or eleventh century, tells us that at the beginning of Mass the pontiff "bowing down prays to God for forgiveness of his sins". So by the eleventh century the preparation is already made at the altar. In the "Canonical Rule" of Chrodegang of Metz (d. 743) the questions put by the priest to the penitent before confession contain a form that suggests our *Confiteor*: "First of all prostrate yourself humbly in the sight of God ... and pray Blessed Mary with the holy Apostles and Martyrs and Confessors to pray to the Lord for you."[1] So also Egbert of York (d. 766) gives a short form that is the germ of our present prayer: "Say to him to whom you wish to confess your sins: through my fault that I have sinned exceedingly in thought, word, and deed." In answer the confessor says almost exactly our *Misereatur*.[2] But it is in *Micrologus* (Bernold of Constance, d. 1100) that we first find the *Confiteor* quoted as part of the introduction of the Mass. The form here is: *Confiteor Deo omnipotenti, istis Sanctis et omnibus Sanctis et tibi frater, quia peccavi in cogitatione, in locutione, in opere, in pollutione mentis et corporis. Ideo precor te, ora pro me*. The *Misereatur* and *Indulgentiam* follow, the former slightly different, but the latter exactly as we have it now.

In the *Ordo Romanus XIV* (by Cardinal James Cajetan in the fourteenth century), we find our *Confiteor* exactly, but for the slight modification: *Quia peccavi nimis cogitatione, delectatione, consensu, verbo et opere*. The Third Council of Ravenna (1314), orders in its Rubric xv our *Confiteor*, word for word, to be used throughout that province. The form, and especially the list of saints invoked, varies considerably in the Middle Ages. Cardinal Bona quotes a number of such forms.[3] In many Missals it is shorter than ours: *Confiteor Deo, beatae Mariae, omnibus sanctis et vobis* (the Sarum Missal). In the Missal of Paul III (1534-1549) it is: *Confiteor Deo omnipotenti, B. Mariae semper Virgini, B. Petro et omnibus Sanctis et vobis Fratres, quia peccavi, mea culpa: precor vos orare pro me*. Since the edition of Pius V (1566-1572) our present form is the only one to be used throughout the Roman Rite, with the exceptions of the Carthusian, Carmelite, and Dominican Offices, whose Missals, having been proved to have existed for more than 200 years, are still allowed. These three forms are quite short, and contain only one *mea culpa*; the Dominicans invoke, besides the Blessed Virgin, St. Dominic. Moreover, some other orders have the privilege of adding the name of their founder after that of St. Paul (the Franciscans for instance), and the local patron is inserted at the same place in a few local uses. Otherwise the *Confiteor* must always be said exactly as it is in the Roman Missal.[4]

2. Use of the Confiteor.—The prayer is said sometimes as a double form of mutual confession, first by the celebrant to the people and then by the people to him, and sometimes only once, as a single form. As a double form it is used: (1) as part of the introductory prayers of Mass said before the priest goes up to the altar, after the Psalm *Judica me*.[5] (2) in the public recital of the Divine Office as part of the *Preces* at Prime (so that it is omitted on doubles and in octaves), and always in the beginning of Compline. As a single form it occurs: (1) during Mass, a second time, if anyone receives Holy Communion besides the celebrant; 2) when Holy Communion is given outside of Mass; (3) before the administration of extreme unction (when it may be said in Latin or in the vulgar tongue; (4) before the Apostolic blessing is given to a dying person; (5) the Ritual further directs that penitents should begin their confession by saying the *Confiteor* either in Latin or in their own language, or at least begin with these words: *Confiteor Deo omnipotenti et tibi pater*; (6) lastly the *Caeremoniale Episcoporum* ordains that when a bishop sings high Mass, the deacon should sing the *Confiteor* after the sermon; the preacher then reads out the Indulgence given by the bishop, and the bishop adds a modified form of the *Misereatur* (in which he again invokes the saints named in the *Confiteor*), the *Indulgentiam*, and finally his blessing. This is the normal ceremony for the publication of Indulgences.[6]

3. Rite of the Confiteor.—The form of words is too well known to need quotation. When it is used as a double form, the celebrant first makes his confession, using the words *vobis fratres* and *vos fratres*, the servers or ministers say the *Misereatur* in the singular (*tui, peccatis tuis*), and then make their confession addressed to the priest (*tibi pater, te pater*). He says the *Misereatur* in the plural (*Misereatur vestri*, etc.), and finally, making the sign of the cross, adds the short prayer *Indulgentiam*. Both the *Misereatur* and the *Indulgentiam* are answered with *Amen*. When used as a single form the priest's confession is left out, the deacon, or server, says the *Confiteor* (*tibi pater*, etc.), the celebrant responds with the *Misereatur* and *Indulgentiam*. A person saying the prayer alone (for instance, in the private recital of the Divine Office) says the *Confiteor* leaving out the clauses *tibi pater* or *vobis fratres*, etc., altogether, and changes the answer to *Misereatur nostri* and *peccatis nostris*. Before Communion at high Mass and before the promulgation of Indulgences the *Confiteor* is sung by the deacon to the tone given in the *Caeremoniale Episcoporum*.[7] The *Misereatur* and *Indulgentiam* are never sung.

Chapter Notes

1   Chrodeg. Met., *Reg. Canon.*, cap. xxxii, in P.L., LXXXIX, 1072.

2   Bona, Bk. II, ii, v.

3   *Ibid.*, II, 5-7.

4   S.R.C.,13 February, 1666; *De SS. Missae*, II, iii, pp. 11-12.

5   *Rit. cel.*, III, 7-9.

6   *Caerimoniale*, I, ch. xxii, 4; II, ch. xxxix, 1-4.

7   *Ibid.*, II, ch. xxxix, 1.

10

KYRIE ELEISON

Kyrie Eleison—Lord have mercy (the Latin transliteration supposes a pronunciation as in Modern Greek) is a very old, even pre-Christian ejaculation used constantly in all Christian liturgies. Arrian quotes it in the second century: "Invoking God we say *Kyrie eleison*."[1] A more obvious precedent for Christian use was the occurrence of the same formula in the Old Testament (Ps. IV, 2; VI, 3; IX, 14; XXV, 11; Isa., xxxiii, 2; Tob., viii, 10, etc., in the Septuagint). In these places it seems already to be a quasi-liturgical exclamation. So also in the New Testament the form occurs repeatedly (Matt., ix, 27; xx, 30; xv, 22; Mark, x, 47; Luke, xvi, 24; xvii, 13).

1. *History.*—It is not mentioned by the Apostolic Fathers or the Apologists. The first certain example of its use in the liturgy is in that of the eighth book of the *Apostolic Constitutions*. Here it is the answer of the people to the various *Synaptai* (Litanies) chanted by the deacon. That is still its normal use in the Eastern rites. The deacon sings various clauses of a litany, to each of which the people answer, *Kyrie Eleison*. Of the Greek Fathers of the fourth century, Eusebius, Athanasius, Basil, Cyril of Jerusalem, and the two Gregories do not mention it. But it occurs often in St. John Chrysostom. Its introduction into the Roman Mass has been much discussed. It is certain that the liturgy at Rome was at one time said in Greek (to the end of the second century apparently). It is tempting to look upon

our *Kyrie Eleison* as a surviving fragment from that time. Such, however, does not seem to be the case. Rather the form was borrowed from the East and introduced into the Latin Mass later. The older Latin Fathers, Tertullian, Cyprian, etc., do not mention it. Etheria (Silvia) heard it sung at Jerusalem in the fourth century (see **GLOSSARY**). It is evidently a strange form to her, and she translates it: "As the deacon says the names of various people (the Intercession) a number of boys stand and answer always, *Kyrie Eleison*, as we should say, *Miserere Domine*." The first evidence of its use in the West is the third canon of the Second Council of Vaison (Vasio in the province of Arles), in 529. From this canon it appears that the form was recently introduced at Rome and in Italy (Milan?): "Since both in the Apostolic See as also in all the provinces of the East and in Italy a sweet and most pious custom has been introduced that *Kyrie Eleison* be said with great insistence and compunction, it seems good to us too that this holy custom be introduced at Matins and Mass and Vespers."[2] The council says nothing of Africa or Spain, though it mentions Africa in other canons about liturgical practices (Can.v). It appears to mean that *Kyrie Eleison* should be sung by the people *cum grandi affectu*. This council represents a Romanizing movement in Gaul.

The next famous witness to its use in the West is St. Gregory I (590-604). He writes to John of Syracuse to defend the Roman Church from imitating Constantinople by the use of this form, and is at pains to point out the difference between its use at Rome and in the East: "We neither said nor say *Kyrie Eleison* as it is said by the Greeks. Among the Greeks all say it together, with us it is said by the clerks and answered by the people, and we say *Christe Eleison* as many times, which is not the case among the Greeks. Moreover in daily Masses some things usually said are left out by us; we say only *Kyrie Eleison* and *Christe Eleison*, that we may dwell longer on these words of prayer."[3] The last words appear to mean that sometimes other prayers are left out that there may be more time for singing the *Kyrie Eleison*. We see also from this passage that in St. Gregory's time the special Roman use of the alternative form *Christe Eleison* (unknown in the Gallican and Eastern rites) existed. It seems inevitable to connect the *Kyrie Eleison* in the Roman Mass with an original litany. Its place corresponds exactly to where it occurs as part of a litany in the Syrian-Byzantine Liturgy; it is still always sung at the beginning of litanies in the Roman Rite too, and St. Gregory refers to "some things usually said" in connection with it. What can these things be but clauses of a litany, sung, as in the East, by a deacon? Moreover there are still certain cases in the Roman Rite, obviously of an archaic nature, where a litany occurs at the place of the *Kyrie*. Thus on Easter Eve the Mass begins with a litany of which the last clause (*Kyrie Eleison*, repeated three times; *Christe Eleison*, repeated three times; *Kyrie Eleison*, repeated three times) is sung as the celebrant says the first prayers of the Mass, and correspond in every way to our usual *Kyrie*. So also at ordinations the Litany is sung towards the beginning of the Mass. In this connection it may be noted that down to the late Middle Ages the *Kyrie* of the Mass was left out when it had just been sung in a Litany before Mass, as on Rogation days. We may suppose, then, that at one time the Roman Mass began (after the Introit) with a litany of general petitions very much of the nature of the third part of our Litany of the Saints. This would correspond exactly to our great *Synapte* (see **GLOSSARY**) in the Syrian Rite. Only, from what has been said, we conclude that the answer of the people was in Latin—the *Miserere Domine* of Etheria, or *Te rogamus, audi nos*, or some such form. About the fifth century the Greek *Kyrie Eleison* was adopted by the West, and at Rome with the alternative form *Christe Eleison*. This was then sung, not as in the East only by the people, but alternately by cantors and people. It displaced the older Latin exclamations at this place and eventually remained alone as the only remnant of the old litany.

The first Roman *Ordo* (sixth-seventh centuries) describes a not yet fixed number of *Kyries* sung at what is still their place in the Mass: "The school [*schola*, choir] having finished the Antiphon (the Introit) begins *Kyrie Eleison*. But the leader of the school watches the Pontiff that he should give him a sign if he wants to change the number of the litany."[4] In the *Ordo of Saint Amand*, written in the eighth century, we have already our number of invocations: "When the school has finished the Antiphon the Pontiff makes a sign that *Kyrie Eleison* should be said. And the school says it (*dicit* always covers singing in liturgical Latin; cf. the rubrics of the present Missal: *dicit cantando vel legendo* before the *Pater Noster*), and the *Regionarii* who stand below the ambo repeat it. When they have repeated it the third time the Pontiff signs again that *Christae* [sic] *Eleison* be said. This having been said the third time he signs again that *Kyrie Eleison* be said. And when they have completed it nine times he signs that they should stop." So we have, at least from the eighth century, our present practice of singing immediately after the Introit three times *Kyrie Eleison*, three times *Christe Eleison*, three times *Kyrie Eleison*, making nine invocations altogether. Obviously the first group is addressed to God the Father, the second to God the Son, the third to God the Holy Ghost. The medieval commentators are fond of connecting the nine-fold invocation with the nine choirs of angels. From a very early time the solemnity of the *Kyrie* was marked by a long and ornate chant. In the Eastern rites, too, it is always sung to long neums. It is still the most elaborate of all our plainsong melodies. In the Middle Ages the *Kyrie* was constantly farced (see **GLOSSARY**) with other words to fill up the long neums. The names of the various *Kyries* in the Vatican Gradual (for instance, *Kyrie Cunctipotens genitor Deus* of the tenth century, *Kyrie magnae Deus potentiae* of the thirteenth century, etc.) are still traces of this. As an example of these innumerable and often very long farcings, this comparatively short one from the Sarum Missal may serve:

Kyrie, rex genitor ingenite, vera essentia, eleyson.

Kyrie, luminis fons rerumque conditor, eleyson.

Kyrie, qui nos tuae imaginis signasti specie, eleyson.

Christe, Dei forma humana particeps, eleyson.

Christe, lux oriens per quem sunt omnia, eleyson.

Christe, qui perfecta es sapientia, eleyson.

Kyrie, spiritus vivifice, vitae vis, eleyson.

Kyrie, utriusque vapor in quo cuncta, eleyson.

Kyrie, expurgator scelerum et largitor gratiae;

quaesumus propter nostras offensas noli nos relinquere,

O consolator dolentis animae, eleyson.

Lord, King and Father unbegotten, True Essence of the
Godhead, have mercy on us.

Lord, Fount of light and Creator of all things, have mercy on
us.

Lord, Thou who hast signed us with the seal of Thine image,
have mercy on us.

Christ, True God and True Man, have mercy on us.

Christ, Rising Sun, through whom are all things, have mercy
on us.

Christ, Perfection of Wisdom, have mercy on us.

Lord, vivifying Spirit and power of life, have mercy on us.

Lord, Breath of the Father and the Son, in Whom are all
things, have mercy on us.

Lord, Purger of sin and Almoner of grace, we beseech Thee
abandon us not because of our Sins,

O Consoler of the sorrowing soul, have mercy on us.

Notice the greater length of the last farcing to fit the neums
of the last *Kyrie*, which are always longer. Sometimes the essential words are mixed up with the farcing in a very curious
mixture of Latin and Greek: *Conditor Kyrie omnium ymas*

creaturarum eleyson. The reformed Missal of Pius V happily abolished these and all other farcings of the liturgical text.

2. In the Roman Rite.—In the Mass, the three groups of invocations are sung by the choir immediately after the Introit. They form the beginning of the choir's part of the Ordinary. A number of plainsong Masses are provided in the Gradual, each characterised and named after the *Kyrie* that begins it. Although each Mass is appointed for a certain occasion (e.g., for solemn feasts, doubles, Masses of the B.V.M., etc.) there is no law against using them without regard to this arrangement. Moreover, except on ferias, which keep their very simple chants, the various parts (*Kyrie, Gloria*, etc.) of different Masses may be combined (see rubric after the fourth Creed in the Vatican "Gradual"). The new Vatican edition also provides a series of other chants, including eleven *Kyries, ad libitum*. The *Kyrie Eleison* (as all the Ordinary and Proper of the choir) may also be sung to figured music that does not offend against the rules of Pius X's *Motu proprio* on church music (22 Nov., 1903). Meanwhile the celebrant, having incensed the altar and read the Introit at the Epistle side, says the *Kyrie* there with joined hands alternately with the deacon, sub-deacon, and surrounding servers. At low Mass the celebrant after the Introit comes to the middle of the altar and there says the *Kyrie* alternately with the server (*Ritus celebratione* in the Missal, iv, 2, 7). The *Kyrie* is said in this way at every Mass with the exception of Holy Saturday and also of the Mass on Whitsun Eve at which the prophecies and litany are chanted. On these occasions the cantors finish the litany by singing the nine invocations of the *Kyrie*. After the prayers at the foot of the altar the celebrant goes up, incenses the altar, and then at once intones the *Gloria*. But he should say the *Kyrie* in a low voice himself first. Besides in the Mass, the *Kyrie* occurs repeatedly in other offices of the Roman Rite, always in the form *Kyrie Eleison, Christe Eleison, Kyrie Eleison* (each invocation once only). It begins the *preces feriales* at Lauds, Terce, Sext, None, Vespers; it begins the *preces* at Prime and Compline. It is sung after the *Responsorium* at funerals, said at marriages and on many other occasions for blessings and consecrations. In these cases it generally precedes the *Pater Noster*. It also begins and ends the Litany of the Saints. As an imitation of this it is always placed at the beginning of the various other private litanies which are imitations of the official one.

3. *In Other Rites*.— In the first place, the invocation *Christe Eleison* is purely Roman. With one exception, obviously a Roman interpolation in the Mozarabic Rite, it does not occur in any other use. Local medieval uses had it, of course; but they are only slight local modifications of the Roman Rite, not really different rites at all. In the Gallican Mass, as described by Germanus of Paris, three boys sing *Kyrie Eleison* three times after the *Trisagion* (see **GLOSSARY**) which follows the Antiphon at the entrance, then follows the *Benedictus*. These chants represent the beginning of the Mass. After the Gospel and Homily comes a litany sung by the deacon like the Syrian and Byzantine *synaptai*. The people answer in Latin: *Precamur te Domine, miserere;* but at the end come three *Kyrie Eleisons*. The Milanese rite shows its Gallican origin by its use of the *Kyrie*. Here, too, the form is always *Kyrie Eleison* three times (never *Christe Eleison*). It occurs after the *Gloria* which has replaced the older *Trisagion*, after the Gospel, where the Gallican litany was, and after the Post-communion always said by the celebrant alone. It also occurs throughout the Milanese offices, more or less as at Rome, but always in the form of *Kyrie Eleison* three times. The Mozarabic Liturgy does not know the form at all, except in one isolated case. In the Mass for the Dead, after the singing of the chant called *Sacrificium* (corresponding to the Roman Offertory) the celebrant says *Kyrie Eleison*, and the choir answers *Christe Eleison, Kyrie Eleison*.[5] This is obviously a Roman interpolation.

All the Eastern rites use the form *Kyrie Eleison* constantly.

It is the usual answer of the people or choir to each clause of the various litanies sung by the deacon throughout the service. It also occurs many other times, for instance in the Antiochene Rite it is sung twelve times, at Alexandria three times just before the Communion. In the Byzantine Rite it comes over and over again, nearly always in a triple form, among the *Troparia*[6] and other prayers said by various people throughout the Office as well as in the Liturgy. A conspicuous place in this rite is at the dismissal. In general it may be said to occur most frequently in the Syrian-Byzantine family of Liturgies. In the Syriac liturgies it is said in Greek, spelled in Syriac letters *Kurillison* so also in the Coptic liturgies (in Greek letters of course—nearly all the Coptic alphabet is Greek); in the Abyssinian Rite it is spelled out: *Kiralayeson*. The Nestorians translate it into Syriac and the Armenians into Armenian. All the versions of the Byzantine Rite used by the various Orthodox and Uniate Churches (Old Slavonic, Arabic, Rumanian, etc.) also translate *Kyrie Eleison*.

Chapter Notes:

[1] *Diatribae Epicteti*, II, 7.

[2] Hefele-Leclercq, *Histoires des Conciles* (Paris, 1908), pp. 1113-1114.

[3] *Ep.* ix in P.L. LXXVII, 956.

[4] *Ordo Rom. I*, p. 130.

[5] *Missale mixtum* in P.L., LXXXV 101, 1018, 1021, 102, etc.—the various Masses for the Dead.

[6] *Troparion*, plural *Troparia*, in the Eastern Church a generic term to designate a stanza of religious poetry. *Troparion* should not be confused with Trope (see **GLOSSARY**) in the Western Church, a short series of words added to a text such as the *Kyrie* to amplify and embelish it (Ed.).

11

Gloria in Excelsis Deo

The great doxology (*hymnus angelicus*) in the Mass is a version of a very old Greek form. It begins with the words sung by the angels at Christ's birth (Luke,ii,14). To this verse others were added very early, forming a doxology. In a slightly different form it occurs at the beginning of a morning prayer in the *Apostolic Constitutions*.[1] The text which has a subordinationist colouring, goes back at least to the third century, some scholars think even to the first.[2] It is sung by the Byzantine Church at the *Orthros* (see **GLOSSARY**). In this form it has more verses than in the Latin, and ends with the *Trisagion* (see **GLOSSARY**). It is not used in the Liturgy by any Eastern Church. Only the first clause (the text of Luke ii,14) occurs as part of the people's answer to the words, "Holy things for the holy", at the elevation in the Liturgy of the *Apostolic Constitutions,* as part of the Offertory and Communion prayers in St. James's Liturgy, at the kiss of peace in the Abyssinian rite, in the Nestorian *Prothesis* (see **GLOSSARY**), and again at the beginning of their Liturgy, in the Byzantine *Prothesis*. The tradition is that it was translated into Latin by St. Hilary of Poitiers (d. 366). It is quite possible that he learned it during his exile in the East (360) and brought back a version of it with him.

The Latin version differs from the present Greek form. They correspond down to the end of the Latin, which however adds: *Tu solus altissimus* and *Cum sancto spiritu*. The Greek then goes on: "Every day I will bless Thee and will glorify Thy name for ever, and for ever and ever", and continues with ten more verses, chiefly from psalms, to the *Trisagion* and *Gloria Patri*.

"The *Liber pontificalis*"[3] says Pope Telesphorus (c.125- c.136) "ordered that...on the Birth of the Lord Masses should be said at night...and that the angelic hymn, that is *Gloria in excelsis Deo*, should be said before the sacrifice"; also "that Pope Symmachus [498-514] ordered that the hymn, *Gloria in excelsis*, should be said every Sunday and on the feasts [*natalicia*] of martyrs." The *Gloria* is to be said in its present place, after the *Introit* and *Kyrie*, but only by bishops. We see it then introduced first for Christmas, on the feast to which it specially belongs, then extended to Sundays and certain great feasts, but only for bishops. The *Ordo Romanus I* says that when the *Kyrie* is finished "the pontiff, turning towards the people, begins *Gloria in Excelsis*, if it be the occasion for it [*si tempus fuerit*]" and notes specially that priests may say it only at Easter. The *Ordo of St. Amand* gives them leave to do so only on Easter Eve and on the day of their ordination. The Gregorian Sacramentary (*dicitur Gloria in excelsis Deo, si episcopus fuerit, tantummodo die dominico sive diebus festis; a presbyteris autem minime dicitur nisi solo in Pascha*). Berno of Constance thinks it a grievance still in the eleventh century, but towards the end of the same century the *Gloria* was said by priests as well as by bishops. The *Micrologus* (by the same Berno of Constance, 1048) tells us that "On every feast that has a full office, except in Advent and Septuagesima, and on the feast of the Innocents, both the priests and the bishop say *Gloria in excelsis*." It then became, as it is now, an element of every Mass except in times of penance. Even in Advent, until it began to be considered such a time, it was said. As early as Amalarius of Metz (ninth century) it was said during Advent "in some places". This would apply, of course, to bishops' Masses on Sundays and feasts at that time. So also Honorius of Autun (1145) in the twelfth century. White vestments were used, and the *Gloria* said, in Rome during Advent to the end of the twelfth century. After that, Advent was gradually considered a time of penance, in imitation of Lent. The *Te Deum* and *Gloria* were left out during it, and the use of purple vestments introduced.

The so-called farced *Glorias* were a medieval development. As in the case of the *Kyrie*, verses were introduced into its text for special occasions. Such expanded forms were very popular, especially one for feasts of the Blessed Virgin that seems to have been used all over Europe. Thus in the Sarum Missal, after the words *Domine Fili unigenite, Jesu Christe, Spiritus et alme orphanorum paraclyte* is added; after *Filius Patris* is inserted *Primogenitus Mariae virginis matris*. Again: *Suscipe deprecationem nostram, ad Mariae gloriam*, and the end: *Quoniam tu solus sanctus, Mariam sanctificans, Tu solus Dominus, Mariam gubernans, Tu solus altissimus, Mariam coronans, Jesu Christe*. The following rubric says: *In omnibus aliis missis quando dicendum est, dicitur sine prosa*; that is, in other Masses than those of the B.V.M., the additional tropes—called *prosa*—are to be omitted. These tropes added to liturgical texts *ad libitum* were contained in special books, *Libri troparii*. In spite of repeated commands to expunge them, they were still sung in places when the Missal was revised by order of Pius V in 1570. In the Bull *Quo Primum* of that year (printed at the beginning of the Missal) the pope forbids anything to be added to, or changed in, the text of the books then published. The popularity of the forms about the Blessed Virgin accounts for the rubric in the Missal after the Gloria: *Sic dicitur Gloria in excelsis, etiam in missis B. Mariae quando dicendum est*. Since then these "farced" forms have happily disappeared. It may be noted here that the *Gloria*, originally foreign to the Milanese and Mozarabic Rites, has displaced the older *Trisagion* in them since the seventh century—an obvious Roman imitation.

The present law about the use of the *Gloria* is given by the *Rubricae generales* of the Missal.[4] It is to be said in Mass whenever the *Te Deum* is said at Matins—with two exceptions. It is therefore omitted on ferias (except in Easter-tide), Ember days, vigils, during Advent, and from Septuagesima till Easter, when the Mass is *de tempore*. The Feast of Holy Innocents, but not its octave, is kept with purple vestments and without the *Te Deum* or *Gloria*. We have seen this already in the *Micrologus* (above). Nor is the *Gloria* said at Requiem or votive Masses, with three exceptions: votive Masses of the Blessed Virgin on Saturdays, of Angels, and those said *pro re gravi* or for a public cause of the Church, unless with purple vestments, have the *Gloria*. The two cases in which it occurs without the *Te Deum* in the Office are Maundy Thursday (when the whole Mass is an exception in Passion-tide and has no correspondence with the canonical hours) and Holy Saturday in the first Easter Mass. The *Gloria* always involves *Ite missa est* at the end of Mass. When it is not said that versicle is changed to *Benedicamus Domino* or, in Requiems, to *Requiescant in pace*.

The manner of saying it is described in the *Ritus celebrandi Missam*.[5] In the *Ordo Romanus I* (above) the celebrant turns to the people to say the first words. That is no longer observed. At high Mass as soon as the *Kyrie* is finished the celebrant, facing the altar in the middle, intones: *Gloria in excelsis Deo*, raising, joining, and lowering his hands, and bowing his head at the word *Deo*. Meanwhile the deacon and subdeacon stand behind him in line. They then come to his right and left and with him continue the *Gloria* in a low voice. All bow at the holy name (it occurs twice) and at the words: *Adoramus Te, Gratias agimus tibi, Suscipe deprecationem nostram,* and make the sign of the cross at the last clause. They then go *per viam breviorem* (genuflecting first, according to the usual rule) to the *sedilia* and sit. Meanwhile the choir immediately continues: *Et in terra pax*, and sings the text straight through. In the former Missal four chants were printed for the celebrant's intonation (for Doubles, Masses of B.V.M., Sundays, and Simples). This intonation ought to be in every way part—the beginning—of the melody continued by the choir; so in the new ("Vatican") edition of the Missal, eighteen alternative chants are given, one for each *Gloria* in the Gradual. Obviously, when a plain-song Mass is sung, the celebrant should intone the *Gloria* to the same chant (and at the same pitch) as its continuation by the choir. The ideal is for the choir to go on at once without any sort of prelude by the organ; *Et in terra pax,* etc., is the second half of the same sentence as *Gloria in excelsis Deo.* In a figured Mass so exact a correspondence is not possible. But in any case the choir may never repeat the celebrant's words. Every *Gloria* in a figured Mass must begin: *Et in terra pax.* The custom—once very common—of ignoring the celebrant and beginning again *Gloria in excelsis* is an unpardonable abomination that should be put down without mercy, if it still exists anywhere. While the *Gloria* is sung, the celebrant, ministers, and servers bow (or uncover) at the holy name and the other clauses, as above. During the last clause the celebrant and ministers rise and go to the altar *per viam longiorem* (genuflecting at the foot, according to rule) and go to their places for the *Dominus vobiscum* before the Collect. At a sung Mass the same order is observed by the celebrant alone. At low Mass he recites the *Gloria* straight through *clara voce,* making the sign of the cross during the last clause (*In gloria Dei Patris. Amen.*).

Mystic and edifying reflections on the *Gloria* will be found in Durandus (see **DURANDUS**) and Gihr.[6] Durandus sees much symbolism in the fact that the Church (that is, men) continues the angels' hymn. By the birth of Christ who restores all things in heaven and on earth (Eph.,i,10), angels and men, separated by original sin, are now reconciled; men may now hope some day to join in the angels' hymns. Gihr gives a devotional commentary on the text, word for word. He sees a mystic reason for the order of the words: *Laudamus, benedicimus, adoramus, glorificamus.* One may be edified by such considerations without attributing so much subtlety to the unknown subordinationist who apparently first arranged them. It will be noticed that the *Gloria* is a hymn of praise addressed to each Person of the Holy Trinity in turn, although the clause about the Holy Ghost is very short (*cum sancto Spiritu*) and is evidently an afterthought. It does not occur in the text of the *Apostolic Constitutions*. It will also be seen that the clauses are arranged in parallels with a certain loose rhythm. This rhythm is much more evident in the Greek original (measured of course by accent).

Lastly, it would be difficult to find in any Liturgy a more beautiful example of poetry than our *hymnus angelicus*. The *Gloria* and the *Te Deum* are the only remains we now have of the *psalmi idiotici* (psalms composed by private persons instead of being taken from the Biblical Psalter) that were so popular in the second and third centuries. These private psalms easily became organs for heretical ideas, and so fell into disfavour by the fourth century. The extraordinary beauty of these two is a witness to the splendour of that outburst of lyric poetry among Christians during the time of persecution.

Chapter Notes

1   *Apost. Const.*, VII, xlvii.

2   Subordinationism—Teaching about the Godhead which regards either the Son as subordinate to the Father or the Holy Ghost as subordinate to both. It is found in the first three centuries to varying degrees even in the writings of otherwise orthodox Fathers such as St. Justin and Origen, and was condemned by the Council of Constantinople in 381 (Ed.).

3   The *Book of the Popes*—a collection of early papal biographies dating back in some cases to the second century. It was constantly updated and eventually included biographies of almost every pope from St. Peter to Martin V (d. 1431)(Ed.).

4   *Rubr. gen.*, VIII, 3 & 4.

5   *Rit. cel.*, IV, 7.

6   Durandus, IV, 13; Gihr, pp. 393-407.

12

Collect

Collect.—the name now used only for the short prayers before the Epistle in the Mass, which occur again at Lauds, Terce, Sext, None, and Vespers. The word *collecta* corresponds to the Greek *synapsis*. It is a noun, a late form for *collectio* (so *missa* for *missio*, *oblata* for *oblatio*, *ascensa*, in the Gelasian Sacramentary, for *ascensio*, etc.). The original meaning seems to have been this: it was used for the service held at a certain church on the days when there was a station somewhere else. The people gathered together and became a "collection" at this first church; after certain prayers had been said they went in procession to the station-church. Just before they started the celebrant said a prayer, the *oratio ad collectam* (*ad collectionem populi*); the name would then be the same as *oratio super populum*, a title that still remains in our Missal, in Lent for instance after the Postcommunion. This prayer, the Collect, would be repeated at the beginning of the Mass at the station itself.[1] Later writers find other meanings for the name. Innocent III says that in this prayer the priest collects together the prayers of all the people.[2] The Secret and Postcommunion are also collects, formed on the same model as the one before the Epistle. Now the name is only used for the first of the three. Originally there was only one Collect (and one Secret and Postcommunion) for each Mass. The older sacramentaries never provide more than one. Amalarius of Metz (d. 847) says that in his time some priests began to say more one Collect,

254

but that at Rome only one was used.[3] *Micrologus* defends the
old custom and says that "one Prayer should be said, as one
Epistle and one Gospel".[4] However, the number of collects
was multiplied till gradually our present rule was evolved. The
way in which our collects are now said at Mass is the fragment
of a more elaborate rite. Of this longer rite we still have a vestige on Good Friday. The celebrant, after greeting the people
(*Dominus vobiscum*), invited them to pray for some intention:
Oremus, dilectissimi nobis, etc. The deacon said: *Flectamus genua*,
and all knelt for a time in silent prayer. The subdeacon then
told them to stand up again (*Levate*) and, all standing, the celebrant closed the private prayers with the short form that is
the Collect. Of this rite—except on Good Friday—the shortening of the Mass, which has affected all its parts, has only left
the greeting *Oremus* and the Collect itself. Here, as always, it
is in Holy Week that we find the older form. It should be noted,
then, that the *Oremus* did not refer immediately to the Collect, but rather to the silent prayer that went before it. This
also explains the shortness of the older collects. They are not
the prayer itself, but its conclusion. One short sentence summed
up the petitions of the people. It is only since the original meaning of the Collect has been forgotten that it has become itself
a long petition with various references and clauses (compare
the collects for the Sundays after Pentecost with those for the
modern feasts). On all feast-days the Collect naturally contains
a reference to the event whose memory we celebrate. Its preparation is the kissing of the altar and the *Dominus vobiscum*. Before inviting the people to make this prayer the celebrant greets
them, and, before turning his back to the altar in order to do
so, he salutes it in the usual way by kissing it. The form *Dominus vobiscum* is the common greeting in the West. It occurs in
the Gallican, Milanese, and Mozarabic Liturgies under the
form: *Dominus sit semper vobiscum*. Germanus of Paris notes it
as the priest's (not bishop's) greeting. It is taken from the Bible.
When Booz came from Bethlehem he said, "The Lord be with

you", to the reapers (Ruth, ii, 4), and St. Gabriel used the same form to Our Lady at the Annunciation (Luke, i, 25; cf. II Thess., iii, 16). A bishop here says, *Pax vobis*, unless the Mass has no *Gloria*, in which case his greeting is the same as that of the priest.[5] This distinction is as old as the tenth century. The Pax is a joyful and solemn greeting to be left out on days of penance. Its connexion with the *Gloria*, that has just gone before (*et in terra pax hominibus*), is obvious. The greeting of peace is the common one in the Eastern liturgies. In either case the answer is: *Et cum spiritu tuo*. This is a Hebraism that occurs constantly in both the Old and the New Testament. "Thy spirit" simply means "thee" (cf. e. g. Dan., iii, 86; Gal., vi, 18; Phil., iv, 23; Philem., 25). Nefesh (Heb.), Nafs (Ar.), with a pronominal suffix, in all Semitic languages means simply the person in question. The Eastern liturgies have the same answer, ("and with thy spirit"), as in the *Apostolic Constitutions*, or *kai to pneumati sou*.

At the *Dominus vobiscum* the celebrant, facing the people, extends and then again joins his hands. It is here a gesture of greeting. With folded hands he turns back to the altar and goes to the Missal at the Epistle side. Here, again extending and joining the hands and bowing towards the cross, he sings or says *Oremus*, and then, with uplifted hands (not above the shoulder),[6] goes on at once with the Collect or collects. The present rule about the collects is this: on doubles only one Collect is said (that of the feast), unless any other feast be commemorated, or the pope or bishop order an *oratio imperata*. The *imperata* is, moreover, omitted on doubles of the first class, Palm Sunday, Maundy Thursday, the eves of Christmas, Easter, and Whitsunday, in Requiems, and solemn votive Masses. On doubles of the second class it is left out in high and sung Masses, and may be said at the others or not, at the celebrant's discretion. For a very grave cause an *imperata* may be ordered to be said always, even on these occasions. It always comes last. The Collect of the Blessed Sacrament, to be said when it is exposed, and that for the pope or bishop on the anniversary of their election, coronation, or consecration, are particular cases of *imperatae*. The rules for commemoration of feasts, octaves, ember days, and ferias of Advent and Lent are given in the rubrics of the Missal.[7] On semi-doubles, Sundays, and days within an octave, three collects must be said; but on Passion Sunday, on Sundays within an octave and throughout the octaves of Easter and Whitsunday there are only two.[8] But in these cases the number may be greater, if there are commemorations. On simples, ferias, and in Requiems and (not solemn) votive Masses, the celebrant may also add collects, as he chooses, provided the total number be an uneven one and do not exceed seven.[9]

The rule about the uneven numbers, on which the Sacred Congregation of Rites has insisted several times (2 December, 1684; 2 September,1741; 30 June, 1896), is a curious one. The limit of seven prevents the Mass from being too long. In any case the Collect of the day always comes first. It has *Oremus* before it and the long conclusion (*Per Dominum*, etc.). The second Collect has a second *Oremus*, and all that follow are joined together without intermediate ending nor *Oremus* till the last, which again has the long conclusion. This separates the Collect of the day from the others and gives it a special dignity, as a remnant of the old principle that it alone should he said. The conclusions of the collects vary according to their form and references. The people (choir or server) answer Amen. During the conclusions the celebrant folds his hands and bows towards the cross at the words *Dominum nostrum Jesum Christum*. It should he noted that the great majority of the collects are addressed to God the Father (so all the old ones; the common form is to begin: *Deus, qui*); a few later ones (as on *Corpus Christi*, for example) are addressed to God the Son, none to the Holy Ghost. At low Mass collects are said aloud so that they can be heard by the people, at high (or sung) Mass they are sung to the festive tone on doubles, semi-doubles, and Sundays. On simples, ferias, and in Masses for the dead, they have the simple ferial tone (entirely on one note, fa). The rules of the tones, with examples, are in the *Caeremoniale Episcoporum*.[10] At high Mass the deacon and subdeacon stand in a straight line behind the celebrant (the deacon on the top step, the subdeacon in plano) with joined hands. At the collects in high Mass, the people should stand. This is the old position for public prayer; originally the sub-deacon explicitly told them to do so (*Levate*). The custom of standing during the collects, long neglected, is now being happily revived. At low Mass they kneel all the time except during the Gospel.[11]

Chapter Notes

[1] Bona, II, 5.

[2] *De Sacr. altaris myst.*, II, 27; see also Benedict XIV, *De SS. Missae*, II, 5.

[3] *De officiis eccl.*, in P.L., CV, 985 sqq.

[4] *De eccl. observ.*, probably by Bernold of Constance (d. 1100), in P.L., CLI, 973 sqq.

[5] *Rit. cel.*, V, 1.

[6] *Ibid.*, V, 1.

[7] *Rubr. Gen.*, VII.

[8] *Ibid.*, IX.

[9] *Ibid.*, IX, 12.

[10] *Caeremoniale* I, xxvii.

[11] *Rubr. gen.*, XVII, 2.

13

LESSONS IN THE LITURGY (EXCLUSIVE OF GOSPEL)

1. *History*.—The reading of lessons from the Bible, Acts of Martyrs, or approved Fathers of the Church, forms an important element of Christian services in all rites from the beginning. The Jews had divided the Law into portions for reading in the synagogue. The first part of the Christian *synaxis* was an imitation or continuation of the service of the synagogue. Like its predecessor it consisted of lessons from the Sacred Books, psalm-singing, homilies, and prayers. The Christians, however, naturally read not only the Old Testament but their own Scriptures too. Among these Christian Scriptures the most important were the histories of Our Lord's life, that we call Gospels, and the letters of the Apostles to various Churches. So we find St. Paul demanding that his letter to the Thessalonians "be read to all the holy brethren" (I Thess., v, 27). Such a public reading could only take place at the *synaxis*. Again, at the end of the Epistle to the Colossians he tells the people to send the letter to Laodicea to be read there, and to demand and read his letter to the Laodiceans (Col., iv, 16). Here too he seems to imply a public reading ("when this epistle shall have been read with you"). That the public reading of lessons from the Holy Books was a well-known incident of Christian services in the first centuries appears also from the common idea that the "Gospel" to which St. Paul alludes as being "through all the churches" (II Cor., viii, 18) was the

259

written Gospel of St. Luke read in the assemblies.[1] The famous text of St. Justin Martyr, (quoted in **GOSPEL IN THE LITURGY**) shows that Biblical texts were read at the Sunday assemblies. So also Tertullian (d. about 240) says of the Roman Church, that she "combines the Law and the Prophets with the Gospels and Apostolic letters" in her public reading.[2] There is evidence that at first, not only the canonical Scriptures, but Acts of Martyrs, letters, homilies of prominent bishops, and other edifying documents were read publicly in the assemblies. St. Cyprian (d.258) demands that his letters be read publicly in church.[3] The first Epistle of Clement to the Corinthians was used for public reading.[4] The Epistle of Barnabas[5] and the "Shepherd of Hermas"[6] are in the *Codex Sinaiticus*.[7] These manuscripts represent collections made for public reading. So also in the East, Acts of Martyrs were read on their anniversaries. Even as late as his time St. John Chrysostom (d. 407) seems to imply that letters from various Churches were still read in the Liturgy.[8] From the third and fourth centuries, however, the principle obtained that in the liturgy only the canonical Scriptures should be read. The Muratorian Canon (third century) expressly forbids the "Shepherd" to be read publicly.[9] The ideas of public reading and canonicity become synonymous, so that the fact that a book is read at the Liturgy in any local Church is understood to be evidence that that Church accepts it as canonical. Readings during the Office (Matins, etc.) outside the Liturgy have always been more free in this regard.

Originally, as we see from Justin Martyr's account, the amount read was quite indeterminate; the reader went on "as long as time allowed". The presiding bishop would then stop him with some sign or formula, of which our clause, *Tu autem Domine, miserere nobis*, at the end of lessons (once undoubtedly said by the celebrant) is still a remnant. The gradual fixing of the whole liturgical function into set forms naturally involved the fixing of the portions of the Bible read. There was an obvious convenience in arranging beforehand more or less equal sections to be read in turn. These sections were called "pericopes", a fragment cut off, (almost exactly the German *Abschnitt*). They were marked in the text of the Bible, as may be seen in most early manuscripts. An index, *capitularium,* giving the first and last words of the pericopes for each Sunday and feast, made it easier to find them. There are many remnants of the practice of naming a pericope after its first words, as in the *capitularium.* The Fathers preach on Gospels which they so call, as if it were a proper name.[10] Eventually, for greater convenience the lessons are written out in their liturgical order in a *lectionarium*, and later still they are inserted in their place with the text of the whole service, in Breviaries and Missals (see **GOSPEL IN THE LITURGY**).

Meanwhile the number of lessons, at first undetermined, became fixed and reduced. The reading of the Gospel, as being the most important, the crown and fulfilment of the prophecies in the Old Law, was put in the place of honour, last. Every allusion to the lessons read in churches implies that the Gospel comes last. A further reason for this arrangement was that in some Churches the catechumens were not allowed to hear the Gospel, so it was read after their dismissal (see **GOSPEL IN THE LITURGY**). We are concerned here with the other lessons that preceded it. For a time their number was still vague. The liturgy of the *Apostolic Constitutions* refers to "the reading of the Law and the Prophets and of our Epistles and Acts and Gospels".[11] The Syriac, Coptic, and Abyssinian Rites have several lessons before the Gospel.[12] In the Roman Rite we still have Masses with a number of lessons before the Gospel. Then gradually the custom obtains of reading two only, one from the Old Testament and one from the New. From the fact that the text read from the Old Testament is looked upon as a promise or type of what followed in Our Lord's life (very commonly taken from a Prophet) it is called the "prophecy". The lesson of the New Testament (exclusive of the Gospel) would naturally in most cases be part of an Epistle of St. Paul or another Apostle. So we have three lessons in the Liturgy - *prophetia, epistola (or apostolus), evangelium*. This was the older arrangement of the liturgies that now have only two. The Armenian Rite, derived at an early date (in the sixth century) from that of Constantinople, has these three lessons. St. John Chrysostom also alludes to three lessons in the Byzantine Rite of his time.[13] In the West, Germanus of Paris (d. 576), describing the Gallican Rite, mentions them: "The prophetic lesson of the Old Testament has its place. . . . The same God speaks in the prophecy who teaches in the Apostle and is glorious in the light of the Gospels", etc. This Gallican use is still preserved in the Mozarabic Liturgy, which has three lessons in the Mass. The Ambrosian Rite has a prophetic lesson on certain days only.

The Roman Rite also certainly once had these three lessons at every Mass. Besides the now exceptional cases in which there are two or more lessons before the Gospel, we have a trace of them in the arrangement of the Gradual which still shows the place where the other lesson had dropped out (see **GRADUAL**). The church of St. Clement at Rome (restored in the ninth century but still keeping the disposition of a much older basilica) has a third ambo for the prophetic lesson. A further modification reduced the lessons to two, one from any book of the Bible other than the Gospel, the second from the Gospel. In the Byzantine Rite this change took place between the time of St. John Chrysostom (d. 407) and the final development of the liturgy. The Barberini manuscript (ninth century, still supposes more than one lesson before the Gospel.[14] The Greek Liturgies of St. James and St. Mark also have only one lesson before the Gospel. This is one of the many examples of the influence of Constantinople, which from the seventh century gradually byzantinized the older Rites of Antioch and Alexandria, till it replaced them in about the thirteenth century. In St. Augustine's sermons we see that he refers sometimes to two lessons before the Gospel (e.g., *Sermo* xl), sometimes to only one (*Sermo* clxxvi, clxxx). At Rome, too, the lessons were reduced to two since the sixth century, except on certain rare occasions. These two lessons then, are our Epistle and Gospel.

2. The Epistle.—In no rite is the first of these two lessons invariably taken from an Epistle. Nevertheless the preponderance of pericopes from one of the Epistles in the New Testament is so great that the first lesson, whatever it may be, is commonly called the "Epistle" (*Epistola*). An older name meaning the same thing is "Apostle" (*Apostolus*). The Gregorian Sacramentary calls this lesson, *Apostolus*, e.g., *deinde sequitur Apostolus*;[15] it was also often called simply *Lectio*. The Eastern rites (Antioch, Alexandria, Constantinople) in Greek still call the first lesson "the Apostle". Originally it was read by a lector. The privileges of the deacon to sing the Gospel and (in the West) of the subdeacon to read the Epistle are a later development (see **GOSPEL IN THE LITURGY**). It seems that in the West lectors read the Epistle as well as the other lessons down to about the fifth century. Gradually, then, the feeling grew that the Epistle belongs to the subdeacon. This is apparently an imitation of the deacon's right to the Gospel. When the custom had obtained of celebrating High Mass with two ministers only—a deacon and a subdeacon—in place of the number of concelebrating priests, regionary deacons, and assistant subdeacons whom we see around the celebrating bishop in the first centuries at Rome, when further the liturgical lessons were reduced to two, and one of them was sung by the deacon, it seemed natural that the subdeacon should read the other. The first Roman *Ordo* (sixth-eighth century) describes the Epistle as read by a subdeacon. But not till the fourteenth century was the subdeacon's peculiar office of reading the Epistle expressed and acknowledged by his symbolic reception of the book of Epistles at his ordination. Even now the Roman Pontifical keeps unchanged the old form of the admonition in the ordination of subdeacons (*Adepturi, filii dilectissimi, officium subdiaconatus*...etc.), which, although it describes their duties at length, says nothing about reading the Epistle. In the corresponding admonition to deacons, on the other hand, there is a clear reference to their duty of singing the Gospel. In the time of Durandus (thirteenth century, see **DURANDUS**) the question was still not clear to every one. He insists that "no one may read the Epistle solemnly in church unless he be a subdeacon, or, if no subdeacon be present, it must be said by a deacon"; but when he treats of the duties of a subdeacon he finds it still necessary to answer the question: "Why the subdeacon reads the lessons at Mass, since this does not seem to belong to him either from his name or the office given to him."[16] We have even now a relic of the older use in the rubric of the Missal which prescribes that in a sung Mass, where there are no deacon and subdeacon, a lector in a surplice should read the Epistle.[17] In case of necessity at high Mass, too, a clerk, not ordained subdeacon, may wear the tunicle (not the maniple) and perform nearly all the subdeacon's duties, including the reading of the Epistle (S.R.C., 15 July, 1698). In the Eastern rites there is no provision for a subdeacon in the liturgy, except in the one case of the Maronites, who here, too, have romanised their rite. In all the others the Epistle is still chanted by a reader.

The Epistle is the last lesson before the Gospel, the first when there are only two lessons. In this case its place is immediately after the Collects. Originally it came between the two chants that we now call the Gradual (see **GRADUAL**). It was read from an ambo, the reader or subdeacon turning towards the people. Where there were two or more ambos, one was used only for the Gospel. The common arrangement was that of an ambo on either side of the church, between the choir and the nave, as may still be seen in many old basilicas (e.g., S. Maria in Cosmedin at Rome, etc.). In this case the ambo on the north side was reserved for the Gospel, from which the deacon faced the south, where the men stood (see **GOSPEL IN THE LITURGY**). The north is also the right, and therefore the more honourable, side of the altar. The ambo on the south was used for the Epistle, and for other lessons if there were only two. In the case of three ambos, two were on the south, one for all other lessons, one for the Epistles. This arrangement still subsists, inasmuch as the Epistle is always read on the south side (supposing the church to be orientated). Where there was only one ambo it had two platforms, a lower one for the Epistle and other lessons, a higher one for the Gospel. The ambo for the Epistle should still be used in the Roman Rite where the church has one; it is used regularly at Milan. In the Byzantine Rite the Apostle may be read from an ambo; if there is none the reader stands at the "high place", the *solea*, that is, the raised platform in front of the iconostasis. Ambos were still built in Western churches down to the twelfth and thirteenth centuries. Since then they have disappeared, except in some old churches. From that time the subdeacon as a rule stands in the choir on the south side of the altar (towards what the rubrics of the Missal call the *cornu epistolae*), facing the altar, as he reads the Epistle. The Byzantine reader, however, faces the people. The Epistle has always been chanted to a simpler tone than the Gospel; generally it is simply read on one note. The answer *Deo gratias* after the Epistle is the common one after the reading of any lesson (e.g., in the Office too). It was originally a sign from the celebrant or presiding bishop that enough had been read. The medieval commentators note that the subdeacon, having finished his reading, goes to make a reverence to the celebrant and kisses his hand. During the Epistle in every rite the hearers sit. They also cover their heads. This is the natural attitude for hearing a lesson read (so also at Matins, etc.); to stand at the Gospel is a special mark of reverence for its special dignity.

3. *Text of the Various Epistles*.—The reason of the present order of Epistles in the Roman Rite throughout the year is even more difficult to find than the parallel case of the Gospels (see **GOSPEL IN THE LITURGY**). In the first period the question does not so much concern what we now call the Epistle as rather the whole group of Biblical lessons preceding the Gospel. We may deduce with some certainty that there was at first the principle of reading successive books of the Bible continuously. The second book of the *Apostolic Constitutions* (third century) says that "the reader standing on a height in the middle shall read the Books of Moses and Jesus son of Nave, and of the Judges and Kings, and of Paralipomenon and the Return (Esdras and Nehemias), after these those of Job and Solomon and the sixteen Prophets (those are the first lessons). The lessons having been read by two (readers), another one shall sing the hymns of David and the people answer back the verses (this is the psalm between the lessons, our Gradual). After this our Acts (the Apostles are supposed to be speaking) shall be read and the letters of Paul, our fellow-worker, which he sent to the Churches."[18] This then implies continuous readings in that order. For the rest the homilies of the Fathers that explain continuous books (and often explicitly refer to the fact that the passage explained has just been read) show us certain books read at certain seasons. Thus, for instance, in Lent Genesis was read in East and West. So St. John Chrysostom (d. 407), preaching in Lent, says: "Today I will explain the passage you have heard read" and proceeds to preach on Genesis i, 1.[19] His homilies on Genesis were held during Lent. It is also probable that St. Basil's sermons on the Hexaemeron were held in Lent. In the Roman Office still Genesis begins at Septuagesima (in Matins) and is read in part of Lent. The reason of this is apparently that the ecclesiastical year was counted as beginning then in the spring. Other books read in Lent were Job, as an example of patient suffering, and Jonas, as a preparation for the Resurrection. During Eastertide the Acts of the

Apostles were read. For special feasts and on special occasions suitable lessons were chosen, thus breaking the continuous readings. In the Middle Ages it was believed that St. Jerome (d. 420), in obedience to an order of Pope Damasus, had arranged the lessons of the Roman Liturgy; a spurious letter of his to the Emperor Constantius was quoted as the first *comes*, or list of lessons, for each day. Dom G. Morin thinks that Victor, Bishop of Capua (541-554), was the author.[20]

From the fifth century various lists of lessons were drawn up. Gennadius of Marseilles (fifth century) says of one Muscus, priest of Marseilles: "Exhorted by the holy Bishop Venerius he selected lessons from Holy Scripture suitable for the feast days of all the year."[21] From this time there are a number of *comites* arranged for use in different Churches. Of these one of the most famous is the *comes* arranged by Albinus (i.e., Alcuin) by command of the Emperor Charles. This contains only the Epistles; it is part of the Roman Rite introduced by Charles the Great in the Frankish Kingdom.

Of the arrangement one can only say that the special suitableness of certain Epistles for the various feasts and seasons soon quite disturbed the principle of continuous reading. Of continuous readings there is now hardly a trace in the Missal. On the other hand, Epistles obviously suitable for each occasion may be traced back through a long list of *comites*. Thus our Epistles from Romans at the beginning of Advent recur in many lists: they are chosen obviously because of their appropriateness to that season. In some cases a connection of ideas with the Gospel seems to be the reason for the choice of the Epistle. In the Missal as reformed by Pius V in 1570 about two-thirds of the Epistles are taken from St. Paul; the others are from other Epistles, the Acts, Apocalypse, and various books of the Old Testament. A principle observed fairly regularly is that on fast days the Epistle is a lesson from the Old Testament. This applies to all week-days in Lent except Maundy Thursday, which has, of course, a festal Mass. The Mass on

Holy Saturday is the first Easter Mass and has an Easter Epistle. So also on most of the ember-days (which still have several lessons); but on the Whitsun ember Wednesday the sense of Pentecost predominates, so that it has two lessons from the New Testament (Acts, ii and v). It may be a remnant of the old system of reading Acts in Eastertide that, except Friday and Saturday, all the Masses of Easter Week have lessons from Acts, though, on the other hand, they are all in themselves appropriate. Practically all feasts and special occasions have Epistles chosen for their suitableness, as far as such could be found.

Occasionally, as on St. Stephen's feast and, to some extent, Ascension Day and Whitsunday, it is the Epistle rather than the Gospel that tells the story of the feast. The three Epistles for Christmas Day are sufficiently obvious: St. Stephen has of course the story of his martyrdom from Acts, vi and vii, Holy Innocents the lesson from Apocalypse, xiv, about the immaculate first-fruits of the saints. The Epiphany has a magnificent lesson about the Gentiles seeing the glory of the Lord in Jerusalem and the people who bring gold and incense; from Isaias, lx. Palm Sunday in its Epistle tells of the obedience of Our Lord to the death of the Cross and of His exaltation (Phil., ii) in the tone of the *Vexilla Regis*. The Easter Epistle could be no other than the one appointed (I Cor., v): Ascension Day and Whitsunday have their stories from the Acts. The feast of the Holy Trinity has the passage in Romans, xi, about the inscrutable mystery of God. *Corpus Christi* brings, of course, St Paul's account of the Holy Eucharist (I Cor., xi). St. John Baptist has a lesson from Isaias, xlix, about vocation and sanctification in the mother's womb. St. Peter and St. Paul have the story of St. Peter's imprisonment in Acts, xii. For All Saints we have the lesson about the saints signed by God and the great crowd around his throne in Apoc., vii. Most of Our Lady's feasts have lessons from the Song of Solomon or Ecclesiasticus applied mystically to her, as in her Office. The commons of saints have fairly obvious Epistles too. It will be seen, then, that a great proportion of our pericopes are chosen because of their appropriateness to the occasion. With regard to the others, in the *Proprium de tempore*, notably those for the Sundays after Epiphany and Pentecost, it is not possible to find any definite scheme for their selection. We can only conjecture some underlying idea of reading the most important passages of St. Paul's Epistles. The fact that every Sunday except Whitsunday has a pericope from an Epistle, that in nearly all cases it is from St. Paul (the Sundays after Easter, 1st, 2nd, 3rd, and 5th after Pentecost have Epistles of other Apostles) still shows that this is the normal text for the lesson before the Gospel; other lessons are exceptions admitted because of their special appropriateness. Of the old principle of continuous readings it is not now possible to find a trace. Our pericopes represent a combination of various *comites* and lectionaries, between which that principle has become completely overlaid.

The Epistle is announced as *lectio*, *Lectio epistolae beati Pauli ad Romanos*, *Lectio libri* Esther, and so on. No further reference is given; when there are several Epistles (e.g., those of St. Peter, St. John) the title read out does not say which it is: *Lectio epistolae beati Petri apostoli*. It should also be noted that all the five books attributed to Solomon and known as the *Libri Sapientiales* (namely, Prov., Eccl., Cant., Wis., Ecclus.) are announced as: *Lectio libri Sapientiae*.

The Epistles read in Eastern Churches are arranged in a way in which there is also no longer any trace of a system. Here, too, the present arrangement is the result of a long series of Lectionaries between which various compromises have been made. The Byzantine Church reads from the Epistles, Acts, and Apocalypse for the first lesson, called the Apostle. We have noted that the Armenians still have the older arrangement of three lessons in every liturgy, a Prophecy from the Old Testament, an Epistle, and a Gospel. The Copts have no Prophecy, but four New Testament lessons, one of St. Paul read from the "Apostle", one from an Epistle by another Apostle, read from another book called the *Katholikon*, then one from the Acts and finally the Gospel; the Abyssinian Church follows the use of Egypt in this as in most liturgical matters. The Syrian Jacobites read first several lessons from the Old Testament, then one from the Acts, an Epistle, and a Gospel. The Nestorians have an Old-Testament lesson, one from the Acts, an Epistle and a Gospel. Between the lessons in all these rites are various fragments of psalms, corresponding to our Gradual. The reading of the Apostle or other lessons before the Gospel is a very simple affair in the East. A reader, who is generally any layman, simply takes the book, stands in the middle of the choir, and sings the text in his usual nasal chant with a few enharmonic cadences which are handed down by tradition and, as a matter of fact, very considerably modified according to the taste and skill of the singer. Meanwhile the celebrant turns towards him and listens. He does not also read the text himself in any Eastern Rite. The Byzantine reader first chants the *Prokeimenon* facing the altar. This is a short verse of a psalm corresponding to our Gradual (which once preceded the Epistle: see **GRADUAL**). He then turns to the people and chants the *Apostolos*. Meanwhile the deacon is incensing the altar.[22]

4. *Ritual of the Epistle in the Roman Rite*.— We have noted that for many centuries the reading of the Epistle is a privilege of the subdeacon. While the celebrant chants the last Collect, the master of ceremonies brings the book containing the Epistle (a *lectionarium* containing the Epistles and Gospels, very often simply another Missal) from the credence table to the subdeacon at his place behind the deacon. The subdeacon turns towards him and receives it, both making a slight inclination. He then goes to the middle and genuflects (even if the Blessed Sacrament is not on the altar) and comes back to a place *in plano* at some distance behind the celebrant. Standing

LESSONS IN THE LITURGY

there, facing the altar, and holding the book with both hands he chants the title *Lectio...*, etc., and goes on at once with the text, to the end. He bows at the Holy Name and genuflects, if the rubric directs it, at his place towards the altar in front. The normal tone for the Epistle is entirely on one note (*do*) without any inflection, except that where a question occurs it sinks half a tone (to *si*) four or five syllables before, and for the last three syllables has the inflection *la*, *si* and a *podatus si-do*. The revised Vatican Missal gives a rather more elaborate chant for use *ad libitum* in the appendix (no. III). While the Epistle is read the members of the choir sit with covered heads. Meanwhile the celebrant reads it (and the Gradual) in a low voice from the Missal at the altar; the deacon stands at his side, turns over the page, if necessary, and answers *Deo gratias* when the celebrant has ended the Epistle. To the Epistle chanted by the subdeacon there is no answer. The last three or four syllables of the Epistle are chanted more slowly, *ritardando* at the end. The subdeacon, having finished, shuts the book, goes to the middle and genuflects; then, still holding the closed book in both hands, he goes round to where the celebrant stands; here he kneels facing sideways (north) on the step. The celebrant turns to him and rests the right hand on the book. The subdeacon kisses the hand and waits with bowed head while the celebrant makes the sign of the cross over him in silence. He hands the book back to the master of ceremonies and then carries the Missal round to the other side for the celebrant's Gospel.

At a sung Mass we have seen that the Epistle may be chanted by a lector in a surplice;[23] the text even says that this should be done: *Epistolam cantet in loco consueto aliquis lector superpelliceo indutus*. In this case he does not go to kiss the celebrant's hand afterwards.[24] Generally, however, the celebrant chants the Epistle himself at the corner of the altar, using the same tone as would a subdeacon. *Deo gratias* should not be answered in this case either. At low Mass the Epistle is read by the celebrant in its place after the last Collect. The server answers, *Deo gratias*.

5. *Other Lessons at Mass*.—There are a good many occasions in the year on which one or more lessons still precede the Epistle, according to the older custom. They are all days of a penitential nature, conspicuously the ember-days. The lessons are always separated by Graduals or Tracts, generally by Collects too. On the Advent ember Wednesday, after the first Collect a lesson from Isaias, ii, is read, then comes a Gradual, the Collect of the day followed by the other two that are said in Advent (or by commemorations), and a second lesson (the Epistle) from Is., vii, and lastly a second Gradual before the Gospel. The Advent ember Saturday has four lessons from Isaias, each preceded by a Collect and followed by a Gradual, then a lesson from Dan., iii (with its Collect before it), which introduces the canticle *Benedictus es, Domine*; this is sung as a kind of Tract. Then come the usual Collects for the day and the Epistle. The Lent ember Wednesday has two, the Saturday five lessons before the Gospel. The Whitsun ember Wednesday has two lessons from Acts, Saturday five prophecies and an Epistle. The ember-days in September have on Wednesday two lessons, on Saturday four lessons and an Epistle before the Gospel. Wednesday in Holy Week also has two lessons from Isaias. In all these cases the arrangement is the same: a collect, the lesson, a gradual or tract. The lessons other than the last (technically the Epistle) are chanted by the celebrant to the Epistle tone; the deacon and subdeacon answer, *Deo gratias*, except in the case of the lesson from Daniel that introduces the canticle. Palm Sunday, in the *missa sicca* in which the palms are blessed, has a lesson from Exodus, xv and xiv, sung by the subdeacon as if it were an Epistle, as well as a Gospel. On Maundy Thursday the Gospel of the Mass is sung again at the Maundy (washing of feet). The Mass of the Presanctified on Good Friday, as part of its archaic character, begins with three lessons. The first is the "Prophecy" from Osee, vi. This is sung by a lector—the only occasion on which such a person is mentioned in the text of the Missal (apart from the preface). A tract and collect follow. Then comes the Epistle (in this case, according to the rule for weekdays in Lent, a lesson from the Old Testament, Ex, xii) chanted by the subdeacon in the usual way, another tract, and the Gospel (the Passion from St. John).

Holy Saturday and Whitsun eve keep a relic of very early times in the long series of lessons (called here too "Prophecies") before the Mass. It is often said that they represent the last instruction of the catechumens before baptism or, rather, a remnant of the old vigil-office of the type of the fourth-century vigil, but now despoiled of the psalms that once alternated with the lessons. The number of the Prophecies on Holy Saturday varied in different churches. Durandus, who explains them in the usual medieval way as instructions for the catechumens, says: "In some churches four lessons are read, in some six, in some twelve, and in some fourteen", and proceeds to give mystic reasons for these numbers.[25] The number at Rome seems to have been always, as it is now, twelve. A tradition ascribes the arrangement of these twelve to St. Gregory I. They were once chanted first in Latin and then in Greek. As they stand in the Missal they represent very well a general survey of the Old Testament as a preparation for Christ; the Collects which follow each emphasise this idea. The eighth and ninth only are followed by Tracts. They are chanted by readers (now practically anyone from the choir) before the altar, while the celebrant reads them in a low voice at the epistle side. They begin without any title. The celebrant, of course, sings the Collect that follows each. Their tone is given in the appendix of the Vatican Missal (no. 11). It agrees with that for lessons at Matins; namely, they are chanted on one note (*do*) with a fall of a perfect fifth (to *fa*) on the last syllable before each full stop, a fall of half a tone (*si*) before a colon, and the same cadence for questions as in the Epistle (see above.

The lessons on Whitsun eve are (like the whole service) an imitation of Holy Saturday. It is supposed that the rites of the Easter vigil, including the baptisms, were transferred to Whitsun eve in the North because of the cold climate. They then reacted so as to produce a duplication, such as is not uncommon in the Roman Rite. The whole rite follows that of Easter eve exactly; but there are only six prophecies, being the 3rd, 4th, 11th, 8th, 6th, and 7th of the Easter series.

6. Lessons in the Office.—Lessons of various kinds also form a very important part of the canonical hours in all rites. The essential and original elements of the Divine Office in East and West are the singing of psalms, the reading of lessons, and saying of prayers. The Canons of Hippolytus (second century) ordain that clerks are to come together at cockcrow and "occupy themselves with psalms and the reading of Scripture and with prayers."[26] The history of these lessons is bound up closely with that of the Office itself. We may note here that in the Office, as in the Liturgy, we see at first the principle of continuous readings from the Bible; to these are added the reading of Acts of Martyrs and then of homilies of approved Fathers. In the West this idea has been preserved more exactly in the Office than in the Mass. In the Roman and indeed in all Western Rites the most important lessons belong to the night Office, the nocturns that we now call Matins. The Rule of St. Benedict (d. 543) gives us exactly the arrangement still observed in the monastic rite. Till the seventh century the ferial Nocturn had no lessons, that of Sunday had after the twelve psalms three lessons from Scripture; the lessons followed from the text of the Bible so that it was read through (except the Gospels and Psalms) in a year. The distribution of the books was much the same as now. In the seventh century lessons began to be read in the ferial Office too. The presiding priest or bishop gave a sign when enough had been read; the reader ended, as now, with the ejaculation, *Tu autem Domine miserere* *nobis*, and the choir answered, *Deo gratias*.

A further development of the Sunday Office mentioned by St. Gregory I (d. 604) was that a second and third nocturn were added to the first. Each of these had three psalms and three lessons taken, not from the Bible, but from the works of the Fathers. For these lessons a library of their works was required, till the homilies and treatises to be read began to be collected in books called *homiliaria*. Paul the Deacon made a famous collection of this kind. It was published by authority of Charles the Great, who himself wrote a preface to it; it was used throughout his kingdom. It became the chief source of our present Roman series of lessons from the Fathers.[27] Eventually then the arrangement of lessons in the Roman Rite has become this: The lessons from Scripture are arranged throughout the year in the *proprium temporis*. They form what is called the *scriptura occurrens*. The chief books of the Bible (except the Gospels and Psalms) are begun and read for a time. The shortening of the lessons, overlapping of seasons, and especially the number of feasts that have special lessons have produced the result that no book is ever finished. But the principle of at least beginning each book is maintained, so that if for any reason the *scriptura occurrens* of a day on which a book is begun falls out, the lessons of that day are read instead of the normal ones on the next free day.

Although the ecclesiastical year begins with Advent, the course of the *scriptura occurrens* is begun at Septuagesima with Genesis. This is a relic of an older calculation that began the year in the spring (see above, 2). The course of the continuous reading is continually interrupted for special reasons. So the first Sunday of Lent has lessons from II Cor., vi and vii ("Now is the acceptable time"). The weekdays in Lent have no *scriptura occurrens* but a Gospel and a homily, according to the rule for the *feriae* that were liturgical from the beginning and have a special Mass. Genesis goes on on the second and third Sundays of Lent; on the fourth comes a pericope from

Exodus. Passion and Palm Sunday have lessons from Jeremias (beginning on Passion Sunday) for a special reason (the connection of the Prophecy of the destruction of the temple with Our Lord's Passion). Easter Day and its octave have only one nocturn, so no *scriptura occurrens*. Low Sunday has special lessons (Col., iii) about the Resurrection. The Acts of the Apostles begin on the day after Low Sunday and are read for a fortnight—according to the old tradition that connects them with Eastertide. The Apocalypse begins on the third Sunday after Easter and lasts for a week. On the fourth Sunday St. Jame's Epistle begins, on the fifth St. Peter's First Epistle. Ascension Day naturally has its own story from Acts, i; but on the next day II Peter begins. The Sunday following brings the First Epistle of St. John; the next Wednesday, II John; the Friday, III John; Saturday, the Epistle of St. Jude. Pentecost and its octave, like Easter, have no *scriptura occurrens*.

It will be noticed that, just as Lent has on its *feriae* only lessons from the Old Testament, even in the Epistles at Mass, so Paschal time has only the New Testament, even in the Office. The feast of the Holy Trinity has special lessons (Is., vi—the Seraphim who cry: Holy, holy, holy); the next day we come back to the normal course and begin the First Book of Kings. II Kings begins on the fifth Sunday after Pentecost, III Kings on the seventh, IV Kings on the ninth. On the first Sunday of August (from which day till Advent we count by the months except for the Mass and the lessons of the third nocturn) the Books of Wisdom begin with Proverbs; Ecclesiastes comes on the second Sunday of August, Wisdom on the third, Ecclesiasticus on the fourth. Job comes on the first Sunday of September, Tobias on the third, Judith on the fourth, Esther on the fifth. October brings on its first Sunday I Machabees, on its fourth II Machabees. The Prophets begin in November: Ezekiel on the first Sunday, Daniel on the third. Osee on the fourth, and then the other minor Prophets in very short fragments, obviously in a hurry, till Advent. Advent has Isaias throughout. The first Sunday after Christmas begins St. Paul's Epistles with Romans; they continue to Septuagesima. I Corinthians comes on the first Sunday after Epiphany, II Corinthians on the second Sunday, Galatians on the third, Ephesians the following Wednesday, Philippians on the fourth Sunday, Colossians on the next Tuesday, I Thessalonians on Thursday, II Thessalonians on Saturday, I Timothy on the fifth Sunday, II Timothy on Tuesday, Titus on Thursday, Philemon on Saturday, Hebrews on the sixth Sunday. We have here again the same crowded changes as at the end of the season after Pentecost. The arrangement then is one of continuous readings from each book, though the books do not follow in order, but are distributed with regard to appropriateness. If we count the Pentateuch as one book (that seems to be the idea), we see that all the books of the Bible are read, in part at least, except Josue, Judges, Ruth, Paralipomenon, and the Canticle of Canticles. Cardinal Quiñones in his famous reformed Breviary (issued by Paul III in 1535, withdrawn by Paul IV in 1558) changed all this and arranged the reading of the whole Bible in a year. His proposal, however, came to nothing and we still use the traditional Office, with the developments time has brought.

The arrangement of Matins is this: On *feriae* and simple feasts there is only one nocturn with its three lessons. On *feriae* all three are from the *scriptura occurrens*: on simples the third lesson is an account of the saint instead of the Scriptural one. The exception is when a *feria* has its own Mass. Such are the days that were originally liturgical days—weekdays in Lent, ember-days, and vigils. In this case the lessons consist of the fragment of the Gospel with a homily as in the third nocturn of semi-doubles. On semi-doubles and all higher feasts (Sundays are semi-doubles) there are three nocturns, each with three lessons. Such days are the *festa novem lectionum*. The first nocturn has always Scriptural lessons—those of the *scriptura occurrens*, or on special feasts, a text chosen for its suitability.

The second nocturn has lessons from a Father of the Church, here called *sermo*, a life of the saint on his feast, or a description of the event of the day. Thus, for instance, St. Peter's Chains (1 August) tells the story of their finding and how they came to Rome; S. Maria *tit. Auxilium Christianorum* (24 May) in the sixth lesson tells *ex publicis monumentis* the story of the battle of Lepanto. Sometimes papal Bulls are read in the second nocturn, as the Bull of Pius IX (*Ineffabilis Deus*) during the Octave of the Immaculate Conception (8 December). The second nocturn continually receives new lessons, written by various people and approved by the Sacred Congregation of Rites. Many of the older ones are taken from the *Liber Pontificalis*. The third nocturn has for its lessons first a fragment (the first clause) of the Gospel read at Mass followed by the words, *et reliqua*, then a sermon (called *Homilia*) of a Father explaining it through the three lessons (the 7th, 8th, and 9th). In cases of concurrence of feasts, the feast commemorated (or the *feria*, if it be a liturgical day) has its own lesson (the life of the saint, or Gospel-fragment, and homily) read as the ninth lesson.

The monastic Office differs only in that it has four lessons in each nocturn (twelve altogether) and the whole Gospel of the day read after the *Te Deum*. This practice of reading the Gospel at the end of Matins was common in many medieval rites. Thus at Christmas in England the genealogy of Our Lord from St. Matthew was read at Christmas, and the one in St. Luke at the Epiphany at this place. So in the Byzantine Rite the Gospel of the day is read at the *Orthros* (see **GLOSSARY**).

The other canonical hours have short lessons called *capitula*, originally *lectiunculae*, sometimes *capitella*. The Ambrosian Breviary calls them *epistolellae* and *collectiones*. These are very short passages from the Bible, generally continuous throughout the hours, connected with the feast or occasion. Very often they are from the same source as the Epistle. At Lauds and Vespers the *capitulum* is chanted by the officiating priest after the fifth psalm, before the hymn. At Terce, Sext, None he chants it after the psalm. Prime and Compline (originally private prayers of monks) are in many ways different from the other hours. They have always the same *capitula*. Prime has I Tim., i, 17 (omitting the word *autem*) chanted in the same place. Compline has Jer., xiv, 9b (adding the word *sanctum* after *nomen* and the final clause, *Domine, Deus noster*). This is sung after the hymn by the celebrant. At Prime the officiating priest chants a second lesson (called *lectio brevis*) at the end, after the blessing that follows the *preces* and the prayer *Dirigere et sanctificare*. For the *proprium temporis* this is given in the Breviary (in the *psalterium*); on feasts it is the *capitulum* of None, with the addition of *Tu autem Domine miserere nobis*. Compline begins after the blessing with a *lectio brevis* from I Peter, v, 8, 9a (with the additional word *Fratres* at the beginning and the clause, *Tu autem*, etc., at the end). All these short lessons are answered by the words *Deo gratias*, but the *capitula* do not have the clause *Tu autem*, etc. The Roman Ritual has a few isolated lessons for special occasions. The Office of the "Visitation and care of the sick" has four Gospels from Matthew, Mark, Luke, and John (all about healing the sick), and the beginning of John. The "Order of commending a soul" has two Gospels —the high-priestly prayer in John, xvii, and the Passion according to St. John. The exorcism has three Gospels (about driving out devils). In the Pontifical, a Gospel (Luke, ix) is appointed to be read at the opening of synods, before the *Veni Creator*, and another one (Luke, x) is given for the end of the blessing of bells. In some countries (Germany and Austria) it is the custom to sing the beginning of each Gospel during the *Corpus Christi* procession at the altars of repose, before the benediction.

All the Eastern rites in the same way have lessons of various kinds as part of the canonical hours. They constantly use psalms as lessons; that is to say, the whole text of a psalm is read straight through by a reader, as we read our lessons. The choral part of the Office consists chiefly of verses, responses, and exclamations of various kinds (the Byzantine *Stichera, Troparia, Kontakia,* etc.) that are not taken from the Bible, but are composed by various hymn-writers. In the Byzantine Office three lessons, generally from the Old Testament are read by a lector towards the end of the *hesperinos.* In the *Orthros* the priest reads the Gospel of the day shortly before the Canon is sung. In the Canon at the end of the sixth ode a lesson describing the life of the saint, or containing reflections on the feast or occasion, is read. If several feasts concur the various *synaxaria* follow each other. The day-hours have no lessons, except that many *troparia* throughout the Office describe the mystery that is celebrated and give information to the hearers in a way that makes them often very like what we should call short lessons. Lessons, Epistles, and Gospels are read at many special services; thus the "Blessing of the Waters" on the Epiphany has three lessons from Isaias, an Epistle (I Cor., x, 1-4), and a Gospel (Mark, i, 9-11).

Chapter Notes

1   Eusebius, *Hist. ecc.*, III, iv, 8; Jerome, *De viris illustr.*, vii.

2   *De praescript. haer.*, 36.

3   e.g., *Ep.* ix, in P.L., IV, 253.

4   It is included (with II Clem. *ad. Cor.*) in the Codex Alexandrinus.

5   An epistle of early Christian times ascribed to the Apostle Barnabas, but it is more probably the work of an unknown Christian of Alexandria who wrote between A.D. 70 and 100 (Ed.).

6   A second-century treatise by the sub-Apostolic writer Hermas who is, however, accounted one of the Apostolic Fathers. Hermas was a freed Christian slave, and his book was a consequence of a series of visions, the fifth of which was that of the Angel of Penance who appeared in the guise of a shepherd, hence the title of the book (Ed.).

7   One of the most famous of all Christian manuscripts. It probably dates

from the end of the 4th century, was discovered in the Monastery of St. Catherine, Mount Sinai in 1844 (hence the name Sinaiticus), sold to the Tsar of Russia, and then by the Soviet Government to the Brish Museum in 1933. It includes the Old and New Testaments, the Epistle of Barnabas, and part of the "Shepherd of Hermas" (Ed.).

8 Hom. 30 on II Cor., in P.G., LXI, 605.

9 The oldest extant canon (list) of New Testament writings, named after the Italian priest scholar L. A. Muratori (d. 1750). It is generally held to date from the second half of the second century. (Ed.)

10 St. Bernard's "Homilies on the *Missus est*" is on Luke, i, 26-38, etc.).

11 *Apost. Const.* VIII, v,11.

12 Brightman, pp. 76-8, 152-4, 212-5.

13 *Hom. 29 on Acts,* P.G., LX,218.

14 Reproduced in Brightman, pp. 309-344.

15 P.L., LXXVIII, 25.

16 Durandus, II, 8.

17 *Rit. cel.* VI, 8.

18 *Apost. Const.,* II, lvii.

19 Hom. vii, de statuis, I.

20 The letter is quoted in Beissel, *Entstehung der Perikopen des Römischen Messbuches* (Freiburg, 1907), 54-5.

21 *De viris illustr.*, lxxix.

22 Fortescue, *Liturgy of St. John Chrysostom* (London, 1908), p.75.

23 *Rit. cel.*, vi, 8.

24 *Ibid.*

25 Durandus, VI, 81.

26 Can. xxi.

27 In P.L., XCV.

14

GRADUAL

(Latin *Graduale*, from *gradus,* a step), in English often called Grail, is the oldest and most important of the four chants that make up the choir's part of the Proper of the Mass. Whereas the three others (Introit, Offertory, and Communion) were introduced later, to fill up the time while something was being done, the Gradual (with its supplement, the Tract or Alleluia) represents the singing of psalms alternating with readings from the Bible, a custom that is as old as these readings themselves. Like them, the psalms at this place are an inheritance from the service of the Synagogue. Copied from that service, alternate readings and psalms filled up a great part of the first half of the Liturgy in every part of the Christian world from the beginning. Originally whole psalms were sung. In the *Apostolic Constitutions* they are chanted after the lessons from the Old Testament: "The readings by the two (lectors) being finished, let another one sing the hymns of David and the people sing the last words after him." This use of whole psalms went on till the fifth century. St. Augustine says: "We have heard first the lesson from the Apostle. Then we sang a psalm. After that the lesson of the gospel showed us the ten lepers healed..."[1] These psalms were an essential part of the Liturgy, quite as much as the lessons. "They are sung for their own sake; meanwhile the celebrants and assistants have nothing to do but to listen to them."[2] They were sung in the form of a *psalmus responsorius,* that is to say, the whole text was chanted by one person—a reader appointed for this purpose. (For some time before St. Gregory I, to sing these psalms was a privilege of deacons at Rome. It was suppressed by him in 595.) The people answered each clause or verse by some acclamation. In the *Apostolic Constitutions* they repeat his last modulations. Another way was to sing some ejaculation each time. An obvious model of this was Ps. cxxxv with its refrain: *quoniam in aeternum misericordia eius*; from which we conclude that the Jews too knew the principle of the responsory psalm. We still have a classical example of it in the *Invitatorium* of Matins (and the same Ps. xciv in the third Nocturn of the Epiphany). It appears that originally, while the number of Biblical lessons was still indefinite one psalm was sung after each. When three lessons became the normal custom (a Prophecy, Epistle, and Gospel) they were separated by two psalms. During the fifth century the lessons at Rome were reduced to two; but the psalms still remain two, although both are now joined together between the Epistle and Gospel, as we shall see. Meanwhile, as in the case of many parts of the Liturgy, the psalms were curtailed, till only fragments of them were left. This process, applied to the first of the two, produced our Gradual; the second became the Alleluia or Tract.

1. *The Name*.—The name Gradual comes from the place where it was sung. In the First Roman *Ordo* it is called *Responsum;* Amalarius of Metz (ninth century) calls it *Cantus Responsorius;* Isidore (seventh century) *Responsorium, quod uno canente chorus consonando respondet.* This name was also used, as it still is, for the chants after the lessons at Matins; so the liturgical *Responsorium* was distinguished later by a special name. The reader who chanted the psalm stood on a higher place, originally on the steps of the ambo. He was not to go right up into the ambo, like the deacon who sang the Gospel, but to stand on the step from which the subdeacon had read the Epistle: "He does not go up higher, but stands in the same place where the reader stood and begins the *Responsorium* alone; and all the choir answer and he alone sings the verse of the *Responsorium.*[3] Later in various local churches, when the ambo was disappearing, other places were chosen, but the idea of a high place, raised on steps, persists. At Reims, the steps of the choir were used, sometimes a special pulpit was erected. Beleth (twelfth century) says that on ordinary days the cantor stands on the altar-steps, on feasts on the ambo. Durandus (see **DURANDUS**) a little later writes: *Dicitur Graduale a gradibus altaris, eo quod in festivis diebus in gradibus cantatur"* ("Gradual is so called from the steps of the altar, on which it was sung on holidays.")[4] There seems then to be no doubt that the name comes from the place where it was sung. Cardinal Bellarmine's idea that the *gradus* in question are those the deacon is climbing for the Gospel while the Gradual is being chanted is a mistake.[5] We have seen that this psalm was not sung to fill up time during the procession to the ambo. Originally the deacon and all the ministers would wait till it was over before beginning their preparation for the Gospel. The older name *Responsorium* lasted, as an alternative, into the Middle Ages. Durandus uses it constantly and gives a mystic explanation of the word: *Responsorium vero dicitur quia versui vel epistolae correspondere debet*, etc., i.e. "Responsory is so called because it ought to correspond to the verse or epistle").[6]

It is difficult to say exactly when the Gradual got its present form. We have seen that in St. Augustine's time, in Africa, a whole psalm was still sung. So also St. John Chrysostom alludes to whole psalms sung after the lessons;[7] as late as the time of St. Leo I (d. 461), in Rome the psalm seems not yet to have been curtailed: "Wherefore we have sung the psalm of David with united voices, not for our honour, but for the glory of Christ the Lord."[8] Between this time and the early Middle Ages the process of curtailing brought about our present arrangement.

2. *Order of the Gradual.*— If we open a Missal, at most of the days in the year (the exceptions will be described below), we find between the Epistle and Gospel a set of verses with some Alleluias marked *Graduale.* Although the whole text follows this heading, although we usually speak of it all as the Gradual, there are here two quite distinct liturgical texts, namely the first part, which is the old *psalmus responsorius* (now the Gradual in the strictly correct sense), and the Alleluia with its verse, the Alleluiatic verse *(versus alleluiaticus).* We have seen that these two chants came, originally, one after each of the lessons that preceded the Gospel. Now that we have only one such lesson as a rule (the Epistle), the Gradual and Alleluiatic verse (or its substitute) are sung together. But there are still cases of their separation. In Lent, as we shall see, the Alleluia is replaced by the Tract. A number of Lenten Masses that have kept the old three lessons also keep the old arrangement, by which the Gradual follows the first, the Tract the second (e.g. Wednesdays in the Lenten Ember week and Holy Week), others (e.g. the Ember Saturday) that have more than three lessons have a Gradual after each of the former ones and a Tract after the Epistle. There are again others (e.g. Tuesday in Holy Week), in which there is no Tract at all, but only a Gradual after the first lesson. And even when they are sung together their essential separation is still marked by the fact that they have quite different melodies, in different modes. Thus, on the first Advent Sunday the Gradual is in the first and second modes mixed, the Alleluia in the eighth; the next Sunday has a fifth-mode Gradual followed by a first-mode Alleluia, and so on. The Gradual itself always consists of two verses, generally from the same psalm. There are however many cases of their being taken from different psalms; some, of verses from other books of Scripture (e.g. those for the Immaculate Conception are from Judith); and a few in which the text is not Scriptural. The feast of the Seven Dolours has such verses, *Dolorosa et lacrymabilis es Virgo Maria* and *Virgo Dei Genitrix.*

So also *Benedicta et venerabilis es Virgo Maria* for the Visitation (July 2) and other feasts of the B.V.M., and the first verse of the Gradual for Requiems (*Requiem aeternam* ...). The first of these two verses keeps the old name *Responsorium*, the second is marked V (for *versus*). It may be that the first represents the former acclamation of the people (like the *Invitatorium* of Matins), and that the second is the fragment of the psalm originally sung by the lector.

The second chant is normally the *versus alleluiaticus* (in this case the shorter one). The use of the word *Alleluia* in the Liturgy is also a very old inheritance from the Synagogue. It became a cry of joy without much reference to its exact meaning in a language no longer understood (as did *Hosanna*). Its place in the Liturgy varied considerably. In the Byzantine Rite it comes as the climax of the Cherubic Hymn at the Great Entrance.[9] In the Gallican Rite it was sung at the Offertory. Its place here before the Gospel is peculiar to the Roman Rite. It appears that before the time of St. Gregory I (d. 604) it was sung only during Eastertide. Sozomen goes further: "At Rome, Alleluia is sung once a year, on the first day of the Paschal feast, so that many Romans use this oath: may they hear and sing that hymn!"[10] This connection with Easter (unknown in the East) afterwards led to additional Alleluias being scattered throughout the Mass in Eastertide (at the Introit, Offertory, Communion, etc.); but its old and essential place for the normal Liturgy is here, where it has displaced the former second *psalmus responsorius*. It will be noticed that the three great Alleluias that usher in Easter on Holy Saturday come here in the place of the Gradual. The chant consists of two Alleluias sung to exactly the same melody. At the end of the second one its last sound *(a)* is continued in a long and complicated neum. This musical phrase (called variously *neuma, jubilatio, jubilus, cantilena*) is a very old and essential element of the Alleluia. A great number of medieval commentators insist on it, and explain it by various mystic reasons. For instance, Rupert of Deutz

(Rupertus Tuitiensis, O.S.B., twelfth century): "We rejoice rather than sing (*jubilamus magis quam canimus*)... and prolong the neums, that the mind be surprised and filled with the joyful sound, and be carried thither where the saints rejoice in glory."[11] So also Sicardus of Cremona: *Congrue quoque in Alleluia jubilamus* (this means singing the neum) *ut mens illuc rapiatur ubi Sancti exsultabunt . . .*[12] Durandus: *Est etiam Alleluia modicum in sermone et multum in pneuma, quia gaudium illud majus est quam possit explicari sermone. Pneuma enim seu jubilus qui fit in fine exprimit gaudium et amorem credentium,* that is, "The Allelula is short in word and long in neum, because that joy is too great to be expressed in words. For the neum or *jubilus* at the end denotes the joy and love of the faithful" etc.[13] The question of the neum is discussed and many authorities quoted in Pothier.[14] It should certainly never be omitted. In the case of a figured Gradual a *jubilus* in figured music should be supplied. After the *jubilus* of the second Alleluia a verse follows. This verse is by no means so commonly taken from the psalms as the verses of the Gradual, and there are a great many cases, especially on feasts of saints, of a fragment of a Christian poem, or other verse not from the Bible. On St. Lawrence's feast (10 August), for example, the Alleluiatic verse is: *Levita Laurentius bonum operatus est, qui per signum crucis caecos illuminavit* ("The Levite Lawrence, who made the blind see by the sign of the Cross, worked a good work"). This Alleluiatic verse is a kind of continuation of the *jubilus* with a text fitted to the long-drawn neums. Then a third Alleluia, the same as the second with its *jubilus*, ends the chant.

There are two exceptions to this order. The first is when the Alleluia is replaced by the Tract. Since this word began to be looked upon as a special sign of joy, most suitable for Eastertide, it followed, as an obvious corollary, that it should not be sung in times of penance or mourning. There is no such idea in the East, where they sing Alleluia always, even in the Office for the Dead, as was once done at Rome too. That

Latins sometimes avoid it was one of their many preposterous grievances at the time of Caerularius's schism.[15] In the West, from Septuagesima to Easter (even on feasts), on Ember days, most vigils, and at Requiems, the Alleluiatic verse disappears. The Vigils in question generally have only the Gradual (but some have the Alleluia, e.g. the eves of Epiphany, Ascension, Whitsunday). On the other days the Gradual is followed by the Tract. The Tract *(tractus)* is the second psalm sung between the lessons, which, although later displaced by the Alleluia on most days, has kept its place here. We find it as an alternative to the Alleluia in the First Roman *Ordo: Postquam legerit cantor cum cantatorio adscendit et dicit responsum. Ac deinde per alium cantorem, si fuerit tempus ut dicatur Alleluia, concinitur, sin autem tractum, sin minus tantummodo responsum cantatur*, i.e. "After the reading (of the Epistle) the cantor ascends with his book and chants the Response. Then, if it be the proper season. another cantor chants the Alleluia; but if the Alleluia have to be omitted (i.e. in times of penance) the Tract or at times (as still on vigils) only the Response is sung."[16] The name "Tract", *psalmus tractus*, was given to it, because it was sung straight through without an answer by the choir *(in uno tractu)*. This was the special note of the second psalm, that distinguished it from the first *psalmus responsorius*. Later authors explain the word incorrectly as describing the slow and mournful way in which it was sung *(a trahendo quia lente et lugubriter cantatur*, from *trahendo*, because it is sung slowly and mournfully. Durandus gives this, with other symbolic reasons, for the name: "It is called tract from *trahendo* because it is sung drawn out *(quia tractum canitur)* and with a harshness of voice and length of words; since it implies the misery and labour of our present life."[17] The text of the *Ordo Romanus I*, quoted above, shows that it was sung from the steps of the ambo, like the Gradual. We have still a few Masses in which the *psalmus tractus* has kept its original nature as a whole psalm. On the first Sunday of Lent it is Ps. xc; on Palm Sunday, Ps. xxi; on Good Friday,

Ps. cxxxix. Otherwise the Tract too has been shortened to two or three verses. It is nearly always taken from Scripture, but not seldom from other books than the Psalter; verses from various psalms or other texts often follow one another, connected only by the common idea that runs through them. Mondays, Wednesdays, and Fridays in Lent are the old *feriae legitimae*, the official days of penance, that still keep certain peculiarities (in choir, on these days, the Office for the Dead, the penitential and gradual psalms are said). Except on Wednesdays in Holy Week they have the same Tract, a prayer for forgiveness from Ps. cii and lxxviii. All feasts that may come between Septuagesima and Easter and all common and votive Masses have a Tract, to be used in that time. Good Friday has two Tracts, one after the Prophecy and one after the lesson from Exodus that takes the place of the Epistle; it has no Gradual. The first Easter Mass on Holy Saturday, among many other peculiarities, keeps so much of the nature of a Lenten vigil that it has, after the great Alleluia and its verse, a Tract. On Whitsun eve the characters of Eastertide and a vigil are combined. It has no Gradual, but first an Allelula, then a Tract. It will be noticed that each verse in the Tracts is marked V. This calls attention to the nature of the old *psalmus tractus* that was sung straight through by the cantor. There are no responses for the choir.

The second exception to the usual order is in Eastertide (from the first Easter Mass to the Saturday after Pentecost). During this time the great Alleluia is sung; it has displaced the Gradual altogether. "Rightly during the fifty days in memory of this our most peaceful and happy deed we are accustomed to sing Alleluia oftener and more joyfully."[18] An exception in this season is the Easter octave. The greatest feasts have always kept older arrangements, so on Easter Day and till the Friday followmg the normal Gradual followed by the Alleluiatic verse (and a sequence) has remained. From Whit-Saturday to the end of paschal time, including all feasts, instead of these two separate chants, one, the great Alleluia, is substituted. Two Alleluias are sung first as a sort of antiphon; the second has a *jubilus*. Two verses follow, each with an Alleluia and *jubilus* at the end. These last two Alleluias have the same melody, different from that of the first two. The verses are taken from all parts of the Bible, in the *Proprium temporis* chiefly from passages in the New Testament about the Resurrection. In this case too feasts and other Masses that may occur in Eastertide are provided with this great Alleluia, as an alternative to be used then. Lastly, five occasions (Easter, Whitsun, *Corpus Christi*, the Seven Dolours, and Requiems) have a sequence after the Gradual. These five are all that Pius V's reform left of the innumerable medieval poems once inserted at this place.

3. *Gradual in Other Rites*.—In the East, too, there are fragments of the psalms once sung between the lessons, that therefore correspond to our Gradual. In the Byzantine Rite the reader of the Epistle first chants "the Psalm of David" and then the "*Prokeimenon* of the Apostle". Both are short fragments of psalms. The *Prokeimenon* only is now usually read. It is printed before each Epistle in the *Apostolos*. After the Epistle the reader should sing Alleluia and another fragment of a psalm. This too is now always omitted by both Orthodox and Melchites; even the *Prokeimenon* seems to be said only on Sundays and feasts in many churches; but I have found churches where it is still used every day. The Armenian Rite, which is only a modified form of that of Constantinople, has however kept the older arrangement of three lessons. Before the Prophecy a fragment called the *Saghmos Jashu* (Psalm of dinnertime) is sung, before the Epistle the *Mesedi*, again a verse or two from a psalm, and before the Gospel the *Alelu Jashu* (Alleluia of dinner-time) consisting of two Alleluias and a verse. Of the two older rites, that of St. James has the same arrangement as Constantinople (a *Prokeimenon* before and an Alleluia after the Epistle), that of St. Mark has a verse and an Alleluia after it.

The Nestorians have hymns (not Biblical texts) before both Epistle and Gospel which they call *Turgama,* and three verses of psalms each followed by three Alleluias (this group is called *Zumara)* after the Epistle. The Gallican Rite in the time of St. Germanus of Paris (d.576) had three lessons. The *Benedicite* canticle (which he calls *Benedictio)* was sung after the second, sometimes by boys, sometimes by a deacon. The place of this canticle was not always the same. At times it followed the first lesson. The present Ambrosian Rite sometimes has a Prophecy before the Epistle. In this case there follows the *Psalmellus,* two or three verses from a psalm. After the Epistle, Hallelujah is sung (on feasts of Christ, except in Octaves, twice), then a verse, then again Hallelujah. In Lent, on vigils and fast days, instead of this the *Cantus* (our Tract) is used. After the Gospel follows the *Antiphona post Evangelium,* from various books of Scripture (except in Lent and on fast days). And on certain great feasts there is also an antiphon before the Gospel. The Mozarabic Rite has three lessons. After the Prophecy follows a chant marked *Psallendo.* It has two verses, then a third marked V, then the second is repeated. The priest says: *Silentium facite* and the Epistle is read. Nothing is sung after the Epistle. In the seventh century a Council of Toledo (633) commanded under pain of excommunication that the Gospel should follow the Epistle immediately. After the Gospel follows the *Lauda,* consisting of an Alleluia, a verse, and a second Alleluia.[19]

4. *Rules for the Gradual.*—The nature and arrangement of the chants that form the Gradual in the Roman Rite have already been explained, so that little need be added here about its use. As a result of the reaction of low Mass upon high Mass (by which everything sung by anyone else must also be read by the priest at the altar), the celebrant at high Mass reads the Gradual with the Alleluia, Tract, or Sequence, according to the form for the day, immediately after he has read the Epistle and at the same place (this is just as at low Mass). As soon as the subdeacon has finished chanting the Epistle, the Gradual (of course, again, in the complete form for the day) is sung by the choir. There is now no rule for the distribution of its parts. All may be sung straight through by the whole choir. It is however usual (partly for the sake of artistic effect) to divide the texts so that some are sung by one or two cantors. A common arrangement is for the cantors to sing the first words of the Gradual (to the asterisk in the choir books), the choir continues, the cantors sing the *versus* and the first Alleluia, the choir the second, the cantors the Alleluiatic verse, and the choir the last Alleluja. Or, all Alleluias are sung by the cantors, the choir only joining in the neum. Similar arrangements may be made easily for the Tract or the great Alleluia in Eastertide. Normally it is all sung to plain-song and, now that we have the Vatican edition, to the form in that book. But there is no law about this, and the Gradual may be sung to any figured music that satisfies the principles of the *Motu Proprio* of 22 November, 1903.

5. *Gradual-book.*—The name Gradual *(Graduale Romanum)* is also used for the book that contains the music sung by the choir at Mass. The name comes from this most important chant, but the book contains the plain-song music for the Ordinary (this part is also published along with the title *Ordinarium Missae* or *Kyriale*) and all the Propers for the year. This book is one of the three parts of the old Roman *Antiphonarium*. Originally all the chants of the choir were contained in that. But by the ninth century it was already divided into three, the *Graduale* or *Cantatorium* for Mass, and the *Responsiale* and *Antiphonarium* (in a stricter sense) for the Office. The history of the book forms part of that of the development of plain-song. An authentic edition (the *Medicaea*) was issued at Rome in 1614. It is now supplanted by the Vatican edition (1908), of which reproductions are being issued by various publishers.

Chapter Notes:

1 *Serm.* CLXXVI, 1.
2 Duchesne, p. 161.
3 *Ordo Rom.* I, III, 9, VI, 5.
4 Durandus, IV, 19.
5 *De Missa*, II, 16.
6 *Loc. cit.*, note 5.
7 *Hom. in Ps.*, CXIV.
8 Serm. ii *in anniv. assumpt.*
9 Brightman, p. 37.
10 *Hist. Eccl.*, VII, xix.
11 *De Officiis*, I.
12 *Mitrale*, III, 3, P.L., CCXIII.
13 Durandus, IV, 20.
14 *Les Mélodies Grégoriennes d'après la tradition* (Tournai, 1881), xi, 170-9.
15 Card. Humbert's *Dialogus* LVI-LVII, in Will, *Acta et Scripta de Controv. Eccl. Graecae et Latinae* (Leipzig, 1861), pp. 122-3).
16 *Ordo Rom. I*, p. 130, supplemented by *Ordo Romanus III.*
17 Durandus, IV, 21.
18 St. Bede, II, Hom.,x.
19 *Missale mixtum*, P.L., LXXXV, e.g. for the first Sunday of Advent, col.110, 112).

15

Gospel in the Liturgy

1. *History*.—From the very earliest times the public reading of parts of the Bible was an important element in the Liturgy inherited from the service of the Synagogue. The first part of that service, before the bread and wine were brought up to be offered and consecrated, was the Liturgy of the Catechumens. This consisted of prayers, litanies, hymns, and especially readings from Holy Scripture. The object of the readings was obviously to instruct the people. Books were rare and few could read. What the Christian of the first centuries knew of the Bible, of Old Testament history, St. Paul's theology, and Our Lord's life he had learned from hearing the lessons in church, and from the homilies that followed to explain them. In the first period the portions read were—like the rite— not yet stereotyped. St. Justin Martyr (d. c.167) in describing the rite he knew (apparently at Rome) begins by saying that: "On the day of the sun, as it is called, all the inhabitants of town and country come together in the same place, and the commentaries of the Apostles or writings of the Prophets are read as long as time will allow. Then, when the reader has stopped, he who presides admonishes and exhorts all to imitate such glorious examples."[1] At this time, then, the text was read continuously from a Bible, till the president (the bishop who was celebrating) told the reader to stop. These readings varied in number. A common practice was to read first from the Old Testament (*Prophetia*), then from an Epistle (*Apostolus*) and lastly from a Gospel (*Evangelium*). In any case the Gospel was read last, as the fulfilment of all the rest. Origen calls it the crown of all the holy writings.[2] "We hear the Gospel as if God were present", says St. Augustine.[3] It seems that in some places (in the West especially) for a time catechumens were not allowed to stay for the Gospel, which was considered part of the *disciplina arcani*. At the Synod of Orange, in 441, and at Valencia, in 524, they wanted to change this rule. On the other hand, in all Eastern Liturgies (e.g. that of the *Apostolic Constitutions*) the catechumens are dismissed after the Gospel.

The public reading of certain Gospels in churches was the most important factor in deciding which were to be considered canonical. The four that were received and read in the Liturgy everywhere were for that very reason admitted to the Canon of Scripture. We have evidences of this liturgical reading of the Gospel from every part of Christendom in the first centuries. For Syria, the *Apostolic Constitutions* tell us that when a bishop was ordained he blessed the people "after the reading of the law and prophets and our Epistles and Acts and Gospels", and the manner of reading the Gospel is described. The *Peregrinatio Silviae* (*Etheriae*) describes the reading of the Gospel at Jerusalem (see **GLOSSARY**).[4] The homilies of St. Basil and St. John Chrysostom explain the Gospel as read at Caesarea, Antioch, Constantinople. In Egypt, St. Cyril of Alexandria writes to the Emperor Theodosius II about the liturgical use of the Gospels.[5] In Africa, Tertullian mentions the same thing, and tells us that the Roman Church "reads the Law and the Prophets together with the Gospels and Apostolic letters".[6] St. Cyprian ordained a certain confessor named Aurelian that he might "read the Gospel that forms martyrs".[7] In every rite then, from the beginning, as now, the reading of the Gospel formed the chief feature, the cardinal point of the Liturgy of the Catechumens. It was not only read in the Liturgy. The *Peregrinatio Silviae* (loc. cit.) alludes to the Gospel read at cock-crow. So in the Byzantine Rite it still forms part of the Office of *Orthros* (Lauds). At Rome the Gospel of the Liturgy was read first, with a homily, at Matins, of which use we have now only a fragment. But the monastic Office still contains the whole Gospel read after the *Te Deum*.

Gradually the portions to be read in the Liturgy became fixed. The steps in the development of the texts used are: first in the book of the Gospels (or complete Bible) marginal signs are added to show how much is to be read each time. Then indexes are drawn up to show which passages are appointed for each day. These indexes (generally written at the beginning or end of the Bible) are called *Synaxaria* in Greek, *Capitularia* in Latin; they give the first and last words of each lesson (*pericope*). The complete *Capitularium* giving references for all the Lessons to be read each day is a *Comes, Liber comitis*, or *comicus*. Later they are composed with the whole text, so as to dispense with searching for it; they have thus become *Evangeliaria*. The next step is to arrange together all the Lessons for each day, Prophecy, Epistle, Gospel, and even readings from non-canonical books. Such a compilation is a *Lectionarium*. Then, finally, when complete Missals are drawn up (about the tenth to the thirteenth centuries), the Lessons are included in them.

2. *Selection of Gospels*.— What portions were read? In the first place there was a difference as to the text used. Till about the fifth century it seems that in Syria, at any rate, compilations of the four Gospels made into one narrative were used. The famous *Diatessaron* of Tatian is supposed to have been composed for this purpose. The Mozarabic and Gallican Rites may have imitated this custom for a time. St. Augustine made an unsuccessful attempt to introduce it in Africa by inserting into one Gospel passages taken from the others.[8] But the commoner use was to read the text of one of the Gospels as it stands. On great feasts the appropriate passage was taken. Thus, we learn from the *Peregrinatio Silviae*, at Jerusalem on Good

Friday: *Legitur iam ille locus de evangelio cata Johannem, ubi reddidit Spiritum.*[9] On Easter Eve *Denuo legitur ille locus evangelii resurrectionis.*[10] On Low Sunday they read the Gospel about St. Thomas: *Non credo nisi videro*", and so on.[11] The *Peregrinatio* gives us the Gospels thus read for a number of days throughout the year. For the rest of the year it seems that originally the text was read straight through (probably with the omission of such special passages). At each *Synaxis* they began again where they had left off last time. Thus Cassian says that in his time the monks read the New Testament through.[12] The homilies of certain Fathers (St. John Chrysostom, St. Augustine, etc.) show that the lessons followed each other in order. In the Eastern Churches the principle obtained that the Four Gospels should be read right through in the course of each year. The Byzantine Church began reading St. Matthew immediately after Pentecost. St. Luke followed from September (when their new year begins), St. Mark began before Lent, and St. John was read during Eastertide. There were some exceptions, e.g. for certain feasts and anniversaries. A similar arrangement is still observed by them, as any copy of their Gospel-book will show. The Syrians have the same arrangement, the Copts a different order, but based on the same principle of continuous readings. It is well known that they name their Sundays after the Sunday Gospel, e.g., the fourth after Pentecost is "Sunday of the Centurion" because Matt., viii, 5 sqq., is read then.

This brings us to a much disputed question: what principle underlies the order of the Gospels in the Roman missal? It is clearly not that of continuous readings. Father Beissel, S.J., has made an exhaustive study of this question (*Entstehung der Perikopen*), in which he compares all manner of *Comites*, Eastern and Western. Shortly, his conclusions are these: The root of the order is the selection of appropriate Gospels for the chief feasts and seasons of the year; for these, the account that seemed most complete was chosen, without regard to the particular Evangelist. The intervals were then filled up so as to complete the picture of Our Lord's life, but without chronological order. First, Easter was considered with Holy Week. The lessons for this time are obvious. Working backwards, in Lent the Gospel of Our Lord's fast in the desert was put at the beginning, the entry to Jerusalem and the anointing by Mary (John, xii, 1, "six days before the Pasch") at the end. This led to the resurrection of Lazarus (in the East, too, always at this place). Some chief incidents from the end of Christ's life filled up the rest. The Epiphany suggested three Gospels about the Wise Men, the Baptism, and the first miracle, which events it commemorates,[13] and then events of Christ's childhood. Christmas and its feasts had obvious Gospels; Advent, those of the Day of Judgement and the preparation for Our Lord's coming by St. John Baptist. Forward from Easter, Ascension Day and Pentecost demanded certain passages clearly. The time between was filled with Our Lord's last messages before He left us (taken from His words on Maundy Thursday in St. John). There remains the most difficult set of Gospels of all—those for the Sundays after Pentecost. They seem to be meant to complete what has not yet been told about His life. Nevertheless, their order is very hard to understand. It has been suggested that they are meant to correspond to the lessons of Matins. In some cases, at any rate, such a comparison is tempting. Thus, on the third Sunday, in the first Nocturn, we read about Saul seeking his father's asses (I Kings, ix), in the Gospel (and therefore in the third Nocturn) about the man who loses one sheep and the lost drachma (Luke, xv); on the fourth Sunday, David fights Goliath *in nomine Domini exercituum* (I Kings, xvii), in the Gospel, St. Peter throws out his net *in verbo tuo* (Luke ,v); on the fifth, David mourns his enemy Saul (II Kings, i), in the Gospel we are told to be reconciled to our enemies (Matt., v). The eighth Sunday begins the Book of Wisdom (first Sunday in August), and in the Gospel the wise steward is commended (Luke, xvi). Perhaps the nearness of certain feasts had an influence, too. In some lists Luke, v, where our Lord says, "From henceforth thou shalt catch men", to St. Peter, came on the Sunday before his feast (29 June),—and the story of St. Andrew and the multiplied bread (John, vi) before 30 November. Durandus (see **DURANDUS**) notices this.[14] Beissel is disposed to think that much of the arrangement is accidental, and that no satisfactory explanation of the order of Gospels after Pentecost has been found. In any case the order throughout the year is very old. A tradition says that St. Jerome arranged it by command of St. Damasus.[15] Certainly the Lessons now sung in our churches are those that St. Gregory the Great's deacon chanted at Rome thirteen hundred years ago.

3. *Ceremony of Singing the Gospel.*—The Gospel has been for many centuries in East and West the privilege of the deacon. This was not always the case. At first a reader *(lector)* read all the lessons. We have seen a case of this in the story of St. Cyprian and Aurelian (see above). St. Jerome (d. 420) speaks of the deacon as reader of the Gospel,[16] but the practice was not yet uniform in all churches. At Constantinople, on Easter day, the bishop did so; in Alexandria, it was an archdeacon, in other places deacons read the Gospel; in many churches only priests. The *Apostolic Constitutions* refer the Gospel to the deacon; and in 527 a council, at Vaison, says deacons "are worthy to read the words that Christ spoke in the Gospel." This custom became gradually universal, as is shown by the formulae that accompany the tradition of the Gospel-book at the deacon's ordination (the eleventh century Visigothic *Liber ordinum* has the form: *Ecce evangelium Christi, accipe, ex quo annunties bonam gratiam fidei populo*). An exception that lasted through the Middle Ages was that at Christmas the emperor, dressed in a rochet and stole, sang the midnight Gospel: *Exiit edictum a Caesare Augusto* etc. Another mark of respect was that everyone stood to hear the Gospel, bareheaded, in the attitude of a servant receiving his master's orders. Sozomenos is indignant that the Patriarch of Alexandria sat ("a new and insolent practice"). The Grand Masters of the Knights of St. John drew their swords while the Gospel was read. This custom seems still to be observed by some great noblemen in Poland. If any one has a stick in his hand he is to lay it down, but the bishop holds his crosier. The Gospel was sung from the ambo, a pulpit generally halfway down the church, from which it could be best heard by every one. Often there were two ambos: one for the other lessons, on the left (looking from the altar); the other, for the Gospel, on the right. From here the deacon faced south, where the men generally gather. Later, when the ambo had disappeared, the deacon turned to the north. *Micrologus* notices this and explains it as an imitation of the celebrant's position at the altar at low Mass—one of the ways in which that service has reacted on high Mass.[17] The Byzantine Church still commands the deacon to sing the Gospel from the ambo, though with them, too, it has generally become only a theoretical place in the middle of the floor. The deacon first asked the blessing of the bishop (or celebrant) then went to the ambo with the book, in procession, accompanied by lights and incense. The ceremonies in the First and Second Roman Ordos are almost exactly our ceremonial. Meanwhile the Gradual was sung (see **GRADUAL**). The *Dominus vobiscum* at the beginning, the announcement of the Gospel *Sequentia sancti Evangelii*, etc.), and the answer, *Gloria tibi Domine*, are also mentioned by the sixth-century Germanus. At the end of the Gospel the people answered *Amen*, or *Deo Gratias*, or *Benedictus qui venit in nomine Domini*.[18] Our present answer, *Laus tibi Christe*, seems to be a later one. The elaborate care taken to decorate the book of the Gospels throughout the Middle Ages was also a sign of respect for its contents. St. Jerome speaks of this.[19] In a collection of manuscripts the *Evangeliaria* nearly always stand out from the rest by their special sumptuousness. They are not uncommonly written in gold and silver letters on vellum stained purple—the extreme limit of medieval splendour.

The bindings, too, are nearly always adorned with special care. It is on Gospel books that one generally sees ivory carvings, metal-work, jewellery, enamel, sometimes relics. The same tradition continues in the East. Allowing for doubtful modern taste in Greece, Russia, Syria, etc., the *Evangelion* (Gospel Book) is still the handsomest book, often the handsomest object in a church. When it is not in use it generally displays the enamels of its cover on a desk outside the *Iconostasis*. To kiss the book was always from early times a sign of respect. This was done at one time not only by the celebrant and deacon, but by all the people present. Pope Honorius III (1216-27) forbade this; but the book is still kissed by any high prelates who may be present. When the ambo disappeared in the West the subdeacon held the book while the Gospel was sung by the deacon. He also carried it first to lay it on the altar.[20] The deacon made the sign of the cross first on the book and then on himself—taking a blessing from the book The meaning of all these marks of reverence is that the Gospel-book, which contains Christ's words, was taken as a symbol of Christ himself. It was sometimes carried in the place of honour in various processions; something of the same idea underlay the practice of putting it on a throne or altar in the middle of the synods. During provincial and general synods the Gospel is to be sung at each session.[21] Superstitious abuses afterwards developed, in which it was used for magic. The Byzantine Church has developed the ceremony of carrying the *Evangelion* to the ambo into the elaborate rite of the "Little Entrance", and all the other Eastern Churches have similar stately ceremonies at this point of the Liturgy. Another special practice that may be noticed here is that at a papal High Mass the Gospel (and the Epistle too) is read in Latin and Greek. This is already noticed by the first Roman *Ordo*. At Constantinople the Patriarch, on Easter Day, reads the Gospel in Greek, and it is then read by other persons in various languages. The same thing is done again at the *Hesperinos*. The little Synopsis of Constantinople

(1883) gives this Gospel of the *Hesperinos* (John, xx, 19-25) in Greek (with two poetic versions, hexameter and iambic), Slavonic, Bulgarian, Albanian, Latin, Italian, French, English, Arabic, Turkish, and Armenian (all in Greek characters). The same custom is observed in Russia, where the Gospel of the Liturgy (John, i) is read in Slavonic, Hebrew, Greek, and Latin.

4. *Present Ceremony of the Gospel.*—Except for the disappearance of the ambo, the rules of the Rubrics in the Missal are still almost exactly those we have seen observed in the Roman Rite since the seventh or eighth centuries.[22] After the Epistle the deacon puts the Gospel book in the middle of the altar (while the celebrant reads his Gospel from the Missal). Liturgical editors publish books containing the Epistles and Gospels, otherwise a second Missal is used (the sub-deacon has already chanted the Epistle from the same book). The celebrant then puts incense into the thurible and blesses it as usual. The subdeacon goes down and waits below, before the middle of the altar. The deacon kneeling by the celebrant just behind him at his right says the *Munda cor meum*. Then, rising and taking the book, he kneels with it before the celebrant (turning towards the north) and says *Jube domne benedicere*. *Jube* with an infinitive is a common late Latin way of expressing a polite imperative. *Domnus* is a medieval form instead of *dominus*, which got to be looked upon as a Divine title. The celebrant blesses him with the form in the Missal, *Dominus sit in corde tuo . . .*), and the sign of the cross; he kisses the celebrant's hand laid on the Missal. The celebrant goes to the Epistle side, where he waits; he turns round towards the deacon when the Gospel begins. The deacon, holding the book lifted up with both hands, comes down to the subdeacon's side; they make the usual reverence to the altar and the procession starts. The thurifer goes first with incense, then two acolytes, then the deacon and sub-deacon side by side, the deacon on the right. We have seen the antiquity of lights and incense at the Gospel.

All this time, of course, the Gradual is being sung. The procession arrives at the place that represents the old ambo. It is still to the right of the altar (north side), but now inside the sanctuary, so that, except in very large churches, there is hardly any way to go; often the old procession to the ambo (the Latin "little entrance") is represented only by an awkward turning round. Arrived at the place, the deacon and sub-deacon face each other, the sub-deacon receives the book and holds it up open before him. Originally the sub-deacon (two are required by the *Ordo Romanus I*, one as thurifer)[23] accompanied the deacon up into the ambo, helped him find his place in the book, and then stood back behind him by the steps. At Milan, where the ambo is still used, this is still done.

In the Roman Rite the subdeacon himself takes the place of the desk of the ambo. But the *Caeremoniale Episcoporum* still allows the use of *legilia vel ambones* if there be any in the church. In that case the subdeacon is to stand behind the desk or at the deacon's right and to turn over the pages if necessary. There is a difficulty about the way they stand. The *Ritus celebrandi* says that the deacon is to stand *contra altare versus populum*.[24] This must mean looking down the church. On the other hand the *Caeremoniale Episcoporum* says that the sub-deacon stands *vertens renes non quidem altari, sed versus ipsam partem dexteram quae pro aquilone figuratur*.[25] This means the way in which they always stand now; namely, the deacon looks north or slightly northeast (supposing the church to be properly orientated); the book is in the same direction as the Missal for the Gospel at low Mass. The acolytes stand on either side of the sub-deacon, the thurifer at the deacon's right. The deacon, *junctis manibus*, sings *Dominus vobiscum* (answered by the choir as usual), then, making the sign of the cross with the right thumb on the book (the cross marked at these words in the Missal is put there to show the place) and signing himself on forehead, lips, and breast, he sings *Sequentia* [or *Initium*] *sancti Evangelii secundum* N…It appears that *sequentia* is a neuter plural. While the choir answers, *Gloria tibi Domine*, he incenses the book three times, in the middle, to its right, and left, bowing before and after. He gives the thurible back and sings the text of the Gospel straight through. He bows at the Holy Name, if it occur, and sometimes (on the Epiphany, at the third Christmas Mass, etc.) genuflects (towards the book). The tones for the Gospel are given at the end of the new (Vatican) Missal. The normal one is a recitative on *do* falling to *la* four syllables before the end of each phrase, with the cadence *si, la, si, si-do* for questions, and a *scandicus la, si (quilisma), do* before the end. Two others, more ornamented are now added *ad libitum*. The celebrant, standing at the Epistle side, looking towards the deacon, hears the Gospel and bows or genuflects with him, but towards the altar. When the Gospel is over the subdeacon brings him the book to kiss, he says: *Per evangelica dicta*, and he is incensed by the deacon. The Mass then continues. We have noted that the only other persons now allowed to kiss the book are the ordinary, if he be present, and other prelates above him in rank.[26] A bishop celebrating in his own diocese reads his Gospel sitting on his throne, and hears it standing there, holding his crosier with both hands.[27] In this case no one else is ever to kiss the book.[28]

In low Mass the ceremonies for the Gospel are, as usual, merely an abridgement and simplifying of those for high Mass. When the celebrant has finished reading the Gradual he says the *Munda cor meum*, etc., in the middle of the altar he says, *Jube Domine benedicere*, because he is addressing God). Meanwhile the server brings the Missal to the north side (this is only an imitation of the deacon's place at high Mass). With the book turned slightly towards the people, the priest reads the Gospel with the same ceremonies (except, of course, for the incense) and kisses it at the end.

5. *The Last Gospel*.—The Gospel read at the end of Mass is a late development. Originally (till about the twelfth cen-

GOSPEL IN THE LITURGY

tury) the service ended with the words that still imply that, *Ite missa est*. The prayer *Placeat tibi*, the blessing, and the last Gospel are all private devotions that have been gradually absorbed by the liturgical service. The beginning of St. John's Gospel (I, 1-14) was much used as an object of special devotion throughout the Middle Ages. It was sometimes read at children's baptism or at extreme unction.[29] There are curious cases of its use for various superstitious practices, written on amulets and charms. It then began to be recited by priests as part of their prayers after Mass. A trace of this is still left in the *Caeremoniale Episcoporum*, which directs that a bishop at the end of his Mass shall begin the Last Gospel at the altar and continue it (by heart) as he goes away to take off the vestments. It will also be noted that it is still not printed in the Ordinary of the Mass, though of course the rubric about it is there, and it will be found in the third Christmas Mass. By the thirteenth century it was sometimes said at the altar. But Durandus still supposes the Mass to be finished by the *Ite missa est*;[30] he adds the *Placeat* and blessing as a sort of supplement, and then goes on at once to describe the psalms said after Mass—*deinde statim dicuntur hymni illi: Benedicite et Laudate*.[31] Nevertheless, the practice of saying it at the altar grew; eventually Pius V made this practice universal for the Roman Rite in his edition of the Missal (1570). The fact that all these three additions after the *Ite Missa est* are to be said, even at high Mass, without any special ceremony, preserves the memory of their more or less accidental connexion with the liturgy. The normal Last Gospel is John,i, 1-14. It is read by the celebrant at the north side of the altar after the blessing. He reads from the altar card with the usual introduction (*Dominus vobiscum... Initium S. Evangelii*, etc.), taking the sign of the cross from the altar. He genuflects at the words, *Et verbum caro factum est*, and the server, at the end, answers Deo gratias". At high Mass the deacon and subdeacon stand on either side, genuflect too, and answer. They do not read the Gospel; it is in no way to be

305

sung by the deacon, like the essential Gospel of the Liturgy. Whenever an office is commemorated, whose Gospel is begun in the ninth lesson of Matins, that Gospel is substituted for John, i, at the end of Mass. In this case the Missal must be brought to the north side (at high Mass by the sub-deacon). This applies to all Sundays, *feriae*, and vigils that are commemorated. At the third Mass on Christmas day (since John, i, 1-14, forms the Gospel of the Mass) that of the Epiphany is read at the end; at low Mass on Palm Sunday the Gospel of the blessing of palms is read. Of Eastern Rites the Armenians alone have copied this practice of the last Gospel from the Latins.

Chapter Notes:

1   *I Apology,* 67.
2   *In Johannem*, i, 4, praef., P.G., XIV, 26.
3   *Ibid.*, tract. xxx, 1, P.L., LXXXV, 1632.
4   Duchesne, p. 493.
5   P.G., LXXVI, 471.
6   *De praeser.*, VI, 36).
7   *Ep.* xxxiii, P.L., IV, 328.
8   *Sermo* 232, P.L., XXXVIII, 1108.
9   Duchesne, p. 492.
10 *Ibid.*, p. 492.
11 *Ibid.*, p. 494.
12 Coll. patr., X, 14.
13 Antiphon *ad Magnificat*, in 2 vesp.
14 Durandus, VI, 142, *De dom.* 25a *post Pent.*
15 Berno, *De officio missae*, i, P.L., CXLII, 1057; *Micrologus*, xxxi, P.L., CLI, 999, 1003.
16 *Ep.* cxlvii, n. 6.
17 *De missa*, ix.

[18] Durandus, IV, 24.

[19] Ep. xxii, 32.

[20] Amalarius of Metz: *De Eccl. offic.*, P.L., CV, 1112.

[21] *Caeremoniale,* I, xxxi, 16.

[22] *Rubr. gen.*, X, 6; *Ritus cel.*, VI, 5.

[23] *Ordo Rom. I*, p. 131. There are sixth century mosaics at Ravenna depicting the bishop attended by a deacon carrying the Gospel-book, and a subdeacon the thurible (Ed.).

[24] *Rit. cel.*, VI, 5.

[25] *Caeremoniale,* II, viii, 44.

[26] *Ibid.*, I, xxx, 1, 3.

[27] *Ibid.*, II, viii, 41, 46.

[28] *Ibid.*, I, xxix, 9.

[29] *De SS. Missae,* II, xxiv, 8.

[30] Durandus, IV, 57.

[31] *Ibid.*, IV, 59.

16

Offertory (*Offertorium*)

The rite by which the bread and wine are presented (offered) to God before they are consecrated and the prayers and chant that accompany it.

1. *History*.—The idea of this preparatory hallowing of the matter of the sacrifice by offering it to God is very old and forms an important element of every Christian liturgy. In the earliest period we have no evidence of anything but the bringing up of the bread and wine as they are wanted, before the Consecration prayer. Justin Martyr says: "Then bread and a cup of water and wine are brought to the president of the brethren".[1] But soon the placing of the offering on the altar was accompanied by a prayer that God should accept these gifts, sanctify them, change them into the Body and Blood of his Son, and give us in return the grace of Communion. The Liturgy of the *Apostolic Constitutions* says: "The deacons bring the gifts to the bishop at the altar . . ."[2] This silent prayer is undoubtedly an Offertory prayer. But a later modification in the East brought about one of the characteristic differences between Eastern and Roman liturgies. All Eastern (and the old Gallican) rites prepare the gift before the Liturgy begins. This ceremony, the *Proskomide*, is especially elaborate in the Byzantine and its derived rites. It takes place on the credence table. The bread and wine are arranged, divided, incensed; and many prayers are said over them involving the idea of an offertory.

The gifts are left there and are brought to the altar in solemn procession at the beginning of the Liturgy of the Faithful. This leaves no room for another offertory then. However, when they are placed on the altar prayers are said by the celebrant and a litany by the deacon which repeat the offertory idea. Rome alone has kept the older custom of one offertory and of preparing the gifts when they are wanted at the beginning of the Mass of the Faithful. Originally at this moment the people brought up bread and wine which were received by the deacons and placed by them on the altar. Traces of the custom remain at a papal Mass and at Milan. The office of the *vecchioni* in Milan cathedral, often quoted as an Ambrosian peculiarity, is really a Roman addition that spoils the order of the old Milanese rite. Originally the only Roman Offertory prayers were the secrets. The Gregorian Sacramentary contains only the rubric: *deinde offertorium, et dicitur oratio super oblata.* The *Oratio super oblata* is the Secret. All the old secrets express the offertory idea clearly. They were said silently by the celebrant (hence their name) and so are not introduced by *Oremus.* This corresponds to the oldest custom mentioned in the *Apostolic Constitutions.* Its reason is that meanwhile the people sang a psalm (the Offertory chant). In the Middle Ages, as the public presentation of the gifts by the people had disappeared, there seemed to be a void at this moment which was filled by our present Offertory prayers. For a long time these prayers were considered a private devotion of the priest, like the preparation at the foot of the altar. They are a Northern (late Gallican) addition, not part of the old Roman Rite, and were at first not written in missals. *Micrologus* says: "The Roman order appointed no prayer after the Offertory before the Secret."[3] He mentions the later Offertory prayers as a "Gallican order" and says that they occur "not from any law but as an ecclesiastical custom". The medieval Offertory prayers vary considerably. They were established at Rome by the fourteenth century. The present Roman prayers were compiled from various sources,

Gallican or Mozarabic. The prayer *Suscipe sancte Pater* occurs in Charles the Bald's (875-877) prayer book; *Deus qui humanae substantiae* is modified from a Christmas Collect in the Gregorian Sacramentary. *Offerimus tibi Domine* and *Veni sanctificator* are Mozarabic. Before Pius V's Missal these prayers were often preceded by the title *Canon minor* or *Secretella* (as amplifications of the Secret). The Missal of Pius V (1570) printed them in the Ordinary. Since then the prayers that we know form part of the Roman Mass. The ideas expressed in them are obvious. Only it may be noted that two expressions: *hanc immaculatam hostiam* and *calicem salutaris* dramatically anticipate the moment of consecration, as does the Byzantine *Cherubikon* (see **GLOSSARY**).

While the Offertory is made the people (choir) sing a verse (the *Offertorium* in the sense of a text to be sung) that forms part of the Proper of the Mass. No such chant is mentioned in the *Apostolic Constitutions*, but it may no doubt be supposed as the reason why the celebrant there too prays silently. It is referred to by St. Augustine.[4] The *Offertorium* was once a whole psalm with an antiphon. By the time of the Gregorian Antiphonary the psalm has been reduced to a few verses only, which are always given in that book. So also the Second Roman Ordo: *Canitur offertorium cum versibus*. Durandus (see **DURANDUS**) notes with disapproval that in his time the verses of the psalm are left out.[5] Now only the antiphon is sung, except at requiems. It is taken from the psalter, or other book of the Bible, or is often not a Biblical text. It refers in some way to the feast or occasion of the Mass, never to the offering of bread and wine. Only the requiem has preserved a longer offertory with one verse and the repetition of the last part of the antiphon (the text is not Biblical).

2. *Present Use.*—At high Mass, as soon as the celebrant has chanted the *Oremus* followed by no prayer, the choir sings the Offertory. When they have finished there remains an interval till the Preface which may (when the organ is permitted) be filled by music of the organ or at any time by singing some approved hymn or chant. Meanwhile the celebrant first says the Offertory chant. The corporal has been spread on the altar during the creed. The subdeacon brings the empty chalice and the paten with the bread from the credence table to the altar. The deacon hands the paten and bread to the celebrant. He takes it and holding it up says the prayer: *Suscipe, sancte Pater*. At the end he makes a sign of the cross with the paten over the altar and slips the bread from it on to the corporal. Soon after the paten is given to the subdeacon's charge till it is wanted again for the fraction. The deacon pours wine into the chalice, the subdeacon water, which is first blessed by the celebrant with the form: *Deus qui humanae substantiae*. The deacon hands the chalice to the celebrant, who, holding it up, says the prayer: *Offerimus tibi Domine*. The deacon also lays his right hand on the foot of the chalice and says this prayer with the celebrant— a relic of the old idea that the chalice is in his care. The celebrant makes the sign of the cross with the chalice and stands it behind the bread on the corporal. The deacon covers it with the pall. The celebrant, bowing down, his hands joined and resting on the altar, says the prayer: *In spiritu humilitatis*; rising he says the *Veni sanctificator* making the sign of the cross over all the *oblata* at the word *benedic*. Then follows the incensing of the altar and the *Lavabo* (see **LAVABO**). The use of incense at this point is medieval and not originally Roman (remnant of the incense at the Gallican procession of the *oblata?*). *Micrologus* notes that the Roman order uses incense at the Gospel, not at the Offertory; but he admits that in his time (eleventh century) the *oblata* are incensed by nearly everyone.[6] Finally, after the *Lavabo* the celebrant at the middle of the altar, looking up and then bowing down, says the prayer *Suscipe, sancta Trinitas* which sums up the Offertory idea. The *Orate fratres* and secrets follow.

At low Mass, the parts of the deacon and subdeacon are taken partly by the server and partly by the celebrant himself. There is no incense. At requiems the water is not blessed, and the subdeacon does not hold the paten. The Dominicans still prepare the offering before Mass begins. This is one of their Gallican peculiarities and so goes back to the Eastern *Proskomide*. The Milanese and Mozarabic Missals have adopted the Roman Offertory. The accompanying chant is called *Sacrificium* at Toledo.

Chapter Notes:

1   *I Apology,* LXV, cf, LXVII.
2   *Apost. Const.,* VIII, xii, 3-4.
3   *Micrologus,* CXI.
4   *Retract.,* II, xi, P.L., XXXII, 63.
5   Durandus, IV, 26.
6   *Micrologus,* IX.

17

LAVABO

The first word of that portion of Ps. xxv said by the celebrant at Mass while he washes his hands after the Offertory, from which word the whole ceremony is named. The principle of washing the hands before celebrating the holy Liturgy—at first an obvious practical precaution of cleanness, then interpreted also symbolically—occurs naturally in all rites. In the Eastern rites this is done at the beginning as part of the vesting; it is generally accompanied by the same fragment of Ps. xxv (vv. 6-12) said in the West after the Offertory. But in the *Apostolic Constitutions*, the hands of the celebrants are washed just before the dismissal of the catechumens, in the Syriac and Coptic rites after the creed. Cyril of Jerusalem (d. 386) also mentions a washing that takes place in sight of the people. So also in the Roman Rite the celebrant washes his hands before vesting, but with another prayer (*Da, Domine, virtutem*, etc., in the Missal among the *Orationes ante Missam*). The reason of the second washing, during the Mass, at Rome was no doubt the special need for it after the long ceremony of receiving the loaves and vessels of wine from the people at the Offertory (all of which is absent from the Eastern rites). The first Roman *Ordines* describe a general washing of hands by the celebrant and deacons, who have received and carried the offerings to the altar, immediately after they have done so. In the St. Amand Ordo the Pontiff washes his hands both before and after the Offertory.[1] There is as yet no mention of any

313

psalm or prayers said at the time. In the Gallican Rite the offerings were prepared before Mass began, as in the East; so there was no Offertory nor place for a *Lavabo* later. At Milan there is now an Offertory borrowed from Rome, but no washing of hands at this point; the Mozarabic Liturgy also has a Romanizing Offertory and a washing, but without any prayer.[2] The Roman Rite had in the Middle Ages two washings of the hands at the Offertory, one just before, while the deacon spread the corporal on the altar, one immediately after the incensing that follows the Offertory.[3] The first of these has now disappeared. The second was accompanied by the verses 6-12 of Psalm xxv. This psalm is first mentioned by the medieval commentators.[4] No doubt it was said from very early times as a private devotion obviously suitable for the occasion. We have noted that it accompanies the washing before the Liturgy in the Byzantine Rite. Benedict XIV notes that as late as his time (eighteenth century) "in some churches only some verses are said", although the Missal requires that all (that is from v. 6 to the end) be recited.[5] Cyril of Jerusalem already explains the washing as a symbol of purity of the soul; all the medieval writers insist on this idea.[6]

The present rule is this: At high Mass (or sung Mass), as soon as the celebrant has incensed the altar after the Offertory and has been incensed himself at the Epistle side, he remains there while his hands are washed by the acolytes, who must be waiting by the credence-table. The first acolyte pours water from the cruet over his fingers into the little dish provided, the second then hands him the towel to dry the fingers. Meanwhile he says: *Lavabo inter innocentes*, etc., to the end of the psalm, with *Gloria Patri* and *Sicut erat*. The *Gloria* is left out in Masses for the dead and in Masses *de tempore* from Passion Sunday to Holy Saturday exclusively.[7] A bishop at high Mass wears the "precious" mitre (*mitra pretiosa*) while he is incensed and washes his hands;[8] in this case a larger silver jug and basin are generally used, though the *Caeremoniale Episcoporum* does not mention them. At low Mass, since there is no incense, the celebrant goes to the Epistle side and washes his hands in the same way immediately after the prayer *Veni sanctificator*. For his convenience the altar-card on the Epistle side contains the prayer said when the water is blessed before it is put into the chalice (*Deus qui humanae substantiae*) and the verses *Lavabo*, etc.

Chapter Notes:

[1] A ninth century manuscript from the monastery of St. Amend-en-Puelle, France (Ed.).

[2] *Missale Mixtum*, P.L., LXXXV, 538.

[3] Durandus, IV, 28; Benedict XIV, *De SS. Missae,* II, 11.

[4] e.g. Durandus, *loc. cit.*

[5] *Loc. cit.*

[6] Durandus, *loc. cit.*; ST, III, Q. LXXXIII, art. 5, ad 1.

[7] *Rit. cel.*, VII, 6, in the Missal.

[8] *Caeremoniale,* 8, 64.

18

ORATE FRATRES

Orate Fratres.—The exhortation ("Pray brethren that my sacrifice and yours be acceptable to God the Father almighty") addressed by the celebrant to the people before the Secrets in the Roman Mass. It is answered: "May the Lord receive the sacrifice from thy hands to the praise and glory of his name, and for our benefit also and for that of all his holy Church." The celebrant adds: *Amen*. The form is merely an expansion of the usual *Oremus* before any prayer. It is a medieval amplification. The Jacobite rite has an almost identical form before the Anaphora; the Nestorian celebrant says: "My brethren, pray for me". Such invitations, often made by the deacon, are common in the Eastern rites. The Gallican rite had a similar one. The Mozarabic invitation at this place is: "Help me brethren by your prayers and pray to God for me." The medieval derived rites had similar formulae. Many of the old Roman Secrets (really Offertory prayers) contain the same ideas. Durandus knows the *Orate Fratres* in a slightly different form.[1] A proof that it is not an integral part of the old Roman Mass is that it is always said, not sung, aloud (as also are the prayers at the foot of the altar, the last Gospel etc.). The celebrant after the *Suscipe, Sancta Trinitas* kisses the altar, turns to the people and says: *Orate fratres*, extending and joining his hands. Turning back he finishes the sentence inaudibly. At high Mass the deacon or subdeacon, at low Mass the server, answers. The rubric of the Missal is: "The server or people around answer, if not the priest himself." In this last case he naturally changes the word *tuis* to *meis*.

Chapter Notes:

[1]   Durandus, IV, 32.

19

Secret

The Secret (Lat. *Secreta, sc. oratio secreta*) is the prayer said in a low voice by the celebrant at the end of the Offertory in the Roman Liturgy. It is the original and for a long time was the only offertory prayer. It is said in a low voice merely because at the same time the choir sings the Offertory, and it has inherited the special name of Secret as being the only prayer said in that way at the beginning. The silent recital of the Canon, which is sometimes called *Secreta*, as by Durandus (see **DURANDUS**),[1] did not begin earlier than the sixth or seventh century, Cardinal Bona thinks not till the tenth.[2] Moreover all our present offertory prayers are late additions, not made in Rome till the fourteenth century (see **OFFERTORY**). Till then the offertory act was made in silence, the corresponding prayer that followed it was our Secret. Already in the *Apostolic Constitions*,[3] the celebrant, receiving the bread and wine, prays silently, doubtless for the same reason, because a psalm was being sung. Since it is said silently the Secret is not introduced by the invitation to the people: *Oremus*. It is part of the Proper of the Mass, changing for each feast or occasion, and is built up in the same way as the Collect. The Secret too alludes to the saint or occasion of the day. But it keeps its special character inasmuch as it nearly always (always in the case of the old ones) asks God to receive these present gifts, to sanctify them, etc. All this is found exactly as now in the earliest Secrets we know, those of the Leonine Sacramentary. Already there the Collect, Secret, Postcommunion, and *Oratio ad populum* form a connected and homogeneous group of prayers. So the multiplication of Collects in one Mass (see **COLLECT**) entailed a corresponding multiplication of Secrets. For every Collect the corresponding Secret is said.

The name *Secreta* is used in the Gelasian Sacramentary; in the Gregorian book these prayers have the title *Super oblata*. Both names occur frequently in the early Middle Ages. In *Ordo Romanus II* they are: *Oratio super oblationes secreta*.[4] In the Gallican Rite there was also a variable offertory prayer introduced by an invitation to the people. It has no special name. At Milan the prayer called *Oratio super sindonem* (*Sindon* for the veil that covers the *oblata*) is said while the Offertory is being made and another *Oratio super oblata* follows after the Creed, just before the Preface. In the Mozarabic Rite after an invitation to the people, to which they answer: *Praesta aeterne omnipotens Deus*, the celebrant says a prayer that corresponds to our Secret and continues at once to the memory of the saints and intercession prayer. It has no special name. But in these other Western rites this prayer is said aloud. All the Eastern rites have prayers, now said silently, after the Great Entrance, when the gifts are brought to the altar and offered to God, but they are invariable all the year round and no one of them can be exactly compared to our Secret. Only in general can one say that the Eastern rites have prayers, corresponding more or less to our offertory idea, repeated when the bread and wine are brought to the altar.

At either high or low Mass the celebrant, having answered *Amen* to the prayer *Suscipiat Dominus sacrificium*, says in a low voice the Secret or Secrets in the same order as he said the Collects, finding each at its place in the proper Mass. He ends the first and last only with the form *Per Dominum nostrum* (as the Collects). The last clause of the last Secret: *Per omnia saecula saeculorum* is said or sung aloud, forming the *ecphonesis* before the Preface.

Chapter Notes:

[1] Durandus, IV, 35.
[2] *Rerum liturgicarum* (Turin, 1763), lib. II, 13, §1.
[3] *Apost. Const.*, VIII, XII, 4.
[4] P.L., LXXVIII, 973.

20

Preface

Preface (Lat. *Praefatio*).—the first part of the Eucharistic prayera (Anaphora or Canon) in all rites, now separated from the rest by the singing of the *Sanctus*.

1. *History*.—According to the idea of thanksgiving which, after the example of the Last Supper, forms a fundamental element of the Eucharistic service, all liturgies begin the Anaphora, the consecration-prayer, by thanking God for His benefits. Almost every account we have of the early liturgy mentions this. Clement of Rome quotes a long example of such a thanksgiving-prayer.[1] So prominent was this idea that it has supplied the usual name for the whole service (Eucharist). The thanksgiving-prayer enumerated the benefits for which we thank God, beginning generally with the creation, continuing through the orders of nature and grace, mentioning much of Old Testament history, and so coming to the culminating benefit of Christ's Incarnation, His life and Passion, in which the story of the Last Supper brings us naturally to the words of institution. In most of the earliest liturgies this enumeration is of considerable length. It is invariably preceded by an invitation to the people: "Lift up your hearts", and then: " Let us give thanks to the Lord", or some such formula. The people having answered: "It is right and just", the celebrant continues, taking up their word: "It is truly right and just first of all to praise (or to thank) Thee"; and so the thanksgiving begins.

Such is the scheme everywhere. It is also universal that at some moment before the recital of the words of institution there should be a mention of the angels who, as Isaias said, praise God and say "Holy, holy, holy" etc., and the celebrant stops to allow the people to take up the angels' words. He then continues his thanksgiving-prayer. But the effect of this interruption is to cut off the part before it from the rest. In the Eastern rites the separation is less marked; the whole prayer is still counted as one thing—the Anaphora. In the West the *Sanctus* has cut the old Canon completely in two; the part before it, once counted part of the Canon, is now, since about the seventh century, considered a separate prayer, the Preface. The dislocation of the rest of the Canon which no longer continues the note of thanksgiving, but has part of its Intercession (*Te igitur*) immediately after the *Sanctus*, and its silent recital, whereas the Preface is sung aloud, have still more accentuated this separation. Nevertheless, historically, the Preface belongs to the Canon; it is the first part of the Eucharistic prayer, the only part that has kept clearly the idea of giving thanks. The name *Praefatio* (from *praefari*) means introduction, preface (in the usual sense) to the Canon. In the Leonine and Gelasian books this part of the Canon has no special title. It is recognized by its first words: *Vere dignum* (Leonine) or the initials "V.D." (Gelasian). In the Gregorian Sacramentary it is already considered a separate prayer and is headed *Praefatio*. Walafrid Strabo calls it *praefatio actionis*, (*actio* for Canon).[2] Sicardus of Cremona says it is *sequentis canonis praelocutio et praeparatio*.[3] Durandus (see **DURANDUS**) writes a whole chapter about the Preface.[4] He explains its name as meaning that it "precedes the principal sacrifice".

The first Roman Prefaces extant are those in the Leonine Sacramentary. They already show the two characteristic qualities that distinguish the Roman Preface from the corresponding part of other rites, its shortness and changeableness. The old thanksgiving (before the *Sanctus*) contained a long enumeration of God's benefits, as in Clement of Rome and the *Apostolic Constitutions*. It is so still in the Eastern rites. At Rome, before the Leonine book was written, this enumeration was ruthlessly curtailed. Nothing is left of it but a most general allusion: "always and everywhere to thank Thee". But the mention of the angels which introduces the *Sanctus* had to remain. This, comparatively detailed, still gives the Roman Preface the character of a prayer chiefly about the angels and makes it all seem to lead up to the *Sanctus,* as the medieval commentators notice. The corresponding prayer in the *Apostolic Constitutions* (VIII) contains two references to the angels, one at the beginning where they occur as the first creatures, the other at the end of the commemoration of Old Testament history (originally written in connexion with Isaias's place in it) where they introduce the *Sanctus*. It seems probable that at Rome with the omission of the historical allusions these two references were merged into one. The *Et ideo* then would refer to the omitted list of favours in the Old Testament (at present it has no special point). So we should have one more connexion between the Roman Rite and the *Apostolic Constitutions*.

The other special note of our Preface is its changeableness. Here, too, the East is immovable, the West changes with the calendar. The Preface was originally as much part of the variable Proper as the Collect. The Leonine book supplies Prefaces all through for the special Masses; it has 267. The Gelasian has 54; the Gregorian has 10 and more than 100 in its appendix. In these varied Prefaces allusions to the feast, the season, and so on, take the place of the old list of Divine favours.

The Preface after the *ecphonesis* of the Secret (*Per omnia saecula saeculorum*—here as always merely a warning) begins with a little dialogue of which the versicles or equivalent forms are found at this place in every liturgy. First *Dominus vobiscum* with its answer. The Eastern rites, too, have a blessing at this point. *Sursum corda* is one of the oldest known liturgical formulas. St. Cyprian quotes it and its answer.[5] It is an invitation to the people eminently suitable just before the Eucharistic prayer begins. Equally old and universal is the people's answer: *Habemus (corda) ad Dominum*, a Greek construction: "We have them [have placed them] before the Lord". Then follows the invitation to give thanks, which very early included the technical idea of "making the Eucharist": *Gratias agamus Domino Deo nostro*. So with verbal variations in all rites. The Jewish form of grace before meals contains the same form: "Let us give thanks to Adonai our God."[6] The people answer with an expression that again must come from the earliest age: *Dignum et iustum est*. This, too, is universal. Its reduplication suggests a Hebrew parallelism. The celebrant takes up their word and begins the Preface always *Vere dignum et iustum est*. The beginning of the Roman Preface is approached among the others most nearly by Alexandria. Our present common Preface represents the simplest type, with no allusions; all the old list of benefits is represented by the words *per Christum Dominum nostrum* only. This is the Preface given in the Canon of the Gelasian book. Most of the others are formed by an intercalation after these words. But there are three types of Preface distinguished by their endings. The first and commonest introduces the angels thus: *per quem maiestatem tuam laudant angeli*; the second (e.g. for Christmas, Epiphany, Easter, Ascension, Apostles) begins that clause: *et ideo cum angelis*; the third and rarest (now only the Whit-Sunday Preface) has: *Quapropter . . . sed et supernae virtutes*". The Trinity Preface (*quam laudant angeli*) is a variant of the first form. All end with the word: *dicentes* (which in the first and second form refers to us, in the third form to the angels), and the people (choir) continue the sentence: *Sanctus, Sanctus, Sanctus*, etc.

There are many prayers for other occasions (chiefly blessings and consecrations) formed on the model of the Preface, with the *Sursum corda* dialogue, beginning *Vere dignum* etc. From their form one would call them Prefaces, though not Eucharistic ones. Such are the ordination prayers, two at the consecration of a church, the blessing of the font, of palms (but this was once a Mass Preface), part of the *praeconium paschale*. They are imitations of the Eucharistic Preface, apparently because its solemn form (perhaps its chant) made it seem suitable for other specially solemn occasions too. The Leonine, Gelasian, and Gregorian Sacramentaries have our ordination prayers, but not yet cast into this Preface form. But through the Middle Ages the Preface form was very popular, and a great number of blessings are composed in it. This is only one more case of the common medieval practice of modelling new prayers and services on others already well-known and popular (compare the hymns written in imitation of older ones, etc).

2. The Preface in Other Rites.—the name *Praefatio* is peculiar to Rome and to Milan, which has borrowed it from Rome. In no other rite is there a special name; it is simply the opening clauses of the Anaphora. In the Syrian-Byzantine-Armenian group, though this part of the Eucharistic prayer is still longer than the Roman Preface and has kept some list of benefits for which we thank God, it is comparatively short. The Byzantine Liturgy of St. Basil has a fairly long form. As usual, there is a much shorter form in that of St. Chrysostom. The Armenian form is the shortest and mentions only the Incarnation. But in the Egyptian group of liturgies the whole Intercession prayer is included in what we should call the Preface, so that this part is very long. This is the most conspicuous characteristic of the Alexandrine type. The prayer begins in the usual way with a list of favours (creation of the world and of man, the Prophets, Christ). Then abruptly the Intercession begins ("And we pray and entreat thee . . ."); joined to it are the memory of the saints and the diptychs (see **GLOSSARY**) of the dead, and then, equally abruptly, the thanksgiving is resumed and introduces the *Sanctus*. It is clear that this represents a later amalgamation; the two quite different prayers are joined awkwardly, so that the seams are still obvious. In all

Eastern rites the Preface, or rather what corresponds to it, is said silently after the first dialogue, ending with an *ecphonesis* (see **GLOSSARY**) to introduce the *Sanctus* (the Alexandrine Liturgy has another *ecphonesis* in its Intercession). This accounts for its being less important an element of the service than in the West.

The Gallican Rite had a great number of Prefaces for feasts and seasons. Even more than in the old Roman Liturgy this prayer was part of the Proper, like the Collects and Lessons. But it was not called a Preface. Its heading in the Gallican books was *Contestatio* or *Immolatio*; the Mozarabic title is *Inlatio*. These names really apply to the whole Eucharistic prayer and correspond to our name Canon (*Inlatio*—anaphora). But as later parts had special names (*Vere sanctus, Post sanctus, Post pridie,* etc.), these general titles were eventually understood as meaning specially the part before the *Sanctus*. Now the Mozarabic *Inlatio* may be taken as equivalent to the Roman *Praefatio*. The Ambrosian Rite has adopted the Roman name. Both Mozarabic and Ambrosian Rites keep the Gallican peculiarity of a vast number of Prefaces printed each as part of the Proper.

3. *Present Use.*—the Roman Missal now contains eleven Prefaces. Ten are in the Gregorian Sacramentary one (of the Blessed Virgin) was added under Urban II (1088-99). The pope himself is reported to have composed this Preface and to have sung it first at the Synod of Guastalla in 1094. The Prefaces form a medium between the unchanging Ordinary and the variable Proper of the Mass. They vary so little that they are printed in the Ordinary, first with their solemn chants, then with the ferial chants, and lastly without notes for Low Mass. The appendix of the new (Vatican) Missal gives a third "more solemn" chant for each, merely a more ornate form of the solemn chant, to be used *ad libitum*. Otherwise the Solemn chant is to be used for semi-doubles and all days above that, the simple chant for simples, ferias, and requiems. The Preface is chosen according to the usual rule for all proper parts of the Mass. If the feast has one, that is used; otherwise one takes that of the octave or season. All days that do not fall under one of these classes have the common Preface, except that Sundays that have no special Preface have that of the Holy Trinity (so the decree of Clement XIII, 3 January, 1759). Requiems have the common Preface, as also votive Masses, unless these latter come under a category that has a proper one (e.g., of the Blessed Virgin, the Holy Ghost, etc.). Votive Masses of the Blessed Sacrament, like *Corpus Christi*, have the Christmas Preface. There are other extensions of use (the Preface of the Holy Cross for the Sacred Heart, etc.), all of which are noted in the Propers of the Missal and in the Calendar.

At High Mass after the last Secret the celebrant at the middle of the altar, resting his hands on it, sings: *Per omnia saecula saeculorum* etc.; the choir answers each versicle. He lifts up the hands at *Sursum corda*; at *Gratias agamus* he joins them, and at *Deo nostro* looks up and then bows. At *Vere dignum* he lifts the hands again and so sings the Preface through. After *dicentes* he joins them and bowing says the *Sanctus* in a low voice, while the choir sings it. The deacon and subdeacon stand in line behind him all the time, bow with him at the words *Deo nostro*, and come to either side to say the *Sanctus* with him.

At Low Mass all is said, the server answering the dialogue at the beginning.

Chapter Notes:

[1] *I Clement ad Cor.*, lx-lxi.

[2] *De eccl. rerum exord. et increm.*, in PL, CXIV, 948.

[3] Mitrale in P.L., CCXIII, 122.

[4] Durandus, IV, xxxiii.

5 *De Orat. Dom.*, xxxi, in PL IV, 539.
6 Mishna, *Berachoth*, 6.

21

SANCTUS

1. *History*.—The *Sanctus* is the last part of the Preface in the Mass, sung in practically every rite by the people (or choir). It is one of the elements of the liturgy of which we have the earliest evidence. St. Clement of Rome (d. about 104, see **GLOSSARY**) mentions it. He quotes the text in Isaias, vi, 3, and goes on to say that it is also sung in church; this at least seems the plain meaning of the passage: "For the Scripture says...Holy, holy, holy Lord of hosts; full is every creature of his glory. And we, led by conscience, gathered together in one place in concord, cry to him continuously as from one mouth, that we may become sharers in his great and glorious promises."[1] It seems clear that what the people cry is the text just quoted. Clement does not say at what moment of the service the people cry these words; but again we may safely suppose that it was at the end of what we call the Preface, the place at which the *Sanctus* appears in every liturgy, from that of the *Apostolic Constitutions* VIII on. The next oldest witness is Origen (d. 254). He quotes the text of Isaias and continues: "The coming of my Jesus is announced, wherefore the whole earth is full of his glory."[2] There is nothing to correspond to this in the Prophet. It seems plainly an allusion to liturgical use and so agrees very well with the place of the *Sanctus*. The Anaphora of Sarapion of Thmuis (Egypt, fourth century) gives the *Sanctus* almost exactly in the form of the Alexandrine Liturgy, but says nothing about its being sung by the people. From the fourth century we have abundance of testimony for the *Sanctus* in every liturgical centre. In Egypt St. Athanasius (d. 373) mentions it; at Jerusalem St. Cyril (d. 386); and at Antioch St. John Chrysostom (d. 407) alludes to it. Tertullian (d. about 220) and Victor of Vite (d. 486) quote it in Africa; Germnanus of Paris (d. 576) in Gaul; Isidore of Seville (d. 636) in Spain. The *Sanctus* is sung by the people in the *Apostolic Constitutions*, and so in almost all rites. The scanty state of our knowledge about the early Roman Mass accounts for the fact that we have no allusion to the *Sanctus* till it appears in the first Sacramentaries. The Leonine and Gelasian books give only the celebrant's part, but their prefaces lead up to it plainly. The Gregorian Sacramentary gives the text exactly as we still have it. But the passage quoted from St. Clement and then the use of Africa (always similar to Rome) leave no doubt that at Rome too the *Sanctus* is part of the oldest liturgical tradition.

The connection in which it occurs in the liturgy is this: in all rites the Eucharistic prayer (Canon, Anaphora) begins with a formal thanksgiving to God for His benefits, generally enumerated at length (see **PREFACE**). This first part of the prayer (our Preface) takes the form of an outline of creation, of the many graces given to Patriarchs and Prophets in the Old Law and so to the crowning benefit of our redemption by Christ, to His life and Passion, to the institution of the Holy Eucharist and the words of institution, all in the scheme of a thanksgiving for these things. Before the prayer comes to the mention of our Lord it always refers to the angels. In the *Apostolic Constitutions* VIII, XII, they occur twice, at the beginning as being the first creatures and again at the end of the Old Testament, history possibly in connexion with the place of Isaias who mentions them. In St. James's liturgy this part of the Anaphora is much shorter and the angels are named once only; so also in St. Mark they come only once. They are always named at length and with much solemnity as those who join with us

330

in praising God. So the description in Isaias, vi, 1-4, must have attracted attention very early as expressing the angelic praise of God and as summing up just the note of the first part of the Anaphora. The *Sanctus* simply continues the Preface. It is a quotation of what the angels say. We thank God with the angels, who say "Holy, holy, holy", etc. Logically the celebrant could very well himself say or sing the *Sanctus*. But apparently from the beginning of its Christian use, one of the dramatic touches that continually adorn the liturgy was added here. We too desire to say with the angels: "Holy, holy, holy"; so when the celebrant comes to the quotation, the people (or choir) interrupt and themselves sing these words, continuing his sentence. The interruption is important since it is the chief cause of the separation of the original first part of the eucharistic prayer (the Preface) at Rome from the rest and the reason why this first part is still sung aloud although the continuation is said in a low voice. The only rite that has no *Sanctus* is that of the Ethiopic Church Order.

   2. *The Sanctus in the Eastern Rites*.—In the liturgies of St. James and St. Mark and the Byzantine Rite the introductory sentence calls it the "Hymn of victory (*Epinikion*)". This has become its usual name in Greek. It should never be called the *Trisagion* (see **GLOSSARY**), which is a different liturgical formula (" Holy God, Holy Strong One, Holy Immortal One have mercy on us ") occurring in another part of the service. In the *Apostolic Constitutions*, the form of the *Epinikion* is: "Holy, holy, holy the Lord of Hosts. Full (are) the heaven and the earth of his glory. Blessed for ever. Amen." St. James has: "Holy, holy, holy , Lord of hosts. Full (are) the heaven and the earth of thy Glory. *Hosanna* (he) in the highest. Blessed (is) he that comes in the name of the Lord. *Hosanna*, (he) in the highest." In this the cry of the people on Palm Sunday (Matt., xxi, 9, modified) is added. Alexandria has only the text of Isaias. In the Greek Alexandrine form (St. Mark) the text occurs twice.

First the celebrant quotes it himself as said by the cherubim and seraphim; then he continues aloud: "for all things always call thee holy and with all who call thee holy receive, Master and Lord, our hallowing who with them sing, saying . . ." and the people repeat the *Epinikion*. The Nestorians have a considerably extended form of Is., vi, 3, and Matt., xxi, 9,in the third person. The Byzantine Rite has the form of St. James, so also the Armenians. In all Eastern rites only the sentence that immediately introduces the *Epinikion* is said aloud, as an *ekphonesis*.

3. The Sanctus in the West.—In Latin it is the *Tersanctus* or simply the *Sanctus*. *Hymnus angelicus* is ambiguous and should be avoided, since this is the usual name for the *Gloria in Excelsis*. Germanus of Paris bears witness to it in the Gallican Rite. Its form was as at Rome. The Mozarabic *Sanctus* is almost the Roman one; but it has for the first *Hosanna*: *Osanna filio David* (more literally Matt., xxi, 9) and the additional exclamations *Agyos, agyos, agyos Kyrie o theos*. Milan has exactly our form. It may be noted that the Gallican and Mozarabic liturgies, following the tradition of Antioch and Jerusalem, continue the Anaphora by taking up the idea of the *Sanctus*: *Vere sanctus, vere benedictus Dominus noster Iesus Christus*, and so coming almost at once to the words of Institution. This prayer, which varies in each Mass, is called *Post Sanctus*, or *Vere Sanctus*. Milan has one remnant of this on Holy Saturday. At Rome the *Sanctus* is described in *Ordo Romanus I*, as *hymnus angelicus, id est Sanctus*. It is sung by the regionary sub-deacons. So also *Ordo Romanus II*, which notes that *Hosanna* is sung twice. In the *Apostolic Constitutions* VIII these verses are sung at the Elevation just before Communion, then they were pushed back to become an appendix to the *Sanctus* where they coincide more or less with the moment of consecration. That the verses of Matthew, xxi, 9, were first used as a salutation to the bishop is quite probable. It is less likely that they are a late Gallican addition at Rome. Their occurrence in the liturgy of

Jerusalem-Antioch may well be one more example of the relation between that centre and Rome from the earliest ages (see **CANON OF THE MASS**). We do not know at what moment the chant of the *Sanctus* was taken from the subdeacons and given to the *schola cantorum*. This is merely part of a general tendency to entrust music that was getting more ornate and difficult to trained singers. So the Gradual was once sung by a deacon. The *Ordo Romanus V* implies that the subdeacons no longer sing the *Sanctus*. In *Ordo XI*, it is sung by the *Basilicarii*. St. Gregory of Tours (d. 593) says it is sung by the people. The notice of the *Liber Pontificalis* that Pope Sixtus I (119-128) ordered the people to sing the *Sanctus* cannot be correct. It seems that it was not sung always at every Mass. The Second Council of Vaison finds it necessary to command that it should not be omitted in Lent nor at requiems. There were also laws in the Middle Ages forbidding the celebrant to continue the Canon before the choir had finished singing it. The ringing of a bell at the *Sanctus* is a development from the Elevation bell; this began in the Middle Ages. Ivo of Chartres (d. 1116) mentions it, and Durandus (see **DURANDUS**). It was rung to call people to church that they might see the Elevation. The *Sanctus* bell is an earlier warning that the Canon is about to begin. The rubrics of the Missal still say nothing about the bell at the *Sanctus*. It was (and in places still is) usual to ring the great church bell at least at high Mass. The handbell was only a warning to the ringers in the tower.

The text of the Roman *Sanctus* is first Isaias, vi, 3 with *pleni sunt coeli et terra gloria tua* instead of *plena est omnis terra gloria eius*. In this way (as at Antioch and Alexandria) it is made into a prayer by the use of the second person. In all liturgies the Hebrew word for "hosts" (sabaoth) is kept, as in the Septuagint (Vulgate, *exercituum*). The "Lord of hosts" is a very old Semitic title, in the polytheistic religions apparently for the moon-god, the hosts being the stars (as in Genesis ii, 1;

Psalm xxxii, 6). To the Jews these hosts were the angels (cf. Luke, II, 13). Then follows the acclamation of Palm Sunday in Matthew,xxi, 9. It is based on Psalm cvii, 25-26); but the source of the liturgical text is, of course, the text in the Gospel. *Hosanna* is in the Greek text and Vulgate, left as a practically untranslatable exclamation of triumph. It means literally "Oh help", but in Matthew, xxi, 9, it is already a triumphant interjection (like Alleluia). In the *Didache* it occurs as a liturgical formula (*"Hosanna* to the God of David").[3] In the medieval local rites the *Sanctus* was often farced (interpolated with tropes), like the *Kyrie* and other texts, to fill up the long musical *neums*. The skeleton of a Mass at the blessing of palms retains not only a Preface but also a *Sanctus*, sung to the original "simple" tone. The many other prayers (blessing of the font, ordinations, etc.) that are modelled on the Preface diverge from its scheme as they proceed and do not end with a *Sanctus*.

4. Present Rite.—At high Mass as soon as the celebrant has sung the last word of the Preface (*dicentes*) the choir begins the *Sanctus*, continuing his phrase. They could sing it straight through including the *Benedictus*. The custom of waiting till after the Elevation and then adding the *Benedictus*, once common, is now abolished by the rubric (*De ritibus servandis in cantu missae*, VII) of the Vatican Gradual. It was a dramatic effect that never had any warrant. *Sanctus* and *Benedictus* are one text. Meanwhile the deacon and subdeacon go up to the right and left of the celebrant and say the *Sanctus* in a low voice with him. Every one in the choir and church kneels. The hand-bell is usually rung at the *Sanctus*; but at Rome there is no bell at all at high Mass. While the choir sings the celebrant goes on with the Canon. They must finish or he must wait before the Consecration. At low Mass the celebrant after the Preface, bowing and laying the folded hands on the altar, continues the *Sanctus* in a lower voice (*vox media*). The bell is rung three times. Although the rubrics of the Missal do not mention this it is done everywhere by approved custom. It may be noticed that of the many chants of the *Sanctus* in the Gradual the simple one only (for ferias of Advent and Lent, requiems and the blessing of palms) continues the melody of the Preface and so presumably represents the same musical tradition as our Preface tone. As in the case of the Preface its mode is doubtful.

Chapter Notes:

[1] I Clement *Ad Cor.*, xxxiv, 6-7.

[2] *In Isa., hom.*, I, n. 2.

[3] *Didache* X, 6.

22

Canon

This article will be divided into four sections: (1) Name and place of the Canon; (2) History of the Canon; (3) The text and rubrics of the Canon; (4) Mystical interpretations.

1. *Name and Place of the Canon*.—Canon (*Canon Missae, Canon Actionis*) is the name used in the Roman Missal for the fundamental part of the Mass that comes after the Offertory and before the Communion. The old distinction, in all liturgies, is between the Mass of the Catechumens (the litanies, lessons from the Bible, and collects) and the Mass of the Faithful (the Offertory of the gifts to be consecrated, Consecration prayer, Communion, and dismissal). Our Canon is the Consecration prayer, the great Eucharistic prayer in the Mass of the Faithful. The name *Canon* means a norm or rule; and it is used for various objects, such as the Canon of Holy Scripture, canons of Councils, the official list of saints' names (whence "canonization"), and the canon or list of clerks who serve a certain church, from which they themselves are called canons (*canonici*). Liturgically it occurs in three senses: (1) The canon in the Byzantine Rite is the arrangement of the nine odes according to the order in which they are to be sung. (2) Like the word *Mass* it has occasionally been used as a general name for the canonical Hours, or Divine Office. (3) Chiefly, and now universally in the West, it is the name for the Eucharistic prayer in the Holy Liturgy. In this sense it occurs in the letters of St.

Gregory I;[1] the Gelasian Sacramentary puts the heading *Incipit Canon Actionis* before the *Sursum Corda*, the word occurs several times in the first Roman Ordo (*Ordo Romanus Primus*)— *quando inchoat canonem*, *finito vero canone*. Since the seventh century it has been the usual name for this part of the Mass. One can only conjecture the original reason for its use. Walafrid Strabo (d. 849) says: "This action is called the Canon because it is the lawful and regular confection of the Sacrament."[2] Benedict XIV says: "Canon is the same word as rule, the Church uses this name to mean that the Canon of the Mass is the firm rule according to which the Sacrifice of the New Testament is to be celebrated."[3] It has been suggested that our present Canon was a compromise between the older Greek Anaphoras and variable Latin Eucharistic prayers formerly used in Rome, and that it was ordered in the fourth century, possibly by Pope Damasus (366-84). The name *Canon* would then mean a fixed standard to which all must henceforth conform, as opposed to the different and changeable prayers used before. In any case it is noticeable that whereas the lessons, collects and Preface of the Mass constantly vary, the Canon is almost unchangeable in every Mass. Another name for the Canon is *Actio*. *Agere* is often used as meaning "to sacrifice". Leo I, in writing to Dioscurus of Alexandria, uses the expression *in qua [sc. basilica] agitur*, meaning "in which Mass is said". Other names are *Legitimum, Prex, Agenda, Regula, Secretum Missae*.

The rubrics of our present Missal leave no doubt as to the limits of the Canon in modern times. It begins at the *Te igitur* and ends with the *Amen* before the Embolism of the *Pater noster* (*omnis honor et gloria, per omnia saecula saeculorum, Amen*). The Missal has the title *Canon Missae* printed after the *Sanctus*, and the Rubrics say: "After the Preface the Canon of the Mass begins secretly" (Rubr. Gen., XII, 6). The ninth title of the *Ritus cel. Missam* is headed: "Of the Canon from the Consecration to the Lord's Prayer." The next title is: "Of the Lord's Prayer and the rest to the Communion." Neither of these limits, however, was always so fixed. The whole Canon is essentially one long prayer, the Eucharistic prayer that the Eastern rites call the Anaphora. And the Preface is part of this prayer. Introduced in Rome as everywhere by the little dialogue *Sursum corda* and so on, it begins with the words *Vere dignum et justum est*. Interrupted for a moment by the people, who take up the angels' words: *Sanctus, sanctus, sanctus*, the priest goes on with the same prayer, obviously joining the next part to the beginning by the word *igitur*. It is not then surprising that we find in the oldest sacramentary that contains a Canon, the Gelasian, the heading *Incipit Canon Actionis* placed before the *Sursum corda*; so that the preface was then still looked upon as part of the Canon. However, by the seventh century or so the Canon was considered as beginning with the secret prayers after the Sanctus. "When they have finished the *Sanctus* the pontiff rises alone and enters into the Canon").[4] The point at which it may be considered as ending was equally uncertain at one time. There has never been any sort of point or indication in the text of the Missal to close the period begun by the heading *Canon Missae*, so that from looking at the text we should conclude that the Canon goes on to the end of the Mass. Even as late as Benedict XIV there were "those who think that the Lord's Prayer makes up part of the Canon".[5] On the other hand the *Ordo Romanus Primus* implies that it ends before the *Pater noster*. The two views are reconciled by the distinction between the *Canon Consecrationis* and the *Canon Communionis* that occurs constantly in the Middle Ages. The *Canon Communionis* then would begin with the *Pater noster* and go on to the end of the people's Communion. The Post-Communion to the Blessing, or now to the end of the Last Gospel, forms the last division of the Mass, the thanksgiving and dismissal. It must then be added that in modern times by Canon we mean only the *Canon Consecrationis*. The Canon, together with the rest of the *Ordo Missae*, is now printed in the middle of the Missal, between the propers for Holy Saturday and Easter Day. Till about the ninth century it stood towards the end of the Sacramentary, among the *Missae quotidianae* and after the Proper Masses (so in the Gelasian book). Thence it moved to the very beginning. From the eleventh century it was constantly placed in the middle, where it is now, and since the use of complete Missals "according to the use of the Roman Curia" (from the thirteenth century) that has been its place invariably. It is the part of the book that is used far more than any other, so it is obviously convenient that it should occur where a book lies open best—in the middle. No doubt a symbolic reason, the connexion between the Eucharistic Sacrifice and the mysteries of Holy Week, helped to make this place seem the most suitable one. The same reason of practical use that gave it this place led to the common custom of printing the Canon on vellum, even when the rest of the Missal was on paper—vellum stands wear much better than paper.

2. *History of the Canon*.— Since the seventh century our Canon has remained unchanged. It is to St. Gregory I (590-604) the great organiser of all the Roman Liturgy, that tradition ascribes its final revision and arrangement. His reign then makes the best division in its history.

Before St. Gregory I (to 590)

St. Gregory certainly found the Canon that has been already discussed, arranged in the same order, and in possession for centuries. When was it put together? It is certainly not the work of one man, nor was it all composed at one time. Gregory himself thought that the Canon had been composed by "a certain Scholasticus",[6] and Benedict XIV discusses whether he meant some person so named or merely "a certain learned man".[7] But our Canon represents rather the last stage of a development that had been going on gradually ever since the first days when the Roman Christians met together to obey Christ's command and celebrate the Eucharist in memory of

Him. Here a distinction must be made between the prayers of the Canon itself and the order in which they are now found. The prayers, or at least some of them, can be traced back to a very early date from occasional references in letters of the Fathers. From this it does not follow that they always stood in the same order as now. Their arrangement in our present Missal presents certain difficulties and has long been a much-disputed point. It is very possible that at some unknown period—perhaps in the fifth century—the Canon went through a complete alteration in its order and that its component prayers, without being changed in themselves, were turned round and re-arranged. This theory, as will be seen, would account for many difficulties.

In the first century, as known, the Church of Rome, like all other Christian Churches, celebrated the Holy Eucharist by obeying Christ's direction and doing as He had done the night before He died. There were the bread and wine brought up at the Offertory and consecrated by the words of Institution and by an invocation of the Holy Ghost; the bread was broken and Communion was given to the faithful. Undoubtedly, too, before this service lessons were read from the Bible, litanies and prayers were said. It is also known that this Mass was said in Greek. Hellenistic Greek was the common tongue of Christians, at any rate outside Palestine, and it was spoken by them in Rome as well as everywhere else, at the time when it was understood and used as a sort of international language throughout the empire. This is shown by the facts that the inscriptions in the catacombs are in Greek, and that Christian writers at Rome use that language. Of the liturgical formulas of this first period little is known. The First Epistle of St. Clement contains a prayer that is generally considered liturgical, though it contains no reference to the Eucharist, also the statement that: "The Lord commanded offerings and holy offices to be made carefully, not rashly nor without order, but at fixed times and hours."[8] It says further: "The high-priest [i.e. bishop] has his duties, a special place is appointed to the priests, and the Levites have their ministry."[9] From this it is evident that at Rome the liturgy was celebrated according to fixed rules and definite order. Chap. xxxiv (of St. Clement's Epistle) tells us that the Romans "gathered together in concord, and as it were with one mouth", said the *Sanctus* from Is., vi, 3, as we do. St. Justin Martyr (died c.167) spent part of his life at Rome and died there. It is possible that his *First Apology* was written in that city, and that the liturgy he describes in it was that which he frequented at Rome.[10] From this we learn that the Christians first prayed for themselves and for all manner of persons. Then follows the kiss of peace, and "he who presides over the brethren" is given bread and a cup of wine and water, having received which he gives thanks to God, celebrates the Eucharist, and all the people answer *Amen.* The deacons then give out Holy Communion. Here is found the outline of our liturgy: the Preface (giving thanks), to which may be added from I Clement the *Sanctus*, a celebration of the Eucharist, not described, but which contains the words of Institution ("by His prayer"), and which corresponds to our Canon, and the final Amen that still keeps its place at the end of the Eucharistic prayer.[11] Perhaps a likeness may be seen between the Roman use and those of the Eastern Churches in the fact that when St. Polycarp came to Rome in 155, Pope Anicetus allowed him to celebrate, just like one of his own bishops.[12] The canons of Hippolytus of Rome (in the beginning of the third century, if they are genuine) allude to a Eucharistic celebration that follows the order of St. Justin, and they add the universal introduction to the Preface, *Sursum corda*, etc.

The first great turning point in the history of the Roman Canon is the exclusive use of the Latin language. Latin had been used side by side with Greek, apparently for some time. It occurs first as a Christian language, not in Rome, but in Africa. Pope Victor I (190-202), an African, seems to have been the first Roman bishop who used it. After this time it soon becomes the only language used by popes; Cornelius (251-53) and Stephen (254-57) write in Latin. Greek seems to have disappeared at Rome as a liturgical language in the second half of the third century, though parts of the Liturgy were left in Greek. The Creed was sometimes said in Greek down to Byzantine times. The *Ordo Romanus Primus* says that certain psalms were still said in Greek, and of this liturgical use of Greek there are still remnants in our *Kyrie eleison* and the *Agios o Theos*, etc., on Good Friday. Very soon after the acceptance of Latin as the only liturgical language we find allusions to parts of the Eucharistic prayer, that are the same as parts of our present Canon. In the time of Pope Damasus (366-84) a Roman writer who was guilty of the surprising error of identifying Melchisedech with the Holy Ghost writes, "The Holy Ghost being a bishop is called Priest of the most high God, but not high priest" (*Sacerdos appellatus est excelsi Dei, non summus*) "as our people presume to say in the Oblation".[13] These words evidently allude to the form "thy high priest Melchisedech" *(summus sacerdos tuus Melchisedech)* in the Canon. Pseudo-Ambrose in *De Sacramentis* (probably about 400 or later) quotes the prayers said by the priest in the Canon: *Fac nos hanc oblationem adscriptam, ratam, rationabilem, acceptabilem, quod figura est corporis et sanguinis Iesu Christi. Qui pridie quam pateretur, in sanctis manibus suis accepit panem, respexit in caelum ad te, sancte Pater omnipotens, aeterne Deus, gratias agens, benedixit, fregit fractumque apostolis suis et discipulis suis tradidit dicens: Accipite et edite ex hoc omnes: hoc est enim corpus meum quod pro multis confringetur. Similiter etiam calicem, postquam caenatum est, pridie quam pateretur accepit, respexit in caelum ad te, sancte Pater omnipotens, aeterne Deus, gratias agens, benedixit, apostolis suis et discipulis suis tradidit dicens; Accipite et bibite ex hoc omnes: hic est enim sanguis meus.* "And the priest says", continues the author: *Ergo memores gloriosissimae eius passionis et ab inferis resurrectionis et in caelum ascensionis, offerimus tibi hanc immaculatam hostiam, hanc panem sanctum et calicem vitae aeternae; et petimus et precamur, ut hanc oblationem suscipias in sublimi altari tuo per manus angelorum tuorum, sicut suscipere dignatus es munera pueri tui iusti Abel et sacrificium patriarchae nostri Abrahae et quod tibi obtulit summus sacerdos Melchisedech.* It will be seen that the whole of this prayer, but for a few unimportant modifications, is that of our Canon. Pope Damasus has been considered one of the chief compilers of the Roman Liturgy. One liturgical change made by this pope is certain. He introduced the word *Alleluia* at Rome.[14] Innocent I (401-17) refers to the Canon as being a matter he ought not to describe—an apparent survival of the idea of the *Disciplina arcani*—and says it is ended with the kiss of peace.[15] "After all the things that I may not reveal the Peace is given, by which it is shown that the people have consented to all that was done in the holy mysteries and was celebrated in the church." He also says that at Rome the names of persons for whom the celebrant prays are read in the Canon: "First the offertory should be made, and after that the names of the givers read out, so that they should be named during the holy mysteries, not during the parts that precede." That is all that can be known for certain about our Canon before Gregory I. The earliest books that contain its text were written after his time and show it as approved by him.

A question that can only be answered by conjecture is that of the relation between the Roman Canon and any of the other ancient liturgical Anaphoras. There are undoubtedly very striking parallels between it and both of the original Eastern rites, those of Alexandria and Antioch. But the Roman Canon shows perhaps more likeness to that of Antioch in its formulae. For instance, the Intercession in the Syrian Liturgy of St. James begins with the prayer: "Wherefore we offer unto Thee, O Lord, this same fearful and unbloody sacrifice for the holy places....and especially for holy Sion....and for thy holy church which is in all the world....Remember also, O Lord, our pious bishops...especially the fathers, our Patriarch Mar N. and our

Bishop" ["and all the bishops throughout the world who preach the word of thy truth in Orthodoxy", Greek Liturgy of St. James]. The whole of this prayer suggests our *Imprimis quae tibi offerimus*, and certain words exactly correspond to *toto orbe terrarum* and *orthodoxis*, as does "especially" to *imprimis*, and so on. Again the Syrian Anaphora continues: "Remember also, O Lord, those who have offered the offerings at thine holy altar and those for whom each has offered [cf. *pro quibus tibi offerimus vel qui tibi offerunt*]. . . . Remember, O Lord, all those whom we have mentioned and those whom we have not mentioned...Again vouchsafe to remember those who stand with us and pray with us [*et omnium circumstantium*]; Remembering. . . . especially our all-holy, unspotted, most glorious lady, Mother of God and ever Virgin, Mary, St. John the illustrious prophet, forerunner and baptist, the holy Apostles Peter and Paul, Andrew . . . . [the names of the Apostles follow] . . . . and of all thy Saints for ever . . . . that we may receive thy help" [*ut in omnibus protectionis tuae muniamur auxilio*, Greek St. James]. The words of Institution occur in a form that is almost identical with our *Pridie quam pateretur*. The Anamnesis begins: "Commemorating therefore [*unde et memores*] O Lord, thy death and resurrection on the third day from the tomb and thy ascension into heaven . . . . we offer thee this dread and unbloody sacrifice [*offerimus* . . . . *hostiam puram*, etc.].

It is true that these general ideas occur in all the old liturgies; but in this case a remarkable identity is found even in the words. Some allusions to what were probably older forms in our Canon make the similarity still more striking. Thus Optatus of Mileve says that Mass is offered *pro ecclesia, quae una est et toto orbe terrarum diffusa*.[16] This represents exactly a Latin version of the "holy Church which is in all the world" that we have seen in the Syrian Anaphora above. The Syrian use adds a prayer for "our religious kings and queens" after that for the patriarch and bishop. So our Missal long contained the words *et pro rege nostro* N. after *et Antistite nostro* N. (see below). It has a prayer for the celebrant himself, where our Missal once contained just such a prayer (below). The treatise *De Sacramentis* gives the words of Institution for the Chalice as *Hic est sanguis meus*, just as does the Syrian Liturgy. There are other striking resemblances. But the other Eastern liturgy, the Alexandrine use, also shows very striking parallels. The prayer for the celebrant, of which the form was *Mihi quoque indignissimo famulo tuo propitius esse digneris, et ab omnibus me peccatorum offensionibus emundare* is an exact translation of the corresponding Alexandrine text: "Remember me also, O Lord, thy humble and unworthy servant, and forgive my sins." The author of *De Sacramentis* quotes the Roman Canon as saying *quod est figura corporis et sanguinis domini nostri Iesu Christi*, and the Egyptian Prayer Book of Serapion uses exactly the same expression, "the figure of the body and blood". In the West the words "our God" are not often applied to Christ in liturgies. In the Gelasian Sacramentary they occur *ut nobis corpus et sanguis fiat dilectissimi filii tui Domini Dei nostri Iesu Christi*, just where they come in the same context in St. Mark's Liturgy. Our Mass refers to the oblation as "thy gifts and favours" (*de tuis donis ac datis*); so does St. Mark. But the most striking parallel between Rome and Alexandria is in the order of the Canon. The Antiochene Liturgy puts the whole of the Intercession after the words of Institution and the *Epiklesis*; in Alexandria it comes before. And in our Canon the greater part of this intercession (*imprimis quae tibi offerimus, Commemoratio pro vivis, Communicantes*) also comes before the Consecration, leaving only as a curious anomaly the *Commemoratio pro defunctis* and the *Nobis quoque peccatoribus* to follow after the Anamnesis (*Unde et memores*).

Although, then, it is impossible to establish any sort of mutual dependence, it is evident that the Roman Canon contains likenesses to the two Eastern rites too exact to be accidental; in its forms it most resembles the Antiochene Anaphora, but in its arrangement it follows, or guides, Alexandria. Before coming to the final definition of the Canon at about the time of St. Gregory, it will be convenient here to consider what is a very important question, namely that of the order of the different prayers. It has been seen that the prayers themselves can be traced back a very long way. Is their arrangement among themselves as old as they are, or is our present Canon a re-arrangement of parts that once stood in another order? Every one who has studied its text has noticed certain grave difficulties in this arrangement. The division of the Intercession, to which reference has been made, is unique among liturgies and is difficult to account for. Again, one little word, the second word in the Canon, has caused much questioning; and many not very successful attempts have been made to account for it. The Canon begins *Te igitur*. To what does that *igitur* refer? From the sense of the whole passage it should follow some reference to the sacrifice. One would expect some prayer that God may accept our offering, perhaps some reference such as is found in the Eastern liturgies to the sacrifices of Abraham, Melchisedech, etc. It should then be natural to continue: "And *therefore* we humbly pray thee, most merciful Father", etc. But there is no hint of such an allusion in what goes before. No preface has any word to which the *igitur* could naturally refer. At any rate there is no trace of it, either in our preface or in any of the other rites.

The prayer *Hanc igitur* has some difficulties. The Greek version adds a rubric before it: "Here he names the dead". What can the *Hanc igitur* have to do with the dead? Yet the Antiochene Liturgy, in which several parallel passages to our Canon have already been noticed, has a parallel to the second half of this prayer too, and that parallel occurs in its commemoration of the dead. There, following a prayer that the dead may rest "in the land of the living, in thy kingdom . . . in the bosom of Abraham, Isaac and Jacob", etc., is found this continuation: "And keep for us in peace, O Lord, a Christian, well-pleasing and sinless end to our lives, gathering us under the feet of thy Elect, when Thou willest and as Thou willest, only without shame and offence; through thy only begotten Son our Lord and God and Saviour, Jesus Christ." We notice here the reference to the elect (*in electorum tuorum grege*), the prayer that we may be kept "in peace" (*in tua pace disponas*], the allusion to the "end of our lives" (*diesque nostros*) and the unusual *Per Christum Dominum nostrum*, making a break in the middle of the Eucharistic prayer. The Syrian form with its plain reference to death ("the end of our lives") seems more clearly to be a continuation of a prayer for the faithful departed. But in the Roman form too is found such a reference in the words about hell (*ab aeterna damnatione*) and heaven (*in electorum tuorum grege*).

The first half of the *Hanc igitur* must now be accounted for down to *placatus accipias*. This first half is a reduplication of the prayer *Quam oblationem*. Both contain exactly the same idea that God may graciously accept our offering. *Hanc oblationem* and *Quam oblationem* differ only in the relative construction of the second form. We know that the relative construction is not the original one. In the *De Sacramentis*, to which reference has several times been made, the *Quam oblationem* occurs as an absolute sentence: *Fac nobis hanc oblationem adscriptam, rationabilem acceptabilemque, quod est figura corporis et sanguinis Domini nostri Iesu Christi*. We also know that the *igitur* in *Hanc igitur* is not original. Moreover, the place and object of this prayer have varied very much. It has been applied to all sorts of purposes, and it is significant that it occurs specially often in connexion with the dead. This would be a natural result, if we suppose it to be a compilation of two separate parts, both of which have lost their natural place in the Canon.

When then may this change be supposed to have been made? It was not made in the time of Innocent I (401-417); it had already occurred when the Gelasian Sacramentary was written (seventh century); it may be taken for certain that in the time of St. Gregory I (590-604) the Canon already stood as it does now. The reason for believing that Innocent I still knew only the old arrangement is that in his letter to Decentius of Eugubium he implies that the Intercession comes *after* the Consecration.[17] He says that the people for whom we pray "should be named in the middle of the holy mysteries, not during the things that go before, that by the very mysteries we should open the way for the prayers that follow". If the diptychs are read after the way has been opened by the holy mysteries, the Roman Canon must follow the same order as the Church of Antioch, and at any rate place the *Commemoratio vivorum* after the Consecration. Supposing, then, that this re-arrangement really did take place, it must have been made in the course of the fifth century.

From the time of St. Gregory I (590 -604).—Certainly when St. Gregory became pope our Canon was already fixed in its present order. There are scarcely any changes to note in its history since then. "No pope has added to or changed the Canon since St. Gregory," says Benedict XIV.[18] We learn from Joannes Diaconus that St. Gregory "collected the Sacramentary of Gelasius in one book, leaving out much, changing little, adding something for the exposition of the Gospels". These modifications seem to concern chiefly the parts of the Mass outside the Canon. We are told that Gregory added to the *Hanc igitur* the continuation *diesque nostros in tua pace disponas,* etc. We have already noticed that this second part was originally a fragment of a prayer for the dead. St. Gregory's addition may then very well mean, not that he composed it, but that he joined it to the *Hanc igitur*, having removed it from its original place. From the time of Gregory the most important event in the history of the Roman Canon is, not any sort of change in it, but the rapid way in which it spread all over the West, displacing the Gallican Liturgy. Charlemagne (742-814) applied to Pope Adrian I (772-95) for a copy of the Roman Liturgy, that he might introduce it throughout the Frankish Kingdom. The text sent by the pope is the basis of what is called the *Sacramentarium Gregorianum*, which therefore represents the Roman Rite at the end of the eighth century. But it is practically unchanged since St. Gregory's time. The Gelasian book, which is earlier than the so-called Gregorian one, is itself later than St. Gregory. It contains the same Canon (except that there are a few more saints' names in the *Communicantes*), and has the continuation *diesque nostros in tua pace disponas*, etc., joined to the *Hanc igitur*, just as in our present Missal. The Stowe Missal, now in Dublin (a sixth or early seventh century MS.), is no longer a sacramentary, but contains already the complete text of a *Missa quotidiana*, with collects for three other Masses, thus forming what we call a Missal. From this time convenience led more and more to writing out the whole text of the Mass in one book. By the tenth century the Missal, containing whole Masses and including Epistles and Gospels, takes the place of the separate books (*Sacramentarium* for the celebrant, *Lectionarium* for the deacon and subdeacon, and *Antiphonarium Missae* for the choir). After the ninth century the Roman Mass, now quite fixed in all its essential parts (though the Proper Masses for various feasts constantly change), quickly became the universal use throughout the Western patriarchate. Except for three small exceptions, the Ambrosian Rite at Milan, the Mozarabic Rite at Toledo, and the Byzantine Rite among the Italo-Greeks in Calabria and Sicily, this has been the case ever since. The local medieval rites of which we hear, such as those of Lyons, Paris, Rouen, Salisbury, York, etc., are in no sense different liturgies. They are all simply the Roman use with slight local variations—variations, moreover, that hardly ever affect the Canon. The Sarum Rite, for instance, which Anglicans have sometimes tried to set up as a sort of rival to the Roman Rite, does not contain in its Canon a single word that differs from the parent-rite as still used by us. But some changes were made in medieval times, changes that have since been removed by the conservative tendency of Roman legislation.

From the tenth century people took all manner of liberties with the text of the Missal. It was the time of farced *Kyries* and *Glorias*, of dramatic and even theatrical ritual, of endlessly varying and lengthy prefaces, into which interminable accounts of stories from Bible history and lives of saints were introduced. This tendency did not even spare the Canon; although the specially sacred character of this part tended to prevent people from tampering with it as recklessly as they did with other parts of the Missal. There were, however, additions made to the *Communicantes* so as to introduce special allusions on certain feasts; the two lists of saints, in the *Communicantes* and *Nobis quoque peccatoribus*, were enlarged so as to include various local people, and even the *Hanc igitur* and the *Qui pridie* were modified on certain days. The Council of Trent (1545-63) restrained this tendency and ordered that "the holy Canon composed many centuries ago" should be kept pure and unchanged; it also condemned those who say that the "Canon of the Mass contains errors and should be abolished."[19] Pope Pius V (1566-72) published an authentic edition of the Roman Missal in 1570, and accompanied it with a Bull forbidding anyone to either add, or in any way change any part of it. This Missal is to be the only one used in the West and everyone is to conform to it, except that local uses which can be proved to have existed for more than 200 years are to be kept. This exception saved the Ambrosian, Mozarabic, and Byzantine Rites, as well as a few ancient modified forms of the Roman Rite, such as the Dominican, Carmelite, and Carthusian Missals. The differences in these Missals, however, hardly affect the Canon, except in one or two unimportant rubrics. Since Pius V our Canon, then, has been brought back to its original simplicity and remains unchanged throughout the year, except that on a few of the very greatest feasts slight additions are made to the *Communicantes* and the *Hanc igitur*, and on one day to the

Qui pridie quam pateretur (see below). Clement VIII (1592-1605), Urban VIII (1623-44), and Leo XIII (1878- 1903) have, each in his own time, re-edited the Missal, and a great number of additional Masses for new feasts or for local calendars have been added to it. But none of these changes have affected the part now under consideration. The Canon that we say is always the one finally restored by Pius V, that remains as it was in the days of Gregory I, and that goes back far behind his time till its origin is lost in the mists that hang over the first centuries when the Roman Christians met together to "do the things the Lord commanded at appointed times."[20] Through all the modifications and additions that, in recent years especially, have caused our Missal to grow in size, among all the later collects, lessons and antiphons, the Canon stands out firm and unchanging in the midst of an ever-developing rite, the centre and nucleus of the whole liturgy, stretching back with its strange and archaic formulae through all the centuries of church history, to the days when the great Roman Caesar was lord of the world and the little community of Christians stood around their bishop while they "sang a hymn to Christ as to a God before day-break."[21] Then the bishop lifted up his hands over the bread and wine, "gave thanks and glory to the Father of all through his Son and the Holy Ghost, and made the Eucharist."[22] So that of all liturgical prayers in the Christian world no one is more ancient nor more venerable than the Canon of the Roman Mass.

3. *The Text and Rubrics of the Canon*.—Following the order of our present text, some remarks will be added about its expression and the ceremonies that accompany it. The whole Canon is now said silently. The priest should just hear his own voice (this is especially important in the case of the words of Consecration, since the form of every sacrament must be sensible), but should not be heard by the bystanders. This law began with the reduplication of the parts of the celebrant and choir. For many centuries the celebrant has not waited till the choir have finished their part, but goes on at once with his prayers—except in the cases of the *Gloria* and Creed, where he has to sing aloud as soon as they have done. Mabillon quotes from the older Roman *ordines* that originally "the priest did not begin the Canon until the singing of the *Sanctus* was over."[23] The singing of the *Sanctus* and *Benedictus* then made it necessary for the priest at the altar to speak the Canon in a low voice. How little this was ever considered really essential is shown by the fact that at an ordination, almost the only case of concelebration left in the West, all the concelebrants say the Canon together aloud. There are also mystic reasons for the silent prayers of the Canon. They are thus shown to be purely sacerdotal, belonging only to the priest, the silence increases our reverence at the most sacred moment of the Mass, removes the Consecration from ordinary vulgar use, and is a symbol of our Lord's silent prayer in the Garden and silence during his Passion.[24] The celebrant lifts up his hands, joins them, also lifting up his eyes, and then bows deeply before the altar, resting his joined hands on it. This ceremony should come *before* the *Te igitur*, so that he does not begin the prayer till he is bowing before the altar. It is an obvious gesture, a sort of mute invocation as the beginning of the Consecration prayer. The first three prayers are always noted as belonging together and making three parts of one prayer (*Te igitur, Memento Domine, Communicantes*), which is closed for itself by the *Per Christum Dominum nostrum, Amen*. It is now a law that a picture of the Crucifixion should be placed at the beginning of the Canon. Innocent III (1198-1216) notes that in his time this was already the custom. The crucifix grew out of the adornment of the letter T with which the Canon begins. Innocent thinks that the presence of the T at that place is a special work of Divine Providence.[25]

Te igitur: We have already considered the *igitur*. At one time the celebrant kissed both the altar and the crucifix in the Missal at the beginning of the Canon.[26] After kissing the altar the celebrant makes three signs of the cross over the bread and wine. It is the first of the many blessings of the gifts in the Canon and is joined to the kiss as one ceremony. He then stands erect and lifts up his hands, as at the collects (now they may not be lifted above the shoulders).[27] This is the traditional attitude of prayer that may be seen in the pictures of *Orantes* in the catacombs. It is observed throughout the Canon. The priest prays first for the Church, then for the pope and diocesan ordinary by name. *Antistes*, from *antisto*, is one of the many older words for "bishop". At the pope's name a slight inclination is made. When the Roman See is vacant, the mention of the pope is left out. In Rome the bishop's name is left out; the pope is local bishop there. The bishop must be canonically appointed and confirmed, otherwise he is not mentioned. But he need not yet be consecrated. It is always the ordinary of the diocese, even in the case of regulars who are exempt. A diocesan bishop in saying Mass changes the form *et Antistite nostro* N. into *et me indigno servo tuo*. The pope naturally uses these words instead of *una cum famulo tuo Papa nostro* N., and omits the clause about the bishop. The mention of the pope always occurs at this place. Otherwise in the Middle Ages there was a great variety in the names. A very old custom was to name the sovereign after the bishop (*et pro rege nostro* N. or *Imperatore nostro* N.). Pope Celestine I (422-32) refers to it in a letter to Theodosius II. Boniface I (418-22) writes to Emperor Honorius: "Behold in the very mysteries, among the prayers which the bishop offers for your Empire." So also the *De Sacramentis* says: "Prayer is offered for the people, for the king, for the others." Throughout the Middle Ages the sovereign was always named. Pius V removed the clause from the Missal. In the case of Catholic princes a privilege is given by which they are put in. In Austria the clause *et pro Imperatore nostro Francisco Josepho* is always added by the celebrant, and in Hungary it becomes of course *pro rege nostro*. At one time the priest went on to pray for himself at this place: *Mihi quoque indignissimo famulo tuo propitius esse digneris et ab omnibus me peccatorum offensionibus emundare*. The word *orthodoxi* that follows is very rare in the West. It is a link between our Canon and the Antiochene Anaphora.

Commemoratio pro vivis: The celebrant does not now name anyone aloud at the "N et N." After *tuarum* he joins his hands and prays silently for anyone he likes. This is the place where the diptychs for the living were read. A diptych was a table folding in two like a book, on which names were written and then read out. Some authorities admit and some deny that the priest in his silent prayer may name people who are outside the Church. As this prayer is a private one (as shown by the folding of the hands) there is no law to forbid him from so doing. He goes on to mention the bystanders, who are thus always specially prayed for at Mass. *Pro quibus tibi offerimus, vel qui tibi offerunt* is a reduplication. The first half (*pro quibus tibi offerimus*) is missing in all early sacramentaries, also in the Greek version. It occurs, however, in the parallel text of the Syrian Liturgy. Both parts refer to the same persons, for whom the priests and his assistants offer the Sacrifice and who themselves also join in the offering by their presence. "Sacrifice of praise" (Ps. xlix, 23), "For the forgiveness of their sins" and "For the hope of their safety and health", are three expressions connoting the threefold character of the Mass as praise, atonement, and petition.

Communicantes: This prayer is headed by the rubric *Infra Actionem*. Why is it put here? The *Communicantes* has a small addition on the five chief days of the year, Christmas, the Epiphany, Easter, Ascension Day, and Whitsunday, referring to the feast. The beginning of the text with these additions is placed among the prefaces, after the corresponding proper preface for each feast. Placed there, the rubric that heads it is obvious. For each feast there is the special preface and, moreover, *Infra Actionem*, that is, "Within the Canon", a further change is made. From its place among the prefaces as a natural heading to the *Communicantes* this rubric has found its way into the Canon, when people had begun to look upon it as the title of that prayer. The Gelasian Sacramentary has it, when the *Communicantes* occurs with an addition among the Propers, but it has not yet found its way into the Ordinary. These five additions to the *Communicantes*, all of them very beautiful and very ancient (they are all, with slight variations, in the Gelasian book), are the only ones left by Pius V, where at one time many more feasts had sometimes long references. *Communicantes* means simply "in union with". The participles here have given rise to much discussion; no finite verb follows, nor does any go before to which they can suitably refer. It is simply a case of late Latin that is not strictly grammatical. It must be understood as standing for a finite verb, as if it were *Communicamus cum eis et memoriam veneramus eorum*. There are parallel examples in the Vulgate of a participle standing for a finite verb (e.g. Rom., ix, 6 sqq., where the Greek has the same anomaly). In the lists of saints that follows, Our Lady of course always holds the first place. She is here named very solemnly with her title of "Mother of God", as in the corresponding Eastern Anaphoras. It is strange that St. John the Baptist, who should come next, has been left out here. He is named in both the Eastern liturgies at this place, and finds his right place at the head of our other list (in the *Nobis quoque*). After Our Lady follow twelve Apostles and twelve martyrs. The Apostles are not arranged in quite the same order as in any of the Gospels. St. Paul at the head, with St. Peter, makes up the number for Judas. St. Matthias is not named here, but in the *Nobis quoque*. The twelve martyrs are evidently arranged to balance the Apostles. First come five popes, then a bishop (St. Cyprian), and a deacon (St. Lawrence), then five laymen. All these saints, except St. Cyprian, are local Roman saints, as is natural in what was originally the local Roman Liturgy. It is noticeable that St. Cyprian (d. 258), who had a serious misunderstanding with a Roman pope, is the only foreigner honoured by the Roman Church by being named among her own martyrs. The fact has been quoted to show how completely his disagreement with Pope Stephen was forgotten, and how Stephen's successors remembered him only as one of the chief and most glorious martyrs of the West. The cult of saints was at first the cult of martyrs; all those in both lists in the Canon died for the Faith. Gregory III (731-41) added to the Vatican basilica a chapel containing a great number of relics and dedicated to All Saints. He ordered the monks who served this chapel to add to the *Communicantes* after the words *et omnium Sanctorum tuorum* the further clause: *quorum solemnitas hodie in conspectu tuo celebratur, Domine Deus noster, in toto orbe terrarum*. The text is found in some medieval Missals. A certain number of Missals also contained additions about special patrons to be used on their feasts.[28] All these clauses disappeared at Pius V's reform, except that in some French churches the names of St. Hilary and St. Martin are still added to the list. This first complex of prayers forms the chief part of the great Intercession that occurs in all liturgies. We notice again the strange fact that at Rome it is divided in two by the Consecration.

Hanc Igitur: This prayer has already been considered, the most remarkable of all in the Canon. Here it need only be added that the *Hanc igitur* receives an addition (after the words *familiae tuae*) on four occasions only, on Maundy Thursday, Easter, Whitsunday, and in the Mass at a bishop's consecration. The additions will be found on the feasts in the Missal, and in the Consecration service in the Pontifical. On Maundy Thursday an allusion is made to "the day on which our Lord Jesus gave the mysteries of his Body and Blood to his disciples to be consecrated"; Easter and Whitsunday have an identical form (a prayer for the newly baptised), and the Consecration Mass has a clause "which we offer to Thee also for this Thy servant [the new bishop says: "for me Thy servant"] whom Thou hast deigned to promote to the order of Episcopacy". The Gelasian Sacramentary has as many as thirty-eight special forms to be intercalated at this place, in which allusions are made to all kinds of special intentions. For instance, in a re-quiem Mass, "which we offer to Thee for the repose of the soul of thy servant N."); for a wedding, "This oblation of thy servants N. and N., which they offer to Thee for thy handmaid N., we beg Thee mercifully to accept, that as Thou hast al-lowed her to come to the fitting age for marriage, so Thou mayest allow her, being joined to her husband by thy grace, to rejoice in the offspring she desires and mayest mercifully bring her with her spouse to the desired length of years; and dispose our days in thy peace." During the *Hanc igitur* the priest, who has joined his hands at the preceding *Per Christum Dominum nostrum. Amen,*, spreads them over the offerings. This is a late ceremony. It occurs first in the fifteenth century. Formerly the celebrant lifted up his hands as before, but made a profound inclination. This older rite is still used by the Dominicans and Carmelites. The imposition of hands seems to have been in-troduced merely as a way of practically touching the sacrifice at this point, at which it is so definitely named in the prayer. At the *Per Christum Dominum nostrum. Amen.* following, the priest again (as always at these words) folds his hands. The *Hanc igitur*, with the two following prayers, may be consid-ered as forming a second member of the Canon, threefold like the first.

Quam oblationem: This prayer has been noticed, as well as its echo of *Hanc oblationem*. The offering is accompanied by five epithets. The *De Sacramentis* has only three, *adscriptam, rationabilem, acceptabilemque*. The word *rationabilis* occurs in Rom., xii, 1. *In omnibus* means "thoroughly". There follows naturally a petition that the offering may "become to us the Body and Blood of thy beloved Son, our Lord Jesus Christ". *De Sacramentis* has: "which is a figure of the Body and Blood", as in Serapion's Prayer and in Tertullian.[29] During this prayer the sign of the cross is made five times over the offering - a further blessing of the bread and wine about to be consecrated.

Qui pridie: Such a form is in all liturgies the connecting link between an allusion to Christ that has gone before and the words of Institution that follow immediately. The short form, "Who, the day before he died, took bread", is in other rites sometimes expanded into a longer account of the Passion.

Gratias agens: The word *Thanksgiving* (Eucharist) always occurs here. Benedict XIV notices that we do not read in the Gospels that Christ lifted up his eyes at the Last Supper, and he says it is a tradition that Christ did so, as He did at the miracle of the loaves and fishes.[30] The words of Institution for the bread are the same in the Synoptic Gospels (Matt., xxvi, 26, Mark, xiv, 22, Luke, xxii, 19) and in I Cor., xi, 23. The Church has added to this form (*Hoc est corpus meum*) the word *enim*, and she leaves out the continuation "which is given for you", that occurs in St. Luke and I Cor. The *enim* seems to have found its way here through analogy with the consecration of the chalice, where it occurs in St. Matthew. This prayer admits of one addition in the year; on Maundy Thursday the form is used: "Who the day before He suffered for our salvation and for that of all men, that is today, He took bread", etc. At the beginning of the *Qui pridie* the celebrant takes the bread (only the host that he himself will receive in Communion) between the forefingers and thumbs of both hands. These fingers are then not separated again, unless when he touches the Blessed Sacrament, till they have been washed at the last ablutions.[31] The reason for this is, of course, lest any crumb may have remained between them. He lifts up his eyes at the words *elevatis oculis*, and makes a sign of the cross over the host at the word *benedixit*. If other hosts are to be consecrated they stay on the corporal. The ciborium (if there is one) is opened before the words: *Qui pridie*. The words of Institution are said "secretly, plainly, and attentively" over the host and over all, if several are to be consecrated. The Catholic Church has always believed that the words of Institution are those that consecrate. Immediately therefore follows the ceremony of the Elevation. The priest genuflects on one knee, still holding the Blessed Sacrament, rises, lifts it up above his head to show it to the people, replaces it on the corporal and genuflects again. An adoration of the Blessed Sacrament at this point is an old rite. The *Ordo Romanus Primus*, which does not give the words of Consecration, says that during the Canon "the bishops, deacons, subdeacons, and priests stay in the presbytery bowing down (*inclinati*)." On account of the heresy of Berengarius (1088), the Elevation was introduced in France in the twelfth, and then throughout the West in the thirteenth, century.[32] Gregory X (1271-76) ordered it to be used throughout the West in his Ceremonial. At first only the Host, not the Chalice, was elevated. The priest's genuflexions were not introduced till later. In the fourteenth century he still only bowed his head. Meanwhile the assistants kneel and bow low. Durandus (see DURANDUS} says "they prostrate themselves reverently on the ground", so also the XIII Roman *Ordo*. However, since the only object of the Elevation is to show the Blessed Sacrament to the people, this does not mean that they should not look up at it. At each genuflexion, and between them at the elevation, the bell is rung. This ceremony also begins in the fourteenth century. Durandus notices it. The bell should be sounded three times at each elevation, or continuously from the first to the second genuflexion.[33] This is the first sounding of the bell ordered by the rubrics after the *Sanctus*. The common practice of ringing at the *Hanc igitur* has no authority.

The server also lifts up the chasuble with his left hand at the elevation, not at the genuflexion.[34] This is to keep back the vestment (which the rubrics always suppose to cover the arms) while the priest elevates. With a modern Roman-shaped chasuble it is a mere form, and a memory of better days.[35] As soon as the celebrant rises from the second genuflexion he continues the Consecration prayer.

Simili modo: *Postquam coenatum est*; the Canon supposes that the cup our Lord consecrated was the last of the Hillel-cups. *Hunc praeclarum calicem*, a dramatic identification of the Mass with the Last Supper. The Consecration-form for the chalice is put together from the four accounts of the Last Supper quoted above. It is mainly from St. Matthew (xxvi, 26); *Calix Sanguinis mei* is adapted from St. Luke and St. Paul, *pro vobis* from St. Luke, *pro multis* from St. Matthew; and the last clause, *Haec quotiescumque feceritis*, etc., is again slightly modified from St. Paul. Moreover, two additions have been made to it that are not in the New Testament at all, *et aeterni* and *mysterium fidei*. This last clause especially has been much discussed. It seems that it was originally a warning spoken by the deacon. The catechumens have been sent away before the Offertory; at the Consecration he again warns the people that it is not for catechumens, it is a "mystery of Faith", that is a mystery for the faithful (the baptised) only. The ceremonies at this Consecration are the same as those for the preceding one, except that the deacon (at low Mass here, as always, the celebrant must supply the deacon's part himself) takes the pall from the chalice before the words of Consecration and replaces it as soon as the chalice is put down after its Elevation. The words *Haec quotiescumque*, etc., are now generally said during the first genuflexion. In the Middle Ages they were often said after the Elevation. At high Mass a certain amount of very natural ritual has been added to both elevations. At least two torches are lit or brought in by the acolytes, which are removed after the elevation (on fast days and for requiem Masses they stay till the end of the Communion). The thurifer puts incense into his thurible, and incenses the Blessed Sacrament thrice at each elevation.

Unde et memores. A solemn memory of Christ's life, death and resurrection (the *Anamnesis*, naturally following the words "as often as you shall do these things, do them in memory of me", comes immediately after the words of Institution in all liturgies). The five signs of the cross made over the Blessed Sacrament during this prayer have often been discussed. Before the Consecration such signs are obviously blessings of the offering. How can blessings be given to what is now consecrated and has become the Real Presence? St. Thomas says the blessings refer to the *terminus a quo*, the bread and wine, not to the *terminus ad quem*, the Body and Blood of Christ.[36] People have seen in them symbols representing our offering to God, memories of the Crucifixion, blessings for the future communicants,[37] or merely a way of pointing to the Blessed Sacrament. It seems that really here again is one more case of what is very common in all our rites, namely, a dramatic representation that does not consider at what moment the effect of a Sacrament is really produced. Such effects must really all happen at one instant, the moment the matter and form are complete. But the Church cannot with words express everything in one instant; moreover before scholastic days people did not ask very closely about the actual moment. So we continually have such dramatic divisions of one simple act, and continually in her prayers the Church goes on asking for something that really must already have been granted. So in our baptism service the devil is driven out before, and the white robe and candle given, after the actual baptism. The truth of these symbols presumably occurs at one instant. Our ordination service is a still more striking instance. Long after the subject is ordained priest, after he has concelebrated, the bishop gives him the power of forgiving sins which is certainly involved in the priesthood he has already received. So these blessings after the Consecration need be only such dramatic forms as our expression, "Receive . . . this *spotless* Host", said at the Offertory long before.

Supra quae: This prayer, too, with its memory of sacrifices in the Old Testament (Abel, Abraham, Melchisedech), is common to other liturgies. St. Mark's Rite mentions the offerings of Abel, Abraham, Zachary's incense, the alms of Cornelius and the widow's mite. The words *sanctum sacrificium immaculatam Hostiam* are said to have been added by St. Leo I (440-61).[38] They do not occur in the text as given in *De Sacramentis*. Grammatically they must refer to Melchisedech's sacrifice.

Supplices te rogamus: This prayer is commonly believed to be the remnant of the Roman *Epiklesis* (see **EPIKLESIS**). It seems certain that our liturgy, like all the others, once had an *Epiklesis*, and this would be its natural place. Even as late as the time of Pope Gelasius I (492-96) there seems to have still been one. He writes: "How shall the Heavenly Spirit, when He is invoked to consecrate the divine mystery, come, if the priest and he who prays Him to come is guilty of bad actions?"[39] *Si sacerdos, et qui eum adesse deprecatur*. By striking out the *et* we have a much plainer sentence: "If the priest who prays Him to come." The chief reason for considering our prayer *Supplices te rogamus* as the fragment of an *Epiklesis* is its place in the Canon, which corresponds exactly to that of the *Epiklesis* (following the Anamnesis) in the Syrian Rite. But its form is hardly that of an *Epiklesis*. The first words of the preceding prayer, *Supra quae propitio ac sereno vultu respicere digneris*, suggest the beginning of the Alexandrine *Epiklesis*: "Look down upon us and upon this bread and this wine", and the last part (*Sacrosanctum Filii tui Corpus et Sanguinem*) have perhaps a vague resemblance; but certainly the chief thing, the Invocation of the Holy Ghost to change this bread and wine into the Body and Blood of Christ is wanting. Moreover there is a prayer in the Alexandrine Liturgy which corresponds singularly to these two prayers (*Supra quae* and *Supplices*): "the Sacrifices . . of them that offer honour and glory to thy holy name receive upon thy reasonable altar in heaven . . . through the ministry of thy holy angels and archangels; like as Thou didst accept the gifts of righteous Abel and the sacrifice of our father Abraham", etc. And this is not an *Epiklesis* but an Offertory prayer, coming in the middle of the Intercession that with them fills up what we should call the Preface. On the other hand, the end of the *Supplices te rogamus* (from *ut quotquot*) corresponds very closely to the end of both Eastern *Epikleses*. Antioch has here: "that it may become to all who partake of it" (*quotquot ex hac Altaris participatione*) "for a forgiveness of sins and for life everlasting" etc., and at Alexandria the form is: "that it may become to all of us who partake of it (a source of) Faith", etc. It seems, then, that this prayer in our Canon is a combination of the second part of an Invocation (with the essential clause left out) and an old Offertory prayer. It has been suggested that the angel mentioned here is the Holy Ghost—an attempt to bring it more into line with the proper form of an Invocation. There is however no foundation for this assertion. We have seen that the Alexandrine form has the plural "thy holy angels"; so has the Latin form in *De Sacramentis*; *per manus angelorum tuorum*. The reference is simply to an angel or to angels who assist at the throne of God and carry our prayers to Him (Tob., xii, 12, etc.). We have already seen that the order and arrangement of our Canon presents difficulties; this is a further case in point. As for the vanished Invocation itself, it will probably always remain a mystery what has become of it. It has been suggested that it was Gelasius himself who removed it from this place and put it before the words of Institution. And indeed the prayer *Quam oblationem* has a curious suggestion of an Invocation in its terms. On the other hand an *Epiklesis* before the words of Institution would be an anomaly unparalleled in any rite in the world. To come back to the rubrics, the celebrant has resumed the normal attitude of standing with uplifted hands after the *Unde et memores*, except that now the forefingers and thumbs remain joined; at the *Supplices te rogamus* he bows deeply over the altar—a ceremony obviously in accordance with the nature of its first words—resting his joined hands on it; and he stays so to the words *ex hac altaris participatione* at which he kisses the altar, rises, joins his hands, and makes the sign of the cross over the Host at *Corpus*, over the chalice at *Sanguinem*, and on himself at *omni benedictione* (while he crosses himself, the left hand is, as always in this case, laid on the breast). He joins his hands for *Per eumdem*, etc., and lifts them up for the next prayer. The next two prayers complete the Intercession, of which we have the greater part before the Consecration.

Commemoratio pro defunctis: The place of this prayer has often been changed. Why *Memento etiam?* This would seem to refer to a commemoration of some one else, that should come just before. This prayer comes naturally just after the Commemoration of the Living and the *Communicantes* (we have seen that such is the order of the Eastern liturgies), and then this *etiam* refers quite naturally to the parallel commemoration of the living. In any case it must always be a mystery that these two last prayers, obviously forming the conclusion of the Intercession, should stand out here by themselves. The ritual is the same as for the other Memento. The celebrant may not now say any names at the place marked "N. et N."; passing on, he reads *Famularumque tuarum, qui nos praecesserunt*, etc., and after *in somno pacis*, folding his hands, he silently prays for anyone he likes. The diptychs of the dead of course once were read here. Now no names are ever read out at either Commemoration. Benedict XIV quotes a case in which names were read out at the "N. et N." in the sixteenth century.[40] At the final clause *Per eumdem*, etc., the priest not only folds his hands but bows the head—a unique case in the Roman Rite, for which there has not been found any satisfactory explanation. Benedict XIV quotes from Cavalieri a mystic reason—because Christ bowed His head when He died, and we here think of the dead.[41] The rubric occurs in Pius V's Missal.

Nobis quoque peccatoribus: A prayer for ourselves that naturally follows that for the faithful departed, although the Commemoration of the Living has gone before. The parallel between this prayer and the latter half of the *Hanc igitur* has already been noticed. It is a petition that we too may find a good death and be admitted to the glorious company of the saints. The names of saints that follow are arranged rhythmically, as in *Communicantes*. Like the others they are all martyrs. First comes St. John the Baptist, as Our Lady before, then seven men and seven women. After the first martyr, St. Stephen, St. Matthias finds here the place he has not been given among the Apostles in the other list. The Peter here is a Roman exorcist martyred at Silva Candida (now part of the Diocese of Porto, near Rome). His feast with St. Marcellinus is on 2 June. The female saints are all well known. Benedict XIV quotes from Adalbert, *De Virginitate*, that St. Gregory I, having noticed that no female saints occur in the Canon, added these seven here.[42] This list of saints, like the other one, was subject to local additions in the Middle Ages.[43] The celebrant strikes his breast and slightly raises his voice at the words: *Nobis quoque peccatoribus*. This rite (the only case of part of the Canon being spoken aloud, if we except the *Per omnia saecula saeculorum* that closes it) is a reminder to the assistants that he has come to the prayer for all of those now present, in which prayer they may join. There is no *Amen* after the *Per Christum Dominum nostrum*, since now the following words, *Per quem*, follow it at once. Nevertheless after it comes a noticeable break in the Canon.

Per quem haec omnia: again a difficult text. It has no connexion with what goes before; the words *haec omnia* refer to nothing in the former prayer. Moreover, the prayer itself is not easily explained. God is said to "sanctify, enliven, bless and give to us these good things". What good things? Such a form as applied to what is already the Blessed Sacrament is very strange. The form must be taken as again a dramatic representation like the sign of the cross after the Consecration. Finally this prayer and the whole Canon ends with a stately doxology. The *Per omnia saecula saeculorum* is said aloud, or sung at high Mass. The answer, *Amen*, of the people, closes the Canon. Signs of the cross are made at the three words: *Sanctificas, vivificas, benedicis*, and the doxology has a special ritual. The celebrant uncovers the chalice and genuflects, makes three signs of the cross with the Host over the chalice at the three forms: *per ipsum et cum ipso et in ipso*, two more signs over the altar in front of the chalice at *Patri omnipotenti* and *Spiritus Sancti*, and finally at *omnis honor et gloria* he slightly elevates the chalice with the left hand, holding the Host above it with the right. He then replaces both, covers the chalice (at high Mass the deacon always uncovers and covers the chalice), genuflects and with joined hands says: *Per omnia saecula saeculorum*. So he goes on to the Embolism of the Our Father. This ceremony went through slight changes in the Middle Ages. St. Thomas Aquinas (d. 1274) notices it.[44] The essence of it is the Elevation, made to show the people the Blessed Sacrament. The reason why these crosses are formed with the Host is that it is just about to be elevated. The priest has already taken it up to elevate it. This corresponds more or less to the point at which the Eastern Churches elevate. It is the original Elevation of the Roman use, and till the heresy of Berengarius it was the only one. We note finally that at and after the Consecration the Host, chalice, ciborium, and all other Hosts that may be consecrated, must always be placed on the altarstone, if it is a movable altar, and on the corporal. Also the celebrant, whenever he lays his hand on the altar before the Consecration, does so outside the corporal; after the Consecration he lays it on the corporal.

4. *Mystical Interpretations.*—It is obvious that in the great days of mystic theology so venerable and sacred a text as the Canon of the Mass should have received elaborate mystical explanations. Indeed, after the Bible it was chiefly to the Canon that these pious writers turned their attention. Equally obvious is it that such interpretations never have any sort of regard to the historical development of the text. By the time they began the Canon had reigned unquestioned and unchanged for centuries, as the expression of the most sacred rite of the Church. The interpreters simply took this holy text as it stood, and conceived mystic and allegorical reasons for its divisions, expressions, rites, even—as has been seen—for the letter T, with which in their time it began. No one who is accustomed to the subtle conceptions of medieval mysticism will be surprised to see that these interpretations all disagree among themselves and contradict each other in every point. The system leads to such contradictions inevitably. You divide the Canon where you like, trying, of course, as far as possible to divide by a holy number—three, or seven, or twelve—and you then try somehow to show that each of these divisions corresponds to some epoch of our Lord's life, or to one of the Gifts of the Holy Ghost, or—if you can make eight divisions somewhere—to one of the Beatitudes. The arrangements are extremely ingenious. Indeed, perhaps the strongest impression one receives from such mystical divisions and explanations is how extraordinarily well their inventors do it. Nor does the utterly artificial nature of the whole proceeding prevent many of the interpretations from being quite edifying, often very poetic and beautiful. To give even a slight account of the endless varieties of these mystic commentaries would take up very much space. One or two of the more interesting or curious examples may be added here. A favourite idea is that the Ordinary to the *Sanctus*, with its lessons, represents Christ's public life and teaching; the Canon is a type of the Passion and death—hence it is said in silence. Christ taught plainly, but did not open his mouth when he was accused and suffered. From Durandus comes the idea of dividing the Mass according to the four kinds of prayer mentioned in I Tim., ii, 1. It is an *Obsecratio* (supplication) to the Secret, an *Oratio* (prayer) to the *Pater noster*, a *Postulatio* (intercession) to the Communion, and a *Gratiarum Actio* (thanksgiving) to the end. Benedict XIV and many others divide the Canon into four sets of threefold prayers: (1) *Te igitur, Memento vivorum, Communicantes*; (2) *Hanc igitur, Quam oblationem, Qui pridie*; (3) *Unde et memores, Supra quae, Supplices te rogamus*; (4) *Memento defunctorum, Nobis quoque, Per quem haec omnia*. This gives the mystic numbers four, three, and twelve. So again each separate expression finds a mystic meaning. Why do we say *rogamus ac petimus* in the *Te igitur*? *Rogamus* shows humility, *petimus* confidence.[45] Why do we distinguish *haec dona* and *haec munera*? *Dona* because God gives them to us, *munera* because we offer them back to Him. Why is there no *Amen* after the *Nobis quoque peccatoribus*? Because the angels say it at that place.[46] *Per ipsum et cum ipso et in ipso est tibi . . . omnis honor et gloria* signifies in its triple form that our Lord suffered three kinds of indignities in His Passion - in His body, soul, and honour.[47] See also the explanations of the twenty-five crosses made by the priest in the Canon suggested by various commentators.[48] Historically, when these prayers were first composed, such reduplications and repetitions were really made for the sake of the rhythm which we observe in all liturgical texts. The medieval explanations are interesting as showing with what reverence people studied the text of the Canon and how, when every one had forgotten the original reasons for its forms, they still kept the conviction that the Mass is full of venerable mysteries and that all its clauses mean more than common expressions. And in this conviction the sometimes naive medieval interpreters were eminently right.

Chapter Notes:

1. I *Epp.*, Lib. VII, lxiv, Lib. XI, LIX.
2. *De exordiis et incrementis rerum eccl.*, XXII, in P.L., CXIV, 919, sqq. XXII.
3. *De SS Missae*, lib. II, XII.
4. *Ordo Rom. I,* p. 138.
5. *De SS. Missae,* CCXXVIII.
6. *Epp.*, lib. VII, no. lxiv, or lib. IX, no. xii.
7. *De SS. Missae,* CLVII.
8. I Clement *Ad Cor.*, lix-lxi.
9. *Ibid.*, xl.
10. *Ibid.*, lxv-lxvi.
11. *Ibid.* lxvi.
12. Eusebius, *Hist. Eccl.*, V, xxiv.
13. *Quaestiones* V. et N. Test." in P.L. XXXV, 2329.
14. Greg. I, *Epp.* IX, xii, in P.L., LXXVII, 956.
15. *Ep. ad Decentium* in P.L., XX, 553.
16. *Adv. Parm.*, III, xii.
17. P.L., XX, 553-554.
18. *De SS. Missae,* CLXII.
19. Sess. XXII., cap. iv. can. vi.
20. I Clement *Ad Cor.*, XL.
21. Pliny, Epp., X, xcvii
22. *I Apology,* III, lxv.
23. *In ord. Rom. comm.*, XXI.
24. Suarez, *disp.* LXXXIII, I, 25
25. Inn. III, *De Sacro altaris myst.*, I, 3, c. ii, P.L., CCXVII.

26 *Ordo Rom.* XIV, 53, fourteenth century.

27 *Rit. cel.*, V, 1.

28 *De SS. Missae,* CLXII.

29 *Adv. Marc.*, III, xix and IV, xl.

30 *De SS. Missae,* p. 160.

31 *Rit. cel.*, VIII, 5.

32 Berengarius of Tours (c. 1010-88) was a scholastic theologian whose teaching called into question the substantial presence of Christ in the Eucharist. He was required by St. Gregory VII to take an oath affirming orthodox belief which has been looked upon since as a touchstone of Catholic orthodoxy. Berengarius was later to attack the formula that he had signed, but before his death he was reconciled to the Church by St. Gregory. The full text of his oath reads:

I, Berengarius, believe interiorly and profess publicly that the bread and wine, which are placed on the altar, through the mystery of the sacred prayer and the words of our Redeemer are substantially changed into the true, proper, and life-giving flesh and blood of our Lord Jesus Christ (*substantialiter converti in veram et propriam ac vivificatricem carnem et sanguinem Iesu Christi Domini nostri*). After the consecration it is the true Body of Christ, which was born of the Virgin, and which hung on the Cross as an offering for the salvation of the world, and which sits at the right hand of the Father. And it is the true Blood of Christ which poured forth from His side. And Christ is present not merely by virtue of the sign and power of the Sacrament, but in His proper nature and true substance as is set down in this summary, and as I read it and you understand it. This I believe and I will not teach any more against this faith. So help me God and this holy Gospel of God! (Ed.)

33 *Rit. cel.*, VIII, 6.

34 *Ibid*

35 "...a memory of better days"—Dr. Fortescue preferred the more flowing Gothic chasuble. (Ed.)

36 ST, III, Q. LXXXIII, art. 5, ad 3.

37 Bossuet, *Médit. sur l'Evang.*, I, 63ᵉ jour.

38 *De SS. Missae,* lib. II, xii.

39 *Ep.*, vii; Thiel, *Ep. Rom. Pont.*, I, 486

40 *De SS. Missae,* p. 220.

41 *Ibid.*, p. 219.

42 *Ibid.*, p. 162.

43 *Ibid.*, p. 223.
44 ST, II, Q. LXXXIII, art. 5, ad 3.
45 Odo Cameracensis, *Exp. in Can. Missae*, dist. III.
46 Albertus Magnus, *Summa de off. Missae*, III, c. ix.
47 *De SS. Missae*, p. 227.
48 N. Gihr, *Das heilige Messopfer, dogmatisch liturgisch und ascetisch erklärt* (6th ed., Freiburg im Br., 1897), p. 550.

23

Libera Nos

The first words of the Embolism (see **GLOSSARY**) of the Lord's Prayer in the Roman Rite. Most liturgies contain a prayer developing the idea of the last clause of the Our Father (But deliver us from evil), and specifying various evils from which we pray to be delivered. This prayer, which always follows the Our Father immediately, is called its Embolism (insertion). In many rites (Antiochene, Alexandrine, Nestorian) it is rather of the nature of an insertion into the Our Father, repeating again and enlarging on its last clauses (e.g. the Antiochene Embolism: "And lead us not into temptation, O Lord, Lord of Hosts Who knowest our weakness, but deliver us from the evil one, and from his works and all his might and art, for the sake of Thy Holy Name invoked upon our lowliness"). The Roman Embolism is said secretly by the celebrant as soon as he has added *Amen* to the last clause of the *Pater noster* sung by the choir (or said by the server). In the middle (after *omnibus sanctis*) he makes the sign of the cross with the paten and kisses it. During the last clause (*Per eundem Dominum nostrum . . .*) he puts the paten under the Host, he (at high Mass the deacon) uncovers the chalice, genuflects, breaks the Host over the chalice, puts a small fraction into the chalice and the rest on the paten. This rite is the Fraction common to all liturgies. The last words (*Per omnia saecula saeculorum*) are sung (or said) aloud, forming the *ecphonesis* (see **GLOSSARY**) before the *Pax*). Only on Good Friday does he sing it aloud, to the tone of a ferial Collect, and the choir answers *Amen*. In this case the Fraction does not take place till the Embolism is finished. In the Milanese and Mozarabic Rites he sings it, and the choir answers *Amen*. The present Milanese form is very similar to that of Rome. It will be found with its chant in any edition of the Ambrosian Missal. The Mozarabic Embolism with its chant is in the *Missale Mistum*.[1] In both rites the Fraction has preceded the Lord's Prayer. In all the Eastern rites the Embolism is said secretly, with the last words aloud (*Ecphonesis*); the people answer *Amen*. The Byzantine Rite has no Embolism of the Lord's Prayer, but only the final clause: "For Thine is the kingdom and the power and the glory, of the Father and the Son and the Holy Ghost, now and for ever and for ages of ages. R. Amen." That it once had this prayer, like the parent Rite of Antioch, seems certain from the fact that there is an Embolism in the Nestorian and Armenian Liturgies, both derived at an early date from Constantinople.

Chapter Notes:

[1] P.L. LXXXV, 559-60.

24

COMMUNION-ANTIPHON

The term Communion (*Communio*) is used, not only for the reception of the Holy Eucharist, but also as a shortened form for the antiphon (*Antiphone ad Communionem*) that was originally sung while the people were receiving the Blessed Sacrament, but which has now been displaced, so as to follow that moment. In the Ambrosian Rite this antiphon is called the *Transitorium*, apparently because the celebrant after Communion goes over (*transit*) to the Epistle side of the altar to read it. It is the fourth and last of the changeable parts of the Mass (*Proprium*) sung by the choir (Introit, Gradual, Offertory, Communion), and is at least as old as the fourth century. In St. Augustine's time (d. 430), together with the Offertory-Antiphon, it had lately been introduced into Africa; he wrote a treatise (*Contra Hilarium*) to defend their use. But the present Communion is only a fragment of the older chant. It was originally a psalm, with the *Gloria Patri*, preceded and concluded by an antiphon. The First Roman *Ordo* (about 770) contains the direction: "As soon as the pontiff begins to give Communion in the *Senatorium* [where the most distinguished people stood] at once the choir begins the antiphon for the Communion, singing it alternately with the subdeacons; and they go until all the people have received Communion. Then the pontiff makes a sign to them to sing the *Gloria Patri*; and so, when they have repeated the antiphon [*repetito versu*] they stop." This is the first definite rubric we have about the

Communio. It shows us that it was to be sung while the celebrant goes around to Communicate the people; and that it consisted of a psalm, sung alternately with its antiphon, as were, at that time, also the Introit and Offertory. So also *Micrologus* (see **GLOSSARY**), Bernold of Constance, d. 1100, says that when the people Communicate, "meanwhile the antiphon is sung which takes its name from the Communion, to which a psalm must be added with its *Gloria Patri* if need be."[1] It was, then, like the other three parts that make up the *Proprium* of the choir, a chant to be sung so as to fill up the time while the clergy were engaged in some action.

The two changes in its history are that it has been removed to its place after the Communion and has been shortened. Its postponement began in the twelfth century. Abbot Rupert of Deutz (d. 1135) says: "The chant that we call the Communion, which we sing after the heavenly food, is a thanksgiving."[2] And Durandus (see **DURANDUS**): "The antiphon, which is called Post-communion by many because it is sung after the Communion . . ."[3] But he goes on to describe the final collect as that which "is properly called Post-communion".[4] There are other instances of this antiphon occasionally being called Post-Communion. The reason of its removal seems to have been, on the one hand, the place of the *Agnus Dei*, which at that time began to be sung during the Communion, and to be repeated thrice, thus taking up more time; on the other hand, the gradual lessening of the number of communicants at high Mass. Its shortened form is part of the curtailing of all the prayers of the Mass that was the result of the multiplication of low Masses. Only in requiems have we a remnant of the older form. Here after the first verse *Lux aeterna* follows an antiphon *Cum sanctis tuis*, then the *Requiem aeternam*—last vestige of the psalm—and the antiphon is repeated. Otherwise the Communion is always one short antiphon, sung by the choir immediately after the *Agnus Dei*, and said by the celebrant after the Communion. It is generally a verse from Holy

Scripture, referring, not to the Holy Eucharist but rather to the feast which is celebrated or to the special season (*de tempore*) or to the purpose (in votives) for which the Mass is offered. But not seldom it is a text taken from some other source, or specially composed for this use. It is always said by the priest at the altar. Since the common use of low Mass, in which he substitutes the choir's part himself, the rule is that the priest also says whatever is sung by them. As soon as he has arranged the chalice and paten in the middle of the altar (at high Mass the subdeacon does this, and takes them to the credence-table) he goes with joined hands to the Missal, which has been replaced at the Epistle side, and there, the hands still joined, reads the Communion from the *Proprium*. He then comes back to the middle for the *Dominus vobiscum* before the Post-Communion.

Chapter Notes:

1   P.L., CLI, 973 sq.
2   *De div. off.*, II, xviii, P.L., CLXX, 13 sq.
3   Durandus, IV, 56.
4   *Ibid.*, p. 57.

25

Postcommunion

The Communion act finishes the essential Eucharistic service. Justin Martyr adds nothing after describing the Communion.[1] However, it was natural that the people should not be dismissed without a final prayer of thanksgiving and of petition, so every rite ends its liturgy with a short prayer or two and a blessing before the dismissal. The earliest complete liturgy extant, that of the *Apostolic Constitutions* VIII, contains two such prayers, a thanksgiving, and a blessing. A significant resemblance between the Roman Rite and that of the *Apostolic Constitutions* is that at Rome, too, there were formerly at every Mass two prayers of the same nature. In the Leonine Sacramentary they have no title; but their character is obvious. As examples, those for the summer ember days may serve, the first *Gratias tibi referimus*, the second *Oculis tuae miserationis intende*. The Gelasian Sacramentary calls the first *postcommunio*, the second *ad populum*. In both sacramentaries these two prayers form part of the normal Mass said throughout the year, though not every Mass has both; the prayers *ad populum* in the later book are comparatively rare. They also begin to change their character. The formerly constant terms *tuere, protege,* etc. are rarer; many are ordinary collects with no pronounced idea of prayers for blessing and protection. In the Gregorian Sacramentary the second prayer, now called *Super populum*, occurs almost only from Septuagesima to Easter; the first, *Ad complendum*, continues throughout the year, but both have lost much of their original character. The *Ad complendum* prayer (Postcommunion) has become a collect formed on the model of the collect at the beginning of Mass, though generally it keeps some allusion to the Communion just received. That is still the state of these prayers after the Communion. The second *Oratio super populum* is said only in ferial Masses in Lent. This restriction apparently results from the shortening of the Mass (which explains many omissions and abbreviations) and the tendency of Lent to keep longer forms. The Mass was shortened for practical purposes except (in many cases) during Lent, which keeps the long *preces* in the Office omitted at other times, sometimes more than two lessons at Mass, and so on. The medieval commentators explain this mystically. Honorius thinks the prayer to be a substitute for the Eastern blessed bread. The *Oratio super populum* is now always the prayer at vespers on the same day. It has been suggested that its use at Mass in Lent may be a remnant of a custom, now kept only on Holy Saturday, of singing vespers at the end of Mass. There remains the first prayer, called *Ad complendum* in the Gregorian Sacramentary. Its name was uncertain through the Middle Ages. Durandus (see **DURANDUS**) calls it merely *Oratio novissima*, using the name *Postcommunio* for the Communion antiphon.[2] The first Roman *Ordo* calls the prayer *Oratio ad complendum*; Rupert of Deutz calls it *Ad complendum*.[3] But others give it the name it had already in the Gelasian book, *Postcommunio*;[4] so also many medieval missals (e.g. the Sarum). This is now its official name in the Roman Rite. The Postcommunion has lost much of its original character as a thanksgiving prayer and has absorbed the idea of the old *Oratio ad populum*. It is now always a petition, though the note of thanksgiving is often included (e.g. in the Mass *Statuit*, for a confessor pontiff). It has been affected by the Collect on which it is modelled, though there is generally an allusion to the Communion.

Every Postcommunion (and secret) corresponds to a collect. These are the three fundamental prayers of any given

Proper Mass. The Postcommunion is said or chanted exactly like the Collect. First comes that of the Mass celebrated; then, if other Masses are commemorated, their Postcommunions follow in the same order and with the same final conclusion as the collects. After the Communion, when the celebrant has arranged the chalice, he goes to the epistle side and reads the Communion antiphon. He then comes to the middle and says or sings *Dominus vobiscum* (in the early Middle Ages he did not turn to the people this time), goes back to the Epistle side, and says or sings one or more Postcommunions, exactly as the collects. At ferial Masses in Lent the *Oratio super populum* follows the last Postcommunion. The celebrant sings *Oremus;* the deacon turning towards the people chants: *Humiliate capita vestra Deo*, on *do* with the cadence *la, do, si, si, do* for the last five syllables. Meanwhile everyone, including the celebrant, bows the head. The deacon turns towards the altar and the celebrant chants the prayer appointed in the Mass. At low Mass the celebrant himself says: *humiliate capita vestra Deo* and does not turn towards the people. The deacon's exclamation apparently was introduced when this prayer became a speciality of Lent.

Chapter Notes:

[1] *I Apology*, LXV-LXVI.

[2] Durandus, IV, 57.

[3] *De divinis officiis*, II, xix.

[4] Sicardus, *Mitrale*, III, viii.

26

Ite Missa Est

This is the versicle chanted in the Roman Rite by the deacon at the end of Mass, after the Postcommunions. It is our formula of the old dismissal still contained in all liturgies. It is undoubtedly one of the most ancient Roman formulae, as may be seen from its archaic and difficult form. All the three oldest Roman *Ordines* contain it. *Ordo Romanus I* says: "When the prayer (Postcommunion) is over, that one of the deacons appointed by the archdeacon looks towards the pontiff to receive a sign from him and then says to the people: *Ite missa est*. They answer: *Deo gratias.*"[1] The medieval commentators were much exercised to explain the meaning of the strange expression. Durandus suggests several interpretations. It has been thought that a word is omitted: *Ite, missa est finita*; or *est* is taken absolutely, as meaning "exists", "is now an accomplished fact".[2] The real explanation seems to lie rather in interpreting correctly the word *missa*. Before it became the technical name of the holy Liturgy in the Roman Rite, it meant simply "dismissal". The form *missa* for *missio* is like that of *collecta* (for *collectio*), *ascensa* (*ascensio*), etc. So *Ite missa est* should be translated "Go it is the dismissal."[3] On certain days which have the character of fasting or penance, this versicle is replaced by the words *Benedicamus Domino*. The fact is noticed by medieval liturgists since about the eleventh century. The three Roman *Ordines* before the tenth century know only the form *Ite missa est*. The explanation is that originally the people were not dismissed on such days, but stayed in church for further prayers after Mass, suitable to fasting days. This is confirmed by a now extinct medieval custom of singing *Benedicamus Domino* at the end of midnight Mass at Christmas, because Lauds follow at once. So the idea obtained that *Ite missa est* implies a festal Mass. Our present rule that it follows the *Gloria in Excelsis* (and therefore the *Te Deum* in the Office) is noted in *Micrologus*.[4] Either versicle was always answered by the obvious response *Deo gratias*, implying thanks that the Sacrifice has been offered—is now complete. At Requiems (since they have no *Gloria*) *Ite missa est* is not said. In this case the versicle is *Requiescant in pace*. R. *Amen*. John Beleth (twelfth century) says that this arose "only from a general custom."[5] Till about the twelfth century the *Ite missa est* really ended the liturgy, as its form implies. In the First Roman *Ordo*, immediately after it the text continues: "Then the seven candlesticks are carried before the pontiff . . . to the sacristy."[6] It was not till the sixteenth century (Missal of Pius V) that the accretions to the Mass that had gradually been introduced (*Placeat*, blessing, last Gospel—all originally private prayers) were definitely recognised as part of the liturgy to be said at the altar.

The corresponding dismissals in the other Western rites are: at Milan, V. *Procedamus in pace*. R. *In nomine Christi*; Mozarabic, *Solemnia completa sunt in nomine D. N. I. C: votum nostrum sit acceptum cum pace*. R. *Deo gratias*. Of the Eastern rites that of the *Apostolic Constitutions* dismisses the people with the form: "Go in peace." The Antiochene and Byzantine Liturgies end with the deacon's announcement: "Let us go forth in peace." R. "In the name of the Lord"; and then a short "prayer of dismissal" said by the celebrant; so also the Alexandrine Rite: while the Nestorians have only a prayer and blessing by the celebrant.

Present Ritual.—At high Mass, as soon as the last Post-Communion is ended, the celebrant and ministers go to the middle of the altar and stand in line. The celebrant turning to the people sings *Dominus vobiscum* (the usual introduction to any announcement), and remains facing them. When the choir has answered, the deacon turns round and, with hands joined, sings *Ite missa est* to its proper tone, the choir answering *Deo gratias* to the same notes. In the former Missal ten melodies were provided for various solemnities. The idea is to sing this last versicle to the tone of the first *Kyrie eleison*, so that Mass ends with the same chant as that with which it began. To carry this out more completely the new Vatican Missal provides nineteen tones, most of them very elaborate (for *Ite missa est* and *Benedicamus Domino*), corresponding to the various masses in the Kyriale. The tone of the first *Kyrie* should always be used. In figured masses the *Ite missa est* should be sung to the tone of the plain-song Mass provided for the occasion. From Holy Saturday till White Saturday (*Sabbatum in albis*), inclusively, two Alleluias are added to both versicle and response; in this case they have a special melody (the first in the Missal), which does not correspond to the *Kyrie*. At Masses that have no *Gloria in excelsis* (therefore in the Office *de tempore* of Advent and Lent, vigils, and ember-days, except Maundy Thursday and Holy Saturday; at Votive Masses, except those of the B. V. M. when celebrated on Saturday, Votive Masses of Angels, and, for a grave cause, when violet vestments are not used in the Mass), the celebrant turns back to the altar after the *Dominus vobiscum*, and the deacon, facing the altar, sings, *Benedicamus Domino*, to the same tone (of the *Kyrie*); the answer is the same, *Deo gratias*. At all Requiems in the same manner he sings, to the tone provided in the Missal. *Requiescant in pace* (in the plural, even when Mass is said for one person). R. *Amen*. As soon as the deacon has finished his versicle the celebrant turns back to the altar and waits; the deacon and subdeacon kneel on the *suppedaneum*. When the answer of the choir is finished the celebrant says the prayer *Placeat* and then gives the blessing. The celebrant himself says *Benedicamus Domino* or *Requiescant in pace* in a low voice while the deacon sings, because these are prayers. He does not say *Ite missa est*, because this is an announcement to the people. At a sung Mass the celebrant sings the deacon's part, at a low Mass he says it. Otherwise there is no change.

Chapter Notes:

1   *Ordo Rom.* I, p. 144.

2   Durandus, IV, 57.

3   See Florus the Deacon, *De expositione Missae*, P.L., CIX, 72.

4   Micrologus, xlvi.

5   *Rat. div. offic.*, P.L., CCII, 49.

6   *Ordo Rom.* I, p. 146.

27

Oremus

Oremus.—Invitation to pray, said before collects and other short prayers and occurring continually in the Roman Rite. It is used as a single ejaculation in the East, or the imperative: "Pray", "Stand for prayer"; most commonly, however, with a further determination, "Let us pray to the Lord" (throughout the Byzantine Rite), and so on. It is not so in the Mozarabic Rite, where the celebrant uses the word only twice, before the *Agios,* and *Pater noster. Oremus* is said (or sung) in the Roman Rite before all separate collects in the Mass, Office, or on other occasions (but several collects may be joined with one *Oremus*), before Postcommunions; in the same way, alone, with no prayer following, before the offertory; also before the introduction to the *Pater noster* and before other short prayers (e.g., *Aufer a nobis*) in the form of collects. It appears that the *Oremus* did not originally apply to the prayer (collect) that now follows it. It is thought that it was once an invitation to private prayer, very likely with further direction as to the object, as now on Good Friday (*Oremus pro ecclesia sancta Dei,* etc.). The deacon then said: *Flectamus genua,* and all knelt in silent prayer. After a time the people were told to stand up (*Levate*), and finally the celebrant collected all the petitions in one short sentence said aloud (see **COLLECT**). Of all this our *Oremus* followed at once by the collect would be a fragment.

28

VOTIVE MASS (*MISSA VOTIVA*)

A Mass offered for a *votum*, a special intention. So we frequently find in prayers the expression, *votiva dona*, meaning "gifts offered with desire of receiving grace in return". The Mass does not correspond to the Divine Office for the day on which it is celebrated. Every day in the year has appointed to it a series of canonical hours and (except Good Friday) a Mass corresponding, containing, for instance, the same Collect and the same Gospel. So Mass and Office together make up one whole. Normally the Mass corresponds to the Office. But there are occasions on which a Mass may be said which does not so correspond. These are votive Masses.

The principle of the votive Mass is older than its name. Almost at the very origin of the Western liturgies (with their principle of change according to the Calendar) Mass was occasionally offered, apparently with special prayers and lessons, for some particular intention, irrespective of the normal Office of the day. Among the miracles quoted by St. Augustine in *De Civitate Dei* is the story of one Hesperius cured of an evil spirit by a private Mass said in his house with special prayers for him—a votive Mass for his cure.[1] The first Sacramentaries contain many examples of what we should call votive Masses. So the Leonine book has Masses *in natale episcoporum*, *de siccitate temporis, contra impetitores*, and so on throughout. Indeed the Masses for ordination and for the dead which occur in this book and throughout the Roman and Gallican Rites, are really examples of votive Masses for all kinds of occasions, for ordinations, for those about to be baptised, anniversaries of ordination, nuns, for the sick, for marriages, kings, travellers, the dead, and a large collection of Masses of general character to be said on any Sunday. In this book the name first occurs, *Missa votiva in sanctorum commemoratione*. The Gregorian Sacramentary, too, has a large collection of such Masses and the name *Missa votiva*.[2]

So all through the Middle Ages the votive Mass was a regular institution. The principle came to be that, whereas one official (capitular) high Mass was said corresponding to the Office, a priest who said a private Mass for a special intention said a votive Mass corresponding to his intention. The great number of forms provided in medieval Missals furnished one for any possible intention. Indeed it seems that at one time a priest normally said a votive Mass whenever he celebrated. John Beleth in the thirteenth century describes a series of votive Masses once said (*fuit quoddam tempus*) each day in the week: on Sunday, of the Holy Trinity; Monday, for charity; Tuesday, for wisdom; Wednesday, of the Holy Ghost; Thursday, of the Angels; Friday, of the Cross; Saturday, of the Blessed Virgin.[3] This completely ignores the ecclesiastical year. But there was a general sentiment that, at least on the chief feasts, even private Masses should conform to the Office of the day. It is well known, for instance that our feast of the Holy Trinity began as a votive Mass to be said on any Sunday after Pentecost, when there was no feast. This idea of allowing votive Masses to be said only when no special feast occurs finally produced the rules contained in our present missal (1570). According to these we distinguish between votive Masses strictly so called and votive Masses in a wider sense. The first are those commanded to be said on certain days; the second kind, those which a priest may say or not, at his discretion.

Strict votive Masses are, first, those ordered by the rubrics of the Missal, namely a Mass of the Blessed Virgin on every

Saturday in the year not occupied by a double, semi-double, octave, vigil, feria of Lent or ember-day, or the transferred Sunday Office.[4] This is the *Missa de S. Maria* in five forms for various seasons, among the votive Masses at the end of the Missal. To this we must add votive Masses ordered by the pope or the ordinary for certain grave occasions (*pro re gravi*). Such are for the election of a pope or bishop, in time of war, plague, persecution, and so on. Such votive Masses may be ordered by the ordinary on all days except doubles of the first or second class, Ash Wednesday, and the ferias of Holy Week, the eves of Christmas and Pentecost; except also days on which the office is said for the same intention or event as would be prescribed by the votive Mass. In this case the Mass should conform to the office as usual. A third kind of strictly votive Mass is that said during the devotion of the so-called "Forty Hours". On this occasion the Mass on the first and third days is of the Blessed Sacrament; on the second day it is for peace. But on doubles of the first and second class, Sundays of the first and second class, on Ash Wednesday, in Holy Week, during the octaves of Epiphany, Easter, Pentecost, on the eves of Christmas and Pentecost the Mass of the day must be said, with the collect of the Blessed Sacrament added to that of the day under one conclusion.

The other kind of votive Mass (*late sumpta*) may be said by any priest on a semidouble, simple or feria, at his discretion, except on Sunday, Ash Wednesday, the eves of Christmas, Epiphany, Pentecost, during the octaves of Epiphany, Easter, Pentecost, Corpus Christi, Holy Week, and on All Souls' Day. Nor may a votive Mass be said on a day whose Office is already that of the same occasion; but in this case the corresponding Mass of the day must be said, according to the usual rubrics. A votive Mass may be taken from any of those at the end of the missal, or of the common of Saints, or of their propers, if the text does not imply that it is their feast. A Sunday or ferial Mass may not be used as a votive

Mass. Nor may it be said of a *Beatus*, unless this be allowed by special indult.

The *Gloria* is to be said in votive Masses *pro re gravi* unless the colour be violet; also in votive Masses of the Blessed Virgin on Saturday, of angels, whenever said, in those of saints, when said on a day on which they are named in the Martyrology or during their octaves. The Creed is said in solemn votive Masses *pro re gravi*. The first and third Masses of the Forty Hours have the *Gloria* and the Creed, not the Mass for Peace (but if said on a Sunday it has the Creed). Solemn votive Masses have only one collect; others are treated as semidoubles, with commemorations of the day, etc., according to the usual rule. The colour used for a votive Mass is the one which corresponds to the event celebrated; except that red is used for Holy Innocents. It is red for the election of a pope, white for the anniversary of a bishop's election or consecration, violet in the general case of asking for some special grace and for the Passion. Requiems and Masses for marriages are really particular cases of a votive Mass.

The unchangeable character of the Eastern liturgies excludes anything really corresponding to our votive Mass. But they have a custom of singing certain *troparia* (see **GLOSSARY**), sometimes of reading special lessons on certain anniversaries and occasions, which is virtually what is done in the Latin votive Masses.

Chapter Notes:

1 *De civ. Dei*, XXII, 8.
2 P.L., LXXVIII, 256.
3 *Explic. div. offic.*, 51.
4 *Rubr. Gen.*, IV, 1.

29

NUPTIAL MASS

Missa pro sponso et sponsa, the last among the votive Masses in the Missal. It is composed of lessons and chants suitable to the Sacrament of Matrimony, contains prayers for persons just married and is interwoven with part of the marriage rite, of which in the complete form it is an element. As the Mass was looked upon as the natural accompaniment of any solemn function (ordination, consecration of churches, etc.), it was naturally celebrated as part of the marriage service. Tertullian (d. about 220) mentions the oblation that confirms marriage (*matrimonium quod ecclesia conciliat et confirmat oblatio*). All the Roman Sacramentaries contain the nuptial Mass, with our present prayers and others (a special *Hanc igitur* and Preface). The Gelasian Sacramentary contains, moreover, the blessing now said after the *Ite missa est*, then said after the Communion, a Gallican addition. Pope Nicholas I (858-867) in his instruction for the Bulgars, in 866, describes the whole rite of marriage, including the crowning of the man and wife that is still the prominent feature of the rite in the Byzantine Church; this rite contains a Mass at which the married persons make the offertory and receive communion.

The present rules for a nuptial Mass are; first, that it may not be celebrated in the closed time for marriages, that is from Advent Sunday till after the octave of the Epiphany and from Ash Wednesday till after Low Sunday. During these times no reference to a marriage may be made in Mass; if people wish to be married then they must be content with the little service in the Ritual, without music or other solemnities. This is what is meant by the rubric: *clauduntur nuptiarum solemnia*; it is spoken of usually as the closed season. During the rest of the year the nuptial Mass may be said at a wedding any day except Sundays and feasts of obligation, doubles of the first and second class and such privileged ferias and octaves as exclude a double. It may not displace the Rogation Mass at which the procession is made, nor may it displace at least one Requiem on All Souls' day. On these occasions its place is taken by the Mass of the day to which commemorations of the nuptial Mass are added in the last place and at which the blessings are inserted in their place. The nuptial blessing is considered as part of the nuptial Mass. It may never be given except during this Mass or during a Mass that replaces it (and commemorates it) when it cannot be said, as above. The nuptial Mass and blessing may be celebrated after the closed time for people married during it. So nuptial Mass and blessing always go together; either involves the other. One Mass and blessing may be held for several pairs of married people, who must all be present. The forms, however, remain in the singular as they are in the Missal. The Mass and blessing may not be held if the woman has already received this blessing in a former marriage. This rule only affects the woman, for whom the blessing is more specially intended (see the prayer *Deus qui potestate*). It must be understood exactly as stated. A former marriage without this blessing, or the fact that children had been born before the marriage, is no hindrance. Nor may the nuptial Mass and blessing be held in cases of mixed marriages (*mixta religio*) in spite of any dispensation.[1] According to the Constitution *Etsi sanctissimus Dominus* of Pius IX (15 November, 1858), mixed marriages must be celebrated outside the church (in England and America this is understood as meaning outside the sanctuary and choir), without the blessing of the ring or of the spouses without any ecclesiastical rite or vestment, without proclamation of banns.

The rite of the nuptial Mass and blessing is this: The Mass has neither *Gloria* nor Creed. It counts as a votive Mass not for a grave matter; therefore it has three collects, its own, the commemoration of the day, and the third which is the one chosen for semi-doubles at that time of the year unless there be two commemorations. At the end *Benedicamus Domino* and the Gospel of St. John are said. The colour is white. The bridegroom and bride assist near the altar (just outside the sanctuary), the man on the right. After the *Pater noster* the celebrant genuflects and goes to the Epistle side. Meanwhile the bridegroom and bride come up and kneel before him. Turning to them he says the two prayers *Propitiare Domine* and *Deus qui potestate* (as in the Missal) with folded hands. He then goes back to the middle and continues the Mass. They go back to their places. He gives them Communion at the usual time. This implies that they are fasting and explains the misused name "wedding breakfast" afterwards. But the Communion is strict law (S.R.C., no 5582, 21 March, 1874). Immediately after the *Benedicamus Domino* and its answer the celebrant again goes to the Epistle side and the bridegroom and bride kneel before him as before. The celebrant turning to them says the prayer *Deus Abraham* (without *Oremus*). He is then told to warn them "with grave words to be faithful to one another". The rest of the advice suggested in the rubric of the Missal is now generally left out. He sprinkles them with holy water; they retire, he goes back to the middle of the altar, says *Placeat tibi*, gives the blessing and finishes Mass as usual.

In the cases in which the *Missa pro sponso et sponsa* may not be said but may be commemorated, the special prayers and blessing are inserted in the Mass in the same way. But the colour must be that of the day. During the closed time it is, of course, quite possible for the married people to have a Mass said for their intention, at which they receive Holy Communion. The nuptial Blessing in this Mass is quite a different thing from the actual celebration of the marriage which must always precede it. The blessing is given to people already married, as the prayers imply. It need not be given (nor the Mass said) by the parish priest who assisted at the marriage. But both these functions (assistance and blessing) are rights of the parish priest, which no one else may undertake without delegation from him. Generally they are so combined that the marriage takes place immediately before the Mass; in this case the priest at the marriage in Mass vestments, but without the maniple. In England and other countries where a civil declaration is required by law, this is usually made in the sacristy between the marriage and the Mass. Canon Law in England orders that marriages be made only in churches that have a district with the cure of souls. This implies as a general rule, but does not command absolutely, that the nuptial Mass also be celebrated in such a church.

Chapter Notes:

[1] Some of the disciplinary rules mentioned by Dr Fortescue were changed in subsequent years, e.g. a Nuptial Mass is no longer forbidden in the case of a mixed marriage. No attempt has been made to update the article which provides a valuable insight into the thinking of the Church on marriage at this time—1913 (Ed.).

30

CONCELEBRATION

Concelebration is the rite by which several priests say Mass together, all consecrating the same bread and wine. It was once common in both East and West. As late as the ninth century priests stood around their bishop and "consented to his sacrifice". The rite of Concelebration was modified at Rome (perhaps in the time of Pope Zephyrinus, 202-218) so that each priest should consecrate a separate host (the deacon holding these in patens or corporals); but they all consecrated the same chalice. In the sixth century this rite was observed on all station days; by the eighth century it remained only for the greatest feasts, Easter, Christmas, Whitsunday, and St. Peter. On other days the priests assisted but did not concelebrate. Innocent III (1198-1216) says that in his time the cardinals concelebrate with the pope on certain feasts. St. Thomas defends its theological correctness.[1] Concelebration is still common in all the Eastern Churches both Uniate and schismatic. In these, on any greater feast day, the bishop says the holy liturgy surrounded by his priests, who consecrate with him and receive Holy Communion from him, of course under both kinds. So also, at any time, if several priests wish to celebrate on the same day, they may do so together.

In the Latin Church the rite survives only at the ordination of priests and bishops.[2] The newly-ordained priests say the Offertory prayers and the whole Canon, including the words of consecration, aloud with the bishop, kneeling around him. The Words of consecration especially must be said "slowly and rather loud" and "at the same moment with the pontiff". They must say the words *significative*, that is with the intention of consecrating, and must be careful not to say them before, but exactly with the bishop. They receive Holy Communion under one kind. The same rite is used at a bishop's consecration, except that in this case the new bishop communicates with the consecrator under both kinds.

Chapter Notes:

1   S.T., III, Q. LXXXII, art. 2.
2   The General Instruction to the 1970 Missal lists a series of occasions on which priests are permitted to concelebrate, but for all practical purposes priests using that Missal now concelebrate whenever they feel so inclined (GIRM, numbers 153-158) (Ed.).

31

LUMEN CHRISTI

Lumen Christi.— the versicle chanted by the deacon on Holy Saturday as he lights the triple candle. After the new fire has been blessed outside the church a light is taken from it by an acolyte. The procession then moves up the church, the deacon in a white dalmatic carrying the triple candle. Three times the procession stops, the deacon lights one of the candles from the taper and sings *Lumen Christi*, on one note (*fa*), dropping a minor third (to *re*) on the last syllable. The choir answers, *Deo gratias*, to the same tone. Each time it is sung at a higher pitch. As it is sung, all genuflect. Arrived at the altar, the deacon begins the blessing of the Paschal Candle (*Exultet*). The meaning of this rite is obvious: a light must be brought from the new fire to the Paschal Candle; out of this the ceremony grew and attracted to itself symbolic meaning, as usual. The triple candle was at first, no doubt, merely a precaution against the light blowing out on the way. At one time there were only two lights. The Sarum Consuetudinary (about the year 1210) says: "Let the candle upon the reed be lighted, and let another candle be lighted at the same time, so that the candle upon the reed can be rekindled if it should chance to be blown out." A miniature of the eleventh century shows the Paschal Candle being lighted from a double taper. The triple candle appears first in the twelfth and fourteenth Roman Ordines,[1] about the twelfth century. Father Thurston suggests a possible connection between it and the old custom of procuring the new fire on three successive days.[2] But precaution against the light blowing out accounts for several candles, and the inevitable mystic symbolism of the number three would naturally apply here too. Durandus (see **DURANDUS**), in his chapter on the Paschal Candle, does not mention the triple candle.[3] In the Sarum Rite only one candle was lighted. While it was carried in procession to the Paschal Candle, a hymn, *Inventor rutili dux bone luminis*, was sung by two cantors, the choir answering the first verse after each of the others. In the Mozarabic Rite the bishop lights and blesses one candle; while it is brought to the altar an antiphon, *Lumen verum illuminans omnem hominem*, is sung. At Milan, in the middle of the *Exultet* a subdeacon goes out and brings back a candle lit from the new fire without any further ceremony. He hands this to the deacon, who lights the Paschal Candle (and two others) from it, and then goes on with the *Exultet*.

Chapter Notes:

[1]   P.L., LXXVIII, 1076, 1218.

[2]   H. Thurston, *Lent and Holy Week* (London, 1904), p. 416.

[3]   Durandus, VI, 80.

32

DOXOLOGY

In general this word means a short verse praising God. The custom of ending a rite or a hymn with such a formula comes from the Synagogue (cf. the Prayer of Manasses: *tibi est gloria in saecula saeculorum. Amen*). St. Paul uses doxologies constantly (Rom., xi, 36; Gal., i, 5; Eph., iii, 21; etc.). The earliest examples are addressed to God the Father alone, or to Him *through* the Son,[1] and *in* or *with* the Holy Ghost.[2] The form of baptism (Matt., xxviii, 19) had set an example of naming the three Persons in parallel order. Especially in the fourth century, as a protest against Arian subordination (since heretics appealed to these prepositions).[3] The custom of using the form: "Glory to the Father, and to the Son, and to the Holy Ghost", became universal among Catholics. From this time we must distinguish two doxologies, a greater (*doxologia maior*) and a shorter (*minor*). The greater doxology is the *Gloria in Excelsis Deo* in the Mass. The shorter form, which is the one generally referred to under the name "doxology", is the *Gloria Patri*. It is continued by an answer to the effect that this glory shall last forever. The form "to God be glory unto the ages of the ages" is very common in the first centuries.[4] It is a common Hebraism meaning simply "forever".[5] The simple form "to him be glory unto the ages" is also common.[6] This expression was soon enlarged into: "now and ever and in ages of ages".[7] In the Latin Rite it seems originally to have had exactly the same form as in the East. In 529 the Second Synod of Vasio (Vaison in the province of Avignon) says that the additional words, *Sicut erat in principio*, are used in Rome, the East, and Africa as a protest against Arianism, and orders them to be said likewise in Gaul. As far as the East is concerned the synod is mistaken. These words have never been used in any Eastern rite and the Greeks complained of their use in the West.[8] The explanation that *sicut erat in principio* was meant as a denial of Arianism leads to a question whose answer is less obvious than it seems. To what do the words refer? Everyone now understands *gloria* as the subject of *erat*: "As it [the glory] was in the beginning", etc. It seems, however, that originally they were meant to refer to *Filius*, and that the meaning of the second part, in the West at any rate, was: "As He [the Son] was in the beginning, so is He now and so shall He be for ever." The *in principio*, then, is a clear allusion to the first words of the Fourth Gospel, and so the sentence is obviously directed against Arianism. There are medieval German versions in the form: "Als *er* war im Anfang".

The doxology in the form in which we know it has been used since about the seventh century all over Western Christendom, except in one corner. In the Mozarabic Rite the formula is: *Gloria et honor Patri et Filio et Spiritui sancto in saecula saeculorum* (so in the Missal of this rite).[9] The Fourth Synod of Toledo in 633 ordered this form. A common medieval tradition, founded on a spurious letter of St. Jerome, says that Pope Damasus (366-384) introduced the *Gloria Patri* at the end of psalms.[10] Cassian (died c. 435) speaks of this as a special custom of the Western Church.[11] The use of the shorter doxology in the Latin Church is this: the two parts are always said or sung as a verse with response. They occur always at the end of psalms (when several psalms are joined together as one, as the sixty-second and sixty-sixth and again the one hundred and forty-eighth, one hundred and forty-ninth and one hundred and fiftieth at Lauds, the *Gloria Patri* occurs once only at the end of the group; on the other hand, each group of sixteen verses of the one hundred and eighteenth psalm in the day Hours has the *Gloria*) except on occasions of mourning. For this reason (since the shorter doxology, like the greater one, *Gloria in Excelsis Deo*, is naturally a joyful chant) it is left out on the last three days of Holy Week; in the Office for the Dead its place is taken by the verses: *Requiem aeternam*, etc., and *Et lux perpetua*, etc. It also occurs after canticles, except that the Benedicite has its own doxology (*Benedicamus Patrem ... Benedictus es Domine*, etc. - the only alternative one left in the Roman Rite). In the Mass it occurs after three psalms, the *Judica me* at the beginning, the fragment of the Introit-Psalm, and the *Lavabo* (omitted in Passiontide, except on feasts, and at requiem Masses). The first part only occurs in the *responsoria* throughout the Office, with a variable answer (the second part of the first verse) instead of *Sicut erat*, the whole doxology after the *Deus in adjutorium*, and in the *preces* at Prime; and again, this time as one verse, at the end of the *invitatorium* at Matins. At all these places it is left out in the Office for the Dead and at the end of Holy Week. The *Gloria Patri* is also constantly used in extra-liturgical services, such as the Rosary. It was a common custom in the Middle Ages for preachers to end sermons with it. In some countries, Germany especially, people make the sign of the cross at the first part of the doxology, considering it as chiefly a profession of faith.

Chapter Notes:

1. Rom., xvi, 27; Jude, 25; I Clem., xli; Mart. Polyc., xx; etc.
2. *Mart. Polyc.*, xiv, xxii, etc.
3. St. Basil, *De Spir, Sancto*, ii-v.
4. Rom., xvi, 27; Gal., i, 5; I Tim., i, 17; Heb., xiii, 21; I Peter, iv, 11; I Clem., xx, xxxii, xxxviii, xliii, xlv, etc.; Mart. Polyc., xxii, etc.
5. Tob., xiii, 23; Ps lxxxiii, 5; repeatedly in the Apocalypse: i, 6, 18; xiv,

11; xix, 3; etc.

6 Rom., xi, 36; Doctr. XII Apost., ix, x; in the Liturgy of the *Apostolic Constitutions*, *passim*.

7 Heb., xiii, 8; *Mart. Polyc.*, xiv, etc.

8 Walafrid Strabo (9th century), *De rebus eccl.*, xxv.

9 P.L., LXXXV, 109, 119.

10 The Benedictine edition, Paris, 1706, V, 415.

11 *De instit. coen.*, II, viii.

33

LIBERA ME

Libera me Domine, de morte aeterna, etc.—the responsory sung at funerals. It is a responsory of redundant form, having two versicles *Tremens factus sum* and *Dies illa.* As in all the Office for the Dead, the verse *Requiem aeternam* takes the place of *Gloria Patri*; then all the first part, down to the first versicle, is repeated. Its form therefore is exceptional, considerably longer than the normal responsory. It is a prayer in the first person singular for mercy at the Last Day. This should no doubt be understood as a dramatic substitution; the choir speaks for the dead person. A great part of our Office for the Dead is made up of such prayers about the Last Day, the meaning of which appears to refer rather to the people who say them than to the dead (the sequence *Dies irae*, most of the Vespers, Matins, and Lauds).

Another dramatic substitution is involved in the prayers of this responsory (and throughout the Office for the Dead) that the person for whom we pray may be saved from hell. That question was settled irrevocably as soon as he died. This is one instance of the dramatic displacement or rearrangement of the objective order of things that occurs continually in all rites (compare for instance in the baptism service the white robe and shining light given after the essential form, in the ordination of priests the power to forgive sins given after the man has been ordained and has concelebrated, the *Epiclesis* in Eastern liturgies, etc.). The explanation of all these cases is the same. Since we cannot express everything at one instant, we are forced to act and speak as if things really simultaneous followed each other in order. And in the eternity of God all things (including our consecutive prayers) are present at once - *nunc stans aeternitas*. The responsory *Libera me* is begun by a cantor and continued by the choir in the usual way (the cantor alone singing the versicles) at the beginning of the "Absolution", that is the service of prayers for the dead person said and sung by the bier immediately after the Mass for the Dead. As soon as Mass is over the celebrant exchanges his chasuble for a (black) cope (all the sacred ministers of course take off their maniples) and chants the prayer *Non intres in judicium*. Then *Libera me* is sung. Meanwhile the celebrant puts incense into the thurible, assisted by the deacon. During the whole Absolution the subdeacon stands at the head of the bier, facing the altar, with the processional cross.

The ninth responsory of Matins for the Dead also begins with *Libera me*, but continues a different text (*Domine, de viis inferni*, etc.). This is built up according to the usual arrangement (with *Requiem aeternam* instead of *Gloria Patri*. But on All Souls' Day (2 November), and whenever the whole Office of nine lessons is said, the *Libera me* of the Absolution is substituted for it. The Vatican Gradual gives the new chant for the *Libera me* after the Mass for the Dead.

34

Epiklesis

The Greek *Epiklesis* (Lat. *invocatio*) is the name of a prayer that occurs in all Eastern liturgies (and originally in Western liturgies also) after the words of Institution, in which the celebrant prays that God may send down His Holy Spirit to change this bread and wine into the Body and Blood of His Son. This form has given rise to one of the chief controversies between the Eastern and Western Churches, inasmuch as all Eastern schismatics now believe that the *Epiklesis*, and not the words of Institution, is the essential form (or at least the essential complement) of the sacrament.

1. *Form of the Epiklesis.*—It is certain that all the old liturgies contained such a prayer. For instance, the Liturgy of *The Apostolic Constitutions*, immediately after the recital of the words of Institution, goes on to the *Anamnesis*—"Remembering therefore His Passion . . ."—in which occur the words: "Thou, the God who lackest nothing, being pleased with them (the Offerings) for the honour of Thy Christ, and sending down Thy Holy Spirit on this sacrifice, the witness of the Passion of the Lord Jesus, to manifest this bread as the Body of Thy Christ and this chalice as the Blood of Thy Christ ...". So the Greek and Syrian Liturgies of St. James, the Alexandrine Liturgies, the Abyssinian Rite, those of the Nestorians, and Armenians. The *Epiklesis* in the Byzantine Liturgy of St. John Chrysostom is said thus: "We offer to Thee this reasonable and unbloody

sacrifice; and we beg Thee, we ask Thee, we pray Thee that Thou, sending down Thy Holy Spirit on us and on these present gifts" (the Deacon says: "Bless, Sir, the holy bread") "make this bread into the Precious Body of Thy Christ" (Deacon: "Amen. Bless, Sir, the holy chalice"): "and that which is in this chalice, the Precious Blood of Thy Christ" (Deacon: "Amen. Bless, Sir, both"), "changing them by Thy Holy Spirit" (Deacon: "Amen, Amen, Amen.").

Nor is there any doubt that the Western rites at one time contained similar invocations. The Gallican Liturgy had variable forms according to the feast. That for the Circumcision was: *Haec nos, Domine, instituta et praecepta retinentes suppliciter oramus uti hoc sacrificium suscipere et benedicere et sanctificare digneris: ut fiat nobis eucharistia legitima in tuo Filiique tui nomine et Spiritus sancti, in transformationem corporis ac sanguinis domini Dei nostri Jesu Christi unigeniti tui, per quem omnia creas ...*" There are many allusions to the Gallican Invocation, for instance St. Isidore of Seville.[1] The Roman Rite too at one time had an *Epiklesis* after the words of Institution. Pope Gelasius I (492-496) refers to it plainly: *Quomodo ad divini mysterii consecrationem caelestis Spiritus adveniet, si sacerdos . . . criminosis plenus actionibus reprobetur?*[2] Some scholars think that several secrets in the Leonine Sacramentary were originally Invocations. Of this Invocation we have now only a fragment, with the essential clause left out—our prayer: *Supplices te rogamus*. It seems that an early insistence on the words of Institution as the form of consecration led in the West to the neglect and mutilation of the *Epiklesis*.

2. Origin.—It should be noticed that the *Epiklesis* for the Holy Eucharist is only one of many such forms. In other sacraments and blessings similar prayers were used, to ask God to send His Holy Spirit to sanctify the matter. There was an *Epiklesis* for the water of baptism. In Egypt especially, *Epikleses* were used to bless wine, oil, milk, etc. In all these cases (including that of the Holy Eucharist) the idea of invoking the Holy Ghost to sanctify is a natural one derived from Scripture (Joel, ii, 32; Acts, ii, 21; Rom., x, 13; I Cor., i, 2). That in the Liturgy the Invocation should occur after the words of Institution is only one more case of many which show that people were not much concerned about the exact instant at which all the essence of the sacrament was complete. They looked upon the whole Consecration-prayer as one simple thing. In it the words of Institution always occur (with the doubtful exception of the Nestorian Rite); they believed that Christ would, according to His promise, do the rest. But they did not ask at which exact moment the change takes place. Besides the words of Institution there are many other blessings, prayers, and signs of the cross, some of which came before and some after the words, and all, including the words themselves, combine to make up the one Canon of which the effect is Transubstantiation. So also in our baptism and ordination services, part of the forms and prayers whose effect is the sacramental grace comes, in order of time, after the essential words. It was not till Scholastic times that theologians began to discuss the minimum of form required for the essence of each sacrament.

3. *The Controversy.*— The Catholic Church has decided the question by making us kneel and adore the Holy Eucharist immediately after the words of Institution, and by letting her old Invocation practically disappear. On the other hand Orthodox theologians all consider the *Epiklesis* as being at least an essential part of the Consecration. In this question they have two schools. Some, Peter Mogilas, for instance, consider the *Epiklesis* alone as consecrating,[3] so that presumably the words of Institution might be left out without affecting validity of the sacrament. But the greater number, and now apparently all, require the words of Institution too. They must be said, not merely historically, but as the first part of the essential form; they sow as it were the seed that comes forth and is perfected by the *Epiklesis*. Both elements, then, are essential. This is the theory defended by their theologians at the Council of Florence (1439). A deputation of Latins and Greeks was appointed then to discuss the question. The Greeks maintained that both forms are necessary, that Transubstantiation does not take place till the second one (the *Epiklesis*) is pronounced, and that the Latin *Supplices te rogamus* is a true *Epiklesis* having the same effect as theirs. On the other hand the Dominican John of Torquemada defended the Western position that the words of Institution alone and at once consecrate.[4] The decree of the council eventually defined this *quod illa verba divina Salvatoris omnem virtutem transsubstantiationis habent*; see also the decree for the Armenians: *forma huius sacramenti sunt verba Salvatoris*.[5] Cardinal Bessarion afterwards wrote a book (*De Sacramento Eucharistiae et quibus verbis Christi corpus conficitur*, 1462,[6] to whom Marcus Eugenicus of Ephesus answered in a treatise with a long title: "That not only by the sound of the Lord's words are the divine gifts sanctified, but (in addition) by the prayer after these and by the consecration of the priest in the strength of the Holy Ghost".

The official *Euchologion* (see **GLOSSARY**) of the Orthodox Church has a note after the words of Institution to explain that: "Since the demonstrative pronouns: This is my body, and again: This is my blood, do not refer to the Offerings that are present, but to those which Jesus, taking in His hands and blessing, gave to His Disciples; therefore those words of the Lord are repeated as a narrative, and consequently it is superfluous to show the Offerings (by an elevation) and indeed contrary to the right mind of the Eastern Church of Christ."[7] This would seem to imply that Christ's words have no part in the form of the sacrament. On the other hand Dositheus in the Synod of Jerusalem (1672) apparently requires both words of Institution and *Epiklesis*: "It [the Holy Eucharist] is instituted by the essential word [i.e. Christ's word] and sanctified by the invocation of the Holy Ghost",[8] and this seems to be the common theory among the Orthodox in our time. Their arguments for the necessity of the *Epiklesis* as at any rate the perfecting part of the form are: (1) that the context shows the words of Institution to be used only as a narrative; (2) that otherwise the *Epiklesis* would be superfluous and deceptive: its very form shows that it consecrates; (3) tradition. The first and second points are not difficult to answer. The words of Institution are certainly used historically (*qui pridie quam pateretur, sumpsit panem...ac dixit: hoc est enim Corpus Meum*", as well as all Eastern forms, is an historical account of what happened at the Last Supper); but this is no proof that they may not be used effectively and with actual meaning too. Given the intention of so doing, they necessarily would be so used. The second point is already answered above: the succession of time in sacramental prayers necessarily involves nothing but a dramatic representation of what presumably really takes place in one instant.[9] As for tradition, in any case it is only a question of Eastern tradition. In the West there has been a great unanimity in speaking of the words of Institution as consecrating, especially since St. Augustine; and the disappearance of any real *Epiklesis* in our Liturgy confirms this. Among Eastern Fathers there is less unanimity. Some, notably St. Cyril of Jerusalem, refer the consecration to the action of the Holy Ghost in a way that seems to imply that the *Epiklesis* is the moment.[10] "He [Christ] says: This is my body. This word changes the offering",[11] quite plainly refers Consecration to Christ's words. It should be noted that these Fathers were concerned to defend the Real Presence, not to explain the moment at which it began, that they always thought of the whole Eucharistic prayer as one form, containing both Christ's words and the Invocation, and that a statement that the change takes place by the power of the Holy Ghost does not necessarily show that the writer attaches that change to this special prayer. For instance St. Irenaeus says that "the bread which receives the Invocation of God is not common bread, but a Eucharist".[12] and, yet immediately before, he explains that that bread is the Body of Christ over which the earlier part of the Anaphora is said.[13] The final argument against the *Epiklesis* as Consecration-form is the account of the Last Supper in the Gospels. We know what Christ did then, and that He told us to do the same thing. There is no hint of an *Epiklesis* at the Last Supper.

It may finally be noted that later, in the West too (since the sixteenth century especially), this question aroused some not very important discussion. The Dominican Ambrose Catharinus (sixteenth century) thought that our Consecration takes place at an *Epiklesis* that precedes the recital of Christ's words. This *Epiklesis* he thinks to be the prayer *Quam oblationem*. A few others (including Renaudot) more or less shared his opinion. Against these Hoppe showed that in any case the *Epiklesis* always follows the words of Institution and that our *Quam oblationem* cannot be considered one at all.[14]

He and others suggest a mitigated theory, according to which the Invocation (in our case the *Supplices te rogamus*) belongs not to the essence of the sacrament, but in some way to its (accidental) integrity. John of Torquemada at the Council of Florence,[15] Suarez,[16] Bellarmine,[17] Lugo,[18] explain that the Invocation of the Holy Ghost is made rather that He may sanctify our reception of the Holy Eucharist. This is a theoretical explanation sought out to account for the fact of the *Epiklesis*, without giving up our insistence on the words of Institution as alone consecrating. Historically and according to the text of the old invocations they must rather be looked upon as dramatically postponed expressions of what happens at one moment. There are many like cases in our rite.[19]

Chapter Notes:

[1] *De eccl. officiis*, I, 15, etc.

[2] *Epp. Fragm.*, vii, in Thiel, *Epp. Rom. Pont.*, I, 486.

[3] Kimmel, *Monumenta fidei eccl. orient.* (Jena, 1850), I, 180.

4   Hardouin, IX, 977 sqq.

5   Denziger, 10th ed., no 698.

6   P.G. CLXI, 494-525.

7   ed. Venice, 1898, p. 63.

8   *Conf. Dosithei*, in Kimmel, op, cit., I, 451.

9   This point is further evolved by Fortescue, *The Orthodox Eastern Church* (London, 1911) pp. 386 sq.

10 St. Cyril, *Cat.* xix, 7; xxi, 3; xxiii, 7, 19.

11 cf. Hom. ii, in II Tim., i.

12 *Adv. haer.*, IV, xviii, 5.

13 IV, xviii, 4.

14 Hoppe, *Die Epiklesis der griech. u. orient. Liturgien u. der röm. Konsekrationskanon* (Schaffhausen, 1864).

15 Hardouin, IX, 976.

16 *De Sacram.*, disp. lviii, 3.

17 *De Euch.*, iv, 14.

18 *De Euch.*, disp. xi, 1.

19 Examples quoted in *The Orthodox Eastern Church*, loc. cit.

35

DURANDUS

Durandus (Duranti or Durantis), William, Canonist and one of the most important medieval liturgical writers; born about 1237, at Puimisson in the Diocese of Béziers, Provence, died at Rome, 1 November 1296. He was called Speculator from the title of one of his works, *Speculum Judiciale*. He studied law at Bologna under Bernard of Parma and then taught it at Modena. Clement IV (Guy Foulques, 1265-1268, also a Provençal) summoned Durandus to Rome, ordained him subdeacon, and gave him titular canonries at Beauvais and Chartres. He was then attached to the papal curia as *Auditor generalis causarum sacri palatii*. He accompanied Gregory X (1271-1276) to the Second Council of Lyons (1274) and, as the pope's secretary, drew up its decrees. In 1279 he was made dean of Chartres, but did not reside there. At about the same time he went to Romagna as papal governor and succeeded in subduing a rebellion under Guy of Montefeltro. He destroyed Guy's fortress della Ripa and founded in its place the town of Urbania. In 1286 he was elected bishop by the chapter of Mende (Mimatum) in the province of Narbonne, but did not go into residence till 1291. Meanwhile his diocese was administered by his nephew, William Durandus the younger. In 1295 he was again in Italy (under Boniface VIII, 1294-1303) as governor of Romagna and Ancona, where the Ghibellines were again in rebellion. He refused the pope's offer to make him Archbishop of Ravenna, came to Rome, and died there. There is no reason to suppose that Durandus belonged to any religious order, though he has been claimed by both the Dominicans and the Austin Canons. He is buried at Rome in Santa Maria Sopra Minerva, where a long epitaph tells the story of his life and gives a list of his works. Of these works the most famous is the *Rationale divinorum officiorum* (first ed. by Fust and Schoeffer at Mainz, 1459, and reprinted frequently). It was written in 1286. Its eight books contain a detailed account of the laws, ceremonies, customs, and mystical interpretation of the Roman Rite. Book I treats of the church, altar, pictures, bells, churchyard, etc.; II of the ministers; III of vestments; IV of the Mass; V of the canonical hours; VI of the *Proprium Temporis*; VII of the *Proprium Sanctorum*; and VIII of the astronomical calendar, manner of finding Easter, Epacts, etc. Durandus's *Rationale* is the most complete medieval treatise of its kind; it is still the standard authority for the ritual of the thirteenth century and for the symbolism of rites and vestments. The allegorical explanation of vestments, for instance, as signifying virtues or the garments worn by Christ in His Passion, is taken from its third book. Other works are *Speculum Legatorum*, afterwards enlarged into *Speculum Judiciale* (four books), a treatise on the canonical rights of legates and the forms of canonical processes (first ed. at Strasburg in 1473; Frankfort, 1668); *Breviarium, sive Repertorium juris canonici* (Rome, 1474), *Breviarium glossarum et textuum juris canonici* (Paris, 1519), both commentaries on the decretals, arranged in the same order, and *Commentarius in canones Concilii Lugdunensis II* (Fano, 1569, with a life of the author by Simon Majolus), a semi-official exposition of the canons of the Second Council of Lyons. Durandus's epitaph also mentions a Pontificale, which is now lost.

GLOSSARY

Agape: The common religious meal which seems to have been in use in the early Church in close relation to the Eucharist. It is referred to in I Cor, xi, 17-34, where abuses which accompanied these common meals which preceded the Eucharist are condemned.

Apostolic
Constitutions: A collection of ecclesiastical law dating from the latter half of the fourth century, almost certainly of Syrian origin, containing a great deal of liturgical material.

Caeremoniale: *Caeremoniale Episcoporum* (Ceremonial) a directory of ceremonies for bishops and others who take part in public services.

Cherubikon: In the Eastern Church at the conclusion of the Mass of the catechumens the deacon says: "All catechumens go away. Not one catechumen shall stay." Needless to say, there are no catechumens present, as in both Orthodox and Uniate churches the faithful are all baptized at birth. The Great Entrance, the most dramatic moment in the Eastern Liturgy, then takes place, when the bread and wine to be consecrated are carried from the *prothesis* to the altar to the accompaniment of the *Cherubikon*, the Cherubic Hymn: "Let us who mystically represent the Cherubim and who sing to the life-giving Trinity the thrice-holy hymn, put away all earthly cares so as to receive the King of all things escorted by the army of angels. Alleluia, Alleluia, Alleluia."

Clement: Clement of Rome, i.e. Clement I, the fourth pope. There is a large corpus of pseudo-Clementine writing, but his First Epistle to the Corinthians is definitely genuine. It was written in about AD 96 to the Church of Corinth to restore peace and unity after a faction of the Corinthian Christians had revolted against their legitimate rulers. It is one of the most ancient and precious documents surviving from early Christian times, and contains valuable information on the early Christian liturgy, including a beautiful Eucharistic Prayer.

Didache: An early Christian manual on morals and Church practice, including two primitive Eucharistic Prayers. The author, date, and place of origin are un known. Some scholars date it as early as A.D. 60.

Diptych: Originally a hinged two-leaved tablet used for writing upon with a stylus. In the early Christian ages it was customary to write on diptychs the names of the living and the dead who were to be considered members of the Church, hence the terms "diptychs of the living" and "diptychs of the dead". To have one's name removed from the diptych was a very severe ecclesiastical penalty eqivalent to excommunication.

Ecphonesis: The concluding words in an audible voice of a prayer, the rest of which has been recited silently.

Embolism: Embolism is derived from the Greek for insertion, and hence a development or expansion of what has come before. The embolism to the *Pater noster* comments on and develops the last petition of this prayer: *sed libera nos a malo*. This embolism is of very ancient origin and is thought to have been inserted after the *Pater noster* by St. Gregory the Great (d. 604). Many Eastern liturgies have a similar prayer at this point.

***Epinikion*:** The name given to the *Sanctus* in the Eastern Rites where it is termed "The hymn of victory *(Epinikion)*."

***Etheria*:** See *Peregrinatio*.

***Euchologion*:** In the Eastern Church the liturgical book containing the essential parts of what in the West is contained in the Missal, Pontifical, and Ritual.

***Farcing*:** See Trope.

***Itala*:** The old pre-Vulgate Latin text of the Bible. *Itala* comes from the Latin for "Italian (version)". The term derives from a passage in St. Augustine (*Doctr. Christ.* ii, 22) where he commends the *Itala* as the best of the Latin texts current in his day. After the publication of the Missal of St. Pius V in 1570, unauthorized changes were made to its text. In his Brief *Cum Sanctissimum*, of 7 July 1604, Pope Clement VIII made particular mention of the fact that: "That very old version of the Holy Bible, which even before St. Jerome's time was held in honour in the Church, and from which almost all the Introits, Graduals, and Offertories of the Masses had been taken, has been entirely removed..." The Pope ordered that such missals be disallowed in the celebration of Mass "unless they be entirely and in everything emended according to the original text."

Justin: *I Apology, First Apology of Justin Martyr* (c. 100—c. 165). The *First Apology* deals with a number of topics, including accounts of the contemporary Christian ceremonies of Baptism and the Eucharist. The fact that St. Justin refers to the celebrant at Mass as "the one who presides" in no way means that during the second century the celebrant was referred to among Christians as "the president", as is mistakenly believed by some contemporary liturgists. He explained the Eucharist in the simplest terms to convince the Romans that Christians did not take part in unspeakable rituals, as was widely believed. To have used the term "priest" would have confused his pagan audience who would have interpreted the word in the sense that they used it.

Micrologus: The word means either a "synopsis" or a "short explanation", and in the Middle Ages was the equivalent of a manual. The best known, and the one cited frequently by Fortescue, is *Micrologus de ecclesiasticis observationibus*. It was compiled in the 11th century, probably by Bernold of Constance (d. 1100), a monk of the Abbey of St. Blasien, Schaffhausen. It is an important source for the history of the Roman Mass. It was first edited in Paris in 1510. It can be found in P.L., CLI, 973-1022.

Ordo: *Ordines Romani*. The word *Ordo* commonly meant in the Middle Ages a ritual book containing directions for liturgical functions, but not including the text of prayers recited by the celebrant or his assistants. These prayers were contained in the separate books, e.g. the Sacramentary, Antiphonary, Psalter, but the *Ordo* concerned itself with ceremonial pure and simple. An excellent description of the principal *Ordines Romani*, by Father Herbert Thurston, can be found in vol. XI of the old *Catholic Encyclopaedia*. The Ordo cited most frequently in this book is the *Ordo Romanus Primus* (see Bibliography).

Orthros: The equivalent in the Eastern Church for the morning office which corresponds to Matins and Lauds in the West.

Perigrinatio: The *Perigrinatio Sanctae Silviae* is an account for her community written by a fourth century Spanish abbess describing her pilgrimage to Egypt, the Holy

Land, Edessa, and Constantinople. The pilgrim, whose real name was almost certainly Etheria, is evidently possessed of great intelligence and powers of observation. Wherever she went the clergy, even bishops, attended her and acted as her guide, while imperial officers escorted her where the road was unsafe. Etheria had a particular interest in the liturgy, and her observations provide a unique contemporary source on the liturgy in the fourth century. Some writers claimed that Etheria was, in fact, St. Silvia, sister of the Roman Prefect, Rufinus, and hence the document became known as *Peregrinatio Silviae*.

Proskomide: Byzantine Offertory, during which the bread and wine are prepared for consecration on a table known as the *prothesis*, the Preparation of the Offering. The name *prothesis* is sometimes given to the rite itself:

The bread is a round loaf marked with divisions, the parts to be consecrated have a cross between the letters IC. XC. NI. KA. (Jesus Christ Conquers). The priest takes the holy lance and cuts away this part and stabs it in the form of a cross, saying, "The Lamb of God is sacrificed." This part of the bread is then commonly called the Lamb. The deacon then pours wine and water into the chalice. The priest then cuts away a particle from the rest of the bread in honour of Our Lady, and nine others for various saints, and others for the bishop and Orthodox clergy and people for whom he wishes to pray. These particles are placed on the *diskos* (the paten, but larger and deeper than the Roman paten as the Eastern Churches use leavened bread) by the Lamb, covered with the *aer* (a large veil which covers both diskos and chalice) and veils, as well as the chalice, and all are repeatedly incensed. The deacon then incenses the prothesis, altar, sanctuary, nave and priest. They both go to the altar, kiss the book of Gospels on it, and the deacon, holding up his *orarion* (stole), says, "It is time to do sacrifice to the Lord" (see A. Fortescue, *The Orthodox Eastern Church*, pp. 413-414).

Prothesis: In the Eastern Church the *prothesis* is the name given to the large credence table on the north side of the altar on which the solemn preparation of the bread and wine for the Eucharist takes place.

Synapte: In the Eastern Church a liturgical prayer constructed in the form of a litany. It consists of short petitions said by the deacon to which the congregation respond with *Kyrie eleison*.

Trisagion: Derived from the Greek "thrice holy"—The refrain "Holy God, Holy and Mighty, Holy and Immortal, have mercy upon us" is chanted with a few exceptions before the readings in most Eastern Liturgies. It should not be confused with the equivalent of the *Sanctus* in the Eastern Liturgies (see *Epinikion*). It occurs in the Good Friday "Reproaches" in the Roman Rite. "Holy God, holy strong One, holy immortal One, have mercy on us," three times, followed by the *Gloria Patri*, *Sicut erat*, and then again "Holy immortal One, have mercy on us," and lastly the whole first verse: "Holy God," etc.

Trope: A trope (*tropus*) is an interpolation in a liturgical text to amplify and embellish it, but which if separated from that text is frequently devoid of any meaning. Thus, for example, the words *Kyrie eleison* are interpolated by the words *qui nos tuae imaginis signasti specie,* ("Thou who hast signed us with the seal of Thine image"),making: *Kyrie, qui nos tuae imaginis signasti specie, eleison.* "Lord, Thou who hast signed us with the seal of Thine image, have mercy on us."

Troping is also referred to as farcing, and a complete example of a farced chant can be found in Chapter X, *Kyrie Eleison*. Tropes, which originated in France, were introduced to fill up the long neums (Gregorian notation) in certain chants and formed an important element in the musical advance between the ninth and twelfth centuries. They were collected together in books called Tropers, e.g. the famous *Winchester Troper*. Sequences, which originated in the eighth century, are sometimes referred to as tropes (*tropi*), as they are insertions between liturgical chants (the Gradual and the Gospel). But, unlike the trope proper, a Sequence is an independent unit complete in itself, and not simply an interpolation into a liturgical text upon which it is dependent to make sense, e.g. if the trope "Thou who hast signed us with the seal of Thine image" is removed from the *Kyrie,* it cannot stand alone.

BIBLIOGRAPHY

Some of the sources quoted in the footnotes have been abbreviated as follows:

I Apology:	*First Apology of Justin Martyr* (c. 100—c.165).
Apost. Const:	The *Apostolic Constitutions*.
Bona:	Bona, *Rerum liturgicarum* (Turin, 1763).
Brightman:	F. Brightman, *Eastern Liturgies* (Oxford, 1896).
Caeremoniale:	*Caeremoniale Episcoporum* .
I Clement *Ad Cor*:	Clement of Rome, *First Epistle to the Corthinthians*.
De SS. Missae:	Benedict XIV, *De Sacrosancto Sacrificio Missae*, lib. III, ed Schneider (Mainz, 1879).
Didache:	The *Didache* or *The Teaching of the Twelve Apostles*.
Durandus:	W. Durandus, *Rationale divinorum officiorum* (Lyons, 1561, Naples 1859).
Duchesne	L. Duchesne, *Origines du Culte chrétien*, 2nd ed. (Paris, 1898).
Gihr:	N. Gihr, *The Holy Sacrifice of the Mass* (St. Louis, 1908).
Micrologus:	*Micrologus de ecclesiasticis observationibus*

	(see GLOSSARY). It can be found in P.L., CLI, 973-1022.
Ordo Rom. I:	*Ordo Romanus Primus*—the First Roman *Ordo* (about 770) found in P.L. LXXVIII, 937-968; translated in: *Ordo Romanus Primus,* ed. Atchley (London, 1905).
P.L.	*Patrologia Latina*, ed. J.P. Migne (221 vols. Paris, 1844-64).
Rit. cel.:	*Ritus servandus in celebratione Missae.*
Rubr. gen.:	*Rubricae generales Missalis.*
ST	*Summa Theologica.*